Notational Analysis of Sport

Systematic notational analysis has debunked many myths inherent in sports. *Notational Analysis of Sport*, Second edition, offers a detailed scientific explanation of how notation is used to assess and enhance sports performance. It shows clearly how a notation system can be constructed and used to provide data to analyse performance in a broad range of sports.

This second edition has been updated to reflect technological developments as well as the growth in knowledge about the practical application of notational systems to help improve performance. The book offers guidance in:

- Constructing a system
- Analysis of data
- Effective coaching using notational performance analysis
- Modelling sport behaviours.

Notational Analysis of Sport
Second edition

Systems for better coaching and
performance in sport

**Edited by Mike Hughes and
Ian M. Franks**

R Routledge
Taylor & Francis Group

LONDON AND NEW YORK

First published 2004 by Routledge
2 Park Square, Milton Park, Abingdon, Oxon, OX14 4RN

Simultaneously published in the USA and Canada
by Routledge
270 Madison Ave, New York NY 10016

Routledge is an imprint of the Taylor & Francis Group

Transferred to Digital Printing 2010

First edition 1997

Typeset in 10/12pt Goudy by Graphicraft Limited, Hong Kong

British Library Cataloguing in Publication Data
A catalogue record for this book is available from the British Library

Library of Congress Cataloging in Publication Data
A catalog record for this book has been requested

ISBN 0-415-29004-x (hbk)
ISBN 0-415-29005-8 (pbk)

Publisher's Note
The publisher has gone to great lengths to ensure the quality of this reprint
but points out that some imperfections in the original may be apparent.

Contents

Illustrations   ix
Contributors   xv
Acknowledgements   xvi

Introduction   1

1   The need for feedback   8
IAN M. FRANKS

1.1   The coaching process and its problems   8
1.2   Feedback   8
1.3   The need for objective information   12
1.4   Summary   15

2   The nature of feedback   17
NICOLA J. HODGES AND IAN M. FRANKS

2.1   Distinguishing information sources   17
2.2   Augmented feedback: knowledge of results (KR) and
      performance (KP)   19
2.3   Demonstrations and instructions   25
2.4   Augmented information summary and conclusions   38

3   The use of feedback-based technologies   40
DARIO G. LIEBERMANN AND IAN M. FRANKS

3.1   Introduction   40
3.2   Video information as a source of feedback   40
3.3   Automated systems as a source of complex information   43
3.4   Training in three-dimensional virtual environments   46
3.5   Tele-remote training and analysis   49
3.6   Laser technology in static and dynamic conditions   50
3.7   Temporal feedback in skill training   51

3.8   The use of force sensors to deliver feedback about
       pressure, time, and direction   55
3.9   Eye-movement recording technology   56
3.10   On coaches' attitudes to the use of feedback-based technology   57
3.11   Conclusions   58

4   Notational analysis – a review of the literature   59
MIKE HUGHES AND IAN M. FRANKS

4.1   Introduction   59
4.2   Historical perspective   60
4.3   Methodological issues   61
4.4   The development of sport-specific notation systems
       (hand notation)   61
4.5   Computerised notation   80
4.6   Summary   103
4.7   The future of notational analysis   104

5   Sports analysis   107
MIKE HUGHES AND IAN M. FRANKS

5.1   Introduction   107
5.2   Creating flowcharts   107
5.3   Levels of analysis – the team, subsidiary units
       and individuals   113
5.4   Summary   117

6   How to develop a notation system   118
MIKE HUGHES AND IAN M. FRANKS

6.1   Introduction   118
6.2   Examples of data collection systems   118
6.3   Data collection systems in general   126
6.4   Examples   128
6.5   General steps in analysis   132
6.6   Different types of data   134
6.7   Summary   140

7   Examples of notation systems   141
MIKE HUGHES AND IAN M. FRANKS

7.1   Introduction   141
7.2   Individual sports   141
7.3   Team sports   151

8   The use of performance indicators in performance analysis   166
MIKE HUGHES AND ROGER BARTLETT

8.1   Summary   166
8.2   Introduction   166
8.3   Analysis of game structures   172
8.4   Conclusions   187

9   Analysis of notation data: reliability   189
M. HUGHES, S.M. COOPER AND A. NEVILL

9.1   Introduction   189
9.2   The nature of the data, the depth of analysis   191
9.3   Consistency of percentage difference calculations 193
9.4   Processing data   194
9.5   Visual interpretation of the data (Bland and Altman plot)   195
9.6   Statistical processes and reliability   201
9.7   Conclusions   203

10   Establishing normative profiles in performance analysis   205
MIKE HUGHES, STEVE EVANS AND JULIA WELLS

10.1   Introduction   205
10.2   Development of the method   207
10.3   Conclusions   225

11   Models of sports contests – Markov processes, dynamical systems and neural networks   227
TIM MCGARRY AND JÜRGEN PERL

11.1   Introduction   227
11.2   Sport and chance   227
11.3   From Markov processes to dynamical systems   236
11.4   Summary   242

12   Measuring coaching effectiveness   243
KEN MORE AND IAN M. FRANKS

12.1   Instruction   243
12.2   Teaching and coaching effectiveness   244
12.3   Systematic observation   244
12.4   Systematic observation and the modification of behaviour   248
12.5   Identification of effective verbal coaching strategies   251
12.6   Summary   256

13   From analysis to coaching   257
MIKE HUGHES AND IAN M. FRANKS

13.1   Examples of the applications of analysis systems to
         coaching practice   257
13.2   Tactical performance profiling in elite level senior squash   263
13.3   Rugby union – a game of change   269
13.4   Summary   271

Glossary   272
References and Bibliography   274
Index   302

Illustrations

Figures

1.1	A simple schematic diagram representing the coaching process	12
2.1	Schematic diagram to illustrate how the learning process is affected by various augmented information sources	18
2.2	Individual trial data represented as Lissajous figures (relative motion plots) across acquisition and in retention for an exemplar participant in the no-instruction group from experiment 1	31
2.3	Individual trial data represented as Lissajous figures (relative motion plots) across acquisition and in retention for an exemplar participant in the in-phase instruction group from experiment 1	32
3.1	A javelin throwing performance and the major variables that could affect the final distance of throw	45
3.2	Examples of the tangential velocity-time profiles of the relevant joints in tennis serve before and after training	53
3.3	Asymmetries between the left and right legs during the support (heel-strike to toe-off time)	54
4.1	The shot codes, or suggestive symbols, used by Sanderson (1983) for his data-gathering system for squash	63
4.2	The data-gathering sheets and example data of the shot codes, or suggestive symbols, used by Sanderson (1983) for his data-gathering system for squash	64
4.3	Example from some of Sanderson's data showing frequency distribution of all shots, winners and errors	65
5.1	Hierarchical structure of a model for representing events that take place in a team game such as field hockey, soccer, basketball, water polo	109
5.2	Simple schematic flowchart for soccer	110
5.3	Core elements of any analysis system of performance	111
5.4	Simple flowchart for squash	112
5.5	Primary level game analysis – team	114

5.6	Individual analysis	116
6.1	Simple scatter diagram for recording position of loss of possession for soccer	119
6.2	Simple scatter diagram for recording position of loss of possession, and the player involved, for soccer	120
6.3	Simple scatter diagram for recording position of loss of possession, and the player, and the action involved, for soccer	121
6.4	Definition of position on a representation of a field hockey pitch	123
6.5	Definition of position on a representation of a field hockey pitch oriented to analysing attacking moves	124
6.6	Alternative definition of position on a representation of a field hockey pitch oriented to analysing attacking moves	125
6.7	Example of the distribution of the frequency of shots per player	136
6.8	A different way of presenting the same data of the distribution of the frequency of shots per player as in Figure 6.7	137
6.9	Example of a frequency distribution of actions in a field hockey match showing numbers of passes, runs, etc. in each area of the pitch	137
6.10	Example of a frequency distribution of errors in a field hockey match showing numbers of errors made in each area of the pitch	138
6.11	Representation of three-dimensional data distribution using two-dimensional graphs	139
6.12	Example of sequential data – path to a shot on goal in field hockey	140
7.1	Division of the court into six cells for analysis of tennis	142
7.2	(a) Notation of data using the system for tennis; (b) schematic representation of data used in the example in (a)	143
7.3	Example of the tennis data – gathering system	144
7.4	Distribution of the types of punches thrown by Tyson in the Bruno-Tyson match (1989)	149
7.5	Distribution of the types of punches thrown by Bruno in the Bruno-Tyson match (1989)	149
7.6	Distribution of jabs by both fighters on a round-by-round analysis (Bruno-Tyson, 1989)	151
7.7	Schematic representation of the basketball court in order to define position cells for a data-gathering system	152
7.8	Representation of the number of completed passes	157
7.9	Representation of the number of uncompleted passes	157
7.10	Representation of the number of clearances	158
7.11	Representation of the percentage of activities throughout the first half	158
7.12	Schematic diagram of a soccer pitch showing suggested divisions of the playing area into a grid for notation	160

7.13   Schematic representation of the netball court for divisions
        of the playing surface   162
8.1   Hierarchical technique model of the long jump   167
8.2   Contour map of the distance a javelin travels as a function
        of two release parameters, with all others held constant   168
8.3   Game classification   173
8.4   Subcategorisation of net and wall games, with some common
        examples   173
8.5   Some factors that contribute to success or improved
        performance in net and wall games   174
8.6   Subcategorisation of invasive games, with some common
        examples   179
8.7   Some factors that contribute to success or improved
        performance in invasive games   179
8.8   Subcategorisation of striking and fielding games, with some
        common examples   183
8.9   Some factors that contribute to success or improved
        performance in striking and fielding games   184
9.1   A correlation of the two sets of data before and after the
        extra lines of data were deleted   192
9.2   Definition of positional cells across the squash court area 194
9.3   The data added by column to give the positional frequency
        of rally-ending shots in the example squash match data   194
9.4   A Bland and Altman plot of the differences in rally length
        plotted against the mean of the rally length from the two tests   196
9.5   The overall data from the reliability study, the intra-operator
        test, presented as a function of the accuracy of each operator   197
9.6   The data from the reliability study, the intra-operator test,
        presented as a function of the action variables and the operator   199
9.7   The data from the reliability study, the inter-operator test,
        presented as a function of the action variables and the
        operators   200
10.1   Examples of the variation of the cumulative mean with
        increasing number of games analysed: mean number of rallies
        per game   210
10.2   Example of percentage difference plot: mean number of shots
        per game   215
10.3   Example of percentage difference plot: mean number of rallies
        per match   215
10.4   Example of percentage difference plot: player A's winners
        when player A loses the game   216
10.5   Example of percentage difference plot: mean number of shpts
        per rally by match   216
10.6   Example of percentage difference plot: player A's errors when
        player A loses the game   217

10.7 Inter-operator reliability and intra-operator reliability, using a modified Bland and Altman plot to demonstrate the percentage differences 217

10.8 Using percentage difference distribution to display the pattern for the number of matches required to establish elite player movement profiles for the shot start position and for the different positions at the 'T' 220

10.9 Aggregate percentage of passes completed in or from each of the selected pitch positions for unsuccessful teams 221

10.10 Aggregate comparison of the percentage of possession that is lost either in or from each of the four positions of the pitch for unsuccessful teams 222

10.11 Number of matches that need to be notated to achieve a critical number of tackles and passes representative of elite-level women's rugby 223

10.12 Number of matches that need to be notated to achieve stability in the number of kicks and rucks representative of elite-level women's rugby 223

10.13 Number of matches that need to be notated to achieve stability in the number of mauls and scrums representative of elite-level women's rugby 224

10.14 Accumulated means of attacking positions of elite volleyball teams 224

10.15 Accumulated means of attacking positions of non-elite volleyball teams 225

11.1 Stochastic (Markov) processes for the sequence of shots and outcomes produced in a squash rally 232

11.2 Learning step and information clusters on a Kohonen feature map 239

11.3 Squash processes on the court and process clusters on a squash network 240

13.1 The prime target area to where the ball should be crossed 260

13.2 Example of 16 cell division of squash court 264

13.3 Example of shot frequency summary data 266

13.4 Examples of various screens of data available 266

13.5 Example of shot option analysis 267

13.6 Example of 'momentum analysis' graph 268

Tables

5.1 Some actions, and their respective outcomes, for soccer 110

6.1 A simple frequency table for basketball 121

6.2 Comparison of descriptive match data for different levels of competitive players 135

6.3 Comparison of nationally ranked players to county players: shot patterns that have differences in frequency 135

6.4   Shooting data from the 1990 soccer World Cup   136
7.1   Symbols used in the data-gathering system for boxing   147
7.2   Sample data from the Tyson-Bruno fight (1989) using the
      data-gathering system for boxing   148
7.3   Collated data of total punches thrown   149
7.4   Analysis of the number of types of punches thrown by both
      boxers   150
7.5   The number of punches thrown while holding   150
7.6   The number of jabs thrown in each round   150
7.7   A demonstration of how the notation system works   153
7.8   Each player has designated areas in which she must play   162
7.9   Example of a record sheet for simple data-gathering for
      notation of netball   163
7.10 Data processed from a notated netball match (part only)   164
8.1   Published performance indicators used in notational analysis   169
8.2   Categorisation of different performance indicators that have
      been used in analyses of net or wall games   174
8.3   Categorisation of different performance indicators that have
      been used in analyses of soccer, an example of invasion games   180
8.4   Categorisation of different performance indicators that have
      been used in analyses of cricket, an example of striking and
      fielding games   184
9.1   An analysis of the different statistical processes used in
      reliability studies in some randomly selected performance
      analysis research papers   189
9.2   An analysis of the different statistical processes used in
      subsequent data analyses in some randomly selected
      performance analysis research papers   190
9.3   The total shots per game   191
9.4   The arithmetic differences in the positions recorded by the two
      analysts   195
9.5   Data from a rugby match notated twice by five different
      operators and presented as an intra-operator reliability analysis   197
9.6   Data from a rugby match notated twice by five different
      operators and the differences for each operator expressed as a
      percentage of the respective mean   198
9.7   Data from a rugby match notated twice by five different
      operators and the mean for each operator expressed as a
      difference from the overall respective mean and then
      calculated as a percentage of the overall mean for each
      respective variable   199
9.8   Data from a rugby match notated twice by five different
      operators and the differences for each operator expressed as a
      percentage of the overall mean for each respective variable   200
9.9   Correlation and X^2 analysis applied to the intra-operator data
      from Table 9.8   201

9.10 Testing and comparing the efficacy of correlation and X^2
      analysis in testing reliability of non-parametric data   201
9.11 Kruksal-Wallis and ANOVA applied to the different variables
      for the five operators for inter-operator reliability   202
9.12 Manipulation of some sample data to test the sensitivity of
      Kruksal-Wallis and ANOVA for inter-operator reliability   203
10.1 Some examples of sample sizes for profiling in sport   206
10.2 Levels of confidence between numbers of matches and playing
      standards   208
10.3 Description information of the matches analysed   211
10.4 The means and limits of error of shots by game (Figure 10.5)   212
10.5 Overall summary of $N_{(E)}$ for all variables measured at each
      limit of error   214
10.6 Analysis of the stability of the profiles of winning shots and
      errors   218
10.7 Games that player A wins – player A data   218
10.8 Number of matches required to establish movement profiles of
      elite women squash players using percentage errors of between
      5% and 10%   219
10.9 Number of matches that need to be analysed to achieve a true
      average that represents the population   222
11.1 Shot – response profile for an individual player   230
11.2 Winner-error profile for an individual player   231
13.1 Comparison of crosses played in front of and behind defences
      in the 1986 and 1998 World Cups with respect to strikes on
      goal and goals scored   259
13.2 Comparison of types of crosses in the 1986 and 1998 World
      Cups with respect to strikes on goals and goals scored   259
13.3 Analysis of shot types from crosses for the 1998 World Cup   262
13.4 Evolution of international rugby union, 1971–2000   269

Contributors

Roger Bartlett is at the Centre for Sport and Exercise Science, Sheffield Hallam University.

S.M. Cooper is at the Centre for Performance Analysis, University of Wales Institute Cardiff.

Steve Evans is at the Centre for Performance Analysis, University of Wales Institute Cardiff.

Ian M. Franks is at the School of Human Kinetics, University of British Columbia, Vancouver.

Nicola J. Hodges is at Liverpool John Moores University.

Mike Hughes is at the Centre for Performance Analysis, University of Wales Institute Cardiff.

Dario G. Liebermann is in the Department of Physical Therapy, Sackler Faculty of Medicine, University of Tel Aviv, Ramat Aviv.

Tim McGarry is in the Faculty of Kinesiology, University of New Brunswick, Fredericton.

Ken More is at Elite Sports Analysis, Edinburgh.

A. Nevill is at the School of Sport, Performing Arts and Leisure, University of Wolverhampton.

Jürgen Perl is at Johannes Gutenberg-Universität Mainz, Institut für Informatik, Mainz.

Julia Wells is at the Centre for Performance Analysis, University of Wales Institute Cardiff.

Acknowledgements

The authors would like to gratefully acknowledge the Social Sciences and Humanities Research Council of Canada for funding material included in the final edition.

Introduction

Welcome to notational analysis

This introduction acts as a simple guide to the rest of the book. The aim of the book is to provide a ready manual on notational analysis. The book is written for the sports scientist, the coach, the athlete, or for anyone who wishes to apply analysis to any performance operation. Although this book is applied directly to sport, notational analysis is a procedure that could be used in any discipline that requires assessment and analysis of performance: nursing, surgical operations, skilled manufacturing processes, unskilled manufacturing processes, haute cuisine, and so on.

To cater for the anticipated spectrum of readership, the book is written to balance the practical approach (giving plenty of examples) with a sound scientific analysis of the subject area. In this way it is hoped that the practitioners of sport, the athletes and coaches, as well as the sports scientists will find the book useful.

About this book

Like most texts, the information within this book is presented in an order that is considered logical and progressive. It is not totally necessary, however, to use the book in this way. It is anticipated that at times certain sections will be needed to be used for immediate practical requirements. At the start of each chapter is advice on how to use that chapter and also which chapters, if any, require reading and understanding beforehand.

Organisation

Chapter 1, The need for feedback (Franks)

Historically, coaching intervention has been based on subjective observations of athletes. However, several studies have shown that such observations are not only unreliable but also inaccurate. Although the benefits of feedback and knowledge of results (KR) are well accepted, the problems of highlighting, memory and observational difficulties result in the accuracy of coaching feedback being very limited. Video (and now DVD) analysis has been shown to benefit advanced athletes, but care must be taken when providing this form of feedback to any other level of athlete.To overcome these problems, analysis systems have been devised. In developing these systems it was necessary to define and identify the critical elements of performance and then devise an efficient data entry method, such that in certain situations a trained observer could record these events in real time. When the demands of the complexity of the systems were such that real-time notation was not possible, post-event analysis has been completed using the slow motion and replay facilities afforded by video (and DVD). The benefits of using computers to record human athletic behaviour in this way can be summarised in terms of speed and efficiency.

Chapter 2, The nature of feedback (Hodges and Franks)

There are many principles based on theory and research in the field of psychology and, more specifically, motor learning that the coach can use to guide their methods of instruction. The aim of this chapter is to provide a discussion of these general principles based on theories of the skill acquisition process and experimental studies where specific information sources have been manipulated.

Chapter 3, The use of feedback-based technologies (Liebermann and Franks)

Skill acquisition may be characterised as an active 'cumulative' process during which a target movement is expected to improve as a function of practice. Only when the performer is able to reproduce a desired pattern systematically and in a satisfactory way can the motor skill be considered as finally acquired. Feedback shortens and improves the acquisition process, but only if appropriately administered (see Schmidt and Lee (1999) for a review). Recent advances in information technology have exploited this fact, and focused on the feedback that athletes receive during training or even during competition.

Some of these technologies allow augmented feedback to be managed by the coach, thus enriching the training experience by stimulating diverse sensory modalities. Such technologies are described. Their advantages and disadvantages are discussed along with practical examples of how augmented feedback, in combination with latest advances in technology, can be used to enhance motor performance skill acquisition.

Chapter 4, Notational analysis – a review of the literature (Hughes and Franks)

This chapter offers as much information about notation systems as possible. It is written in the form of a literature review of the research work already published in this field. Although this is written for, and by, sports scientists, it is hoped that anyone with an interest in this rapidly growing area of practice and research will find it equally interesting and rewarding.

The review is aimed at being as comprehensive as possible but, as some published work will inevitably be missed, it is structured to follow the main developments in notational analysis. After tracing a historical perspective of the roots of notation, the application of these systems to sport are developed. These early systems were all hand notation systems; their emerging sophistication is followed until the advent of computerised notation. Although the emphasis is on the main research developments in both hand and computerised notational systems, where possible the innovations of new systems and any significant data outputs within specific sports are also assessed.

Chapter 5, Sports analysis (Hughes and Franks)

The aim of this chapter is to provide an insight into how sports can be broken down into their inherent logical progressions. The construction of flowcharts of different sports is examined, together with the definition of key events in these respective sports. The whole process is integrated into a complete and logical analysis for these sports. The next step is to design a data collection and data processing system, so anyone interested in designing a notation system should read this chapter first.

Chapter 6, How to develop a notation system (Hughes and Franks)

This chapter will enable you to develop your own hand notation system for any sport: no matter how simple or complicated you wish to make it, the underlying principles apply. If you are hoping to develop a computerised system, the same logical process must be followed, so this chapter is a vital part of that developmental process too. It will help understanding a great deal if Chapters 4 and 5 have also been read.

Chapter 7, Examples of notation systems (Hughes and Franks)

The best way to appreciate the intricacies of notational analysis is to examine systems for the sport(s) in which you are interested, or sports that are similar. Presented here are a number of examples of different systems for different sports. They have been devised by students of notational analysis and are therefore of differing levels of complexity and sophistication, but there are always lessons to be learnt, even from the simplest of systems. Some of the explanations and analyses are completed by beginners at notational analysis; coaches of these sports should not therefore be irritated at the simplistic levels of analysis of the respective sports. The encouraging aspects about these examples is the amounts of information that even the simplest systems provide. Examples 1–6 are for individual sports; examples 7–15 are for team games, which are often more difficult to notate.

Chapter 8, *The use of performance indicators in performance analysis* (Hughes and Bartlett)

Performance indicators are variables or, more likely, combinations of variables by which we determine that a performance has been successful or otherwise. The aims of this chapter are to examine the application of performance indicators in different sports from a performance analysis perspective and, using the different structural definitions of games, to make general recommendations about the use and application of these indicators. Formal games are classified into three categories: net and wall games, invasion games, and striking and fielding games. The different types of sports are also subcategorised by the rules of scoring and ending the respective matches. These classes are analysed further, to enable definition of useful performance indicators and to examine similarities and differences in the analysis of the different categories of game. The indices of performance are subcategorised into general match indicators, tactical indicators, technical indicators and biomechanical indicators. Different examples and the accuracy of their presentation are discussed. It is very easy to use simple data analyses in sports that are too complex to justify that utilisation; more care needs to be taken in presenting performance indicators in isolation.

Chapter 9, *Analysis of notation data: reliability* (Hughes, Cooper and Nevill)

It is vital that the reliability of a data gathering system is demonstrated clearly and in a way that is compatible with the intended analyses of the data. The data must be tested in the same way and to the same depth in which it will be processed in the subsequent analyses. In general, the work of Bland and Altman (1986) has transformed the attitude of sport scientists to testing reliability; can similar techniques be applied to the non-parametric data that most notational analysis studies generate? There are also a number of questions that inherently recur in these forms of data-gathering – this chapter aims to demonstrate practical answers to some of these questions. These ideas have been developed over the past couple of years and represent a big step forward in our understanding of the reliability of systems in this area of sports science.

The most common form of data analysis in notation studies is to record frequencies of actions and their respective positions on the performance area; these are then presented as sums or totals in each respective area. What are the effects of cumulative errors nullifying each other, so that the overall totals appear less incorrect than they actually are?

The application of parametric statistical techniques is often misused in notational analysis – how does this affect the confidence of the conclusions to say something about the data, with respect to more appropriate non-parametric tests? By using practical examples from recent studies, this chapter investigates these issues associated with reliability studies and subsequent analyses in performance analysis.

Chapter 10, Analysis of notation data: performance profiling (Hughes, Evans and Wells)

It is an implicit assumption in notational analysis that in presenting a performance profile of a team or an individual a 'normative profile' has been achieved. Inherently this implies that all the means of the variables that are to be analysed and compared have stabilised. Most researchers assume that this will have happened if they analyse enough performances. But how many is enough? In the literature there are large differences in sample sizes. Just trawling through some of the analyses in a variety of sports shows the differences.

There must be some way of assessing how data within a study is stabilising. The nature of the data itself will also affect how many performances are required – five matches may be enough to analyse passing in field hockey; would you need ten matches to analyse crossing or perhaps 30 for shooting? The way in which the data are analysed will effect the stabilisation of performance means – data that are analysed across a multi-cell representation of the playing area will require far more performances to stabilise than data that is analysed on overall performance descriptors (e.g. shots per match). Further, it is misleading to test data of the latter variety and then go on to analyse the data in further detail.

This chapter aims to explore strategies in addressing these problems for the practical analyst. It uses two sports, squash and badminton, as examples in depth, and then presents further examples from a multiplicity of other sports.

Chapter 11, Models of sports contests (McGarry and Perl)

The purpose of this chapter is to provide a summary review of ideas and theories written on modelling in competitive sport, and also to outline other practical means of modelling that could be developed further in sports, such as chaos theory. Teams and performers often demonstrate a stereotypical way of playing and these are idiosyncratic models, which include positive and negative aspects of performance. Patterns of play will begin to establish over a period of time but the greater the database, the more accurate the model will be. An established model provides for the opportunity to compare single performances against it.

The modelling of competitive sport is an informative analytic technique because it directs the attention of the modeller to the critical aspects of data that delineate successful performance. The modeller searches for an underlying signature of sport performance, which is a reliable predictor of future sport behaviour. Stochastic models have not yet, to our knowledge, been used further to investigate sport at the behavioural level of analysis. However, the modelling procedure is readily applicable to other sports and could lead to useful and interesting results.

Chapter 12, Measuring coach effectiveness (More and Franks)

Effective instruction is crucial to the pursuit of optimal sporting performance. The more effective the instruction, the more fully the instructor's role will benefit athlete performance. Such instruction requires the application of skills that range from the planning, organisation and presentation of learning experiences to the provision of appropriate feedback information. Previous research attempted to analyse the verbal coaching behaviours of coaches during a coaching practice. However, analysing coaching behaviour with the intent of improving their instructional effectiveness assumes the existence of a 'best practice' template for coaches. This chapter will review recent empirical literature pertaining to this template of effective instruction and question existing concepts of 'best practice' behaviours for coaches.

Performance analysis of sport has been used primarily to inform the coaching process. That is, objective information about an athlete's performance is used by the coach to design the practice environment and subsequently aid in the modification of athlete behaviour. Therefore, the 'practice session' itself can be considered a critical element in the development of skilled athletic performance. Although we do accept the fact that the coach is involved in many other activities (from nutritional guide to public relations spokesperson), instructing athletes on their performance remains a priority for most sports. During the 'practice session' effective instruction is crucial to the pursuit of optimal sporting performance, as the more effective the instruction, the more fully the instructor's role will benefit athlete performance. Instructional strategy therefore can be viewed as a particular arrangement of antecedents and consequences that are designed and implemented by the coach in order to develop and control the behaviour of their athletes. This instruction requires the application of skills that range from the planning and organisation of learning experiences to the presentation of instructional and feedback information. Hence, one of the defining roles of the coach is that of instructor and, as an instructor, the coach is responsible for teaching the athlete what to do, how to do it, and hopefully how to do it well.

Chapter 13, From analysis to coaching (Hughes and Franks)

The ultimate problem facing the coach and the analyst now is the transformation of these oceans of data into meaningful interpretations with respect to their sport. There is no set paradigm for this process as yet, so specific analyses of three sports will be presented and discussed as examples of good practice. Perhaps, as the theoretical work in analysis progresses, set parameters of analysis will be defined, but at the moment we are all working empirically, so let us see what we can learn from others' ideas. In this chapter practical examples of work from leading practitioners are examined in three different applications of notational analysis for the respective sports:

1   using analysis to define optimal performance patterns, and then using these to design practices to improve techniques
2   performance profiling to define strengths and weaknesses – to enable improvement of the coach's athletes by the correctly applied practices, and also to enable tactical analyses of future opponents
3   using detailed objective analyses to determine rule changes in sport.

1   The need for feedback

Ian M. Franks

1.1 The coaching process and its problems

Traditionally, coaching intervention has been based on subjective observations of athletes. However, several studies have shown that such observations are not only unreliable but also inaccurate. Franks and Miller (1986) compared coaching observations to eyewitness testimony of criminal events. Using methodology gained from applied memory research, they showed that international level soccer coaches could recollect only 30 per cent of the key factors that determined successful soccer performance during one match. In another study, a forced choice recognition paradigm was used by Franks (1993), who found that experienced gymnastic coaches were not significantly better than novice coaches in detecting differences in two sequentially presented front hand-spring performances. An additional finding of interest in this study was that experienced coaches produced many more false positives (detecting a difference when none existed) than their novice counterparts, and were also very confident in their decisions, even when wrong. This finding led to the speculation that the training undertaken by coaches predisposes them to seek out and report errors in performances even when none exist.

The evidence from these studies, combined with many others from the field of applied psychology (such as experiments that investigate the reliability of eyewitness testimony of criminal events), leads one to believe that the processing of visual information through the human information processing system is extremely problematic (Neisser, 1982) if one requires an objective, unbiased accounting of past events. Hence, the solution is to collect relevant details of performance during a live event and then recall these details at the termination of that event. Although many recording devices (e.g. a tape recorder) would serve equally well as an external memory aid, the computer appears to be ideally suited for such a task.

1.2 Feedback

Information that is provided to the athlete about action is one of the most important variables affecting the learning and subsequent performance of a skill (see Franks (1996a) for a practical review). Knowledge about the proficiency with which athletes perform a skill is critical to the learning process and in certain circumstances a failure to provide such knowledge may even prevent learning from taking place. In addition, the nature of the information that is provided has been shown to be a strong determinant of skilful performance. That is, precise information about the produced action will yield significantly more benefits for the athletes than feedback that is imprecise (Newell, 1981). However, the process of skill acquisition and the effects of feedback at different stages of learning is a complex issue and is dealt with in greater detail in Chapters 2 and 3.

How then does the athlete acquire this vital information about action? Firstly, a major contributor to the athlete's knowledge base about the performance of a skill is that of intrinsic feedback. This has been defined as information that is gained from the body's own proprioceptors, such as muscle spindles, joint receptors etc. (for a more detailed description of this internal process see Rothwell 1994, Chapters 4–6). A second source of feedback is that which augments the feedback from within the individual. This can be thought of as extrinsic information, or 'knowledge of results' (KR). The term 'knowledge of performance' (KP) has also been used to differentiate between information about the outcome of the action (KR) and information about the patterns of action used to complete the skill (KP). A full discussion of these terms is given in Gentile (1972), Salmoni *et al.* (1984), and Chapter 2 of this text.

Although intrinsic feedback is of vital importance to the performance of skill, it remains the responsibility of the coach to offer the best possible extrinsic feedback that will enable the athlete to compare accurately 'what was done' with 'what was intended'. Clearly, the use of video or film has the potential to provide such feedback. The benefits of using such aids are intuitively obvious. In the case of video, the information can be played back on a TV screen only a few seconds after the event has taken place. There is no delay period that may hamper the comparison of performances being made by the athlete, the motivation to perform is enhanced by individuals wanting to see themselves on TV and, in addition, the whole performance can be stored in its entirety or edited for later analysis. The videotape can therefore provide error information, can be a reinforcer when performance is correct, and can be a strong motivating force. However, the videotape should be used under the watchful eye of the coach who is able to draw the athletes' attention to key critical elements after complete analysis.

Given the fact that video offers the potential to be an excellent source of information feedback, the research into the effects of video feedback on the skill learning process should show positive benefits. Surprisingly, however, there are few research studies that have shown a clear superiority of using video as a form of KR that will effect the learning of a skilled motor act. An excellent review of 51 studies using several sport skill examples was completed by Rothstein and Arnold (1976). While the results of these studies did not offer unequivocal support for the use of video as an essential component in the process of coaching and instruction, there was uniform agreement on one aspect: the interaction of the level of skill at which the athlete was performing and the method of giving the video feedback. Athletes that are at the early stages of learning a skill cannot improve their performance by observing videotapes without the assistance of the coach who can draw their attention to the key elements of performance competency. Also, some evidence (Ross et al., 1985) shows that indiscriminate viewing of videotape by early learners may even retard the learning process. One possible explanation of this phenomenon is that there is too much information for the beginner athlete to assimilate. Furthermore, these novice athletes have a good probability of paying attention to the non-critical elements of performance. The practical implication of this finding is that coaches should either edit the videotape before showing it to their athletes, or highlight by instruction or slow motion, the response cues that are responsible for correct performance.

On a practical level, therefore, two problems seem to arise for the coach when considering the use of video feedback. The first problem is that of identifying the 'critical elements' of successful athletic performance. Then, having identified these elements, the second problem is a technological one. Can systems be developed that can provide fast and efficient feedback that pertains only to the critical elements of performance? These problems are of concern to notation analysts. We adopted a systems approach to the analysis of athletic performance (Franks and Goodman, 1986a), and developed several computer-aided sport analysis systems (Franks et al., 1986a; Franks and Goodman, 1986b; Franks et al., 1987; Partridge and Franks, 1993, 1996; McGarry and Franks, 1996a) that captured the critical elements of competition, stored these events in a computer's memory, computed specified analyses on these data and produced the results immediately following competition. Earlier work (Reilly and Thomas, 1976; Sanderson and Way, 1979) developed templates of hand notation systems, while Hughes and colleagues (Hughes, 1985; Hughes and Charlish, 1988; Hughes and Cunliffe, 1986; Hughes and Franks, 1991; Taylor and Hughes, 1988; Hughes and Knight, 1995; Hughes, 1995b) created computerised systems for most sports as well as researching the problems of voice interactive and generic systems. In developing these systems it was necessary to define and identify the critical elements of performance and then devise an efficient data entry method, such that in certain situations a trained observer could record these events in real time. When the demands of the complexity of the systems are such that real-time notation is not possible, post-event analysis has been completed using the slow motion and replay facilities afforded by video and digital technology. The benefits of using computers to record human athletic behaviour in this way can be summarised in terms of speed and efficiency.

Once the concept of interfacing video and computer technologies became a reality within the field of quantitative sport analysis, it was obvious that the data from athletic performance that was stored in the computer could be linked directly to a pictorial image that corresponded to a particular coded athletic behaviour. Digital or video scenes of performance could therefore be pre-selected and edited automatically. The advantages of using computer–video interactive systems in sport analysis was originally detailed by Franks and Nagelkerke (1988). In this paper we outlined the procedures and hardware that was needed to undertake such an analysis. The observed athletic behaviour was recorded and stored along with its corresponding time. A concurrent video recording of the performance was made, and a computer produced time code dubbed onto the second audio-channel of the videotape, giving the computer data and video data a common time base. At the commencement of the competition, the coach (or analyst) not only accessed, via the computer, a digital and graphic summary of athletic performance, but also viewed the video scene that corresponded to one, or a classified group of, specified athletic behaviours.

The use of such computer-aided analysis has since been expanded and elaborated within the coaching process, especially for team sports. While a trained observer enters a sequential history of coded events into a computer, a digital record is taken of the competition. Having made the comparison between the observed data and the expected data, the coach highlights several priority problems associated with the performance. These itemised problems are automatically edited from stored images and assembled for viewing by individuals or groups of athletes. After these excerpts from competition have been discussed, the athletes engage in a practice session organised by the coach. Several analytic techniques have been developed that examine in detail the behavioural interaction between the coach and athlete during this practice session (Franks *et al.*, 1988; More and Franks, 1996; More *et al.*, 1996). It is now possible to have feedback about athletic performance available throughout this cyclical process of competition, observation, analysis and practice.

The majority of computer-aided analysis systems that have been developed collect data on relatively gross behavioural measures of performance. These measures include such elements as 'a shot at goal' in soccer, a 'check' in ice hockey, a 'possession change' in basketball, and a 'penalty corner' in field hockey. Whereas this information, logged in the manner mentioned above, is extremely valuable to the overall improvement in performance of the various teams that use it, the need for more precise and sophisticated analysis is evident when considering the individual closed sport skills (environmental uncertainty is at a minimum) such as diving, gymnastics and golf (see Poulton (1957) for a complete definition and delineation between open and closed skills). In these skills the movement patterns themselves are fundamental to the overall performance. For that reason, the athlete should be able to view the details of the pattern of movements that are used to produce the skill. It is also important for the athlete to be able to highlight the differences between a criterion movement pattern that is to be produced and the movement pattern that was actually completed. There are however, several problems associated with this comparison process. Firstly, the criterion performance itself should be a model movement pattern. Secondly, the angle of viewing must be from a position that can pick up key points in the movement pattern. Several simultaneous recordings from various specified angles are preferable. Thirdly, there should be a relatively short time delay between performing and viewing, and also between viewing and performing again. Fourthly, the athletes should have control over such functions as 'slow motion', 'pause' and 'replay' to allow them to analyse the performance fully at their own pace. Finally, the athlete must have some method of identifying the errors in his/her movement pattern in order that changes can be made on subsequent attempts.

1.3 The need for objective information

The essence of the coaching process is to instigate observable changes in behaviour. The coaching and teaching of skill depends heavily on analysis in order to effect an improvement in athletic performance. It is clear from the arguments in section 1.2 that informed and accurate measures are necessary for effective feedback and hence improvement of performance. In most athletic events, analysis of the performance is guided by a series of qualitative assessments made by the coach. Franks *et al.* (1983a) defined a simple flowchart of the coaching process (see Figure 1.1).

The schema in Fig. 1.1 outlines the coaching process in its observational, analytical and planning phases. The game is watched and the coach will form an idea of positive and negative aspects of performance. Often the results from previous games, as well as performances in practice, are considered before planning and preparing for the next match. After this game is played the process repeats itself. There are, however, problems associated with a coaching process that relies heavily on the subjective assessment of game action.

During a game many occurrences stand out as distinctive features of action. These range from controversial decisions given by officials to exceptional technical achievements by individual players. While these types of occurrence are easily remembered, they tend to distort the coaches' assessment of the game in total. Most of the remembered features of a game are those that can be associated with *highlighted* features of play.

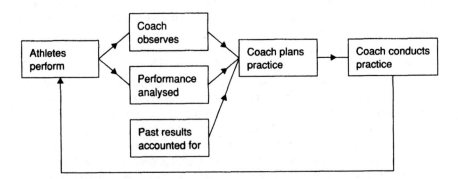

Figure 1.1 A simple schematic diagram representing the coaching process.

Human memory systems have limitations, and it is almost impossible to remember accurately all the meaningful events that take place during an entire competition. Our studies (Franks and Miller, 1986, 1991) have shown that soccer coaches are less than 45 per cent correct in their post-game assessment of what occurred during 45 minutes of a soccer game. While there is considerable individual variability, this rapid forgetting is not surprising, given the complicated process of committing data to memory and subsequently retrieving it. Events (considered non-critical) that occur only once in the game are not easily remembered and forgetting is rapid. Furthermore, emotions and personal biases are significant factors which affect storage and retrieval processes of memory.

In most team sports an observer is unable to view, and assimilate, all the action taking place on all the playing area. Since the coach can only view parts of game action at any one time (usually what are considered to be critical areas), most of the peripheral play action is lost. Consequently the coach must base post-match feedback on only partial information about a team's, unit's or individual's performance during the game. This feedback is often inadequate and, as such, the opportunity is missed to provide the players and teams with information that could improve their performance.

Problems associated with subjective assessments would seem to present the coach with virtually insurmountable difficulties. The whole process of coaching, achieving improvement of performance of the athlete, hinges on the observational abilities of the coach. Despite the importance of observation within the coaching process, very little research has been completed in the specific area of observational accuracy. Hoffman and his co-workers (Armstrong and Hoffman, 1979; Skrinar and Hoffman, 1979; Imwold and Hoffman, 1983) attempted to define the different observational processes 'expert' and 'novice' coaches exhibit while monitoring athletic performances such as gymnastics, golf and softball. One conclusion made was that 'experts' (experienced coaches) do not appear to have any standard and predefined system of monitoring performance, and therefore a diagnostic strategy that can be used to train pre-service and in-service coaches remains elusive.

Despite this dearth in the literature of the sport science discipline, there has been a considerable body of applied research that quantitatively measured the accuracy of observers in criminal eyewitness situations. There are a number of similarities between the situation of the coach observing an athletic performance and that of the eyewitness to the criminal event. Wells and Loftus (1984) prefaced their text on eyewitness testimony by stating that 'Testimony by an eyewitness can be an event of profound importance.' This is equally true for criminal and sporting situations. The accurate analysis of competition is fundamental to the entire coaching process and underlies improvement in performance; consequently the research completed on eyewitness testimony is very relevant to the sport coach/scientist.

Generally, it appears that eyewitnesses to criminal events are unreliable and in some cases inaccurate. One reason that was put forward by Clifford and Hollin (1980) was the high level of arousal that the violent crime instilled in its victims. They found that eyewitness testimony was less accurate following the witnessing of a violent incident, and the decrease in accuracy appeared to be a function of the number of the perpetrators involved in the crime, especially under violent conditions. A further factor influencing the accuracy of the witnessing of the event was the seriousness of the crime, defined by the value of the material stolen. Leippe *et al.* (1978) examined crime seriousness as a determinant of accuracy in eyewitness identification. The witness observed a staged theft, in which either an expensive or an inexpensive object was stolen. Subjects either had prior knowledge of the value of the stolen article or learned of its value only after the theft. When witnesses had prior knowledge of the value of the stolen item, accurate identification of the thief was more likely. Leippe *et al.* concluded that the effect of perceived seriousness of the criminal act is mediated by processes that operate during, rather than after, the viewing interval: processes such as selective attention and stimulus encoding.

Regarding the actual details of the crime itself, Wells and Leippe (1981) found that the focus of attention during the crime was a critical factor. The results from eyewitnesses viewing a staged theft showed that those who accurately identified the thief averaged fewer correct answers on the peripheral details test than did eyewitnesses who identified an innocent person. Therefore, witnesses attending to the thief's characteristics processed little information about the peripheral factors. Moreover, subjects who attended to the peripheral factors had trouble identifying the thief. In a study by Malpass and Devine (1981) it was found that line-up instructions to the witness had an effect on identification. If biased instructions were given, it was implied that the witnesses were to choose someone, whereas unbiased instructions included a 'no-choice' option. The results showed that identification errors were highest under biased instructions without decreasing correct identifications.

In making the comparison between criminal and sporting situations, although there are many differences, the similarities are very significant. For example, in competition the arousal level of the coach fluctuates markedly (Clifford and Hollin, 1980). Also, the sports environment differentiates between what is considered to be important and non-important competition. For example, Olympic events are considered more important than provincial competitions. In addition, the coach has the problem, especially in team games, of directing attention away from peripheral non-critical elements of the performance towards the more central features of performance. Finally, personal biases will always distort any subjective interpretations of observed competition or practice and will therefore render inaccurate the observational accuracy of the coach of any event (McDonald, 1984).

We (Franks and Miller, 1986) addressed these problems by undertaking a comparison between eyewitnesses to criminal situations and observations made by coaches and teachers following a sporting performance. An experiment was designed in which novice coaches were tested on their ability to observe and recall critical technical events that occurred during one half of an international soccer game. Three experimental groups received instructions either prior to or following a game. These instructions varied in the amount of information that was given to direct the observations of the coaches toward a final post-game questionnaire. The results showed that the overall probability of recalling critical events correctly for all coaches was approximately 0.42. There were no statistically significant differences between experimental groups, but there were differences in the ability of the coaches to recall certain categorised events more accurately than others. In particular, coaches in all three experimental groups recalled 'set-piece' information (corners, free kicks, throws-in, etc.) more accurately than all other categories.

The surprisingly high probability of correctly recalling information about set pieces was thought to be due to the discontinuity that is inherent in the set piece. That is, the continuous nature of a soccer game is stopped for a period of time while penalties are awarded and play is restarted in some organised format. These pauses in action may be used by the observer as some framework around which the game events can be organised. The game itself has within it organising principles that are used by coaches. This point was made previously by Newtson (1976), who defined action that is perceived as a change of a stimulus array. (See Chapter 11 for a discussion on the nature of perturbations in squash and soccer. These perturbations may also be candidates for anchors about which observations are made.)

One of the coach's main tasks is to accurately analyse and assess performance. It would seem then that this function cannot be expected to be carried out by any subjective method. Any hopes for improvement through feedback may be reduced to chance if objective methods of analysis are not used. How can this situation be rectified?

The main methods used in objectifying the process are through the use of notational analysis.

1.4 Summary

Historically, coaching intervention has been based on subjective observations of athletes. However, several studies have shown that such observations are not only unreliable but also inaccurate. Although the benefits of feedback and KR are well accepted, the problems of highlighting, memory and observational difficulties result in the accuracy of coaching feedback being very limited. Video (and now DVD) analysis has been shown to benefit advanced athletes, but care must be taken when providing this form of feedback to any other level of athlete. On a practical level, therefore, problems seem to arise for the coach when considering the use of this type of feedback. The major problem is that of identifying 'critical elements' of successful athletic performance.

To overcome these problems, analysis systems have been devised. In developing these systems it was necessary to define and identify the critical elements of performance and then devise an efficient data entry method, such that in certain situations a trained observer could record these events in real time. When the demands of the complexity of the systems were such that real-time notation was not possible, post-event analysis has been completed using the slow motion and replay facilities afforded by video (and DVD). The benefits of using computers to record human athletic behaviour in this way can be summarised in terms of speed and efficiency.

2 The nature of feedback

Nicola J. Hodges and Ian M. Franks

There are many principles based on theory and research in the field of psychology and, more specifically, motor learning that the coach can use to guide their methods of instruction. The aim of this chapter is to provide a discussion of these general principles based on theories of the skill acquisition process and experimental studies where specific information sources have been manipulated.

2.1 Distinguishing information sources

As discussed in Chapter 1, many sources of information are available to the learner during performance. Some of these information sources are naturally available as part of performing the skill (referred to as intrinsic information feedback). These include outcome information from vision, proprioception (i.e. feel) and audition. In putting a golf ball, the performer can see where the ball lands, how the shot felt and how the ball sounded when it was struck. However, there are certain sources of information that are somewhat impoverished in this example, and the coach has a role to play in determining how to augment these sources of information. For example, the golfer may know how the shot felt, but does not have visual information about how the shot looked. Video, mirrors or a visual demonstration might be used to provide this information. Augmented information about how a movement was executed (i.e. technique) is referred to as knowledge of performance (KP). This knowledge might relate to the arm, to the club or even to the flight of the ball and can be conveyed via video, mirrors or verbal statements. As should become clear in later discussions, attention (directed by performance feedback) can affect how effectively the information can be used to change and correct the skill.

Additionally, the performer might not realise by how much the shot was off target (i.e. the precision of the shot). This can be augmented by specific feedback about accuracy in terms of the nearest metre or degrees of error from the target. Information about the outcome or success of the movement is referred to as knowledge of results (KR). Bilodeau and Bilodeau (1961, p. 50) argued that 'there is no improvement without KR, progressive improvement with it and deterioration after its withdrawal'. We will discuss the validity of this statement below when we evaluate how KR works to affect the learning process.

Sources of information that are augmented through external means are often referred to as extrinsic feedback. It is these extrinsic sources of information which we are particularly interested in exploring.

In addition to the error-alerting role of feedback (whether this is through intrinsic or extrinsic sources), the important role of information is an error-correcting role. Seeing that a putt was mis-hit contains little or no information about how the shot should be changed or corrected on the next attempt. At a very basic level the performer might know that a correction to the right will be needed if the ball goes too far left, but how to control the ball to effect this change needs to be discovered through practice or taught by a coach or companion. This error-correcting role can at a very basic level be encouraged through outcome feedback, but more frequently instructions and demonstrations are provided to alert what to change. Combining demonstrations with verbal cues is a common technique for alerting to errors and also to ways of correcting these errors. Combining demonstrations with video feedback helps the performer evaluate what to change to perform more like a skilled performer. In Figure 2.1 we have illustrated how augmented information affects performance and subsequently learning through the processes of error detection and correction. More specifically, we have tried to show simply how the intentions and goals of performance are influenced by feedback (both intrinsic and extrinsic) and also by augmented information in the form of demonstrations, instructions and verbal and visual cues.

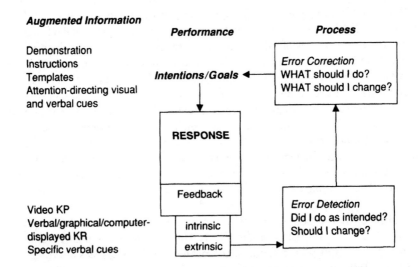

Figure 2.1 Schematic diagram to illustrate how the learning process is affected by various augmented information sources. Error-detection and correction processes are informed by augmented information in the form of feedback and pre-practice information. This information influences the intention and goals of the performer and subsequently the movement response.

In the following sections we evaluate these information sources in terms of their potentially positive and negative roles in the learning process. Various methods are compared to ascertain how effectively they alert to error throughout performance and how effectively they help change performance when required. What should be clear from this review is that more information is not necessarily better than less, instructing is not always better than a more hands-off method where the learner is encouraged to discover a motor solution, and what might work in one situation for one person will not necessarily be the most effective under different conditions and at a different level of skill.

2.2 Augmented feedback: knowledge of results (KR) and performance (KP)

Feedback provides both a motivational and an informational role, encouraging repeated performance and performance directed to reducing discrepancy between a desired and an actual outcome. It is this second, informational role that is of most concern in this review. Although the motivational role of the coach is undoubtedly critical to performance change and performance generally, it is the type of information that is delivered and how it is delivered that is most important in encouraging specific changes in performance in the direction of a to-be-acquired movement or outcome goal(s).

2.2.1 Positive effects

KR and KP at a very basic level serve to confirm a person's own judgement about outcome success based on intrinsic information sources (see Magill, 2001). Alerting to success of an outcome will lead to continued performance if the result was successfully achieved and a change in performance if it was not (see Figure 2.1). Outcome information has been distinguished in two ways: either qualitative, whereby a general statement alerting to the success of the action is provided, such as good or bad; or quantitative, whereby the extent of error is conveyed through exact measurements. The amount of information conveyed by either source will be somewhat dependent on the task, and the knowledge of the performer, such that distinctions between qualitative and quantitative KR might be less important than distinctions between the amount or degree of information. In the past, there have been many experiments directed towards the precision of KR. Early in practice at relatively simple timing or distance skills (e.g. Magill and Wood, 1986), qualitative and quantitative KR typically have similar effects on performance (or refinement), as the learner gradually gets closer to the goal and begins to reduce variability in attempts. After this initial period of practice, more precise quantitative information can be used more effectively to reduce error and perform more accurately.

In general, the positive effects of KR have been observed during the practice or acquisition phase of skill learning. Repeated feedback from trial to trial will lead or guide the learner to the correct response, encouraging the degree of change that is needed from trial to trial. KR and KP can help to make errors salient to the performer such that corrections can be put in place next trial to alleviate these errors. It has been shown that so powerful are the effects of outcome feedback that even when it is erroneous, learners use the information and downgrade valid intrinsic sources, from vision for example, to 'correct' performance erroneously (e.g. Buekers et al., 1992). During practice, providing KR after every trial, in what has been termed a frequent schedule of feedback, has generally shown to be beneficial to performance (see Winstein and Schmidt, 1990). As long as the learner knows whether an error has been made, there is a strong likelihood that changes in performance will be observed. Even with-holding KR can be informational if the performer realises that error information is only provided once performance falls outside a certain criterion or bandwidth (see Lee and Carnahan, 1990).

In relatively complex skills, where a new movement pattern needs to be acquired, feedback about outcome success can also promote a change in the movement response without additional information alerting what to change (e.g. Hodges and Franks, 2000, 2002a; Swinnen et al., 1993). There have been a number of studies where the type of information available in the feedback has been manipulated, i.e. information about outcome success generally (i.e. KR) or information about how the task was achieved (i.e. KP). For example, Swinnen et al. (1993) conducted a dual arm movement task where the arms were required to perform simultaneous yet non-symmetrical tasks. This decoupling of the limbs to perform a movement skill is typical for many sporting actions, such as executing a serve in tennis, where one hand needs to throw the ball in the air while the other is responsible for timing the swing of the racket (see Sherwood and Rios, 2001). In this dual-arm movement task, Swinnen et al. (1993) found that feedback about the degree of coupling between the limbs (i.e. KR) was equally effective at encouraging the correct movement as feedback about the displacements of the limbs (i.e. KP).

In a similar bi-manual task, requiring a spatial and temporal decoupling of the limbs, it has been shown that a change in movement response can be effectively encouraged by feedback concerning the relationship between the limbs (see Hodges and Franks, 2001, 2002a). This feedback does not need to contain information about what needs changing, only that a change is required. This role of KR as an instigator for change is undoubtedly its most important func-tion. If a change in a response is not encouraged through KR and the skill has not been performed to the degree of required success, then the information is not sufficient. These instances include times when error information concern-ing only one component of the action or goals of the action are available, such as either the spatial or temporal component, or the movement of only one limb. In addition, when the feedback relates to components that cannot easily be changed, such as the force imparted onto an object due to strength or height limits in the performer, the role of feedback is likely to be diminished.

These principles hold for both KR and KP. More detailed knowledge of performance might fail to change performance as effectively as KR if the skill level of the performer does not allow the degree of control over specific components to change the skill, or if they do not know how the movement should be changed. For example, Newell *et al.* (1990) showed that the value of KR and KP was dependent on the novelty of the task goal, such that knowledge about how the movement was performed was only useful if criterion information about how it should be performed was also available. If the task goal was unfamiliar or novel, the quality of the feedback was unimportant. Similarly, Brisson and Alain (1997) showed that KP about how a movement was performed in a coincident timing task, presumed to be somewhat analogous to intercepting a ball with a bat, was useful only if suitable reference information was provided to interpret or calibrate the KP. This reference role could be provided by KR (i.e. whether the target was correctly intercepted) or by an expert template of correct performance.

2.2.2 Negative effects

Precise information about performance, and frequent feedback generally, can have the negative effect of producing variable performance during the practice phase. Knowledge of an error (whether this is within one second, or one millisecond) could lead to over-correction of performance (see Sherwood, 1988). If the level of feedback is too specific for the level of control that the performer is able to exert over the skill, then this feedback could prevent stable performance and hinder outcome success.

Despite this instability which might result from frequent provision of precise KR, very rarely are negative effects from providing KR observed during the practice phase of learning. However, learning can only be effectively assessed at a later time period. Performance changes during practice might reflect only temporary changes and not relatively permanent long-term adjustments (see Schmidt and Lee, 1999). To separate these temporary from more long-term effects, the acquisition or practice phase has been distinguished from the retention phase. During retention, performance is evaluated after cessation in practice and typically augmented feedback is withheld to evaluate performance. The retention phase of testing is meant to represent those conditions where performance itself will be evaluated. For example, a long-jumper who is provided with augmented feedback about error in footfall, in relation to the take-off board during practice, will not typically have this information available under competitive conditions. The important question then is whether augmented information provides a long-term benefit when it is no longer available. As will be shown, there is considerable evidence that performance will suffer when this information is withdrawn. In contrast to augmented information about footfall placement, outcome information concerning the length of the long-jump remains during the test phase, so the assessment of the skill with this information is a valid and realistic measure of learning. These distinctions are important as the effects of feedback are remarkably dependent on the phase and conditions of learning. In fact, these effects are so strong that researchers have observed an inverse relationship between practice and retention, such that the greater the benefits of feedback seen during the practice phase of skill acquisition, the greater are the detriments observed in the test or retention phase (see Salmoni et al.,1984).

One of the most serious effects of regular performance feedback is its overly guiding role, such that the learner becomes dependent on this information to their detriment when performance is required at a later date in the absence of this information. This has been referred to as the guidance hypothesis (Salmoni et al., 1984; Winstein and Schmidt, 1990). This dependency on feedback during the practice phase of the skill has been proposed to hinder self-generated error detection processes and the use of intrinsic sources of information which remain throughout testing conditions (see Swinnen, 1996). The amount of feedback and when it is delivered will have a significant impact on the dependency of the performer on this information. Very generally, concurrent feedback provided throughout the execution of continuous, rhythmic tasks has been found to be more guiding and promote greater dependency than feedback about task success provided after the movement has been completed (i.e. terminal feedback). For example, Vander Linden et al. (1993) found that concurrent feedback about the amount of force expended during an elbow extension task was more helpful at reducing error in acquisition than terminal feedback. However, when performance was assessed in retention, the concurrent feedback group performed with the most error. Concurrent feedback guides the performer to the correct response such that they are not equipped for reducing error based on other sources of intrinsic information. There is no incentive to engage in the error-detection process and actively work out why an error occurred and what changes in the movement led to the correction of this error.

Similar to the mechanism underpinning the negative effects of concurrent feedback, feedback provided immediately after executing the action has also been shown to discourage the learner from actively being involved in the error-detection process and interpreting intrinsic information sources (e.g. Swinnen et al., 1990). Although feedback needs to be tied to the response and therefore given in relatively close proximity to the actual movement, when it is provided too soon after movement completion negative effects in retention are likely to result.

Finally, there have been a number of manipulations on KR frequency which have demonstrated that a high frequency of experimenter-provided augmented feedback is detrimental for later performance in retention tests. Again, the mechanisms behind frequent KR relate to a decreased reliance on other natural information sources available from performing the action (such as the feel and the visual consequences of the movement) and a failure to evaluate actively how effective the actions were in achieving the desired outcome.

As should be clear from these studies, the negative effects of feedback provision can in most cases be quite simply overcome by reducing the frequency of feedback and increasing the time delay between feedback provision and successive practice attempts. Even encouraging learners to evaluate their own performance in the interval between the end of the action and KR can help to overcome potentially negative consequences in retention (e.g. Hogan and Yanowitz, 1978). Such reductions in frequency measures include:

1 an overall reduction in the relative frequency of feedback, for example on 50 per cent of the trials
2 fading schedules of feedback, whereby the frequency gradually reduces as a function of practice
3 bandwidth feedback, which is provided only when error falls markedly outside performance guidelines (which might work in a similar way to a fading schedule, as the frequency of feedback is reduced as participants learn)
4 summary feedback, provided after a block of practice trials relating to all the trials in a general manner, or perhaps only the previous trial
5 self-selected feedback, whereby the learner governs the amount of information they need concerning task success.

The optimal amount of feedback to provide is difficult to prescribe accurately. Very generally, the reduction in the relative frequency of KR provision is more important than the actual amount of feedback (Goodwin and Meeuwsen, 1995). Also, Schmidt *et al.* (1990b) found that there was an inverted 'U' relation between accuracy in retention and the interval between the provision of summary KR. Providing feedback too infrequently was shown to be somewhat equivalent to providing feedback after every trial. An optimal frequency allows for self-directed error detection, but does not allow performance to depart too markedly from the goal or criterion. A slightly lower rate of acquisition as a result of a reduction in feedback will be evidenced in enhanced performance in retention relative to a group that is provided with feedback every trial. This reduction in feedback frequency will also prevent the over-correction of errors during performance that can produce high variability in trial-to-trial responses.

2.2.3 Additional feedback issues: interactions with task complexity and movement features

Despite these long-term negative effects of frequent feedback, there has been evidence that dissociations in performance effects between the practice and test phase are dependent on the type of task and specific features of the task. Generally it has been shown that more frequent feedback is beneficial for absolute features of a movement (such as the overall timing, force and movement distance), but that relative features of the movement, such as the relative timing between components and the sequencing of components, are enhanced via a reduction in feedback. For example, Wulf and Schmidt (1996) found that the relative timing between a sequence of key-presses was learnt more effectively under reduced frequency of feedback conditions, whereas a relative reduction in feedback was actually somewhat harmful to scaling the movement correctly to respond in the desired time. However, reduced feedback regarding relative timing was also more beneficial during practice than 100 per cent KR, questioning the interpretation that it is the guiding properties of KR that are harmful in later retention performance. Rather, reduced feedback produced increased stability in the practice phase (i.e. a reduced need to over-correct errors), which seemed to benefit the performance and learning of the invariant features of the movement (see Lai and Shea, 1998).

In general, where tasks are somewhat deprived in the amount of intrinsic feedback available from naturally performing the movement, KR is likely to be critical in its role as long as it is not provided too frequently such that the learner cannot perform without it when it is removed in retention or final testing conditions. Some reduction of KR in acquisition can also be beneficial to this phase of learning if the desired movement goal is consistent production, rather than the acquisition of a novel movement pattern.

In addition to feedback interactions as a result of specific features of the movement, there is also evidence that the effects of feedback are dependent on the complexity of the skill to be acquired. Although the removal of feedback might impact negatively on performance, the degree of performance detriment does not always take performance to the level observed by reduced feedback groups. For example, Swinnen et al. (1997) examined the acquisition of a difficult two-handed coordination movement under various feedback conditions. In retention and transfer to new feedback conditions, although the group that was provided with augmented feedback about the relationship between the limbs, and therefore task success, was affected by its removal, the performance of this group was still better than a blindfold and regular vision group. Also, Wulf et al. (1998) found that when trying to perform fast and wide movements on a ski-simulator, more frequent provision of feedback about movement amplitude and speed was actually better for learning than reduced feedback provided during practice.

It seems that for tasks that are rich in intrinsic information about how the movement feels, frequent feedback helps the learner know how to calibrate the intrinsic feedback to success, thus enabling more refined judgements of success based on this information alone. As a result of this research and similar studies where task complexity has been increased, Swinnen (1996) has recommended that optimal summary length should become close to every trial as the complexity of the task increases. Although there are no specific criteria that can describe a task as more complex than others, typically more complex tasks require the learning of new relationships between a number of body segments and might involve more degrees of freedom (such as whole body movements) in comparison to more simple tasks. Wulf and Shea (2003) have also suggested that feedback provided in more complex skills typically serves less of a guiding role in comparison to its role in relatively simple skills. Where a number of options are available for attaining success (e.g. a penalty shot in soccer), or different components have to be achieved (e.g. both a fast and wide movement on a ski-simulator), feedback alerts to errors but typically does not prescriptively alert performers as to how to change their actions to achieve success. Under these conditions, the performer will need to rely on their own error-detection and correction capacities to improve performance and therefore will not show a strong dependence on feedback when it is later removed in retention tests. These dual roles of augmented information as a description of what was done and a guide as to what should be done (as illustrated in Figure 2.1) are elaborated below when we discuss the role of demonstrations and instructions in the motor learning process.

2.3 Demonstrations and instructions

The error-alerting role of feedback is undoubtedly important. Before changes in the movement will be observed, some knowledge that change is required is necessary. A number of authors (e.g. Hodges and Franks, 2002b; Newell, 1991; Swinnen, 1996) have pointed to the dual roles of feedback in not only providing information as to movement success (i.e. detection of error), but also establishing a goal for the movement. If feedback is provided about the success in throwing a ball to a target (e.g. a basketball free-throw shot), goal information is also indirectly available concerning the task demands. If feedback is provided about the manner of achieving the shot, then goal information is also provided in as much as the learner is directed to changing this feature of the movement. Additional goal information might be relayed through movement templates, demonstrations or verbal instructions. For economy we will refer to this information generally as pre-practice information. However, it is important to appreciate that this type of information is often provided throughout the learning process and interspersed with practice attempts, such that the term is not all-encompassing. It is this error-correcting role of augmented information to which we now turn our attention. The aim of this review is to evaluate the empirical evidence concerning the value of pre-practice information in acquiring and refining motor skills. How much should coaches instruct, and can instruction actually be detrimental for performance and learning?

2.3.1 Positive effects

2.3.1.1 The reference role of pre-practice information

There is no doubt that one of the important components of motor skill acquisition is adequate goal-related information. Without guidance as to what is required and perhaps indirectly measures of performance that reflect the task goals, the attempted response will be undirected. Various environmental and task constraints will indirectly dictate how a skill is to be performed (e.g. certain equipment will constrain how a person can stand, hold an object or impart force onto an object); more often, however, additional constraints will be needed in terms of instructions or demonstrations, which more directly limit the manner of attaining a task goal.

Movement goals conveyed through instructions, demonstrations and criterion templates (e.g. computer displays such as those in simulators and virtual reality devices) help to provide a reference-of-correctness (see Swinnen, 1996), so it is possible for the performer to judge whether their actions matched those required. In this way comparisons are made across the sensory experiences of performing and the desired technique or movement, alerted via instructions and demonstrations. When a desired sequence of movements or a specific movement is the intended goal of instruction (e.g. a pike jump on the trampoline, the performance of a cartwheel in gymnastics or a choreographed dance sequence), then it is important that reference information is provided so that the intended movement(s) can be determined. Feedback can direct attention onto specific components of the action and encourage change, but without a clear reference goal as to what is required, feedback might have little value. For example, in a study comparing verbal instructions to video feedback about an over-arm throwing action, Kernodle et al. (2001) found that verbal information, which alerted participants as to errors and how to correct them, was more beneficial for acquiring a desired throwing pattern than only providing video feedback. The authors concluded that because reference information was not provided to the video feedback group, they were unable to perform comparisons and thus detect errors in performance over and above their existing knowledge concerning how to throw over-arm.

2.3.1.2 Effectively conveying information through demonstrations?

Beyond the important reference role of this type of information, additional questions concern how effectively the goal of the action can be conveyed through demonstrations and instructions and whether repeated exposure to this information before practice helps the learner acquire a novel motor skill. Some of the most convincing research that demonstrations help to effectively convey important features of the movement, which are then translated into effective motor reproduction, comes from Carroll and Bandura (1982, 1985, 1987). These researchers have shown that a discrete sequence of arm movements can be learnt via a series of demonstrations. Measures of recognition and recall show that repeated demonstrations help the learners encode the information, such that errors can be detected (i.e. desired performance determined) and subsequently corrected. Very few studies have tried to untangle these two components of learning, i.e. conceptual understanding as assessed through measures of recognition and the ability to use this information to perform the skill correctly, as assessed through motor recall. The issue of conceptual understanding (i.e. the ability to determine the task requirements and understand the critical features of a demonstration) is especially pertinent with young children. Not only will the inexperience of young children affect their ability to discern correctly what to do, but also underdeveloped cognitive skills (i.e. attention span, verbal skills and memory capacity) will cause problems in understanding. As detailed below, additional information, such as feedback or visual cues, is sometimes required to help learners extract the important information from a display. Indeed, Carroll and Bandura (1990) found that verbal cues, alerting to sequencing and timing, helped participants reproduce the spatial components of the action in the correct order more effectively.

2.3.1.3 Conveying a strategy

In addition to information about the spatial features of a to-be-produced action and the correct ordering of these components, demonstrations and instructions also help to convey a strategy. In some situations the success of a movement is not automatically determined by its closeness to a specified criterion. For example, the success of a throw is judged by its end result (i.e. whether it reached the intended target), not whether the technique matched a desired criterion. In fact, sometimes the method for attaining a goal is not clear-cut and may depend on many factors such as the novelty of the task, the strength and height of a performer, the environmental conditions on the day. Therefore, one of the roles of instructions and demonstrations is to relay a strategy for achieving success, which might be in terms of a general technique or form (e.g. how to throw a javelin), a specific cue (e.g. the position of the arm during the backswing of a javelin throw) or a reliable method (e.g. the cascade method of juggling). In some early research looking at the effectiveness of visual demonstrations in teaching an unusual motor skill (i.e. shoot-the-moon task where a ball had to be moved to the top of two hand-held rods), Martens et al. (1976) found that demonstrations alerted participants to an effective strategy for achieving the task goal (i.e. a ballistic rather than creeping strategy). In this way, ineffective strategies and perhaps valuable practice time were avoided so that practice could be devoted to refining a technique. Similarly, Vogt (1996) found that a technique for performing a moving, pendulum swing task (where the swing of the pendulum was to be minimised at the end of its movement) could be effectively encouraged through observation of a practised model.

For skills with relatively simple motor responses, but perhaps a significant problem-solving component (as in the shoot-the-moon task), technique or strategy information would be expected to facilitate acquisition rate. A strategy can be relayed via instructions or demonstrations and if it is the only, or at least the most effective or efficient, way for performing the skill, then information concerning this strategy should be beneficial. A study by Al-Abood et al. (2001), where participants were required to practise landing a modified dart on a target board placed on the floor, serves to illustrate this point. An under-arm throwing strategy was conveyed through either verbal instructions or visual demonstrations and the performance of these two groups was compared to a control condition where no strategy information was provided. The control group failed to spontaneously adopt this strategy for performing the task in comparison to the two strategy-instructed groups (supporting previous research). However, in terms of performance error (i.e. target accuracy), the control group did not perform significantly worse than the other two groups. What this study shows is that when a strategy is not obvious, or perhaps not even optimal for successful performance, it will not be spontaneously adopted without further constraining information. In instances where goal attainment can be achieved successfully through other means, the motivation for changing technique will be substantially diminished.

2.3.1.4 A comparison across pre-practice methods

In the study by Al-Abood et al. (2001), the authors also found that the visual demonstration more effectively constrained performance than the verbal instructions. There have been a number of experiments comparing across these different mediums to examine which method is the most effective for encouraging correct technique and successful performance (when these can be differentiated). For example, Magill and Schoenfelder-Zohdi (1996) showed that demonstrations were more effective at encouraging the acquisition of a rhythmic-gymnastic's rope-skill than a series of instructions which contained essentially the same information. The authors concluded that for skills with complex features, visual demonstrations most effectively conveyed these features and the relationships between components. It is the general consensus that more information can be conveyed more simply by a visual demonstration than by verbal instructions (see McCullagh and Weiss, 2001; Newell et al., 1985). It has additionally been shown that the attentional demands associated with taking information from a visual display are decreased in comparison to written or verbal instructions (see Craik and Lockhart, 1972). However, Annett (1993) has suggested that the effectiveness of a specific medium for conveying a motor action will be judged in terms of how it is able to generate a motor image. The implication is that if verbal instructions can activate an image of the action to the same degree as a visual demonstration, the value of these two mediums will be similar.

There has also been considerable evidence in the motor skill acquisition literature to show that a combination of verbal and visual information aids the retention and subsequent recall of an act (e.g. Hall et al., 1997). Although verbal labelling is sometimes engaged spontaneously, especially by adults or more skilled learners, there is evidence that children in particular do not attach labels to actions, which is subsequently detrimental for recall (e.g. Cadopi et al., 1995). In addition, because young children have a tendency to focus on the outcome effects of an action, rather than the actual movements required to attain them, verbal or visual cues might help children attend to important features of the movement. For example, Bekkering et al. (1996) showed that four-year old children imitated correctly a movement to the left ear, but failed to imitate the action when the right arm moved across the body to touch the left ear. Similarly, Hayes et al. (2003) showed that a novel bowling movement, demonstrated by a model, is somewhat ignored by 7-year old children when a ball is supplied. If a specific movement form is the intended goal of instruction then additional information might be required to direct young children to this information. The combination of visual and verbal cues in this case would also help later recall of these features.

2.3.2 Negative effects

Although there are undoubtedly positive benefits from providing pre-practice information which prescribes what to do, there are conditions where this type of augmented information is ineffective and, more worryingly, detrimental to the skill acquisition process. Across a series of experiments we have examined how demonstrations and instructions impact on the acquisition of a difficult and unfamiliar dual limb coordination task, requiring spatial and temporal decoupling (see Hodges and Franks, 2002b, 2003 for a review). To perform this movement correctly, participants are required to inhibit the production of more stable, yet undesirable, coordination tendencies where the arms show a preference to move symmetrically in and out together at the same time, or in an alternating fashion. As remarked earlier, many sport skills require coordinated yet non-symmetrical coupling of the limbs involved in the skill (e.g. juggling, dancing, butterfly stroke in swimming).

Correct production of the required coordination movement in these experiments was alerted by outcome feedback, provided either during the movement (concurrently) or at the end of the movement (terminal). The feedback was actually a graphical plot of the relationship between the left and right hand movements, such that a quarter of a cycle phase lag between the arms resulted in a circle pattern. Participants were required to move continuously at a regular speed to try to produce the required movement, which was alerted directly by instructions or demonstrations or somewhat indirectly by the movement feedback (i.e. correct production of a circle). The intrinsic feedback available from performing this task is relatively high, such that augmented feedback should help initially to encourage change in movement production, but also enable the calibration of intrinsic feedback such that the movement can be performed by this information alone (see Swinnen et al., 1997). The main question of concern, however, was whether additional information, specifying how to reach the goal (i.e. a method for error-correction), would facilitate performance beyond that provided by feedback.

In an initial study, Hodges and Lee (1999) found that written instructions, which gave either a general rule specifying the desired relation between the limbs or a schematic specifying the exact positions of the arms every quarter of a cycle, did not enhance performance beyond a non-instructed control group. In a follow-up experiment, similar results were observed when visual demonstrations rather than written instructions were provided during the practice phase (Hodges and Franks, 2001). It was not only that the additional information provided in the form of instructions and demonstrations failed to encourage adoption of the desired movement, but also in some cases it was actually detrimental to performance and learning. Even instructions which served to warn participants of initial biases in performance, and how to adapt these to produce the newly required movement, failed to aid either rate of acquisition or learning generally (Hodges and Franks, 2002a) and again negatively impacted on performance. The question of what information is extracted from a demonstration becomes important in this context to help answer why this information was insufficient to speed acquisition above non-prescriptive feedback and also, more importantly, why performance was negatively affected. A number of variables that could account for these effects are discussed in the following sections.

2.3.2.1 Ineffective strategy information

As discussed earlier, one of the critical information roles of pre-practice information is to alert to a strategy. For movements that require the limbs to move in a somewhat complex spatial and temporal coordination pattern, the strategy that is alerted from a demonstration or instruction might not be that intended by a coach or teacher. Participants in our experiments were able to pick up a strategy that symmetrical movements were not required. However, this strategy was not sufficient at guiding them to the correct response, but rather encouraged another incorrect, alternating movement strategy to be adopted. In fact, it proved to be a somewhat harmful strategy, as symmetrical movements were avoided and little variability in movement production was demonstrated within and between practice attempts. Example data from two participants attempting to produce circle patterns by moving their arms in the desired coordination pattern are shown in Figures 2.2 and 2.3.

In Figure 2.2, individual trial data across acquisition and retention is displayed for a participant in the no-instruction group. A positive sloping line illustrates a tendency to perform symmetrical movements initially. This very quickly gives way to more varied performance across practice and a greater tendency to perform alternating movements and eventual ability to offset the limbs by a quarter of a cycle to produce circle patterns. In contrast, exemplar data from a participant in the instruction group has been illustrated in Figure 2.3. This participant received instructions and demonstrations detailing how symmetrical, in-phase movements could be adjusted to effect a quarter of a cycle lag enabling correct production of the circle pattern. Despite the considerable instruction, the effect of this information was to encourage avoidance of symmetrical movements, and the adoption of another undesired movement (alternating flexion and extension of the arms) illustrated by the negative sloping lines in Figure 2.3. Although after 80 practice trials some circular tendencies were noted in the feedback (i.e. an offset in the limbs), in retention, only alternating movements were displayed. As such, the demonstrations and instructions served to constrain the movement, but not effectively so that the required movement was produced. Although stable performance is desirable if a movement has been performed correctly and the performer is trying to refine the movement, when the movement is wrong and the performer is having difficulty resisting other more comfortable movements, this lack of change in the movement response is problematic (see Lee et al., 1995).

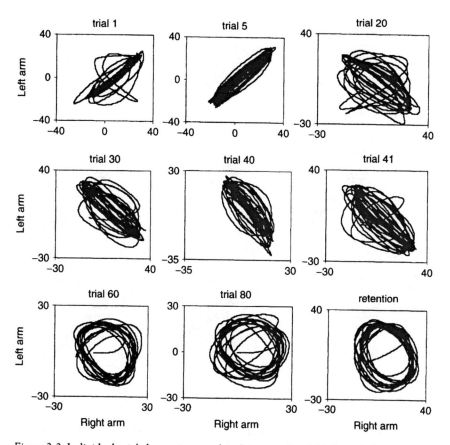

Figure 2.2 Individual trial data represented as Lissajous figures (relative motion plots) across acquisition and in retention for an exemplar participant in the no-instruction group from experiment 1 (Hodges and Franks, 2002a).

Strategy or technique information can also be detrimental for performance and learning in tasks where the desired movement is not the goal of the action. For example, Vereijken (1991) found that individuals learning to perform slalom ski-movements on a simulator, where success in achieving fast and wide movements was not dependent on a specific method, were actually more successful when a skilled model was not available for them to copy. Vereijken argued that in tasks where there are both outcome and technique goals, performers might trade-off performance in one against trying to improve in another. Again, constraints imposed by demonstrations or instructions had a negative impact on task success.

Therefore, it is important that the learner and coach or teacher is aware as to the critical goals of the task. If outcome attainment is the only requirement of

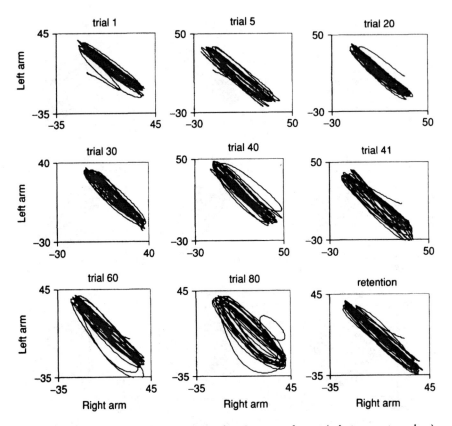

Figure 2.3 Individual trial data represented as Lissajous figures (relative motion plots) across acquisition and in retention for an exemplar participant in the in-phase instruction group from experiment 1 (Hodges and Franks, 2002a).

a skill (such as is the case with a javelin throw), then additional technique goals can interfere with attainment. However, coaches often have dual goals of attaining a specific outcome, in a specific manner (perhaps as a result of experience with other athletes, mechanical principles, or aesthetics). In these conditions, the coach needs to be clear as to the critical goal, perhaps at different points in acquisition. Although there have been very few empirical studies where instructions have been manipulated at different points in the learning process (see Wulf and Weigelt, 1997), a possible method for instruction might be to encourage outcome goals initially, then to follow-up this method with technique-based instruction, if success is not forthcoming. This information does not need to be comprehensive, but perhaps only specific verbal cues directing to change and critical features for achieving that change. Fronske *et al.* (1997) found that verbal cues not only led to better technique but also improved performance in comparison to intense guided practice which comprised detailed instruction and guidance.

In summary, strategy information conveyed through instructions or demonstrations, which supposedly convey what to do, might not be that intended and can detrimentally constrain performance. Second, in many sporting skills, the success of the action is not directly dependent on the technique and movement form. Especially early in practice, very rarely are success and technique perfectly in tune. What should be apparent is that trade-offs in performance might result due to augmented information directed to one, rather than another. Learning is a process of discovering how movements and effects are related, not the acquisition of one in isolation (see also Van Rossum, 1997). As will be discussed in the following sections, an increased focus on the effects of an action is more beneficial for performance and learning than an increased focus on the cause (i.e. technique and form).

2.3.2.2 Critical information is difficult to discern in novel and complex skills

Returning to the discussion as to why the instructions or demonstrations in our experiments failed to facilitate learning (i.e. Hodges and Franks, 2000, 2001, 2002a), an important question concerns why demonstrations in particular were not able to inform about the desired movement. In other words, why wasn't it possible to alert the performer to the desired coordination pattern and effectively encourage error-correction? Among others, Scully and Newell (1985) have proposed that the critical information relayed by a demonstration is the relative motions of the limbs (i.e. the spatio-temporal relationship of the body). However, this information is not in fact easily detected in unfamiliar and complex movements and subsequently will not be well produced in movement recall. Collier and Wright (1995) showed that extraction of relative timing information might only be possible for simple, more natural movements such as walking and running and that for unusual or sport-specific tasks, other information might be more important. Features such as absolute motion seem to be replicated or, as seen in our research, performers are alerted to specific characteristics of the display, such as the fact that symmetrical movements are not produced.

There has been very little empirical evidence to show that relative motion information is extracted from a demonstration by an observer. For example, Horn *et al.* (2002) showed that in learning a soccer-chip shot, a model conveys information about more global parameters of the movement, such as the number of approach steps to the ball, rather than the relative motions *per se*. This was irrespective of whether a video model was shown, or a point-light model where the relative phasing between the limbs was made salient.

In the dart-throwing study by Al-Abood *et al.* (2001) detailed earlier, the authors concluded that performers were extracting relative phase information from a demonstration because participants who watched a model performed better in terms of form reproduction than a verbal instruction group. However, rather than extracting relative motion information, it might be that participants focused on the displacements of one specific joint angle (e.g. the elbow) and the relative motion pattern emerged as a consequence of trying to replicate the movements of this one limb. Indeed, absolute timing information from one joint might be as easy, or easier to perceive than relative timing from a number of joints. Additionally, Blandin et al. (1999) showed that absolute timing was learnt before relative timing in a barrier knock-down task (i.e. the timing of one segment, rather than the proportion of time between segments). While we might recognise the movements of a spin bowler, an overhead kick in soccer, the scaling of a hurdle, or a complicated turn on the ice or in the air by a figure skater, whether we understand what we see (i.e. the relationship between the joints and the relative motions in general), and can effectively relate what we see to our own bodies, is questionable. Indeed, the perceptual skill of differentiating across different spins or gymnastic stunts takes experience and knowledge of how these actions are performed.

These conclusions were supported by the results from a recent experiment (Hodges et al., 2003a) where the movement goal was conveyed only through demonstrations and not via augmented feedback. Under these circumstances, demonstrations alone were not sufficient at specifying the desired movement. Due to the novelty and difficulty of the task, participants had problems understanding what was required (i.e. a problem in error detection). This was confirmed in error-detection tests provided at the end of practice, where a number of individuals were unable to differentiate the required movement pattern from incorrect yet somewhat similar movements. Therefore, not only was an undesirable strategy adopted due to difficulties in performing the required movements, but participants were not aware that the movements were wrong.

Interestingly, video feedback about the learner's own movement (i.e. KP) helped to overcome some of these difficulties in error detection and subsequently correction. If the performer is able to compare and contrast across information sources (i.e. this is what I should do and this is what I did), then subtle differences in the information content of the two displays should help make salient the required features of the movement. There are many examples in sports and arts where demonstrations need to be supplemented with video or mirrors to alert the performer to discrepancies between their performance and that which is required. For example, in learning to perform a dance or martial arts move, it is sometimes difficult to know whether one's own movements are the same as those demonstrated and related – whether the critical features of the demonstrated movement are understood.

2.3.2.3 Attentional focus

Another important mechanism influencing the effectiveness of instructions and demonstrations during skill acquisition is that of the type of attentional focus encouraged by augmented information. There has been considerable evidence to show that limb-related instructions and demonstrations are actually harmful to performance and learning. In a series of experiments, Wulf and colleagues (see Wulf and Prinz (2001) for a review) manipulated attentional focus to encourage attention either to the limbs or internal features of the movement, or to the effects of the action on the environment, referred to as an external focus of attention. In skills such as pitching and putting a golfball, serving a shot in tennis and volleyball, an attentional focus onto the club, racket or the ball and its effects was more beneficial for performance and learning than an attentional focus onto the limbs required to execute these skills (i.e. the arm and hands). Even in skills requiring balance and slalom-like movements on a ski-simulator, again a focus onto an external cue, such as the apparatus or even a marker placed in a position far from a participant's feet, facilitated performance relative to a focus on the feet or a near cue.

The potentially negative effects of instructions that are related to the limbs rather than the effects of the action on the environment have potentially serious implications for how motor skills should be taught. Novel methods of instruction need to be implemented that encourage change and focus attention on task success, but also manage to help offer some prescriptions as to what and how to change in performance. In an experiment designed to prescribe what to change, but also to decrease the attentional focus on to the limbs in a dual limb coordination task, Hodges and Franks (2000) provided movement demonstrations in conjunction with instructions that directed the performer's attention to the feedback and the relationship between their arms and the feedback (i.e. an external focus). Although no detrimental effects of this type of instruction were observed and this group outperformed a demonstration-only group, there was no significant benefit of this type of information over that of a control group who only received feedback. This finding leads to the conclusion that instructions and demonstrations have a negative impact on performance when they encourage a focus onto the limbs and the movement itself, yet even without this detrimental focus, 'how to' information relayed through demonstrations and instructions is not easily perceived and understood.

In addition to augmented information methods, which encourage attention onto the effects of the movement, other more prescriptive methods might encourage learning without causing an inward attentional focus to the limbs. For example, criterion templates and instructions could be provided which alert the performer to the movements of an expert's racket and/or ball flight information. With this template of the external effects of the action the performer is then able to focus on an external cue, but also to refine their movements from trial to trial based on the degree of discrepancy between their trajectories and the trajectories of an expert. Indeed, some success has been demonstrated from using these strategies to teach motor skills. Todorov *et al.* (1997) found that providing the trajectory of a player's paddle and ball concurrently with those of a skilled player (through a computer simulation) facilitated performance relative to a group provided with verbal feedback statements. Hodges *et al.* (2003b) directly compared demonstrations and feedback relating to either movement form or ball trajectory in a soccer chip-shot. Preliminary results showed that the ball-trajectory group was more accurate in achieving the height and distance requirements of the task than the movement form group, even though both groups received outcome error at the end of each trial.

There are obvious interactions that need to be considered in these situations which relate to the attainment of specific task components. Although outcome success in terms of distance and accuracy in a golf or soccer chip-shot is encouraged by effects-related templates, if a specific technique is the intended goal of the action, an important question concerns whether effects-related templates are able to bring about task success in a method that is considered optimal. Although Hodges et al. (2003b) found that there were some significant features about the movement form group's technique which were more similar to the skilled model than the ball-trajectory group (e.g. number of approach steps), analysis on knee and hip angles showed that both groups displayed similar kinematics to the model. The implication is that the ball-flight information was sufficiently constraining, such that only certain movements emerged as a consequence of trying to match these end-point templates. Similarly, Wulf et al. (2002) found that externally-related feedback statements provided during volleyball training improved service accuracy relative to internal or limb-related feedback statements, but that both types of feedback produced similar improvements in movement form.

In summary, prescriptive, 'how to' instructions should not be considered the default instructional method for teaching motor skills. Changes in movement form can be encouraged through the manipulation of other variables, such as externally-directed feedback statements. Although there are situations where a specific technique or form is the intended goal of the action (as with skills such as gymnastics, diving, dancing, ice-skating), techniques for teaching these skills do not have to be heavily prescriptive in terms of how the joints are interrelated and the angles etc. of the joints. While there is evidence that reduced frequency of feedback relating to movement-related features of an action benefits acquisition and retention, in comparison to the same information provided, there have not been studies designed to look at the amount of internally-related feedback or instruction given on a specific trial.

This type of research obviously has important implications for sport's practitioners. If it is the case that one internally-related movement cue is not as harmful to acquisition as three-internally related cues, then the practitioner can perhaps use a small number of internal statements and cues to inform as to critical aspects of technique. It might be that a combination of internally- and externally-related instructions is optimal in terms of encouraging the desired response in the most effective manner. There also might be interactions with the skill level of a performer in terms of the amount of internally-related instructions that can be given. For example, Beilock et al. (2002) found that manipulations which encouraged attention onto the feet for novice soccer players when dribbling did not negatively impact on performance in comparison to more skilled players.

2.3.2.4 Implicit learning/reinvestment

A final caution concerning the provision of instructions relates to the conditions of practice where performance is required and the explicit nature of the rules underlying successful performance. In a number of studies by Masters and colleagues (e.g. Masters, 1992; Masters and Maxwell, 2003; Maxwell et al., 2001), benefits from withholding instructions and preventing learners from engaging in explicit hypothesis testing have been demonstrated under conditions of attentional load and pressure or anxiety. Masters and colleagues have generally observed a discrepancy between performance of explicitly-instructed groups and implicit or even non-instructed groups. Although in practice of golf putting and table tennis skills the explicitly instructed or non-instructed groups outperformed the implicit groups, who were required to perform secondary, attention-demanding tasks during acquisition, under manipulations which were supposed to elicit stress in retention, the implicit groups and to a somewhat lesser degree the non-instructed groups were less, or not, affected by this manipulation than groups who learnt explicitly. It has been suggested that the mechanism underlying these effects under stressful performance conditions is reinvestment of knowledge into the control of actions, which are better performed at a non-rule-based, non-conscious level of control.

Despite the fact that implicit learning results in performance benefits under conditions of anxiety, this condition of administering practice is somewhat impractical. This is not only because of the difficulty of learning under secondary task conditions; the research has also failed to show that implicit learning groups are able to acquire the skills as well as explicit groups. In an effort to rectify this position, Liao and Masters (2001) required participants to learn a table tennis serve with either explicit instructions, implicitly (while performing a secondary task), or by analogy to coming up the hypotenuse of a right-angled triangle. Analogy learning was found to be somewhat impervious to secondary task and stress interventions, which interfered with the performance of the explicit learning group. Additionally, the learning encouraged by analogy did not affect acquisition performance, in contrast to many implicit learning manipulations. In the most recent review of this research, Masters and Maxwell (2003) suggest that learning with visual demonstrations, rather than verbally-based instructions, should be less impervious to this reinvestment under stress because of the role of verbally-based memory processes interfering with the control of motor performance. Again, although this research has only briefly been highlighted, what it shows is that the conditions of testing need to be considered when deciding the best methods for augmenting learning through the various information sources available. Knowledge-rich strategies for conveying information might not be the most effective for later performance under competitive conditions.

2.3.3 Overview of instructions and demonstrations

Information which specifies what to do and how a movement should be changed can be beneficial to learning under conditions (a) where it dictates what the goal of the action should be, (b) when it provides a clear and obtainable reference, such that comparisons with performance can effectively be achieved, and (c) when valuable practice time can be circumvented by the conveyance of a strategy that has been shown to be the most effective and/or the only way for performing the skill. Some of the negative effects of demonstrations and instructions relate to the fact that an unintended strategy might be conveyed in complex tasks where individuals have difficulty extracting the critical information and under-standing the requirements. Even when this information can be adequately per-ceived and used by a performer, there are situations where it might be ineffectual or indeed detrimental to success on the task. For example, in situations where outcome success is not dependent on a specific technique or strategy, this type of technique instruction in isolation might fail to bring about success. The fact that augmented information also directs attention is an important consideration when deciding how best to facilitate learning. The work of Wulf and colleagues strongly cautions against providing information which directs the learner's attention to the movement (i.e. internally) at the expense of a more effects-related, external focus of attention onto the apparatus, implement or even the augmented feedback (see Shea and Wulf, 1999).

2.4 Augmented information summary and conclusions

What has been highlighted in this review of the literature on augmented infor-mation is that there are no easy, hard and fast rules for effectively providing information to individuals wishing to acquire motor skills. What might be beneficial to performance in one situation will not necessarily be beneficial in another, and therefore it is critical to consider both the conditions of practice and later testing conditions where the skill will be required. The cognitive processes underlying improvements in practice, especially when a skill is being refined through augmented feedback, might be degraded in later conditions when the skill is required in the absence of the augmented information.

While it should be clear that feedback plays primarily an error-detection role and instructions and demonstrations play an error-alerting role, these roles are not always effectively served unless certain conditions are also met. For example, feedback presented on every trial during practice of a relatively simple motor skill will fail to encourage self-generated error-detection mechanisms necessary to ensure effective production when that information is no longer available. Even though a demonstration might effectively convey a strategy for performing a motor skill, under conditions where many different techniques can lead to successful performance or the technique is complicated such that little understanding is gained by merely watching, demonstrations alone are unlikely to facilitate learning and may fail to alert adequately to the desired movement.

Combining different forms of augmented information might help to increase the saliency of desired movement features, as has been suggested in earlier reviews of the feedback literature (e.g. Rothstein and Arnold, 1976), and also the combination of verbal and visual information might benefit later retention and recall.

Although we have discussed a number of reasons why instructions, demonstrations and indeed feedback might have negative consequences for performance and learning, it is important to remember that all these mechanisms could interact during the learning process. If a performer is unable to discern effectively what the task requirements are from a demonstration, then an ineffective strategy might be implemented on the basis of this information. This strategy could lead to a decrease in early variability in initial movement attempts, hindering the discovery of the required movement or a successful strategy for attaining task success. Additionally, the information conveyed could lead to a detrimental focus onto the movements and away from the effects of the movement on the environment. Finally, if the information is conveyed through detailed task instructions, under competitive situations performance might break down, in comparison to the performance of athletes whose practice conditions were less knowledge-heavy.

Both roles of augmented information, as error-alerters and error-correctors, are obviously critical from a coaching perspective. Very generally, the coach needs to consider these roles when deciding what information to provide and how it will work in performance and retention. Often feedback will indirectly specify to the performer what needs changing without the need for additional instruction or demonstration. However, if change is not forthcoming from feedback alone, supplemental information will be needed. Whether this needs to relate to a desired form so that a reference-of-correctness can be formulated will be somewhat dependent on the type of skill to be acquired and perhaps the experience of the learner and conditions under which the skill will be required. Other, less knowledge-rich methods of instruction which encourage variability, problem-solving and attention to intrinsic sources of error might be effective for encouraging outcome and/or movement success. Indeed, although we have presented little discussion as to the importance of cognitive effort in aiding memory and later retention, there is considerable research in the field of education to show that active, problem-based methods of instruction and learning are more effective at encouraging long-term retention of information. Discovery-based methods of instruction, where the learner is encouraged to find the solution or strategy for task success, should help promote a deeper level of learning and understanding and later recall and transfer to new skills.

3 The use of feedback-based technologies

Dario G. Liebermann and Ian M. Franks

3.1 Introduction

Skill acquisition may be characterised as an active 'cumulative' process during which a target movement is expected to improve as a function of practice. Only when the performer is able to reproduce a desired pattern systematically and in a satisfactory way can the motor skill be considered as finally acquired. Feedback shortens and improves the acquisition process, but only if appropriately administered (see Schmidt and Lee (1999) for a review). Recent advances in information technology have exploited this fact, and focused on the feedback athletes receive during training or even during competition.

Feedback is a concept that originated in control theory for close-loop systems (Shannon and Weaver, 1949) designed to keep homeostasis or equilibrium around a reference value a priori set. Such systems are designed to sense information about their actual state, and if any differences between actual and reference values appear, they are corrected in order to restore homeostasis. Motor control in humans is far more sophisticated but, as a conceptual framework, close-loop theory has had very practical implications for motor skill acquisition: firstly, concerning the use of feedback in motor learning, and secondly, concerning the development of specific technologies applied to sports.

Coaches have long assumed their role as feedback facilitators, but they recognise to a lesser extent their role in the correct administration of feedback (its type, quantity and frequency). It is in their power to decide if and how to integrate feedback-based technologies into their training protocols. Some of these technologies allow augmented feedback to be managed by the coach, thus enriching the training experience by stimulating diverse sensory modalities. Such technologies are worth mentioning and are described in the present chapter. Their advantages and disadvantages are discussed along with practical examples on how augmented feedback, in combination with latest advances in technology, can be used to enhance motor performance skill acquisition.

3.2 Video information as a source of feedback

During training, athletes are active in correcting errors in performance and normally use different feedback sources, such as vision and proprioception. On some other occasions, however, they are passive. The question of concern here is to what extent feedback is effective when an athlete is a passive observer: for example, when coaches use alternative training aids such as videotaped replays of previous performances.

Extrinsic video information without a coach's guidance would be rather ineffective in many cases. Video technology has significantly influenced training methods mainly because its relatively low cost, accessibility and portability had already made it the most popular technology among coaches in many sporting events. Individuals watching their performances on videotape cannot regulate the feedback they receive, and sometimes the information available might exceed the athletes' processing ability. Therefore, the intervention of a coach is required, particularly with inexperienced or young athletes. Coaches could help in pinpointing the relevant information captured on video. Then, they could use it as feedback that would help the performer to associate errors in performance, their correction, and the expected movement pattern. From videotaped replays coaches may extract two main kinds of feedback information: one relating to qualitative aspects of performance, and the other relating to the quantitative information. The relation of these two types of video feedback and other technologies will be described in the following paragraphs.

3.2.1 Qualitative video feedback

Video is mostly recognised as an appropriate medium for obtaining qualitative information about performance. Video in combination with TV and PC technology is suitable for enhancement of feedback during the replays. A very promising use of video replays is related to playback technology that allows for a comparison between one's performance and that of other athletes. The technology may be used to imitate movements. One remarkable fact of comparison and imitation is that, as a learning strategy, it has behavioural and neurobiological basis. Humans and other primates imitate movements soon after birth (Meltzoff and Moore, 1977). Moreover, there is evidence showing that specific neurons in the pre-motor cortex of the brain (an area highly associated with planning motor acts) are responsive to movements of others ('mirror neurons') as well as to motor actions carried out by the observer (Rizzolatti *et al.*, 2001). A possible benefit of visually imitating and comparing movements is that imitation is based on observable (extrinsic) kinematics. This strategy might actually serve to bypass the computational burden imposed on the brain during planning motion because it need not consider movement dynamics (muscle moments and joint torques) during computation (Wolpert *et al.*, 1995). This has obvious practical implications for machine learning. In this area of research, imitation is effectively implemented to accelerate robot motor learning (see Schaal, 1998, 1999).

In sport, software developed for implementing the imitation strategy is available. One such technology enables a user to split the computer screen in two halves, and observe in one half the actual performance and in the other half the model performance. The same technology enables a user to blend two synchronised video footages, one from an expert and another from a less experienced individual, which are enhanced, fitted to each other and appropriately transformed (scaled, translated and rotated) (www.quintic.com; www.dartfish.com; for a review of these types of technology see Hughes *et al.* (2002)). To extract meaningful visual information, the videotaped performances can be viewed as continuous replays or as single frames (one frame after an other). Digital blending may be more useful to expose essential differences between two performances, and therefore it may lead to a more effective use of visual feedback. A drawback in comparing and imitating the performance of an expert athlete is that no two performers are identical. What is optimal for one athlete is not for another (Bartlett, 1999). Therefore, the general use of superposition of videotaped replays should be carefully examined in each case. For example, mechanical demands are maximised only at high competitive levels, and therefore mechanical solutions are constrained to only a few, of which some are worth imitating. At low competitive levels, it is suggested to use this technology only to compare video-recorded movements of one's own performance in repeated trials during training or even during competition. For beginners, such visual feedback may be ineffective if the coach does not guide the performer about the interesting foci of attention.

3.2.2 *Quantitative video feedback*

Relevant feedback about the performance is sometimes less explicit than that provided by just showing a videotaped replay. Quantitative information about segmental and joint kinematics (paths, velocities and accelerations) can sometimes provide the basis for changes and corrections based on objective and comprehensible data. For example, vector graphics describing the direction and magnitude of a movement (e.g. the ball path and velocity in a football match) are easily captured today using event-tracking software combined with video or TV technology (www.orad.co.il/sport/index.htm). Basic kinematic information may be used on site or in remote locations for immediate notational analysis if TV broadcasting is available.

When the kinematic feedback needs to be more specific (e.g. joint rotations), the appropriate video technology is different. Video cameras are required to record on-site both the performer in action and a calibration frame of known dimensions, and from a constant perspective. It also requires suitable means for offline video projection, and software to extract digital information and analyse the data. Most video systems for movement analysis require manual coding and visual detection of points of interest on the single images (video frames or fields), one at a time. A data transformation process follows to convert video-coded images in pixel units to some real unit. Displacements as a function of time could therefore be obtained and higher-order time derivatives (e.g. segmental velocities) could be calculated (see Ariel Dynamics, Inc., www.arielnet.com for illustrative examples). Common video analysis systems have become affordable for coaches, and are adaptable to most PC platforms and video cameras. However, a disadvantage of such kinematic analysis systems is that detection of points on the computer screen is manual. This is rather tedious work, and without the expertise, it may sometimes result in unreliable data. Another disadvantage of most affordable commercial systems is their low frame rate, normally ranging between 50 and 60 Hz for European PAL or North American NTSC systems, (0.02s or 0.016s between frames respectively). At these sampling rates, important fast events might not be captured (e.g. the exact moment of heel-strike during running). Although such systems are cost-effective, the quantitative feedback that finally reaches coaches and athletes is delayed with respect to the time of performance. The time taken to record manually the specific points of interest can be rather long (Ay and Kubo, 1999), and this precludes immediate feedback of anything other than the video images themselves. Because of the delay in the provision of the quantitative feedback, videotaped performances cannot always be associated with the internal sensory experience at the time of motor execution. To solve this problem, automatic or semi-automatic video-based commercial systems for movement analysis have been developed and are available. They allow the same information to be gathered more easily and immediately, but are significantly more expensive.

3.3 Automated systems as a source of complex information

Immediate and detailed kinematic analyses require fully automated and technical expertise. Automatic tracking systems use different technologies to track and record motion events in real time (e.g. Charnwood Dynamics, Inc., www.charndyn.com, Motion Analysis Corp., www.motionanalysis.com, Optotrak – Northern Digital Ltd, www.northerndigital.ca, ProReflex and QTM – Qualisys Ltd, www.qualisys.se, Vicon – Oxford Metrics Inc., www.vicon.com). Most are not based on video, but are optic systems adapted to capture light, either passively from light-reflecting markers or actively from pulsed light arrays synchronised with multiple cameras. They are particularly attractive for rapid feedback provision in non-competitive sport settings and for analysing fast motion. Their development has been parallel to that of computer technology that facilitates the task of computation, and to computer vision that allows automatic recognition of markers. The feedback information that can be provided to the athlete is almost immediate and may touch most important aspects of movement. The appropriate way to exploit such technologies is to focus only on the relevant kinematic parameters that answer specific questions because the information that can be retrieved using such systems is too large. This approach accompanied the development of the technologies, and became popular during the past decade to bring athletes to maximal performance (see Kearney (1996) for illustrative examples).

However, most automated systems do not work on video images, and only work on selective marker information. Only a few systems allow video image collection in parallel with marker data collection. Usually these systems are only adapted to combine video recording with the automatic marker recording from separate cameras, all synchronised at start, but not necessarily working at the same sampling frequency. To compensate for the lack of video recording, some other systems combine marker data with simulations of the performance. The assumption is that a virtual performer would add some realism to the numerical marker data, and thus they put an emphasis on the translation of the real-time marker positions into solid body models by using appropriate software packages and body scanning technology (see for example www.polhemus.com/ FTcasestudyl.htm#skill). It should be noted that any advantage of receiving feedback from three-dimensional graphics (compared to only two-dimensional simple video replays) during training or competition is not well documented. It appears that systems that can overlap real video with the solid body models may become a choice of preference of coaches and athletes, because these systems combine the advantage of video with quantitative data and simulations.

3.3.1 *Quantitative feedback derived from simulated performance*

An alternative use of high-precision systems is the inclusion of the kinematic information obtained to build models and to simulate sport techniques (see Winters and Woo (1990) for a review on modelling). Using models may allow coaches to become aware of unnoticed errors and act as feedback mediators in passing pre-elaborated model information to the performers. This is particularly useful when very subtle changes in a skill are required in order to achieve optimal or maximal performance. For example, in javelin throwing the athlete's goal is to achieve a given maximal distance. For that subject only a few mechanically defined movement patterns would probably lead to acquisition of the target distance, because maximisation constrains the solution of the problem to only a few possible solutions. These (few) possible ways to achieve a near maximum distance in javelin throwing can be estimated using a biomechanical optimisation process. By 'optimisation' we mean an interplay between variables that are maximised, minimised, or tuned to a criterion defined as a set of kinematic and/or dynamic equations of constraint. A model could be built based on such equations and the underlying computer algorithm could be designed to calculate prospective outcomes of performance before and after changing some parameters of movement. Model algorithms are often built to simulate body motion using suitable computer graphics, and therefore a visual comparison between real and computer-simulated (optimised) performances is allowed. In the javelin-throwing example mentioned previously, a performer may be able to control release velocity, release angle, and height of release (see Figure 3.1), but not air friction, air density and humidity that interact with the javelin surface. Using Newton's laws of motion to make model calculations, the combination of parameters necessary to achieve any distance of throw can be predicted. Feedback about the differences between expected (modelled) and observed results (obtained, for example, from videotape analysis) could be used to change the technique and to perform closer to the model. In doing so, it is assumed that the chance to throw the javelin at the larger expected distance will increase.

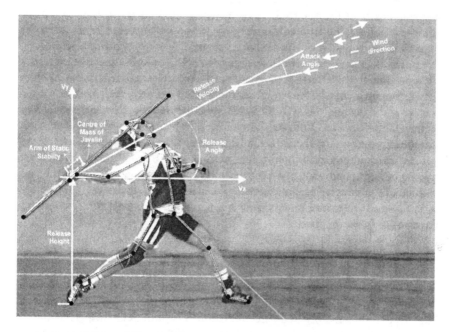

Figure 3.1 A javelin throwing performance and the major variables that could affect the final distance of throw. Some are used as the input to a biomechanical model of the javelin flight. These variables are presented to the coach, who can experiment on the computer with the effects of modifying them. The athlete could be trained to change some variables, and in doing so to perform close to the mechanical model.

A problem with such an approach is, again, that the calculated parameters cannot always be made available immediately. Therefore, much effort has been dedicated to develop video systems and computer applications that can provide the essential modelled information as soon as possible, and not only in laboratory conditions. Hubbard and Alaways (1989) reported an early implementation of such an approach, and measured kinematics at release during a series of javelin throwing trials. Optimisation of the javelin flight for a thrower was based on a constant release speed assumption, while the angle of release, the angle of attack, and the pitch rate were manipulated to optimise performance. Immediate feedback about actual and expected results was provided after each throw to allow the athlete to improve in the next throw.

Some concerns arise regarding the use of the feedback even if the information is immediately available. First, not enough attention has been paid to whether immediate feedback of such a complex kind could improve performance. The common assumption is that the more immediate the feedback that is available, the more effective the use of the information (however, it is important to read the research evidence regarding this issue: see Chapter 2). A second concern is the complexity of the feedback. Athletes need information on how to change their techniques, and the optical technologies coupled to the system of model equations provide it. It might be that a change in the angle of the arm prior to the forward throw is sufficient to lead to a change in all other parameters, rather than needing to try to change all parameters separately (see Kugler *et al.*, 1980). There is some evidence showing that the critical variables, such as the angle of release of the javelin, relate to the distal musculature or implements required to achieve an effect (see Wulf and Prinz, 2001). With this knowledge, the coach can direct attention to one critical kinematic variable, decreasing the attentional burden of simultaneously monitoring many different components. In spite of the higher costs, automated systems have become more popular in recent years, particularly among sport professionals but mainly for indoor uses. Further research is needed because an extensive outdoor use of automatic tracking systems has not yet been reported.

3.4 Training in three-dimensional virtual environments

The use of videotaped replays exploits the ability of athletes to translate two-dimensional visual feedback into meaningful motor actions. Nevertheless, humans perceive and act in a three-dimensional world. Self-motion relative to the surroundings initiates perception of the three-dimensional environment as a precursor to action; that is, action and perception are not separated (Gibson, 1979). This action–perception link can be used to enhance the acquisition of skill because movement affects the way we perceive, while changes in perception affect the way we move (Michaels and Carello, 1981). In practice, computer applications have been specifically developed to create virtual environments that simulate real conditions in sports by using three-dimensional visual effects combined with auditory and/or kinesthetic feedback.

3.4.1 How does the three-dimensional virtual technology work?

Stereovision is a common method used to create a three-dimensional effect from a two-dimensional projection. This is based on the principle that when each eye receives a slightly different perspective of the same visual object, fusion of the two planar views (one for each eye of the same object) occurs at higher brain centres that interpret the resulting image as one three-dimensional view. Various techniques are used to create this illusion. In its simplest version, computer programs can generate two superimposed images. One image is presented in one colour (red) and seen by one eye, and the other image is presented in another colour (green or blue) and seen by the contra-lateral eye, but from a slightly different perspective (that depends on the separation between the two eyes). During the presentation of the images, the subject wears appropriate filter glasses, such that an eye sees one image but not the other. Movement and shading effects help to achieve a more realistic three-dimensional virtual reality experience. Active methods are also available. This method depends on which full-colour image can be displayed to each eye alternately (usually on small video monitors the size of eyeglasses). Again, each eye receives a slightly different image because the monitors are rotated with respect to each other (www.3d-video.de). A more recent technology uses non-rotated glasses that provide continuously different TV displays for each eye (see www.i-glasses.com). A major disadvantage of this sophisticated but relatively inexpensive technology is that subjects cannot see the peripheral surroundings as in reality.

Yet another active method worth mentioning has been developed based on polarised transparent glasses. The individual wears normal eyeglasses, but the crystals are of electronically polarised materials. The technology is based on synchronisation of the right and left polar lenses of the eyeglasses with the pixel lines that compose the images projected on a high-resolution graphic computer monitor (Silicon Graphics Ltd). Monitor lines coded with odd numbers are activated and blank after a fraction of a second and perceived only by one eye, and alternately even-numbered lines are activated to display a rotated version of the same image, but seen only by the other eye. A realistic three-dimensional experience is achieved using this method, and in addition, it does not preclude peripheral vision of the surroundings. This technology is widely used to create virtual environments or complete immerse virtual-reality settings (see www.sgi.com/virtual_reality/Immerse_Reality). Augmented virtual reality using three-dimensional technologies might soon become commonplace, where different practical situations that require motor skills converge. For example, these technologies would aid in the training of surgeons, army personnel, and athletes (Feiner, 2002).

A disadvantage of virtual reality is associated with 'cybersickness'. This is a form of motion sickness, common in 'immerse' virtual environments when subjects experience fast motion three-dimensional virtual performances. The symptoms are similar to those observed during or after training in flight simulators (Crowley, 1987), such as head spinning, vestibular disturbances, and nausea, which commonly appear when a subject cannot cope with minor sensory conflicts between what the eyes see and what the vestibular system perceives.

3.4.2 Advantages of three-dimensional technology in coaching

A potential advantage of using a virtual environment to enhance and train skills is that external and internal feedback, in isolation or combined, may be manipulated to enhance motor learning. Another advantage is that such environments allow practising in unknown conditions without the risks that might be involved in practising in reality. In a simulated three-dimensional virtual environment, a coach can regulate many perceptual factors to train motor reactions to unexpected changes in the environment. Recognising this fact and its contribution to success in sports, some technologies have specifically been developed to enhance feedback in three-dimensional virtual settings, for example, in bicycle riding (CompuTrainer™, RaceMate Inc.) and windsurfing (Force[4] WindSurf Simulator, Force[4] Enterprises Inc.). Kelly and Hubbard (2000) reported a further use of this technology in the design of a bobsled simulator that comprised a cockpit, a motion control system, and a graphics workstation. Such a system allows control of speed, orientation, and direction of movement, and can even add unexpected perturbations (virtual obstacles) in the course of the performance. The simulation and the mechanical components are synchronised and provide a more realistic training. The coach can control parameters such as the type of track, sceneries, steering forces, or weather conditions. Skill training in such virtual settings may bring a better adaptation to reality. Moreover, it can lead to the adoption of more effective anticipatory strategies. Current research suggests that visual feedback during virtual reality training may accelerate the learning process compared to standard coaching techniques (Todorov *et al.*, 1997). However, other evidence suggests that information presented in three-dimensional virtual environments does not always result in the formation of a strategy that is used in reality. For example, judgements based on the information presented in a virtual environment may lead to a different visual-search strategy to the one used when individuals are asked to estimate where a ball would really land (Zaal and Michaels, 1999). One byproduct of training in a virtual reality may be its effects on motivation to learn and perform.

In clinical environments, virtual reality can be effective in the recovery of normal function in children or in adult patients (for example, see www.irexonline.com/software.htm, www.irexonline.com/how_it_works.htm and www.health.uottawa.ca/vrlab/research.html), because mere practice in a novel setting is enough to captivate some individuals. Merians *et al.* (2002) reported the use of virtual reality in stroke patients in the chronic recovery phase, and suggested that the augmented feedback received in standard training combined with virtual reality has led to positive effects in motor function.

A concept that is worth investigating is that of a 'multi-sensing environment', which might also have motivating effects on motor skill acquisition. The Media Laboratory of the Massachusetts Institute of Technology (MIT) has been working on this idea, and developed a virtual 'kids' playground' that reacts to a child's verbal commands or motion (www.whitechapel.media.mit.edu/vismod/demos/kidsroom/kidsroom.htlm). Walls, floors, and furniture interact with the performer, and in doing so, the environment augments feedback and stimulates motor responses that would otherwise be more difficult to elicit. As far as elite sports and athlete training are concerned, no implementation of such facilities is reported, but an exception that might get close is the virtual Tai-Chi trainer developed by the research group of the Entertainment Technology Center of the Carnegie Mellon University in Pennsylvania (www.etc.cmu.edu/projects/mastermotion/overview.htm). This is an ideal example that combines a virtual environment with a virtual trainer, and further links the performer to the computer via optical wireless technology. The individual receives continuous feedback (verbal, tactile vibratory or visual) about his/her movements and the accuracy, posture, and timing of the actions. During skill acquisition in Tai Chi, performers implement an imitation learning strategy. The aim is to master movement by intentionally carrying segmental motion as slowly and as accurately as possible in a quasi-static environment. Therefore, this VR technology combined with the proposed Tai Chi training system might even bypass the problem related to motion sickness.

It should be mentioned that there is not much information on whether training in virtual environments is effective in sports. Most current research focuses on the use of virtual reality in clinical conditions, industry and in the military. Further research is thus required to support the use of such virtual settings in sports and motor skill training.

3.5 Tele-remote training and analysis

Remote coaching using the Internet is a recent concept. People today may carry out a computerised exercise program while a third party supervises the routines and controls the resistance mechanism of the machines (e.g. a 'servo valve' in an isokinetic fitness machine). Speed, resistance, and other parameters may be adjusted from a remote location using the Internet or simply via the phone line (see Ariel Dynamics Ltd; www.arielnet.com).

Some additional possibilities of tele-remote technology including video and other digital technologies are currently being explored, for example via cellular phones or hand-held computers interfaced to GPS (global position system) services. Having an appropriate interface (a CPG card), the images recorded on digital video could be downloaded on hand-held computers, and sent to a remote server where offline analysis takes place. Consider the impact of taking advantage of such a combination of technologies (video, communications and notational analysis online) in field conditions during a golf match. The performer could send video information directly from the cellular videophone (www.j-phone.com; see www.3g.co.uk/PR/December2002/4564.htm), and in a matter of minutes, the quantitative feedback would be sent back via MMS (Multimedia Messaging Service), also available among some phone services. A similar concept but with slightly different technology has been already implemented using hand-held computers (www.arielnet.com).

Online remote coaching is an option that is now also applied in running on a treadmill, cycling or training on a stepper (see NetAthlon™ or UltraCOACH VR® software, IFT Ltd, www.fitcentric.com). The service is managed and controlled via the Internet. The performer can train and even compete in a virtual environment that is shared by others on the net. Sceneries of preference can be displayed on a screen during jogging or riding. If the performer wears appropriate glasses, it also allows a three-dimensional virtual experience during training. Lately, 'web racing' has become possible in sports like bicycle riding, fitness rowing, and even wheelchair racing (www.fitcentric.com).

Another concept that is under development is based on complete personalised fitness protocols (for muscle strength and endurance) that can be totally controlled without the intervention of a human personal trainer by combining broadband Internet communications, robotics, and virtual reality (KnowledGym®, contact fitness@knowledgym.com for information). In this case, a tele-operated robotic arm is used to carry out a set of robot-guided resistance exercises (selected from a personalised library of exercises). A set of sensors allows correcting of posture, segmental displacements, and timing, and a virtual trainer (a digital humanoid) displayed on a computer screen provides verbal feedback online and interactively. The question of concern is whether the feedback provided and the environment benefit performance. The concept has some potential also for recreation, skill learning, and mainly rehabilitation. Hogan has made some initial attempts with his research group (Krebs *et al.*, 1998) at the Massachusetts Institute of Technology to develop robot-aided rehabilitation methods specifically adapted to work with stroke patients (see www.mit.edu/hogan/www for illustrative example). While it is still difficult to measure the success of such a method, it is clear that the technology may lead to positive results. More importantly, the robot may be controlled from a remote site by patients: this may allow future in-house motor rehabilitation (see www.ranier.hq.nasa.gov/ telerobotics_page/realrobots.html for examples of tele-operated robots over the net or via telemetry).

3.6 Laser technology in static and dynamic conditions

During aiming sports that require accuracy such as Olympic shooting or archery, vision is a primary feedback channel. Diverse technologies have been developed to improve the aiming skill by enhancing feedback provision. Perhaps a most representative and clear example is in the use of laser-guided guns to train Olympic shooters. Laser technology has been used to correct for deviations from aiming targets within very narrow margins of error. Technically, a laser beam (e.g. attached to a rifle) hits a laser-sensitive grid that generates an on–off pulse captured by a computer through an interface. The software transforms the pulses generated by those sensors in the array that are hit into relevant coordinates. A graphic display of deviations from the aiming centre is provided for offline analysis, but also online auditory feedback is provided in such form that a proportionally higher pitch sound plays as the distance from the centre increases. Visual feedback in combination with computer-generated auditory feedback has made the training process of shooters very efficient. It allows athletes to immediately correct arm and body posture before pulling the trigger (Noptel Oy Company, Finland; www.noptel.fi/nop_eng/shooter.html).

Laser technology can also be used in dynamic sports, such as speed skating and athletics. Split times and sprint velocities during speed skating, otherwise difficult to obtain on site, were measured by Liebermann *et al.* (2002b) using a Laveg™ laser device especially adapted for sports (Jenoptik, Optik Systeme GmbH, Germany; www.jenoptik-los.de/lasersensor/english/ range_finder/laveg.html). The device allowed for the measuring of linear displacement during the first 100 m of a 500 m sprint within a spatial accuracy of 1 mm and a temporal resolution of 20 ms (50 Hz). The advantage of such a device, compared to video analysis, is that raw displacement data and higher order derivatives were relatively accurate and easy to obtain in the stadium. Liebermann *et al.* (2002b) calculated the different variables (e.g. start velocity, peak velocity, and the time when acceleration dropped to zero) from time differentiation of the horizontal displacement–time function. Athletes and coaches could receive most information immediately, and could use such elaborated kinematic feedback to correct the following trials.

3.7 Temporal feedback in skill training

One important element in skill performance is timing. While people are trained to perform a skill, the duration of the movement is perceived and learned better than some spatial aspects even if the person pays attention only to the latter (Liebermann *et al.*, 1988). In practice, the information conveyed in temporal structures or rhythms may sometimes override the need to define the spatial configuration of a movement. The use of temporal information fed back as a visual or auditory stimulus is not new in sports. Coaches often use rhythmic structures intuitively to link performance and timing (e.g. clapping their hands). Temporal information has been used to train individuals during aerobic workouts, and for this purpose, Davis and Bobick (1998) developed the concept called interactive personal aerobic training (virtual PAT). Their approach was based on a combination of technologies applied to physical fitness training. Using this system, individuals are instructed to perform exercises (e.g. calisthenics) between a video camera and a large screen that is back-projected with an infrared light source. When the performer stands in front of such a screen, his/her body eclipses the infrared light. The cameras interfaced to a computer filter out infrared from other existing light sources, and an edge-detection algorithm extracts the video image of a performer from the background. This pattern recognition algorithm is designed to discriminate between black (the performer's silhouette) and white (the screen) within each video frame. Changes in spatial coordinates of the silhouette, from frame to frame, are interpreted as body motions and temporally coded by the computer (the video sampling rate defines the time lapse from frame to frame). The real sequences are online compared to predefined templates that describe a desired pattern of performance. The computer provides an auditory feedback when major differences between expected and observed performance are found (e.g. negative or positive verbal feedback). The algorithm also sets a rhythm for the personalised aerobic workout and may adjust interactively during the performance. The message that transpires from this example is that an apparent technological complexity in the process of extracting essential information can reduce feedback to an elementary factor such as the rhythmical structure of the movement.

Vision is particularly effective in capturing movement from structured time. That is, the spatial configuration of a movement pattern might be reconstructed or extracted from temporal information. Johansson (1975) showed that people could visually identify different movement patterns from a limited source of visual information. Johansson used a set of light-reflecting markers distributed over the body joints of performers, and showed that passive observers could identify the type of movement (e.g. dancing) and other features, but only when the movement of the random set of points was allowed (Johansson, 1975).

Based on the empirical facts that show that time is an essential element of the movement experience, a time learning approach was expanded to the acquisition and training of high-level skill performance. Liebermann (1997) tested a skill acquisition strategy that exploited the advantage of learning temporal structures (rhythms). A mechanically advantageous movement pattern, such as the whip-like action in tennis (Chapman and Sanderson, 1990) was characterised by a specific rhythmical structure. A basic assumption was that the pattern-related rhythm would lead a subject to use the appropriate inter-segmental coordination associated with the whip-like action. Such a pattern was assumed to allow an efficient impulse transmission between the different joints in the kinematic chain, as suggested by Chapman and Sanderson (1990). For this purpose, Liebermann (1997) conducted a pilot experiment, in which two national-level juvenile tennis players were trained to follow the new temporal structure during the performance of the serve. The goal of the performance was to generate higher end-point tangential velocities at contact with the ball. The modified temporal pattern was computed for each player according to the whip-like action applied to the arm–racket system (shoulder, elbow, wrist and racket). This rhythmical structure was taped and replayed to the players in the tennis court (100 trials). The feedback consisted of auditory tones of different frequencies ('beeps') that delineated the successive onsets of the shoulder, elbow, and wrist–racket movements. Kinematic data were collected before and after the provision of the temporal feedback (ten serves each). The data showed that learning the new rhythm took only a few trials. A comparison between movements, prior to and after training, showed slight differences in the specific relative timing among peak angular tangential velocities as expected from the whip action, and both performers showed a mean increase in tennis ball velocity at strike (Liebermann, 1997). Figure 3.2 illustrates this procedure in one of the participants.

Note that in the top plot all joints are locked, and reach peak tangential speed simultaneously (i.e. segments are aligned as in near full arm extension). This pattern resembles a catapult-like action (Wilson and Watson, 2003), which exploits the elastic characteristics of the arm system. The second plot (bottom) shows a pattern in which each joint contributes maximally to end-point tangential velocity, in an orderly and sequential manner following a pattern that resembles the whip-like strategy.

Unlike such discrete skills as the tennis serve, continuous skills (e.g. running, swimming, rowing, or cycling) have no clear onset and offset. Thus, duration feedback can only be based on arbitrary landmarks within the cycle. In walking, for example, a landmark that could be used is the time when the heel touches the ground (heel-strike) and the time when the toe leaves the ground (toe-off time). Both time events define the step duration and the duration of the leg swing. Such information could be used, for example, to correct for inter-limb

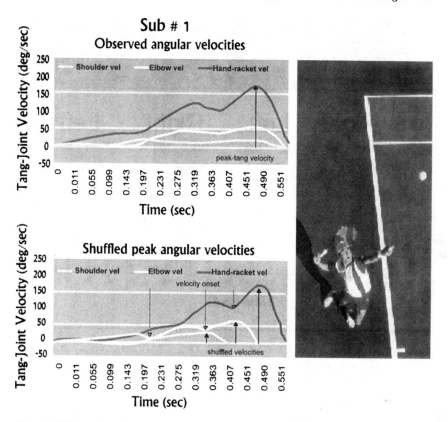

Figure 3.2 Examples of the tangential velocity–time profiles of the relevant joints in tennis serve before and after training. Top plot: actual angular velocity during a serve before training the new temporal pattern (subject #1). Bottom plot: shuffled angular velocities (same subject #1) where peaks are moved with respect to each other to allow a different torque interaction that leads to the whip-like strategy. Arrows show points in time at which an auditory feedback is provided.

asymmetries. To explore the potential of temporal auditory feedback, Liebermann (1997) installed membrane switches in the insole of a pair of running shoes to measure times of heel-strike and toe-off of the left and right legs, and further trained subjects to correct performance if needed. These pilot experimental trials showed that individuals were able to perceive and correct asymmetries easily. An example is presented in Figure 3.3.

Dobrov and Liebermann (1993) extended this time training strategy to Olympic walkers and runners. Subjects were instructed to follow optimised patterns that resulted from a computer simulation, which provided temporal feedback (heel-strike and toe-off times for the left and right legs) as the main output. They built a kinematic model based on a simple inverted pendulum system (Alexander McNeill, 1992, 1999), and constrained the motion of the

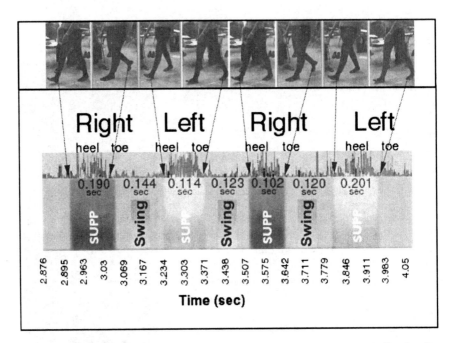

Figure 3.3 Asymmetries between the left and right legs during the support (heel-strike to toe-off time) and swing phases. The duration of these epochs should be similar for both legs. That is, a nearly symmetrical rhythmical pattern would normally be expected. Auditory feedback provides information about the duration of the step phases, and allows for the correction of existing differences between legs.

centre of mass to follow a minimum mechanical energy criterion (i.e. changes in horizontal and vertical velocities were minimised). It was assumed that as long as the individual kept the optimised temporal structure, a target time of performance would be achieved with minimal mechanical energy expenditure (Dobrov and Liebermann, 1993). Training was carried out on a treadmill while performers received computer-generated tempos (auditory and visual feedback) to match their steps with the rhythmical structure prescribed by the model. The preliminary data suggested that the new temporal information converged in a kinematic solution that forced performers to follow closely the optimised pattern of movement. This was confirmed in walkers but not in runners. Presumably, this was the case because during running subjects were unable to perceive differences between the support times from step to step (during running this time is sometimes less than 75 ms, which is the minimal duration that can be perceived as an auditory stimulus). Therefore, this training strategy for runners might not be efficient and other parameters should be used.

3.8 The use of force sensors to deliver feedback about pressure, time, and direction

Paradiso *et al.* (1999a, 1999b) brought the concept of rhythm learning to the state of the art in technology applied to dancing. These authors developed a cybershoe-based Wearable Computer systems technology that includes a sophisticated set of sensors and switches that send relevant information via telemetry to a receiver that is interfaced to a computer unit during dancing (Paradiso *et al.*, 1999b). The system allows mapping of data, which arrives from the shoe sensors, into a musical structure. For example, the different sensors (accelerometers, resistance and pressure-sensitive membrane, and gyros) capture identifiable dancing actions (such as sudden stops, support steps and rotations). These gestures are then translated into different instrumental or harmonic tones by the computer algorithm (percussion for a sudden stop or a harmonic chord for a roll along the longitudinal axis). In a sense, the dancer writes with his actions a melody that could later be matched to a desired pattern. There is no doubt that such a principle can successfully be applied to skills other than dancing, such as sports or the functional rehabilitation of patients (Morris and Paradiso, 2002).

Force sensing has been used in some sports unrelated to the rhythm of movement. For example, athletes and coaches may simply need to know immediately the precise timing of their actions and the force–time distribution in critical periods of the performance of a skill. Sprinters need to know reaction times. In athletics, the reaction times are obtained from the moment a start gun is triggered until the athlete leaves the blocks. Sanderson *et al.* (1991) installed a set of force sensors at the starting blocks used by track and field sprinters. Using these sensors they provided feedback about the linear dynamics and reaction times that could be used to improve technique. Later, McClements *et al.* (1996) reported that the immediate feedback about the reaction time and about the force–time distribution on the starting blocks had positive effects in correcting errors and improving the results of the performance.

Feedback about the forces has been used not only in track and field but also in other sports. Force sensors were used in cycling to provide information about dynamics of pedalling (e.g. Sanderson and Cavanagh, 1990; Broker *et al.*, 1993). In this case, whether such feedback is more effective if provided immediately remains open to question. Immediate provision of summary feedback about the forces applied, for example, on pedals during cycling makes no difference in modifying the pedalling technique in inexperienced cyclists (Broker *et al.*, 1993). Forces have been also measured to obtain the moments applied on oars or oarlocks during rowing (e.g. Dal Monte and Komar, 1988; Smith *et al.*, 1994), and such information has been considered important not only for evaluation of rowing technique but also for crew selection (e.g. Gerber *et al.*, 1985). Recent technological developments of force sensing have even allowed measurement of all forces that significantly affect boat speed. Knowledge about the application of such forces and their resulting propulsive component are relevant for improving rowing performance (Smith and Loschner, 2002).

3.9 Eye-movement recording technology

A line of research based on eye-movement recording technology has been promoted lately to determine where an athlete focuses gaze. The underlying assumption is that through training to search visually for those aspects and features of objects that are most relevant, athletes may improve performance. This assumption is based on evidence that shows that eye movements in expert athletes lock momentarily on what is perceived as the relevant information (Vickers, 1996; see Quiet Eye, www.pbs.org/saf/1206/video/watchonline.htm). The expectation is that by learning the important foci of attention in experts, coaches may be able to instruct less expert athletes where to look during the acquisition of a skill. This approach is reflected in the research of Vickers and Adolphe (1997), who recorded continuously and compared eye movements of expert volleyball players and near-experts. From their results it appears that near-experts do not fixate their eyes for as long as experts on the important events and locations (Adolphe *et al.*, 1997). The underlying assumption of this line of research is that continuous visual information is necessary to learn and perform. However, this assumption is challenged by the finding that athletes might only take advantage of visual input obtained at the beginning and/or the end of the performance and use it to interpolate the necessary anticipatory information to perform correctly (Land and McLeod, 2000). For example, in sports such as cricket, table tennis, ice hockey, or baseball (see e.g. www.pbs.org/saf/1206/video/watchonline.htm, Baseball Tech), expert players may be able to predict and organise motor actions based on snapshots of visual information, although the eyes may move continuously.

This is implied in the approach of Franks and Hanvey (1997) and Franks (2000), who developed a training programme for goalkeepers based on previous measurements of their eye movements. The purpose of the training was to improve their ability to save a penalty shot. The information collected to assess changes in performance before and after training eye movement included: goalkeeper movement (movement time, incorrect or correct prediction of ball placement, and save percentage), penalty taker's non-kicking foot placement, ball time, and final ball position. After a pre-test, the goalkeepers were asked about the strategies they commonly use to predict the shot direction. Training sessions followed in which the goalkeepers were shown, first, how a visual pre-cue about 'placement of the non-kicking foot' was reliable enough for detecting shot direction, and later, they were given a simulated training session that involved confronting a videotaped performance of a penalty taker approaching them in normal size. At near ball contact the screen would blank and the goalkeepers would indicate with their right or left arm in which direction they would dive to catch the ball. During this training intervention, goalkeepers also wore an eye movement recorder that provided feedback about their gaze. The feedback about gaze was recorded on video and superimposed on the scene. Goalkeepers were then given feedback on a monitor regarding the focus of their gaze during the penalty taker's run-up. The training phase that followed also simulated penalty kicks (60 trials) but stressed gaze fixation on the non-kicking foot before that foot landed, and on the events leading up to the run-up. The experiments showed that goalkeepers could use the feedback provided by eye movement recording to reduce the variability of their eye scan path and concentrate on the direction of the penalty taker's non-kicking foot before the shot. That is, the technology maximised the benefits of training and using the advanced response cue.

Finally, a more realistic set-up was used in the post-training phase, in which goalkeepers still wore the eye movement recorder and faced a real penalty (120 trials). Goalkeepers adopted a 'ready stance' and were instructed to move their hands to the right or the left as soon as they detected shot direction without diving to catch the ball. Before the feedback intervention, the goalkeepers' ability to predict correct direction of the penalty kick was approximately 46%, but after training, this figure improved significantly to 75%. Thus, it is clear that goalkeeper training using eye movement recording helped them to concentrate their gaze in relevant events, and consequently to improve. Presumably, the feedback available through the eye recording technology facilitated the process.

3.10 On coaches' attitudes to the use of feedback-based technology

A few words should be added on the attitudes to science and technologies in skill acquisition and sport training. In a recent survey, Katz *et al.* (2001) enquired about the attitude towards science and technology in sports among 30 Canadian certificated coaches (at different levels). One main finding from this initial survey was that most coaches recognise that technology and scientific knowledge are helpful in achieving better performance. Still, many practitioners are often sceptical about the advantages of using sophisticated technology and prefer using simple methods to deal with the training process. According to the survey, coaches show interest in the results of scientific enquiries and in the understanding of how the motor function can be enhanced in training and competition. However, they sometimes perceive negatively the use of expensive technology. They see it as a major investment of effort, time, and money, which, compared to other needs, is considered 'lower priority'. Moreover, not all coaches see themselves handling complex technologies. Therefore, they attribute to sport technology and science a dependency on scientists and/or technicians, which they do not favour. They regard this dependency as a potential source of interference with their normal working scheme. From the sample in the survey of Katz *et al.* (2001), it appears that technological education received by coaches during their coaching certificate programme does not match the developments of feedback-based technologies in sports. Therefore, coaches may sometimes be reluctant to adopt notational analyses and augmented feedback technologies in their training protocols.

3.11 Conclusions

The present chapter suggests that technology may be helpful as a means to enhance sensory mediated and abstract information. Technology may be used to reduce a motor performance to its most essential and representative data units, and might further allow immediate feedback for coaches and athletes. Augmented feedback allowance should be regulated according to the needs of the athlete. Sometimes, commercially available technologies add more feedback than is actually required for enhancing the acquisition of a skill. In light of the costs of some such technologies, coaches should critically evaluate their use based on scientific information and experiment. Some coaches might find it hard to adapt to the rapid development of feedback-based technologies in sports, even if they are scientifically based and very practical. There is no doubt that such advances accelerate the skill acquisition process at early learning stages, and might further provide the leading edge in elite competitive sports. Unless this is recognised, many practitioners might remain locked in traditional training views.

4 Notational analysis – a review of the literature

Mike Hughes and Ian M. Franks

4.1 Introduction

The aim of this chapter is to offer as much information about notation systems as possible. It is written in the form of a literature review of the research work already published in this field. Although this is written for, and by, sports scientists, it is hoped that anyone with an interest in this rapidly growing area of practice and research will find it interesting and rewarding.

It is not possible to trace the work of all those coaches and sports scientists who have contributed in one way or another to notational analysis. A large number of these innovative people did not see the point of publishing the work that they did, regarding it as merely part of their job, and consequently cannot receive the acclaim that they deserve here in this compilation. There is no doubt that all the published workers mentioned in this chapter could cite five or six other 'unsung' innovators, who either introduced them to the field or gave them help and advice along the way.

Literature in notational analysis has been difficult to find until recently. Researchers have had to find different types of journals that would accept their papers, and so they are spread throughout many different disciplines. This chapter should help readers to initiate a search for information on a specific sport or technique.

A number of texts contain sections devoted to research in notational analysis. The best of these, until recently, were the proceedings of conferences on football (Reilly *et al.*, 1988, 1993, 1997; Spinks *et al.*, 2002) and racket sports (Reilly *et al.*, 1995; Lees *et al.*, 1998). There is also a book, *Science of Soccer*, again edited by Reilly (1997), which is a compendium of contributions by different sports scientists on the application of their own specialisms to soccer. Three chapters in this book are based on notational analysis and review current developments and ideas in the field.

A big step forward, to enable notational analysts to share their research and ideas, has been the introduction of world conferences on notational analysis of sport. The proceedings of these conferences offer an invaluable compilation of notational analysis. The presentations of the first two conferences, held in Liverpool and Cardiff respectively, are compiled in one book, *Notational Analysis* of *Sport I & II* (Hughes, 1996b) and the first section has a number of keynote speakers who present a varied but enlightened overview of different aspects of notational analysis. The third conference was in Turkey; Hughes (2000a) edited the proceedings, *Notational Analysis of Sport III*. The fourth was in Porto, Portugal, and the book *Notational Analysis of Sport IV* was produced by Hughes and Tavares (2001). *Pass.com* is the proceedings of the Fifth World Conference of Performance Analysis of Sport, which was combined with the Third International Symposium of Computers in Sports Science (Hughes and Franks, 2001). Over the 18 months preceding this conference, biomechanists and notational analysts had come together, at the request of the British Olympic Association, to explore common areas of interest and had agreed on a generic title of 'performance analysis' – hence the change in the title of the world conference. Each of these books of proceedings is sectionalised – firstly the keynote presentations and then into different sports or equipment development – for ease of access for the reader.

The most recent development in gathering research in this area is the founding of an electronic journal, the *International Journal of Performance Analysis of Sport* (eIJPAS) (http://ramiro.catchword.com/). This is organised and managed by the Centre for Performance Analysis in UWIC, Cardiff. So now we have, at last, a research journal that is for performance analysis; at the moment not many biomechanists are using it, so it is principally concerned with notational analysis.

This review is aimed at being as comprehensive as possible but, as some published work will be missed, it is structured to follow the main developments in notational analysis. After tracing a historical perspective of the roots of notation, the applications of these systems to sport are then developed. These early systems were all hand notation systems; their emerging sophistication is followed until the advent of computerised notation. Although the emphasis is on the main research developments in both hand and computerised notational systems, where possible the innovations of new systems and any significant data outputs within specific sports are also assessed.

It should also be stressed that, although hand and computerised notation are presented in separate sections, this division is just a way of presenting the material: there is no real difference in the basic philosophy behind the methodology of these two ways of gathering data. Indeed, many systems being used at the time of writing, with National Governing Bodies or professional sports clubs, combine data gathering using hand and computerised notation systems.

4.2 Historical perspective

General, rudimentary and unsophisticated forms of notation have existed for centuries. A summary review of the history of notational analysis can be found in Hughes and Franks (1997). Initially a large amount of work was completed in soccer and squash, but this has changed considerably now and work and publications can be found on most sports. Some have inevitably attracted more attention than others: in the following sections these bodies of work are analysed to trace the developments in each of these sports. There is not room to cover all sports, so some omissions are made deliberately; some will be made through ignorance – apologies to all concerned. The selections have been made in an attempt to create a starting point from which the reader can then approach the literature in an informed way. If you cannot find the sport in which you are interested, look for a similarly structured sport – there will be lessons that you can learn from the developments and analyses in that sport.

4.3 Methodological issues

Research in sports science has become more concerned with accuracy of methodology over the past decade or so (Atkinson and Nevill, 1998), and this has been mirrored in performance analysis. These issues are very important in such a practical, applied discipline as performance analysis: so much so that several chapters in this book cover these areas in some depth.

4.4 The development of sport-specific notation systems (hand notation)

The earliest publication in notation of sport is that by Fullerton (1912), which explored the combinations of baseball players batting, pitching and fielding and the probabilities of success. But probably the first attempt to devise a notation system specifically for sport analysis was that by Messersmith and Bucher (1939), who attempted to notate distance covered by specific basketball players during a match. Messersmith led a research group at Indiana State University that initially explored movement in basketball, but went on to analyse American football and field hockey. Lyons (1996) presented a fascinating history of Messersmith's life for those interested in understanding the man behind the work.

Notation systems were commercially available for American football play-analysis as early as 1966 (Purdy, 1977), and the Washington Redskins were using one of the first in 1968 (Witzel, cited by Purdy, 1977). Interestingly, American football is the only sport that has as part of its rules a ban on the use of computerised notation systems in the stadium. How this could be enforced is not clear; however, all clubs that have been contacted have been very helpful. All claim to use a similar hand notation system, the results of which are transferred to computer after the match. Clubs exchange data just as they exchange videos on opponents. Because of the competitive nature of this and other 'big money', sports, little actual detailed information was available.

Although some sports have little notational research published, it does not mean that systems do not exist or are not used in these disciplines. For purposes of clarity and reference the following section has been subdivided into specific sports, even though in some areas there is not a great deal of information to report.

4.4.1 Tennis

The first publication of a comprehensive racket sport notation was not until 1973, when Downey developed a detailed system which allowed the comprehensive notation of lawn tennis matches. Detail in this particular system was so intricate that not only did it permit notation of such variables as shots used, positions, etc., but it catered for type of spin used in a particular shot. The Downey notation system has served as a useful base for the development of systems for use in other racket sports, specifically badminton and squash.

Sailes (1989) studied the difference between three different methods of target-oriented hitting of ground strokes from the back of the court. Sixty tennis academy players were split into three groups: those with no targets, those with court targets and those with net targets. Each player hit ten forehands and ten backhands, with five going cross-court and five going down the line. The court was divided into three scoring zones – one, three and five – in terms of closeness to the baseline. Even though this study was performed in a non-competitive environment, the principle of splitting the court into sections is a scientific way of collecting accurate data: for example, looking at what shots are used in those positions and where they are hit from and to; discovering which shots are likely to cause error.

A movement analysis of elite male 'serve and volley' tennis players was undertaken by Hughes and Moore (1998), who found that the average number of shots per rally on grass was 2.97 and concluded that the efficiency of movement was much higher than expected. A study of the time use of energy systems in elite tennis by Richers (1995) concluded that the non-aerobic (ATP-PC) system was the primary energy source used on hard, clay and grass court surfaces. He found mean rally times of 4.3 ± 2.7 s on grass and 7.6 ± 6.7 s on clay but the sex of the subjects was not stated in the study.

Furlong (1995) analysed the service effectiveness in lawn tennis at Wimbledon and on clay at the French Open in 1992 as a comparison. Furlong notated both men's and women's singles and doubles events to standardise for the fastest and slowest surface. The results showed that the service in doubles was more effective because most serves were slower to compensate for accuracy so that a strong attacking position at the net could be achieved, which would help in scoring more points.

Hughes and Taylor (1998) compared the patterns of play between six top British under-18 (U18) players in comparison to six top U18 European and three top U18 American/Canadian elite performers. The hand notation system recorded data using symbols based in four positional zones of the court; data gathering was performed post-event from video. These researchers analysed two tournaments just before the 1996 Wimbledon, which are perceived as 'warm-up' tournaments. These tournaments were Imber Court, London and the ITF Group 1 tournament held in Roehampton, London, both on a grass surface. Eight matches were recorded over the two venues and the following conclusions were generated:

- U18 British players made more unforced errors from the back of the court
- Europeans seem to hit more attacking shots from the back of the court
- U18 British players made more defensive shots from the back of the court
- U18 British players won more points at the net, while Europeans won more at the back of the court
- U18 British players executed a low number of winning passing shots in comparison to both Europeans and Americans/Canadians.

4.4.2 Squash

Several systems have been developed for the notation of squash, the most prominent being that by Sanderson and Way (1979). Most of the different squash notation systems possess many basic similarities. The Sanderson and Way method made use of illustrative symbols to notate 17 different strokes, as well as incorporating court plans for recording accurate positional information. The major emphasis of this system was on the gathering of information concerning 'play patterns' as well as the comprehensive collection of descriptive match data. Sanderson felt that 'suggestive' symbols were better than codes, being easier for the operator to learn and remember, and devised the code system shown in Figure 4.1. These were used on a series of court representations, one court per activity, so that the player, action and position of the action were all notated (see Figure 4.2). In addition, outcomes of rallies were recorded, together with the score and the initials of the server. The position was specified using an acetate overlay with the courts divided into 28 cells. The system took an estimated 5–8 hours of use and practice before an operator was sufficiently skilful to record a full match as it was in progress. Processing the data could take as long as 40 hours of further work. Sanderson (1983) used this system to gather a database and show that squash players play in the same patterns, winning or losing, despite the supposed coaching standard of 'if you are losing change your tactics'. It would seem that the majority of players are unable to change the patterns in which they play.

Drive					
Drive		│			
X-drive		/			
Drop		•			
Boast	(back hand)	⊂;	(fore hand)	⊃	
Volley		V			
Lob		L			
Serve		S			

Combinations
e.g.   X-drop   /·
       Volley-lob VL

Figure 4.1 The shot codes, or suggestive symbols, used by Sanderson (1983) for his data-gathering system for squash.

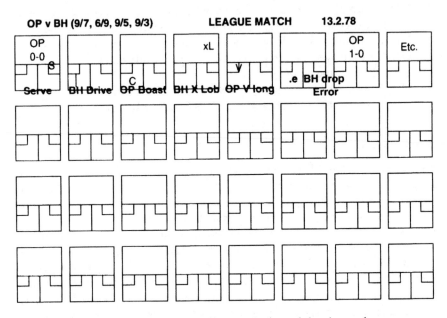

Figure 4.2 The data-gathering sheets and example data of the shot codes, or suggestive symbols, used by Sanderson (1983) for his data-gathering system for
squash.

Most of the data that Sanderson and Way presented were in the form of frequency distributions of shots with respect to position on the court. This was then
a problem of presenting data in three dimensions – two for the court and one
for the value of the frequency of the shots. Three-dimensional graphics at that
time were very difficult to present in such a way that no data was lost, or, that
was easily visualised by those viewing the data. Sanderson overcame this problem
by using longitudinal and lateral summations (Figure 4.3). Not only were the
patterns of rally-ending shots examined in detail, but also those shots (N − 1)
that preceded the end shot, and the shots that preceded those (N − 2). In
this way the rally-ending patterns of play were analysed. The major pitfall
inherent in this system, as with all longhand systems, was the time taken to
learn the system and the sheer volume of raw data generated, requiring so much
time to process it.

4.4.3 Soccer

Science and Soccer II (Reilly, 2003) contains three chapters relating to match
analysis and presents a sound source of background reading for the application
of this discipline to soccer.

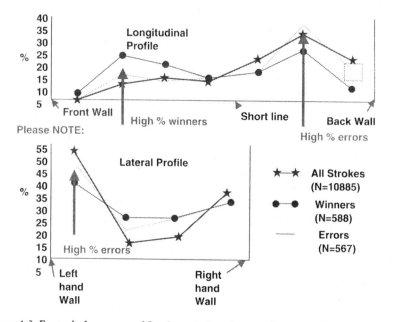

Figure 4.3 Example from some of Sanderson's data showing frequency distributions of all shots, winners and errors.

4.4.3.1 *Patterns of play*

An alternative approach to match analysis was exemplified by Reep and Benjamin (1968), who collected data from 3,213 matches between 1953 and 1968. They were concerned with actions such as passing and shooting rather than work-rates of individual players. They reported that 80 per cent of goals resulted from a sequence of three passes or fewer. Fifty per cent of all goals came from possession gained in the final attacking quarter of the pitch.

Bate (1988) found that 94 per cent of goals scored at all levels of international soccer were scored from movements involving four or fewer passes, and that 50–60 per cent of all movements leading to shots on goal originated in the attacking third of the field. Bate explored aspects of chance in soccer and its relation to tactics and strategy in the light of the results presented by Reep and Benjamin (1968). It was claimed that goals are not scored unless the attacking team gets the ball and one, or more, attacker(s) into the attacking third of the field. The greater the number of possessions a team has, the greater chance it has of entering the attacking third of the field, therefore creating more opportunities to score. The higher the number of passes per possession, the lower the total number of match possessions, the total number of entries into the attacking third, and the total chances of shooting at goal. Thus Bate rejected the concept of possession football and favoured a more direct strategy. He concluded that to increase the number of scoring opportunities a team should play the ball forward as often as possible; reduce square and back passes to a minimum; increase the number of long passes forward and forward runs with the ball; and play the ball into space as often as possible.

These recommendations are in line with what is known as the 'direct method' or 'long-ball game'. The approach has proved successful with some teams in the lower divisions of the English League. It is questionable whether it provides a recipe for success at higher levels of play, but this data has fuelled a debate that continues to the present day. Hughes and Franks (2003) tried to demonstrate that perhaps these analyses of the data were simplistic and that broader non-dimensional analyses give a different answer.

Pollard et al. (1988) used Reep and Benjamin's (1968) method of notation in order to quantitatively assess determinants and consequences of different styles of play. It was suggested that elaborate styles relied on multi-pass sequences of possession and that direct styles of play significantly relied on long forward passes and long goal clearances. In addition it was found that there was no relation between the degree of elaborate style and the use of width. Pollard et al. concluded that it was important for the coach to build up a style profile of each opponent for future analysis by using this type of quantitative assessment of playing style.

A hand notation system developed by Ali (1988) recorded 13 basic factors of the game: dribbling, short pass, long pass, goal, offside, shot on target, ball intercepted by goalkeeper, header on target, header off target, intercepted short pass, intercepted long pass, shot off target and the position of the restarts. The system attempted to ascertain whether there were specific and identifiable patterns of attack and how successful each pattern was in influencing the result of the match. It thus considered only sequences in the attacking half of the field: these patterns were recorded on the prepared pitch diagram in graphic form. The data were entered into a computer in terms of X and Y coordinates on the pitch diagram and compared in relation to pattern and constituent. The final action of each type of pattern was analysed to determine its influence on the game. Ali found that attacking patterns that proceeded along the length of the wing were more successful than those through the centre, the most likely result of a long pass is offside, and that plays involving a great number of passes increased the likelihood of a goal.

Ali (1992) went on to analyse patterns of play of an international soccer team by considering five matches played by Scotland during 1986–8. He identified five types of attacking patterns of play, each of which represented large numbers of attacks. Nine different types of final action were also defined, and the analysis showed that there were significant relationships between final actions and patterns of play. Ali claimed that the large number of attacks for each pattern overcame the low number of matches analysed, citing numbers in the mid to high forties, but with nine possible final actions, this leaves the ratio of frequency of attack to final action to be about five. This would seem low for statistical significance.

Harris and Reilly (1988) considered attacking success in relation to team strategy and the configuration of players around the point of action, by concentrating mainly on the position of attackers in relation to the defence and the overall success of each attacking sequence. This was a considerable departure from many of the systems previously mentioned, which have tended to break each sequence into discrete actions. Harris and Reilly provided an index describing the ratio of attackers to defenders in particular instances, while simultaneously assessing the space between a defender and an attacker in possession of the ball. These were analysed in relation to attacking success, whereby a successful attack resulted in a goal, an intermediate attack resulted in a non-scoring shot on goal, and an unsuccessful attack resulted in an attack ending without a shot. Successful attacks tended to involve a positive creation of space, where an attacker passes a defender; an unsuccessful attack involved a failure to use space effectively due to good organisation of defensive lines.

Olsen (1997), who was the coach to the Norway team, discussed the need for closer links between the 'academic' and the 'practical', and he cited this as a key reason for Norway's success in international football in recent years. Their aim in doing the analysis was:

1 to measure the team's effectiveness through counting scoring opportunities
2 to measure the types of attacks and their efficiency
3 to gain more knowledge of the match syntax in general
4 to have a quantitative and qualitative analysis of each player.

It was particularly refreshing to appreciate the views of Olsen, as someone who was not just a theoretician but a practical and applied source.

Rico and Bangsbo (1996), in designing their notation system for soccer, clearly delineated their operational definitions – an excellent example of how to utilise a well-designed system. They used examples of the Danish soccer team in the European Championship (1992) to demonstrate the analyses. Potter (1996a) also presented a system for notation of soccer, and a database of the 1994 World Cup in soccer (all 52 matches). The validity tests in this paper are sound and very clearly explained, and the data are presented in a way that it is hoped other researchers might follow.

These examples represent the different purposes that notational analysis can fulfil. More recent research using hand notation tends to use a data-gathering system and then process the data in a computerised database. Pettit and Hughes (2001) used a hand notation system to analyse all the matches from the 1998 World Cup, through the aid of a database into which the data was entered. The system was designed in an order like a flowchart so as each action occurred the operator inputted the data from field to field; for example, firstly the time was inputted then the event that led to the cross, crossed from and to, and so on. If a shot was taken the data was added; otherwise the process was started again to input the data for the next cross. Abbreviations were used to help speed up the process of inputting the data. The system, designed to analyse crossing and shooting, was based on that used in the study by Partridge and Franks (1989a, 1989b). All 64 matches from the 1998 World Cup were notated post-event over a period of 90 minutes plus injury time, although extra time and penalty shootouts were omitted from the analyses. The time the cross occurred, events leading up to, team, area crossed from, area crossed to, type of cross, in front or behind the defence, result of cross, if applicable; whether or not a pass was made, number of passes in sequence, shot type, height of shot, direction in relation to goalkeeper, speed and intent of shot, contact, direction GP, outcome and possession were analysed, which enabled the frequency of the actions to be recorded. A chi-square test was used as a statistical process to determine whether differences occurred between the 1986 and 1998 World Cup Finals.

4.4.3.2 Penalty kicks

Penalties are now a subject of myth, romance, excitement, dread, fear and pressure – depending on whether you are watching or taking them. They have either helped careers of footballers or destroyed them. Yet little research has been completed on penalty kicks. Using a hand notation system, Hughes and Wells (2002) notated and analysed 129 penalties with the intention of examining:

- the time in preparing the shot
- the number of paces taken to approach the ball
- the speed of approach
- the pace of the shot
- its placement and the outcome.

In addition, the actions of the goalkeeper were notated – position, body shape, movements as the player approached, his first movements and the subsequent direction, the outcome. Not all video recordings enabled all of these data to be notated, so in the subsequent analyses some of the totals are 128 and 127.

   The findings can be summarised as follows.

- One in five penalties were saved (20 per cent; 3/15), one in fifteen missed (7 per cent; 1/15) and three in four resulted in a goal (73 per cent; 11/15).
- Players using a fast run-up had 25 per cent of their efforts saved, because the player then tried either 50 per cent or 75 per cent power.
- Best success ratios are from an even run-up of four, five and six paces.
- There is no laterality in the success ratios – left-footers and right-footers have the same success percentages.
- No shots above waist height were saved.
- In every case, the goalkeeper moved off the line before the ball was struck.
- Although there is only a small data set, the goalkeepers who did not dive to either side while the striker approached the ball had the best save and miss ratios.

This is a good example of hand notation providing accurate data in this age of computers. In fact, the data were then entered into Access, and analysed through this database – a method used more and more. In addition, because of the nature of these data, and a performance analysis of what is virtually a closed skill situation, the data analysis provides a clear picture of the most efficient ways of penalty taking and saving.

4.4.3.3 *Movement analysis in soccer*

Brooke and Knowles (1974) conducted a study into the description of methods and procedures for the recording and subsequent analysis of field movement behaviour in soccer, and to consequently establish the reliability of that method. Shorthand symbols were utilised to represent variables and parameters to be measured. Validation of the system was never clear, and some of the data has to be questioned.

The definitive motion analysis of soccer, using hand notation, was by Reilly and Thomas (1976), who recorded and analysed the intensity and extent of discrete activities during match-play. They combined hand notation with the use of an audio tape recorder to analyse in detail the movements of English First Division soccer players. They were able to specify work-rates of the players in different positions, distances covered in a game and the percentage time of each position in each of the different ambulatory classifications. They also found that typically a player carries the ball for less than 2 per cent of the game. Reilly (1997) has continually added to this database, enabling him to define clearly the specific physiological demands in soccer, as well as all the football codes. The work by Reilly and Thomas has become a standard against which other similar research projects can compare their results and procedures. A detailed analysis of the movement patterns of the outfield positions of Australian professional soccer players was completed in a similar study to that described above (Withers *et al.*, 1982). The data produced agreed to a great extent with that of Reilly and Thomas (1976); both studies emphasised that players cover 98 per cent of the total distance in a match without the ball, and were in agreement in most of the inferences made from the work-rate profiles.

Withers *et al.* (1982) classified players into four categories: full backs, central defenders, midfield and forwards ($n = 5$ in each group of player positions). Players were videotaped while playing; at the end of the match they were informed that they were the subject and were then required to 'calibrate' the different classifications of motion. The subject was videotaped while covering the centre circle as follows from a walking start of 3–5 m: walking, jogging, striding, sprinting, moving sideways, walking backwards and jogging backwards. The average stride length was then calculated for each of these types of locomotion. The data produced by Withers *et al.* agreed to a great extent with that of Reilly and Thomas (1976): both studies showed that players spend 98 per cent of the match without the ball, and were in agreement in most of the rest of the data, the only difference being that the English First Division players (Reilly and Thomas) were stationary a great deal more (143 s) than the Australian players (45 s). Withers et al. went on to link their analysis with training methods specific to the game and position.

4.4.4 Netball

The growth of netball internationally has undoubtedly led to an increase in the amount of scientific investigation and literature. However, notational netball research is still limited in comparison with other sports such as soccer and squash, where research is extensive. Much of the research was completed in the late 1970s and early 1980s; these pieces of research formed a foundation for future research. Researchers at this time included Embrey (1978), Barham (1980), Otago (1983), Elliott and Smith (1983) and Miller and Winter (1984).

Embrey (1978) may have prompted research in the area, having commented that 'there is a paucity of material to describe what actually happens in a game ... the time is now ripe for planned investigation of the game'. Embrey's own research analysed the use of specific skills, game structures and various successes of individuals and combinations used by teams.

The system was sophisticated and recorded data retaining its sequence to highlight the passages of successful and unsuccessful play, in order to determine the reasons for losing or converting possession. The information it produced was valuable to a coach planning effective strategies and set-plays tailored specifically for the analysed team's strengths and weaknesses. The system was successful but required significant learning and practice time.

Barham (1980) produced a system that analysed play in real-time and provided the coach with immediate courtside information. The system allowed the coach to make objective informed decisions regarding individual players and game strategies and tactics. The data could also be retained and used for future reference on performances and training implications. The system was simple and effective in collating the required data, but unfortunately was not sophisticated enough for teams of international standard. The reasoning of the data was well planned but the system was not globally accepted. Barham also produced other research and resources in the field of netball including books, coaching aids and videos.

Otago (1983) became one of the first netball researchers to analyse the activity patterns of the players. The reasoning behind the research was the lack of specific information available for netball conditioning despite its importance. Otago highlighted the fact that the specificity of training is very important in any sport. This means that the work done at any training should be similar to the game. The research determined the characteristics of each position and the typical movements players make throughout a game, such as lengths of rest periods and work-to-rest ratios. The information the analysis collated reported the activity levels of different positions of international netball players to enable the development of exercise routines that are specific to position and activity in match conditions. The system produced large amounts of data of which a limited amount was discussed, the remainder being left open to inter-pretation. Otago concluded that the field of investigation into netball is wide open. A more detailed study could be performed by individually videotaping players in each position for a number of games.

Elliott and Smith (1983) analysed the vital technique of shooting. The research was a statistical analysis of netball shooting, observing netball shooters over a whole season. The 12 subjects for the study were aged between 16 and 27, highly skilled netball shooters from Grade A netball teams in Western Australia. Elliott and Smith outlined the lack of match statistics related to shooting under game conditions; for example, what is a good shooting percent-age that a coach can expect from her shooters during a game? Pelcher (1981) identified that most basketball coaches look for an individual efficiency of 80 per cent from professional players. The research also analysed how many points per game per shooter can be expected, and aimed to provide benchmarks for coaches to expect and players to achieve.

Miller and Winter (1984) completed research similar to that of Otago and Embrey. It identified specific movement patterns unique to different positions, defined specific training patterns for positions and indicated the importance of specific and progressive practices. Analysis of the accuracy of passing subject to varying degrees of pressure was also made.

4.4.5 Field hockey

A study by Miller and Edwards (1983), using almost exactly the same technique as Withers *et al.* (1982) but only for the analysis of one match, showed that the field hockey player studied spent 47 min 10 s walking (66.4 per cent), 10 min 52 s running (15.3 per cent), 1 min 16 s sprinting (1.8 per cent), and 11 min 42 s standing (16.5 per cent).

An analysis system specifically for analysing attacking circle play was de-veloped by Andrews (1985). Five international matches were studied using video recordings of the games; three were men's hockey played on artificial turf and two were women's games played on grass. The attacking circle was divided into nine segments and each segment was further subdivided into ten segments. When a shot was made its position in the circle was recorded. Play was also recorded diagrammatically from the time the ball entered the attacking 25-yard area to the time it left this area. The results showed that 51.8 per cent of attacks entered on the right-hand side of the circle, but that shots from the left-hand side of the circle were more successful. Although the research is detailed, the system had major disadvantages, as the research was confined to a small area of the game and did not display the game as a whole.

Howells (1993) performed a study on five women's international hockey teams to identify and analyse defensive patterns of play. Twenty-five whole game videos were notated using a hand notation system. The results showed Korea to be the most successful of the five teams in the study, playing 25.8 per cent of passes from the right side of the pitch to the left side, and successfully distributing 29 per cent of passes to attackers on the left side of the pitch. Howells found that Korea were the only team to double their number of positive passes as opposed to negative passes. Argentina proved to be the least successful team, producing the most negative passes and fewest positive passes of all the five teams in the study.

Boddington et al. (2001) examined the physical demands of the 'modern' hockey match using video analysis and hand notation to quantify the displacement of the female players ($n = 11$) every 15 seconds during a league match ($n = 3$). These data for each match were analysed using ANOVA with repeated measures and a covariance for playing time. The mean total displacement was $3,914 \pm 770$ m in 63.3 ± 9.5 minutes or approximately 61 m per minute of playing time. The total displacement in match 1 ($4,250 \pm 752$ m) was greater than match 2 ($3,850 \pm 642$ m; $P = 0.0002$) and match 3 ($3,864 \pm 632$ m; $P = 0.001$). Displacement per minute playing time was greater in match 1 (65 ± 8.4 m min^{-1}) than in match 2 (58 ± 3.7 m min^{-1}; $P = 0.005$) and match 3 (59 ± 4.6 m min^{-1}; $P = 0.046$). There were significant decreases in displacement in the second half compared to the first ($P = 0.01$ total displacement and $P = 0.009$ displacement per minute playing time). There were no significant differences between the mean displacement and the mean speed ($P = 0.33$ and $P = 0.31$ respectively) for the three matches or the two playing halves ($P = 0.19$ and $P = 0.20$ respectively).

Mean heart rate was significantly higher during match 1 (176 ± 5 beats min^{-1}) than matches 2 and 3 (162 ± 5 beats min^{-1} and 166 ± 4 beats min^{-1}, matches 2 and 3 respectively). The mean heart rate during the first half (171 ± 7 beats min^{-1}) was higher than the second (165 ± 9 beats min^{-1}) ($P = 0.03$).

An analysis of the subjective data found that the players perceived match 1 to be harder than match 2 or 3 ($P < 0.05$) and match 3 to be harder than match 2 ($P < 0.05$). The preparation and the subjective feelings prior to the three matches were perceived to be the same ($P = 0.67$ and 0.09 respectively).

It was concluded that the average displacement during a match was approximately 4 km and the average displacement covered during each 15-second period was about 15 m, which included frequent changes in direction and speed.

4.4.6 Rugby union

Rugby union presents unique problems for analysis with its set-piece moves, the 'scrum' and the 'line-out', and also the activity ensuing from a tackle in either 'rucks' or 'mauls'. Lyons (1988) gathered data by hand on the Home International Championship for a period of ten years and created a sound database. From this database he claimed to predict the actions, e.g. the number of scrums, line-outs, passes, kicks and penalties, in the England–Wales match in the 1986–7 season to within three passes and two kicks.

Treadwell (1992) presented a summary of the work completed at Cardiff by the team working there, demonstrating that game models were clearly tenable for rugby union regardless of weather, selection, refereeing or even coaching style. Over 40 different action variables were defined and data collection was completed live using hand notation. This was validated using a computerised system to analyse matches from video, post-event. Data from the Five Nations Championships over four years was presented to confirm the hypothesis that the game of rugby union provides a rhythm for prediction of certain variables.

Research into movement analysis and definition of fitness profiles is of value to rugby union coaches, players and others but it does have its limitations and there is a need for some other important aspects to be considered. For any fitness or training norms to be taken from such studies then there is a need to ensure the following.

1   A specific player/position is tracked for the entire match and for a series of matches. This will then give a global figure which will also have accounted for environmental factors such as weather and pitch conditions, importance of the match, and personal attitude of the player.
2   The nature of the game is accounted for. The work-rates of players may vary from position to position according to whether the game is fast and fluid or whether they are on the winning or losing side.

Carter (1996) combined quantitative and qualitative information in a time-and-motion analysis and heartrate monitoring of a back-row forward. The results showed that the requirements for playing in each of the three back-row positions did vary. The qualitative recording of game incidents and training methods added another dimension to the research. A clear analysis of the performance of England (Potter, 1996b), as an example of one of the international teams in the Five Nations Tournament (1992–1994), demonstrated the power of notational analysis in a team sport, but this type of research might benefit from a directed hypothesis rather than just reporting data.

Limited research exists on the analysis of the performance of referees, although Catterall *et al.* (1993) and Asami *et al.* (1988) both found that soccer referees typically covered between 9,500 m and 11,200 m during matches. No similar research appears to have been completed for rugby union referees, although the Welsh Rugby Union has cited data that claims a referee walks 0.5 miles, runs at medium pace for 1.5 miles and sprints for 0.75 miles. One of the first analyses of officials in this sport (Hughes and Hill, 1996) demonstrated the difficulties that rugby union has with its complex laws, in particular in the line-outs. This type of analysis is surely the way forward for the training and development of professional officials in all the professional team sports.

Hughes and Blunt (2001) analysed the complexity of the task facing the rugby union referee, which is increasing with each change in the laws of the game – especially since the more recent changes have been motivated to make the play 'more open', faster and more attractive to spectators. The aim of the study was to develop and validate a hand notation system to assess and analyse the movement of rugby union referees, post-event from videos of referees in match. Chi-square and percentage error were used to compare the reliability data sets; a percentage agreement of 93.8 per cent was accepted. Six referees were observed: four were WRU officials, one was an English panel referee with international experience, and the final referee was an Australian representative referee in charge of an Australian inter-state match.

The referees covered an average of 5,588 m per game, there was no significant difference between the mean of the first half (2,853 ± 278 m) and that of the second half (2,736 ± 366 m). The different ambulatory modes were also analysed – 2,380 m of the match distance was in the jogging mode. The movement of the referees is mainly aerobic: 55 per cent of the time was spent in little or no locomotor activity, only 8 per cent of the overall ambulatory modes being stressful to the anaerobic systems. A referee typically changed locomotor modes over 800 times per match. The nature of the data gave clear signals for the type of training needed for referees. In addition the individual differences between the referees indicate strong individual styles in the data, signified by some large standard deviations, which may be a function of either personal traits or match characteristics.

Potter and Carter (2001a, 2001b) and Carter and Potter (2001a, 2001b) conducted an analysis into the Rugby World Cup finals in 1991 and 1995. They considered the changes that had occurred during the four-year gap, and the effect that these changes had on the game. They analysed the amount of second-phase possession, the amount of kicking and passing of the ball during each of the finals, the number of set-pieces in particular, scrums and line-outs, and the tries scored. In effect they created a map of the game as it had developed over this period of time. This mapping of the game has been continued by the International Rugby Board, who have established an Analysis Centre in Cardiff, with a number of full time staff who access and analyse all important games played throughout the world, using post-event computerised systems designed and written in-house.

4.4.7 Badminton

Full-time notational analyst for the Badminton Association of England, Steve Evans, has developed various hand notation systems to provide information on badminton play patterns, work-to-rest ratios and movement analysis. Using the 1998 ladies singles final of the All England Championship, Evans (1998b) analysed rally-ending situations so as to provide tactical match plans for future training sessions. Within the study it was noted that a low winner-to-error ratio was apparent. The players also showed an increased number of errors when playing the clear in comparison to other shots. This could have been due to the surrounding environment or increased pressure: it is usually expected that a clear will produce a low winner-to-error ratio. The smash, though, will usually have a winner-to-error ratio greater than one (in men's singles the ratio is 2.2:1 (Evans, 1998a)). Within this study only one match was analysed, therefore care must be taken when interpreting the data. Evans (1998b) outlined that ideally a good player profile can be established by using a collection of five matches:

'the more matches one can notate the more accurate an emerging pattern will be' (Evans, 1998b, p. 9).

Hong and Tong (2000) performed a notational analysis investigation into playing patterns of the world's top singles badminton players in competition. The aims of the study were to analyse the percentage distribution of shots and their placement within the court-areas; the frequency of different serves; how playing effectiveness corresponded with court-area; and the crucial factors that influenced winning or losing a match. The results showed that for male singles players the low serve was most preferable, the majority of shots were returned to the forecourt, and the lob was the most popular shot followed by the smash, net and clear. The forecourt was also where the most 'effective' shots were returned, with the rearcourt producing the majority of 'ineffective' shots. Furthermore, it was found that each game contained on average 47.61 rallies, with a mean of 7.37 shots played in each rally. The study concluded that for top-level international players the most important strategy for producing a winning performance was a pressure and attack game.

More recently an unpublished study by Dobson (2001) compared the patterns of play of elite and sub-elite ladies singles badminton. The world's top ten ranked ladies were used for the elite subjects and the ladies ranked 40–50 worldwide were used for the sub-elite subjects. The study used 17 matches taken from the All England Open and the Korean Open to analyse the variables:

- frequency of all shots by position and match
- outcome by match
- outcome by position by match
- outcome by shot type by match.

Using a hand/computerised notation system it was discovered that the only significant difference ($P < 0.1$) for positional shots was found in position 5 (the centre of the court). Sub-elite players were shown to make a significantly higher percentage of errors ($P < 0.05$) than elite players, but no difference was found between the two standards with respect to the percentage of winners.

The study concluded that there was a difference in the patterns of play for elite and non-elite players, but also identified other reasons for the differences that the system could not analyse. These influencing factors included the general fitness of players and their injury status, the techniques adopted within the game and the financial support available.

4.4.8 Basketball

The research around performance analysis of basketball usually focuses its attention on the players and game evaluation, trying to understand those aspects related to the optimisation of subjects resources and, on the other hand, to enlighten the understanding of competition demands (Janeira, 1994). This section demonstrates how a group working in one centre can advance the knowledge of a particular sport – the group in Porto have really worked well to illuminate the analysis of this complex sport.

The evaluation of players in research publications generally focuses its attention on somatotype and body composition, on the physiological profile of athletes and on the evaluation of specific capacities and abilities (Bale, 1991; Janeira and Maia, 1991; Maia, 1993; Janeira, 1994; Pinto, 1995; Brandão, 1995). Some authors also tried to acknowledge the players relative to the game indicators (two-point shots, three-point shots, assists, free throws, rebounds, turnovers, fouls, interceptions, fast-breaks) and relate these values with somatic indicators (Alexander, 1976; Janeira, 1988).

For a better understanding of the game some authors resorted to the time-and-motion analysis. This type of analysis enables the identification of the activity patterns of players in the competition context. Research has described distances covered by players, the intensity of actions and the number of jumps (Riera, 1986; Janeira, 1994).

The investigators also compare players or teams of different levels of perform-ance, based on the indicators usually used to evaluate players or game situations (Alexander, 1976; Bale, 1986; Janeira, 1994; Pinto, 1995) with the purpose of finding the factors that define teams or players.

In this context, basketball research has focused its attention on the efficiency indicators of the game. Competition seems to be the most adequate moment to evaluate performance and the results are a criterion to judge the quality of players or teams. The game situation allows the identification of some variables that can distinguish the good teams and players from the less good ones, and consequently lead to better sport results.

Marques (1990) developed a study which related the game efficiency indic-ators with the success of teams. The author considered different perspectives of study. First Marques considered teams with success and without success, and found differences in the percentage of offensive and defensive rebounds and in the second shots. According to the author, winner teams try more often to score, are more efficient in shooting, try the fast-break more often and get more offensive and defensive rebounds. After that study he analysed equilibrate games (results with two points of difference), normal games (three to ten points of difference in result) and games with large differences in results (more than ten points). Marques (1990) found that in the less equilibrate games, all the differences found in the first analysis are more relevant and in the normal games some differences are not so relevant (two point shots and fast-break). In the equilibrate games there were not large differences in the indicators studied.

Marques (1990) used univariate analysis. This type of analysis only allows one variable of one group to be compared to the same variable of the other group. Thus, it would be important to develop more studies of this type using multivariate analysis, which is considered more powerful, to compare groups of different performance levels.

The research group in Porto have tried to find the variables that determine the efficiency of a team and consequently lead to better results (Mendes and

Janeira, 2001; Cruz and Tavares, 2001; Silva, 2001; Tina, 2001). The purpose of the study by Mendes and Janeira was to identify the efficiency indicators in the game, which have the power to discriminate between winning and losing teams. The data was collected by specialist technicians from *Infordesporto*. They analysed the 70 games of the first 12 rounds in the 1995/96 season. The study was based on three different perspectives. In the first they considered the totality of the games, in the second they reported the games with differences in the final score of less than ten points, in the third, they analysed games with final score margins of ten or more points. Mendes and Janeira considered the following variables: total made assists, scored assists, fouls, interceptions, two-point shots, three-point shots, free-throws, ball steals, defensive rebounds, offensive rebounds, total of rebounds, second shots and turnovers. The mean and standard deviation were calculated. They used *T*-test with independent measures to compare the dependent variables of the two groups (winners and losers), and then applied Manova and discriminate analysis to find the smallest group of variables which can classify teams in their real groups. Finally, they used 'Jacknife' to reclassify the groups. The significance level was 5 per cent. The results from the multivariate study of the game efficiency indicators showed in all analyses the discriminatory power of defensive rebounds. In games with differences in final score greater than ten points, the percentage of two-point shots showed a high discriminant power. Finally, in the games where final scores differed by less than ten points the fouls, assists and defensive rebounds all seem to discriminate winning teams from losing teams. The other research listed above, all of which appears in the proceedings of *Notation of Sport IV*, used similar methodologies for different levels of performance.

4.4.9 Individual (closed performance) sports

Historically, match analysis has concentrated on the frequencies of occurrence of actions that make up the elements of a performance. By applying these methodologies to different sports, analysts have defined work-rates, tactical models of success and failure, technical models of elite performance and predictive models of performance of athletes, coaches and officials in events. More and more, coaches and athletes require not just a quantitative analysis of the elements that make up a performance, but also some qualitative assessment of these factors critical to success. This is true now for most sports, and a great deal of experience of this type of analysis has been gathered lately, particularly in the closed performance sports such as dance, gymnastics, diving and athletics.

Hughes and Crowley (2001) explored the potential of notation to analyse performance in acrobatic dance that is based on qualitative elements of assessment, typified by gymnastics and dance. But these qualitative forms of assessment are inherent in the provision of feedback in any performance in sport where the boundaries of success and failure are determined by the quality rather than the frequency of the actions.

A hand notation system was designed to record the skill sequences in sports acrobatics with respect to time and position. Three specifically designed data collection sheets were used to gather data for each performance. The system was tested for intra-observer reliability on actions (100 per cent), position (98 per cent) and time (98.5 per cent). The data was gathered post-event from video from the 1993 World Cup and the 1996 World Championships; performances ($N = 99$) from all the respective groups of acrobats were analysed.

Pearson product correlation showed that, in three disciplines, more time spent in preparation and dancing between the elements led to increased success in the performance of skills ($P < 0.05$). The remaining disciplines showed an opposite trend ($P < 0.05$): a lower amount of time spent between elements led to an increase in success in performance of skills. It was found in individual disciplines that skills recorded a higher complexity score when there was a lower amount of dance and preparation time prior to performing that skill. It was concluded that this methodology and analysis were capable of reducing the qualitative essence of these performances to quantitative analysis and feedback.

At present, very little research in terms of notation has been carried out in athletics, though individual sports such as squash have been well notated. Track athletics, the most obvious sport that can be examined by movement analysis, has been almost completely overlooked. Examples of past research include Fowler (1989), and later Evans (1997) and Hubball (1999) analysed the velocities of middle distance male and female runners, respectively, and the effect of race position in relation to the winner at set points of the race. Parker and Hughes (2002) analysed male and female elite-level 100 m athletics sprinters, in order to identify the effect of stride length and stride frequency when racing. To achieve this a hand notation system was developed and tested for reliability of both the system and the user. The different phases of a 100 m race were identified and commented on during the study.

The notation was completed from video coverage of the Sydney 2000 Olympics. The 100 m race was divided into four intervals. The athletes' positions, times, velocities and stride lengths and frequencies were recorded and calculated for each interval. The results of the research showed that the last 10 m was significantly faster ($P < 0.05$) than the first 10 m and that the first 40 m interval (10–50 m) was significantly faster ($P < 0.05$) than the second 40 m interval (50–90 m). There was no significant relationship ($r = 0.127$, $P = 0.787$) between the time taken by the athletes and number of strides taken. All the finalists in the men's 100 m recorded faster times in the final than in the heats, but only two athletes in the final of the women's 100 m produced faster times than in the heats. The effect of stride frequency and stride length on performance in a 100 m race seems to be individual. The physiological structure of athletes to a certain extent determines stride length and frequency, but identifying competitors' race components could influence how athletes propose to run a race.

Duckenfield and Hughes (2002) extended these types of systems and analysed elite-level 400 m runners, in order to identify what varying tactics and techniques separate the winners from the rest of the field. A system was designed, and then tested for validity and reliability. Notation was carried out via video coverage of the Sydney 2000 Olympics, with athletes' split times, stride count and race position at each 100 m interval recorded onto notational analysis sheets.

Research results showed no significant difference ($P < 0.05$) for all measured variables between the winners, second, third and fourth place athletes. For total stride count measurements, a mean stride count for first place male athletes of 171.73 strides ±8 SD represented a large amount of variation at this level. Fourth place female athletes recorded a mean total stride count of 185.3 strides ±7.73 SD, further quantifying this finding. The proposed application of 'percentage difference' as a more appropriate analytical technique for performance variations as small as those found in this piece of research indicated that differences did exist on all variables considered. A significant difference was found between the split times of all four 100 m sections ($P < 0.01$), with 100–200 m and 200–300 m identified as significantly faster than the first and last 100 m sections.

Analysis of winning males' race positions signified that 31 per cent were in first place by 200 m and 63 per cent by the 300 m mark. None of the winning athletes were further down the field than fourth place by 300 m. Analysis of female results indicated that all winning athletes were in the top three by 200 m. On reaching the 300 m mark, 69 per cent were in first position with no athletes further down the field than second place. Comparisons between winning male and female 400 m athletes identified a significant difference ($P < 0.01$) between total stride count and stride length. No difference in stride rate was found ($P < 0.01$).

The subjective judging and assessment of qualitative sports, such as ice dance, gymnastics or diving, over the past few decades has proved to be problematic, which has recently been highlighted by the controversies at the 2002 Winter Olympics. Hughes and Houlton (2003) investigated the judging of qualitative sports using quantitative methods. The sport of diving was used as a case study.

Ten competitions were analysed live, using a devised hand notation system to record the judges' scores. The same ten competitions were also analysed by two independent judges post-event from video recordings. The two judges awarded scores using the current judging format as well as an alternative method called component analysis.

The originality of the study has meant that the results are unique in their findings. Results show that clear distinctions exist between the competition judges and the independent post-event judges, although the judges at the event were in agreement. The conclusions from the results illustrated that the post-event judges awarded a far wider range of marks for dives than the competition judges and that 'component analysis' (analysing the dive by dividing the performance into separate components) was potentially a beneficial learning tool for inexperienced judges, enabling them to gain the necessary knowledge and apply it to competition settings.

4.4.10 Summary

Hand notation systems and computerised notation systems have now been applied to virtually all sporting situations, and can provide very rich data. The distinctions between hand and computerised systems are blurring even more now as the hand-gathered data is often processed by way of databases such as Excel. These hand notation systems could then use the Excel data broadsheet to gather the data (post-event from video) – is it then hand notation or computerised notation? It does not matter.

Hand notation systems are in general very accurate but they do have some disadvantages. The more sophisticated systems involve considerable learning time. In addition, the amount of data that these systems produce can involve many man-hours of work in processing them into forms of output that are meaningful to the coach, athlete or sports scientist. Even in a simple game like squash the amount of data produced by the Sanderson-Way system of notation required 40 man-hours of work to process one match.

The introduction of computerised notation systems has enabled these two problems, in particular the data processing, to be tackled in a positive way. Used in real-time analysis or in post-event analysis in conjunction with video recordings, they enable immediate easy access to data. They also enable the sports scientist to present the data in graphical forms more easily understood by the coach and athlete. The increasing sophistication, and reducing cost, of video systems has greatly enhanced the whole area of post-event feedback, from playback with subjective analysis by a coach to detailed objective analysis by means of notation systems.

4.5 Computerised notation

Using computers introduces extra problems of which the system-users and programmers must be aware. Increases in error possibilities are enhanced by either operator errors or hardware and software errors. The former type of error is when the system-user unintentionally enters incorrect data, e.g. presses the wrong key on the keyboard. Any system is subject to perception-error where the observer misunderstands an event or incorrectly fixes a position, but the computer–operator interface can result in the operator thinking the correct data is being entered when it is not. This is particularly so in real-time analysis when the data must be entered quickly.

Hardware and software errors are introduced by the machinery itself, or the programs of instructions controlling the operation of the computer. Careful programming can eradicate the latter problem.

To minimise both types of problem, careful validation of computerised notation systems must be carried out. Results from both the computerised system and a hand system should be compared and the accuracy of the computerised system quantitatively assessed.

Computers have only relatively recently impinged on the concept of notation analysis. Franks *et al.* (1983a) maintained that this form of technology is likely to enhance manipulation and presentation due to improved efficiency. This view is supported by the work of Hughes (1985).

Four major purposes of notation have been delineated:

1   analysis of movement
2   tactical evaluation
3   technical evaluation
4   statistical compilation.

Many of the traditional systems outlined above are concerned with the statistical analysis of events which previously had to be recorded by hand. The advent of online computer facilities overcame this problem, since the game could then be first digitally represented via data collection directly onto the computer, and then later documented via the response to queries pertaining to the game (Franks *et al.*, 1983a). The major advantage of this method of data collection is that the game is represented in its entirety and stored in ROM or on disk. A database is therefore initiated and is a powerful tool once manipulated.

Team sports have the potential to benefit immensely from the development of computerised notation. The sophistication of data manipulation procedures available would aid the coach in his efforts to ameliorate performance.

The information derived from this type of computerised system can be used for several purposes, as suggested by Franks *et al.* (1983a):

1   immediate feedback
2   development of a database
3   indication of areas requiring improvement
4   evaluation
5   as a mechanism for selective searching through a video recording of the game.

All the above functions are of paramount importance to the coaching process, the initial *raison d'être* of notational analysis. The development of a database is a crucial element, since it is sometimes possible, if the database is large enough, to formulate predictive models as an aid to the analysis of different sports, subsequently enhancing future training and performance.

4.5.1 Soccer

One of the major developments in computerised notation has been the development of a mini system devised by Franks *et al.* (1983a). Franks configured a keyboard on a mini-computer to resemble the layout of a soccer field and designed a program which yielded frequency tallies of various features of play. The path of the ball during the game was followed, so off-ball incidents were considered extraneous. A video was time-locked into the system so that relevant sections of the match could be replayed visually alongside the computer analysis.

Mayhew and Wenger (1985) calculated the time spent by three professional soccer players in different matchplay activities by analysing videotapes using a specially designed computer program. The results indicated that soccer is predominantly an aerobic activity, with only 12 per cent of game time spent in activities that would primarily stress the anaerobic energy pathways. The mean time of 4.4 s for such high-intensity work indicated the lactic acid energy supply system was the anaerobic system of primary importance. The interval nature of soccer was partly described, and suggestions for the design of soccer-specific training programmes were offered. The work did not extend in any way the previous efforts of Reilly and Thomas (1976) or Withers et al. (1982).

Evaluation is an essential component of sport because it provides the coach with a means of establishing norms from the model based on the 'post-mortem' in order to fulfil selection and scouting needs. An essential prerequisite of evaluation in that it must be carried out as objectively as possible. Franks et al. (1983b, p. 77) maintained that 'if it can be measured – it is fact, if it cannot be measured – it remains opinion' and that this applies to the coaching arena.

One of the major conclusions related to previously noted observations (Hughes, 1987) concerning the number of passes leading to a goal. It was suggested as a result of the analysis that it would be extremely beneficial to performance if coaches could advise players to keep the number of passes in sequence down to three or fewer. This application of the research could be improved and a more thorough analysis of the parameters required to enhance the result. Minimal consideration was given to the number of games to be notated prior to the establishment of a recognised system of play. This is an important point, since any fluctuation in the patterns and profile will affect the deduced consequences, particularly with reference to the match outcome. Teams may also vary their system and pattern of play according to opponents, although these factors are not considered. Furthermore, the existence of patterns of play peculiar to individual players was not illustrated. It is in this area that the study by Church and Hughes (1986) concentrated, in an attempt to investigate the presence of patterns of play in a soccer team and whether any reasons can be found to explain the results.

Church and Hughes developed a computerised notation system for analysing soccer matches using an alternative type of keyboard, called a concept keyboard. This is a touch-sensitive pad that can be programmed to accept input to the computer. This permitted pitch representation to be graphically accurate and action and player keys to be specific and labelled. This considerably reduced the learning time of the system, and made the data input quicker and more accurate. The system enabled an analysis of patterns of play on a team and player level, and with respect to match outcome. An analysis of six matches played by

Liverpool during the 1985/6 season resulted in a number of conclusions, the most important of which were:

1   a greater number of passes were attempted when losing than when winning
2   possession was lost more often when losing
3   a greater number of shots were taken when losing than when winning.

Hughes *et al.* (1988) used the same concept keyboard and hardware system developed by Church and Hughes (1986), but with modified software, to analyse the 1986 World Cup finals. Patterns of play of successful teams, those teams that reached the semi-finals, were compared with those of unsuccessful teams, i.e. teams that were eliminated at the end of the first rounds. A summary of the main observations is as follows.

1   Successful teams played significantly more touches of the ball per possession than unsuccessful teams.
2   The unsuccessful teams ran with the ball and dribbled the ball in their own defensive area in different patterns to the successful teams. The latter played up the middle in their own half, the former used the wings more.
3   This pattern was also reflected in the passing of the ball. The successful teams approached the final sixth of the pitch by playing predominantly in the central areas while the unsuccessful teams played significantly more to the wings.
4   Unsuccessful teams lost possession of the ball significantly more in the final sixth of the playing area, both in attack and defence.

Lewis and Hughes (1988) extended this work, analysing attacking plays only, to examine whether such unsuccessful teams use different attacking patterns to successful teams. An attack was defined as any move or sequence of moves that culminated, successfully or otherwise, in an attempt on goal. A total of 37 individual action variables and 18 different pitch divisions were employed in the data collection programme. The data analysis programme employed chi-square test of independence to compare the frequency counts of each action available, with respect to positon on the pitch, between successful and unsuccessful teams.

It was concluded that successful teams passed the ball more than unsuccessful teams when attacking, particularly out of defence and in the final attacking end of the pitch. As in the previous work by Hughes *et al.*, the successful teams used the centre of the pitch significantly more than unsuccessful teams. Further differences demonstrated that successful and unsuccessful teams used patterns of play that vary significantly in attack. Implications were drawn with respect to the optimisation of training and preparation for success in elite soccer match-play.

Partridge and Franks (1989a, 1989b) produced a detailed analysis of the crossing opportunities from the 1986 World Cup. They carefully defined how they interpreted a cross, and gathered data on the following aspects of crosses:

1   build-up
2   area of build-up
3   area from which the cross was taken
4   type of cross
5   player positions and movements
6   specific result of the cross
7   general result, if the opportunity to cross was not taken.

Fifty of the 52 games of the competition were analysed from video tape, using specifically designed software on an IBM XT microcomputer that enabled each piece of information relating to crossing opportunities to be recorded and stored. The program recorded the time at which all actions took place during the match, for extracting visual examples post-analysis, in addition to the usual descriptive detail about the matches, i.e. venue, teams, etc. A second programme was written to transform and download this data into dBASE III+, after which this database was queried to reveal selected results. The authors summarised their results by considering what they termed 'key factors'. These were as follows.

1   Take the opportunity to cross the ball if (a) a target player can contact the cross, (b) you have the chance to play the ball behind defenders and eliminate the goalkeeper.
2   The cross should be played (a) first time, where possible, (b) behind defenders, (c) past the near post, (d) without loft and hang time.
3   Target players should be in position to contact the cross by (a) individual moves to get goal-side of the marking defender, (b) being as direct as possible, (c) not running past the near post to contact the ball, (d) always making an attempt to contact the ball.
4   Supporting players should position themselves to (a) seal off the top of the penalty area, (b) seal off the back-post area (not allow any ball to go through the back-post area).
5   Crosses should not be taken from areas close to the corner flag. Instead, the crosser should dribble towards the goal and either win a corner or get into the penalty area and cross to a particular player.

In conclusion, the authors related their results to the design of practices to help players understand their roles in the successful performance of crossing in soccer.

At the World Congresses of Science and Football a considerable amount of work on computerised analysis of football has been presented; this is all collated in the proceedings (Reilly et al., 1988, 1993, 1997). Similarly, the proceedings of the World Conferences in Notational Analysis of Sport (Hughes, 1997; Hughes, 2000a; Hughes and Tavares, 2001; Hughes and Franks, 2001) offer a large amount of work on analysis of soccer. A number of these have already been considered because of their contribution to the development of hardware and software as well as their contributions to research. The more significant applications will be reviewed.

Gerisch and Reichelt (1993) used graphical representation of their data to enable easier understanding by the coach and players. Their analyses concentrated on the one-on-one confrontations in a match, representing them in a graph with a time-base, so that the development of the match could be traced. Their system can also present a similar time-based analysis of other variables, interlinking them with video so that the need for providing simple and accurate feedback to the players is attractively achieved. Despite the limited amount of data presented, the results and their interpretation were very exciting in terms of their potential for analysis of the sport.

Winkler (1993) presented a comprehensive, objective and precise diagnosis of a player's performance in training and match play using a computer-controlled dual video system. This was employed to assess physical fitness factors employed in training contexts. In addition, he used two video cameras, interlinked by computer, to enable a total view of the playing surface area. This, in turn, permitted analysis of all the players in a team throughout the whole match, on and off the ball – something that not many systems have been able to produce.

Dufour (1993) presented an analysis, using computer-assisted video feedback and a specific algorithm for the statistics, of an evaluation of players' and team performance in three fields: physical, technical and tactical. He demonstrated the ability of his computerised systems to provide accurate analysis and feedback for coaches on their players and teams. Yamanaka et al. (1993), using an updated version of the systems used by Hughes et al. (1988), demonstrated the ethnic differences in international soccer by analysing the 1990 World Cup. They defined four groups, British Isles, European, South American and Developing Nations, and by analysing the respective patterns of play in matches with respect to pitch position were able to conclude on the different playing styles of these international groups. They also presented data in a case study of Cameroon, who had had such a successful World Cup, comparing their data to that of the other groups to examine the way in which they had developed as a footballing nation. Jinshan et al. (1993) completed an analysis of the goals scored, and the techniques used, in this World Cup and compared these with those scored in the 1986 World Cup. They found few differences between the two competitions. Partridge and Franks (1993) used a digitisation pad similar to that used by Hughes et al. (1988) and used this sophisticated system to compare the World Cup with the World Collegiate Championships. They found significant levels of differences in the skill levels of the two sets of players, particularly in dribbling and passing, and made positive suggestions to coaches at the collegiate level.

A sophisticated analysis of the definion of playing space in which players perform (Grehaigne et al., 1996) introduced new ideas and directions for research in soccer. A more practical approach by Tiryaki et al. (1997) demonstrated how analysis can help some sides achieve unexpected results: this research team had worked with the Turkish team that surprised Switzerland and qualified for the 1996 European Championship finals. In another practical example of the uses of notational analysis as a form of feedback, Partridge and Franks (1996) researched the actual effect of feedback on performance. Although limited by the number of subjects, the research demonstrated that the feedback did produce beneficial changes in nearly all the subjects, and that the best aspect of the feedback was the change in attitude of the players in thinking about and analysing their own performances.

In international tournaments, teams are judged on their ability to win matches. To achieve these victories, the teams must have effective ways to win the ball, create successful attacks first by reaching the attacking third of the field, create scoring chances and complete them by scoring goals with a high efficiency. Luhtanen et al. (2002) selected offensive and defensive variables of field players and goalkeepers in the Euro 2000 competition and attempted to relate the results to the final team ranking in the tournament. The final ranking order in the WC '98 tournament was explained by calculating the rank correlation coefficients between team ranking in the tournament and ranking in the following variables: ranking of ball possession in distance, passes, receptions, runs with the ball, shots, interceptions, tackles and duels. Selected quantitative and qualitative sum variables were calculated using ranking order of all obtained variables, only defensive variables and only offensive variables. The means and standard deviations of the game performance variables were calculated and ranking order in each variable was constructed. Spearman's correlation coefficients were calculated between all ranking game performance variables. Only the variable of successful passes at team level explained success in Euro 2000.

France was the best team in the performance of passes, receptions, runs with ball and tackles. In percentage of the successful passes, France was the top team. The strengths of Italy were in defence. The Italians were best in interceptions and third best in tackles. In the passing activity their position was 15th, but in the percentage of successful passes second. In the overall ranking taking into account all analysed variables, Italy was 13th. This analysis would give Holland a better place than third. Holland was first in ball possession (8.9 km) and second in the number of passes and shots, and also close to the top place in the corresponding successful executions. Because Holland controlled the ball a lot, it didn't have many chances for interceptions or duels. This can be seen in the number of interceptions and duels. Germany was strong in having the ball in possession (second), in passing play (second) and in the number of goal-scoring trials (fourth). However, weaknesses were found in defence activity of interceptions (16th) and tackles and duels (15th).

Usually, notational analysis uses numerical data to study and assess the quality of a match. As far as the analysis of the tactical aspects of the game is concerned, there is a dearth of published research with regard to their theoretical bases. Grehaigne et al. (1996) tried to construct a knowledge base about soccer using some qualitative observational tools. In a soccer match, structures and configurations of play should be considered as a whole rather than examined a piece at a time. Systems with many dynamically interacting elements can produce rich and varied patterns of behaviours that are clearly different from the behaviour of each component considered separately. To that effect, effective space game, action zone, and configurations of play were examined to show that this type of analysis is complementary more than opposed to the numerical data analysis systems. This work demonstrates the growing awareness of the need for qualitative factors investing the quantitative nature of notation data with a far greater wealth of relevance to an overall performance.

Luhtanen (1993) carried out a statistical evaluation of the offensive actions at the 1990 World Cup. He compared the number of offensive actions and the efficiency of these actions between teams in respect to their final ranking in the competition. The results showed that in 69 per cent of attacks possession was not lost (free-kick, corner, throw-in or penalty won in the attacking third), 28 per cent of attacks produced a scoring opportunity, and 9 per cent resulted in a goal. They also found that successful teams (with the exception of Argentina) mastered the game in terms of numbers in the attacking third, and created greater scoring opportunities than the unsuccessful teams. The World Cup winners, Germany, proved to have the greatest efficiency when attacking, as they possessed the highest number of attacks, the lowest number of lost attacks and the highest number of scoring opportunities. Partridge and Franks (1993) also found that they lost the highest percentage of possession in the attacking third (61 per cent), and the lowest percentage in the defending third (7 per cent).

Tiryaki *et al.* (1997) completed an analysis of offensive patterns of Switzerland during the 1994 World Cup. Matches against USA, Colombia, Romania and Spain were analysed using a computer notation system developed in the Notational Analysis Centre at Liverpool John Moores University. The study found that the Swiss team were more successful in midfield and less effective in offensive areas. Notational analysis can help some sides achieve unexpected results. For example, Tiryaki *et al.* (1997) worked with Turkey, who surprised Switzerland to qualify for the 1996 European Championships Finals.

Luhtanen *et al.* (1997) used a new notational analysis system to compare Brazil and their opponents during the 1994 World Cup. A video recording-based system was constructed to input data of different time, space and manoeuvre per player. The qualitative manoeuvre variables include:

1   the number of successful attacking trials for the attacking third
2   scoring chances created in the vital area
3   scoring trials
4   goal standardised for the normal playing time.

The qualitative variables included:

1   cumulative time of the ball in possession for each team
2   distance covered by the ball under control of each team.

The results found that Brazil had the highest number of successful attacking trials in the attacking third, the highest number of scoring opportunities in vital areas, and the highest number of shots from scoring opportunities. They also found that the highest number of successful attacks originated from interceptions in the middle third of the field; they used more change-over when passing; used a free style of play with fewer long passes; used long runs with the ball; and used more overlap and wall passing than their opponents.

Although soccer has received a major share of the research by notational analysts over the past five decades and substitutes have been positively or negatively affecting the results of soccer matches since the change in the rules in the 1960s, no analyses had been completed on this critical area of the game until Pearce and Hughes (2001) analysed substitutions during the European Football Championships 2000. The study was divided into two sections. Firstly, general characteristics were recorded from all 176 substitutions that were made during the tournament. Secondly, 24 substitutes were analysed to assess their impact on the teams' performance and whether the substitute's performance was better than the player he replaced.

The research was carried out using a computerised notation system in conjunction with video, post-analysis. Data collection involved gathering data from a match 15 minutes prior to the substitution and 15 minutes post-substitution. The data were analysed by comparing the number of actions that occurred by a team/individual during the first 15 minutes to the number of actions that occurred in the second period of 15 minutes. A total of 24 matches were selected from Euro 2000, and substitutions chosen so that the respective teams were equally balanced in winning, losing and drawing situations. Performances between the two periods were evaluated by the use of an evaluation matrix that enabled variables to be ranked in order of importance. These matrices were then applied to both the team performance and the respective individual performances for 15 minutes before and after substitution.

The majority of substitutions took place during the second half of the match and primarily for tactical reasons. The most frequent position for substitutions was in midfield, possible reasons for this could include the high work-rate associated with these positions. Results also suggested that substitutions might influence teams' performances, with 60 per cent of substitutions analysed having a positive influential effect on performance. Little difference was found between the actions of the substitute and the actions of the player replaced. The findings suggested that substitutes play an important role in their contribution towards team performance and can provide coaches with greater flexibility.

When these sophisticated analysis systems are truly integrated with the video analysis and editing suites such as Noldus Oberver or Sportscode (see Hughes et al., 2002b), then the task of the analyst and coach will be more immediate but never simpler.

4.5.2 Squash

Hughes (1985) modified the method of Sanderson and Way so that the hand-notated data could be processed on a mainframe computer. The manual method was modified so that a match could be notated live at courtside using a micro-computer. Because of difficulties with the speed of the game and the storage capacity, only one player was notated. Hughes established a considerable database on different standards of squash players and reviewed his work in squash in 1986. He examined and compared the differences in patterns of play between recreational players, country players and nationally ranked players, using the computerised notational analysis system he had developed. The method involved the digitisation of all the shots and court positions, and entered these via the QWERTY keyboard.

A detailed analysis of the frequency distribution of shots showed that the recreational players were not accurate enough to sustain a tactical plan, being erratic with both their straight drives and their cross-court drives. They played more short shots, and although they hit more winners they also hit more errors.

The county players played a simple tactical game generally, keeping the ball deep and predominantly on the backhand, the weaker side of most players. They hit significantly more winners with straight drives. Their short game, consisting of boasts, drops and rally-drops, although significantly less accurate than the nationally ranked players, was significantly more accurate than the recreational players.

The nationally ranked players, because of their far greater fitness, covering ability and better technique, employed the more complex tactics, using an 'all-court' game. Finally, the serves of the county players and the recreational players, because of shorter rallies, assumed greater importance than the serves of the ranked players.

In an unusual but very interesting piece of sports analysis, Alexander *et al.* (1988) used the mathematical theory of probability to analyse and model the game of squash. Mathematical modelling can describe the main features of a game such as squash and can reveal strategic patterns to the player. They suggested that squash is an example of a Markov chain mathematical structure, i.e. a series of discrete events each having associated probability functions:

The probability that A wins a rally when serving is P_a

The probability that A wins a rally when receiving is Q_a

The probability that B wins a rally when serving is $P_b = 1 - Q_a$

The probability that B wins a rally when receiving is $Q_b = 1 - P_a$

If two opponents are of the same standing then P_a, P_b, Q_a, $Q_b = 0.5$

The probability of A winning a point when serving is the sum of each winning sequence of rallies:
$P_a = 1/2 + 1/2^3 + 1/2^5 + 1/2^7 + \ldots = 2/3$ (geometric series)
P_a wins 9–0 = $(2/3)^9 = 0.026$
If A is a stronger player, with $P_a = 2/3$ and $Q_a = 3/5$, then:

Probability that A wins when serving is 5/6; when receiving is 1/2

Probability of A being in a serving state is 3/4

The probability of winning a game is the sum of all the probabilities of each possible score, i.e. sum of $p(9–0)$, $p(9–1)$ . . . $p(9–8)$, $p(10–9)$. The model ignores off-days, fatigue, etc. By presenting all these associated probabilities Alexander *et al.* were able to compute the potential benefits of winning the toss, so as to serve first – a surprisingly large advantage. Also, they were able to recommend strategies for players having to choose how to 'set' the game, when the score reaches 8–8, depending on the respective skill and fitness levels.

In an attempt to circumvent the problems posed by presenting frequency distributions on two-dimensional representations of the playing area, Hughes and McGarry (1989) developed a system that updated the Hughes's (1984) system, using a concept keyboard for input and using an Acorn BBC micro-computer. They specifically tackled the problem of three-dimensional graphical output of the data from a squash match. Their system enabled the presentation of the frequency distributions in colour 3D histograms, with the capability of rotation. Comparative presentations of data were also possible. It is interesting to compare this form of presentation with that of Sanderson, who did not have the facility of computers, and the present-day analysis systems that are integrated into their respective graphics and database systems.

Hughes *et al.* (1989) were interested in analysing the motions of athletes of any sport, without having to resort to the long and arduous job of cinemato-graphic analysis or the semi-qualitative methods associated with notational methods, used live or from video. They attempted to combine the best of both systems without the faults of either. They designed a tracking system that enabled the use of the immediacy of video, and, by using mixed images on the same VDU screen, accurate measurements of the velocities and accelerations of the players, usually associated with film analysis. A 'Power Pad' was used to gather positional data along with the time base. The playing area representation on the Power Pad was videotaped and its image mixed with that of the subject tape. Careful alignment of the images of the two 'playing areas' enabled the subject, and the tracking stylus on the bit pad, to be viewed at the same time, and an accurate tracing of the movements of the player onto the simulated playing area in real time. A careful validation of the system showed its accuracy and the short learning time required by operators.

Hughes and Franks (1991) utilised this system and applied it to squash, comparing the motions of players of differing standards. They presented com-parative profiles for four different standards of players, spanning club players to the world elite. The profiles consisted of analyses of distance travelled, velocities and accelerations during rallies. The work provides reference data against which physiological studies of squash play can be compared. In addition, the distance travelled during rallies by both recreational and regular club players was surprisingly short, the mean distance being approximately 12 m for both top club players and recreational players. Hughes and Franks were able to present suggestions about specific training drills for the sport. Their system could also compare the individual profile of a player to those of his peer group, so giving a direct expression of his relative fitness; as an example they chose to analyse some of the reasons why the seven times World Champion, Jahangir Khan, dominated squash for so long. Khan was compared to the top six in the world (which data included his own profile). The data clearly showed the vast physical advantage that he has over the best athletes in the world at this sport.

A fairly recent innovation in attempting to solve the problems of data entry was the utilisation of a new language, visual BASIC, which enables a graphical user interface, i.e. the operator enters data by moving an arrow round the screen using the mouse and clicking to enter a selected item. All IBM-compatible systems can run these software packages. This language was used to write a system for squash, which was used by Brown and Hughes (1995) to examine the effectiveness of quantitative feedback to squash players. While this system of data entry will not be as quick as the concept keyboard, when used by a fully trained and experienced operator, it is again very easy to use, attractive to the eye and the extra hardware requirements are nil. It was used by Hughes and Knight (1995) to examine the differences in the game of squash when played under 'point-per-rally' scoring as opposed to the more traditional English scoring. The former had been introduced to most senior international tournaments because it was believed to promote more 'attacking' play and shorter rallies, and hence make the game more attractive. It was found that the rallies were slightly longer on average, not significantly so, that there were more winners and the same errors – this being attributed to the lower height of the 'tin' under these new rules.

A similar system was used by Hughes and Clarke (1995) to analyse the differences in the playing patterns of players at Wimbledon, on grass, to those of players at the Australian Open, on a synthetic surface. They found very significant differences between the two surfaces, particularly with the ball-in-play time. This averaged about 10 per cent for the synthetic surface (14 minutes in an average match of just over two hours), while it was as low as 5 per cent on grass (7 minutes in an average match of just over two hours). This work, that of Hughes and Knight (1995) and some analyses of squash tournaments using tennis scoring, prompted Hughes (1995a) to analyse and recommend a new scoring system in squash to try to make the game more attractive. Hughes recognised the need to shorten the cycles of play leading to 'critical' points in squash – currently it takes about 15–20 minutes to reach a game-ball; by having more, shorter games, more critical points will arise and this will raise the levels of excitement and crowd interest. Badminton has the same problems with its scoring systems and the ensuing activity cycles.

McGarry and Franks (1994) created a stochastic model of championship squash match-play which inferred prospective from previous performance through forecasting shot response and associated outcome from the preceding shot. The results were restricted because it was found that players produced the same patterns of responses against the same opponent ($P > 0.25$) but an inconsistent response was found when competing against different opponents ($P < 0.25$). This contradicts earlier work by Sanderson (1983) who found that squash players played in the same patterns against different opponents, whether winning or losing, but this may well be a function of the finer degree to which McGarry and Franks were measuring the responses of the players. However, these results led to further analysis by these authors (McGarry and Franks, 1995) of behavioural response to a preceding athletic event, and they again found the same results. They confirmed that sport analysis can reliably assume a prescriptive application in preparing for future athletic competition, but only if consistent behavioural data can be established. The traditional planning of match strategies from a priori sport information (scouting) against the same opponent would otherwise seem to be an expedient and necessary constraint. A review of work completed in the computerised analysis of racket sports (Hughes, 1995b), together with a number of papers in match analysis of racket sports, is included in *Science and Racket Sports* (Reilly *et al.*, 1995).

Murray *et al.* (1998) researched the effect of computerised notational analysis as feedback on improving squash performance. This study used a similar method to that of Brown and Hughes (1995) on the effectiveness of quantitative and qualitative feedback in squash. It was concluded that both groups reacted positively to the feedback provided and the feedback from notation analysis accounted for an increase in the number of winners and a decrease in the number of errors. From this evidence it is clear that notation analysis has its uses as an effective practical tool during the coaching of performance.

'A comparison of the game strategies employed by national and international squash players in competitive situation by notation analysis' is the title of a paper by Hong *et al.* (1996a). Ten male matches from the Perrier Hong Kong Closed Championship '94 were recorded. Strokes and where the ball landed were recorded; they were identified according to 13 well-known types, namely as straight drive (SDr); cross-court drive (XDr); boast (Bo); reverse boast (RB); straight volley drive (SVDr); cross-court volley drive (XVDr); straight volley drop (SVDp); cross-court volley drop (XVDp); volley boast (VB); straight lob (SL); cross-court lob (XL); straight drop (SDp); and cross-court drop (XDp). The quality of the return shot was depicted by four different categories: 'effective', 'ineffective', 'winning' and 'losing'. The results obtained from this study coincide with those of Hughes (1996b). In the front of the court, for instance, the national players played a significantly higher percentage frequency of both all returns and 'losing' shots than the international players. National players played both a significantly higher percentage of 'ineffective' shots and a lower percentage of 'effective' shots than their international counterparts. They also played significantly more shots from the front of the court and fewer from the back, played significantly more 'ineffective' drive, drop and volley shots and less effective shots than the international players.

All the research carried out on playing patterns in squash has observed male subjects only, apart from a recent study by Hughes *et al.* (2000d), who analysed female squash players. The aim of the study was to define models of patterns of play at different levels in squash for women and analyse the demands placed on players as they ascend through these levels. An additional aim was to define a 'normative profile' and explore how much data was required to reach a 'normal playing pattern'. Using a computerised notation system (Brown and Hughes, 1995), post-event analysis for elite ($N = 20$), county ($N = 20$), and recreational ($N = 20$) players was conducted. A dependent t-test was used to establish whether a normative profile had been reached; the profiles of eight matches were compared with those of nine and ten matches for each of the categories of players. Analysis of variance and chi-square analysis were used to test for differences in the overall match totals and distributions of shots.

The results produced in this study have clearly distinguished between the playing patterns of women at the different levels of play. It was discovered that elite and county players did establish a playing pattern that could be reproduced reasonably consistently. The recreational players did not produce a normal playing pattern due to lack of significance at a suitable level. Hughes *et al.* (2000d) felt that a normative playing pattern is only achieved when a player plays at top level; the subsequent differences of the recreational player exist not because of chance but because they do not possess a fixed pattern. As players work their way up the different standards of play, set patterns emerge. The county playing standards showed a set pattern forming, but this will not be fully achieved until that county playing standard reaches the top level of squash: elite level. (Hughes *et al.*, 2000d, p. 91.)

Significant differences were produced on a number of key elements of play across the three standards. There was a significant difference in the total number of shots played per match ($P < 0.05$) and standards of play. There was also significant difference ($P < 0.05$) between all three groups for the total number of shots per rally.

The conclusions drawn from this study have similarities to the work of Hughes (1986) concerning male subjects. The elite players employed an 'all-court' game, using more complex tactics, creating more pressure, due to their higher levels of fitness, covering ability, speed and skill levels. County players showed a consistent attempt to hit the ball into the back of the court and predominantly on the backhand side. Their shots were less accurate than those of the elite players, but significantly more accurate than those of the recreational player. Recreational players adopted a 'hit and run' game due to their inability at tactics. They were erratic with their distribution of shots, hitting a high percentage loose to the middle of the court. These studies by Hughes (1986) and Hughes *et al.* (2000d), although they distinguish between playing patterns of various standards for both genders, are not representative of the junior game in any way. This is due to the differing physiological factors between the two subject areas, for instance being able to retrieve the ball, and also other factors that might contribute to the variance in playing patterns, such as quality of coaching.

Many studies that analyse the performance of a certain groups of people, and try to highlight relationships and differences between them, fail to examine raw data in order to establish whether a 'normal playing pattern' had been established (Hughes and Knight, 1995; Hong *et al.*, 1996a; Hughes and Robertson, 1998). Studies have failed to answer the question of how many matches should be analysed before a 'normal playing pattern' is reached. Hughes *et al.* (2000d) identified that the method they used to establish a normative playing profile was significant by comparing the profiles of eight matches with those of nine and ten matches.

Future studies including performance profiling should ensure that the subject number is distinct enough for a normative profile to be reached. This study has established specific reference data on the playing patterns of female squash players and has paved the way for further research to be carried out on the women's game. (This concept is discussed in detail in Chapter 10.)

4.5.3 Tennis

There are many areas of the game of tennis that have been researched and these include statistical analysis, biomechanical analysis, movement analysis and time-motion analysis. Elite tennis strategy has been studied using timing factors, shot details (Hughes and Clarke, 1994; O'Donoghue and Liddle, 1998; O'Donoghue and Ingram, 2001), positional play, distance covered (Underwood and McHeath, 1977) and point profiles (O'Donoghue and Liddle, 1998).

Hughes and Clarke (1995) undertook an investigation into the strategies used in rallies at Wimbledon and at the Australian Open 1992 Grand Slam events. Their analysis found mean rally lengths of 2.50 s and 4.72 s respectively. The main cause of rallies ending was identified as errors rather than winners on both grass and acrylic. The ace and service winner frequencies were similar for both tournaments, but the number of serves returned was 11 per cent more at the Australian Open than at Wimbledon. Their study also analysed the distribution of player position: this was slightly skewed to the left, indicating that many players use the inside-out forehand tactic to open the court up for the next shot. Both the mean number of shots in a rally and the mean rally length were lower at Wimbledon. Hughes and Clarke's conclusions suggest that the service is more effective on grass, as is net play, while baseline play is more dominant on the synthetic surface. Statistically, there were more winners at Wimbledon while more errors were made on the synthetic surface of the Australian Open. More service games were held at Wimbledon, as were more winners, while more errors were evident at the Australian Open. The time analysis showed that there was 5 per cent ball-in-play time (7 min in 2 h 7 min) at Wimbledon and 11 per cent ball-in-play time in Australia (14 min in 2 h 14 min) in an average match.

Further investigation into strategy for males and females and different court surfaces was proposed. O'Donoghue and Liddle (1998) analysed whether elite female players win a greater proportion of points on serve and at the net on the grass at Wimbledon than on the clay at the French Open during the 1996 Grand Slams. They identified that more points were won on serve and at the net on grass than on clay and there were more baseline rallies in clay court competitions. They also examined the cause and effect of coming to the net and concluded that there is a higher chance of winning the point if a player draws the opposition to the net on clay than on grass.

The study by O'Donoghue and Ingram (2001) analysed male versus female players, and all four Grand Slam surfaces. They examined 31,558 points in Grand Slam events from May 1997 to January 1999. Rallies of 7.1 ± 2.0 s in women's singles were significantly longer than those of 5.2 ± 1.8 s ($p < 0.001$) in men's singles. The rallies were significantly longer at the French Open and significantly shorter at Wimbledon than any of the other tournaments. The rally times for women were 4.3 ± 1.6 s at Wimbledon, 6.3 ± 1.8 s at the Australian Open, 7.7 ± 1.7 s at the French Open and 5.8 ± 1.9 s at the US Open. The results indicated that the court surface and sex of a player influenced the characteristics of singles tennis at Grand Slam tournaments.

4.5.4 Netball

Steele and Chad (1991, 1992) used Miller (1988) as a foundation for the analysis of movement patterns of netball players during match play to form designs for training programmes. Steele and Chad (1992) noted that 'A fundamental pre-requisite for developing training programmes specific to the requirements of any sport is an understanding of the physiological demands placed on each individual team member during a game'.

The study analysed four one-hour matches, three between NSW State League teams and one between the Illawarra Academy of Sport and a district representative side. The average age of the players in the study was 19.7 ± 3.4 years. All players matched in ability as closely as possible and maintained the same playing positions throughout. Movement patterns (locomotor activities) were classified as standing, walking, jogging, running, sprinting and shuffling. The non-locomotor activities were shooting, successful goal, unsuccessful goal, centre pass, catch, toss-up, jump, leap, rebound, defend and guard. The coding of the movement patterns was derived using the 'time analysis' program, as follows:

1   number of repetitions of each locomotor/non-locomotor activity during play
2   average time spent performing the locomotor/non-locomotor activity
3   total time spent performing locomotor and non-locomotor activities during the match
4   relative contribution of each locomotor and non-locomotor activity to the total time available in match play expressed as a percentage of the total time of the game.

Steele and Chad concluded in terms of both the muscle groups and the energy sources that similarity should exist between training and match play. Training activities should be tailored to suit the needs of particular positions on court; they should also replicate as closely as possible the movement patterns found in a game. Steele hoped information provided from the study would allow netball coaches to review their current training programmes and use the research as a criterion model for the basis of new training programmes for specific positions.

Croucher (1997) designed a computer program for netball known as NETSTAT. This sophisticated program analyses the data entered and provides invaluable analyses for the coach. NETSTAT was designed to provide a detailed look at all aspects of play in a game of netball. The data were preferably collected by two individuals, one to call out the action and the other to record. Specific recording sheets were designed simultaneously with the program to simplify the data entry process. The system was successful in providing the detailed and extensive analysis it suggested, but did not prove to be a popular method of data collection and analysis.

Palmer et al. (1994) produced research analysing patterns of play, specifically the centre pass. The study was a comparison of successful and non-successful teams and their centre-pass movements. It aimed to dichotomise the characteristics of successful and non-successful netball teams. Palmer et al. selected England as the non-successful team and New Zealand and Australia, the two top nations in the world, as the successful teams. Four matches of each team were notated using a computerised notation system completed post-event from video. The research found that the skill level of a team differentiated on the basis of their ability to create goal-scoring opportunities and to score off centre-pass play. The standard of teams also differentiated in their ability to play the ball forward on the first and second passes of the centre pass. The research was limited but provided a starting block for other researchers to 'advance the existing methodology and attempt to develop more player-specific systems modelled on those that differentiate players of successful and non-successful teams' (Palmer et al., 1994).

Netball research spans many aspects of the game of netball, and the spectrum of research is broad. Largely, research focuses on an important aspect of play. The importance of centre-pass play and the conversion of possession are highlighted in the Palmer et al. research, and these are arguably the most effective components of play in the game. The skill level of the team dictates the quality of centre-pass play and scoring opportunities.

4.5.5 Field hockey

Franks et al. (1987) developed an analysis program using the Apple IIe computer. The analyst viewed the game from a central and elevated position and recorded the flow of play. During half time and after the game the sequential data (some 2,000 events) were stored on disk and a menu-driven analysis program was accessed. The analysis selection was made and the results were computed and printed.

The key factors of performance were identified as: goals scored and conceded; shots taken and the results of such shots; possession of the ball and where possession was lost or gained; types and number of passes made; success or failure at set-plays, including free hits, sideline hits, penalty corners and corners; and information relating to the goalkeeper's performance. At first, the field hockey analyst used the computer keyboard as a representation of the field to enter the data. However, after extensive preliminary experiments, it was decided to use a Power Pad to ease the data entry.

Hughes and Cunliffe (1986) observed the England ladies' hockey team to study the effect of different surfaces on the patterns of play in field hockey, and to provide feedback on performance to the England coaching staff. This consisted of the patterns in which the team was playing and also individual player profiles, i.e. analyses of all actions by each individual, to whom they passed and where, from whom each received passes, tackles, free hits and so on. The data were entered via the QWERTY keyboard. It was concluded that tactics adopted on artificial turf differ from tactics applied on grass. The rolling resistance on artificial surfaces is less than that on grass; an artificial surface is also more uniform so that the ball rolls more evenly. These were thought to be the major reasons that players ran more with the ball on artificial surfaces than on grass, and that there were more touches per possession in play on artificial surfaces.

The printed feedback provided for the coaches was modified to meet their own perceived requirements. These requirements inevitably changed each time they received analyses of matches, so the data processing software had to be continually modified. This would seem to be a natural and inevitable part of this feedback process.

Hughes and Billingham (1986) developed another system for field hockey that analysed patterns in passing sequences among team members. All data were entered via a digitisation pad in the specific order of player number, pitch position and action variable. The system was applied to analyse six women's international hockey teams, with match data for the analysis provided in the form of pre-recorded video tapes. Results showed that the successful teams made significantly greater use of the right-hand side of the pitch, forced more short corners and were tackled in possession significantly fewer times than the non-successful teams. Significantly more successful shots were taken from the left-hand side of the shooting circle for all teams, although successful teams took a significantly greater number of shots at goal than non-successful teams. The significance of the former is linked with the successful teams attacking significantly more on the right wing, from which crosses would enable players on the left-side of the circle greater shooting opportunities.

4.5.6 Volleyball

Franks and Goodman (1986a) highlighted the pressure that the sequential nature of team sport places on the human memory system: often only after a critical moment in a game does a previous event become significant. This is very much the case in volleyball, where the quality of the skill being notated is highly dependent on the skill preceding it. Eom (1988) designed a computer interactive recording system to store and analyse a sample of 164 games from the 3rd FIVB Korean Cup (1987). Playing actions were quantified using a five-point numerical rating system, which ranked the different outcomes of six key skill components (serve, reception, setting, attack, block and defence). Stochastic analysis using a Markov model (first and second order) was applied to detect the sequential dependencies of the events in each process. The data, represented in the form of a transitional matrix, was analysed using a chi-square test to investigate whether a skill that occurred at time $(t + 1)$ or time $(t + 2)$ was dependent on a skill occurring at time t. Further analyses were conducted to compare a transitional matrix in the attack process with that in the counter-attack process and among the quick, medium, and high attacks. Initial work with this system found that transition probabilities between the serve reception and set (0.81), and between the set and the spike (0.83), were highly significant. Among the types of spike, successes in first and second tempo attacks were highly dependent on the quality of the set 0.87 and 0.92 respectively. The investigation did not find dependencies between the set and third tempo attacks; this was probably due to the nature of the skill. Third tempo attacks are characterised by a slow, high ball trajectory, which gives the hitter time to adjust if the set isn't spatially and temporally accurate.

Work done on spiking data of Italian volleyball teams (Van Hal, 1999) showed a kill percentage of 51.9 per cent for 8.15 error. The kill total relates to the percentage of spikes that the player scores points from directly; the error total indicates when a point is lost as a direct result of a spike (hit out, into the block or into the net). A good player will be characterised by a high kill total and low error total.

Dividing the court up into zones and recording the position of different actions presents the coach with a collection of spatial information relevant to the game, for example through which court positions are players spiking more successfully. The analyst must decide the best method for dividing the court; use of a large number of zones will be very specific but may lack reliability in the recording.

The most notable contemporary volleyball study is a quantitative computerised system devised by Handford and Smith (1996) to assess the development and application of a systematic approach to performance analysis in volleyball. It looked to address the tactical implications of previous research, investigating skill quality and frequency on a rotation-by-rotation basis. They incorporated a number of variables in the development of their system, namely the involvement of coaches, methods of reducing data input time, and the development of a 'user-friendly' system. They produced what they perceived as 'a computerised programme that combined the best features of existing systems'. They also produced inter- and intra-operator reliability tests for the proposed system, and illustrated the results with accurate, simple graphs and diagrams essential for game analysis.

4.5.7 Badminton

The need to apply computerised notational analysis techniques to the study of badminton has been recognised (Liddle et al., 1996). A rally analysis system was used to compare men's and ladies' singles and doubles badminton in European Circuit competition (Liddle and O'Donoghue, 1998). The European Circuit involves players from many nation including New Zealand and Chinese Taipei. It is a competition competed in by individuals and doubles pairs at various venues on the circuit. The Europe Cup, on the other hand, is a single tournament between top European badminton clubs that takes place over a four-day period. The purpose of a study by O'Donoghue (2001a) was to investigate differences in shot rates between all five singles and doubles games using a computerised system. This would provide knowledge of the slightly lower level of competition of the Europe Cup, allowing a contrast with European Circuit matches.

The findings of O'Donoghue (2001a) were in disagreement with those of Liddle and O'Donoghue (1998), as no significant differences were found between men's and ladies' singles in European Circuit rallies. There were also no significant differences between the shot rates of men's and ladies' games in singles or doubles. This was due to the smaller variances in shots found in O'Donoghue (2001a). Overall the results showed that there were differences between the five games, concluding that particular disciplines should be made specific to badminton training.

4.5.8 Rugby union

Rugby union presents slightly different problems for analysis with its set-piece moves, the scrum and the line-out, and also the action after a tackle: either rucks or mauls. Treadwell (1988) developed software that utilises the concept keyboard to analyse rugby union. Hughes and Williams (1988) developed software using a similar system of hardware (cf. previous work on soccer). The system was designed to notate the matches post-event using video tapes. Four computer programs were written. The data collection program was constructed with the help of an international coach, who helped define the most important variables to be recorded. The other three programs analysed the data and provided the output. Once again the concept keyboard was used to help gather the data. The pressing of the sub-routine keys 'scrum', 'line-out', 'ruck', or 'maul' caused the software to direct the input back to the QWERTY keyboard where additional data was entered, such as the order in which players arrived (ruck or maul), and quality of ball (scrum, ruck or maul).

The developed system was used to notate five matches from the Five Nations Series over the previous two years, involving all the participating nations. A comparison was made for each match between the two playing sides, and then the results were collated and analysed statistically for differences in the patterns of play between the French, Scottish and Irish compared to the English and Welsh sides.

No significant differences were found between the patterns of play for successful and unsuccessful teams, although a number of differences were found between the patterns of play of the three nations compared to the other two ($P < 0.05$). France, Scotland and Ireland played in different patterns to England and Wales.

Docherty et al. (1988) analysed 27 players during matches to assess the time spent in the various activities of the game. Computerised notation of the frequency and total, mean and percentage times of six activities was undertaken. The players selected were either centres or props; eight players were tracked by four cameras in five-minute intervals for a minimum of 40 minutes per match. The findings were that:

1   players spent 47 per cent of the time walking and jogging
2   players spent 6 per cent of the time running and sprinting
3   players spent 9 per cent of the time tackling and competing for the ball
4   players spent 38 per cent of the time standing
5   centres sprinted for 3 per cent of the time, the props for less than 1 per cent of the time
6   players spent 85 per cent of the match in low-intensity activity.

The system of Hughes and Williams (1988) was upgraded and transferred to IBM software architecture and used to investigate the effects of the rule changes in rugby union in the 1991–92 season. It was found that the ball in play time actually decreased and the only other significant changes were to the rucks and mauls. These systems were also used to investigate the 1991 World Cup (Stanhope and Hughes, 1996; Hughes and White, 1996), with comprehensive analyses of the way in which points were scored, and how the successful and unsuccessful teams used their respective threequarters and forwards. This analysis of this tournament places all these data onto a database which will be invaluable as it will enable longitudinal comparisons across tournaments to be made.

Recent rugby union studies have examined rule changes. Hughes and Clarke (1994) studied the effects of the new law changes on patterns of play. The new laws included the 'use it or lose it' rule at the breakdown. The results of the study showed that the number of possessions during a match decreased, while the number of passes per possession increased. Also, more tries were scored after three, four or five phases, but there were no differences between the numbers of breakdowns created during the matches. The differences found may be caused not only by the new laws but by increasing standards of play.

Hughes et al. (1997) used some of the data from the 1991 World Cup as a comparative norm with which to compare similar analyses of women's international rugby matches taken from the Five Nations championship. These data showed very clearly the result of the stark physiological differences between male and female rugby players in the comparative figures in distances gained from kicks and yardage gained, in all positions, in running with the ball. There were also indications that the women's game is still in the early stages of technical development and further studies should be undertaken in years to come to help the coaches remain aware of the shortcomings.

McCorry et al. (1996) developed a manual match analysis technique for post-match video analysis of rugby union that addressed positive and negative attacking and defensive play, possession changes and methods of gaining territory. Although McCorry *et al.*'s (1996) results did not reveal any significant differences between winning and losing sides in the knock-out stages of the 1995 Rugby Union World Cup, the method allowed the effectiveness of the four semi-finalists to be compared over three matches. Hunter and O'Donoghue (2002) extended McCorry *et al.*'s (1996) technique to a larger number of matches from the 1999 Rugby Union World Cup to compare further the performances of winning and losing teams. Twenty-two matches were analysed including 15 group matches, three play-off matches and four matches from the knock-out stages.

'Positive offence' was measured by the number of occasions a team entered the opposition's last third through positive offensive play; 'negative offensive play' was the number of occasions play exited the opposition's last third as a result of negative offensive play; 'negative defensive play' was the number of occasions play entered a team's own last third as a result of negative defensive play; 'positive defensive play' was the number of occasions play exited the team's own last third as a result of positive defensive play. Possession gains from set and lose play were recorded as well as the number of occasions where a team gained territory by going around (running and passing), over (kicking) and through (driving, rucking and mauling) the opposition. Seven of the 11 variables were positively skewed ($z_{Skew} > +2$), therefore the winning and losing teams were compared using a series of non-parametric Wilcoxon signed ranks tests. The winning team scored 2.7 ± 1.0 points per occasion in the opponent's last third, which was significantly greater than the 1.2 ± 0.6 for the losing team ($z = 3.9, P < 0.001$). Play entered the losing team's last third significantly more than the winning team's last third, with the successful teams tending to perform more positive offensive play and using running/passing moves to gain territory to a greater extent than their opponents.

Martin *et al.* (2002) also examined the effect of recent rugby union rule changes, including foul play incidents, line-out contesting and the impact of sin-bins. The main conclusions of the study showed that foul play penalties decreased during the year 2000 compared to 1999, and line-out possession retention reduced from 89 per cent in 1999 to 83 per cent in 2000, with the average number of line-outs contested rising from 53 per cent to 58 per cent. Finally, they concluded that sin-bins could have a possible impact or significance on the results of perhaps as few as three of 69 matches.

Studies comparing successful and unsuccessful teams have been popular in many sports, as they can identify the reasons why some individuals or teams dominate the sport. In rugby union a recent study by Jackson and Hughes (2001) found that when successful and unsuccessful women's rugby union teams were compared, there were a few significant differences. It was found that successful teams had a higher number of passes per possession rate, a higher tackle count and a greater number of players in each ruck and maul situation.

4.5.9 Computer-controlled video

One of the most exciting and potentially significant outgrowths of computerised sport analysis has been the advent of interactive video technology. The ability of computers to control the video image has made it possible to enhance existing sport-specific analytical procedures. An inexpensive IBM-based system was described by Franks et al. (1989). The system operates in conjunction with an IBM XT (or compatible) and requires a circuit board to be resident within the computer. The system was designed to interact with a video cassette recorder (VCR) that has a 34 pin remote control outlet (some Sony and Panasonic AG and NV series). The interaction between the computer and the VCR was outlined as well the technical details of the circuit boards. In addition, several software programs were given that demonstrate the control features of the circuit board.

Franks and Nagelkerke (1988) developed such a system for the team sport of field hockey. The analysis system, described by Franks and Goodman (1986b), required a trained analyst to input, via a digitisation pad, the game-related data into a microcomputer. Following the field hockey game, a menu-driven analysis program allowed the analyst to query the sequentially stored time–data pairs. Because of the historical nature of these game-related sequences of action, it was possible to perform both post-event and pre-event analysis on the data. That is to say, questions relating to what led up to a particular event or what followed a particular event could now be asked. In addition to presenting the sports analyst with digital and graphical data of team performance, the computer was also programmed to control and edit the videotape of the game action.

The interactive video computer program accessed from the stored database the times of all specific events such as goals, shots and set plays. Then, from a menu of these events, the analyst could choose to view any or all of these events within one specific category. The computer was programmed to control the video such that it found the time of the event on the video and then played back that excerpt of game action. It was also possible to review the same excerpt with an extended 'lead-in' or 'trail' time around that chosen event. This system is at present being tested and used by the Canadian national women's hockey team.

The system was modified for use to analyse and provide feedback for ice-hockey and soccer. A number of professional ice-hockey clubs are currently using it, as well as the national Canadian team.

A number of commercial systems are now available for the notational analyst that can considerably enhance the power of feedback, through the medium of video replays and edited video clips. Some of the more successful are appraised by Hughes et al. (2002b); much more detail can be found on the appropriate website for each system reviewed: Sportscode, Quintic, SiliconCoach, Tracksys and Purple VAIO.

4.6 Summary

To summarise the developments in computerised notational analysis, one can trace the innovative steps used in overcoming the two main problems of dealing with computers – data input and data output.

The initial difficulty in using a computer is entering information. The traditional method is using the QWERTY keyboard, but, unless the operator possesses considerable skills, this can be a lengthy and boring task. If codes are assigned to the different actions, positions or players that have some meaning to the operator, then the key entry can be easier. The next step is to assign areas of the keyboard to represent areas of the pitch, numbers for the players, and another section of the keyboard for the actions (see Hughes and Cunliffe, 1986). An alternative is to use a specifically designed keyboard (Franks *et al.*, 1983a; Alderson and McKinnon, 1985, cited in Brackenridge and Alderson, 1985) that has key entry designed ergonomically to meet the particular needs of the sport under analysis.

The major innovation, however, in this area, which eased considerably the problems of data entry in terms of both skill requirements and learning time, was the introduction of the digitisation pad. In Britain most workers have utilised the 'concept keyboard' (Hughes and Feery, 1986; Sharp, 1986; Treadwell, 1988) while in Canada, Ian Franks, at his Centre for Sport Analysis at UBC, Vancouver, has utilised another pad that has the trade name 'Power Pad' (Franks *et al.*, 1986a). These are programmable touch-sensitive pads, over which one can place an overlay that has a graphic representation of the pitch and aptly labelled keypad areas for the actions and the players. This considerably reduces the skill required for fast data entry, and the learning time required to gain this level of skill. These digitisation pads have gradually given way to the use of the graphical user interface (the mouse) and on-screen graphics, but this is not as quick as the use of the digitisation pads, because of their easy 'point and click' demands. But the mouse is universal, and a lot more convenient than trying to get the extra 'add-on' hardware to work, which is not always 100 per cent compatible from country to country.

Another highlight, which is still awaited, is the introduction of voice entry of data into the computer. Although Taylor and Hughes (1988) were severely limited by the amounts of funding for their research, they were still able to demonstrate that this type of system can and will be used by the computer 'non-expert'. Although systems are expensive at the moment, computer technology is an environment of rapidly decreasing costs, even as the technology races ahead, so one can expect that this will be the next big step forward in the use of computers in general, and sports systems in particular. It is strange, given the advance in electronic technology, that 15 years on from this research and the comments made above, they are still true today.

Notational analysis, while having been the platform for considerable research, has its foundations in practical applications in sport. In these situations, it is imperative that the output is as immediate as possible and, perhaps more important, clear, concise and to the point. Consequently, the second strand of innovation that one can trace through the development of different systems is that of better output.

The first systems produced tables and tables of data, incorporated with statistical significance tests, that sport scientists had difficulty in interpreting: pity the coach or the athlete attempting to adopt these systems. Some researchers attempted to tackle the problem (Sanderson and Way, 1979), but not everyone would agree that this type of presentation was any easier to understand than the tables of data. Representations of frequency distributions across graphics of the playing area, traces of the path of the ball prior to a shot or a goal (Hughes and Cunliffe, 1986; Franks and Nagelkerke, 1988), and similar ploys have made the output of some systems far more attractive and easier to understand. The system developed by Hughes and McGarry specifically tackled this problem and produced some 3-D colour graphics that presented the data in a compact form, very easy to assimilate. Finally, the computer-controlled video-interactive systems (Franks et al., 1989) initiated the idea that the users of analysis systems could utilise the potential of immediate analysis combined with the visual presentation of the feedback of the action. This has led now to the edited video image being the medium of feedback, the story-board of which is created by the detailed analyses provided by hand or computerised notation systems (or a combination of both) (see Murray and Hughes, 2001).

4.7 The future of notational analysis

In terms of technological development, notational analysis will undoubtedly move as rapidly as the developments in computer technology and video technology as we journey through the twenty-first century. The integration of these technological developments in computerised-video feedback will enable both detailed objective analysis of competition and the immediate presentation of the most important elements of play. Computerised systems on sale now enable the analysis, selection, compilation and re-presentation of any game on video to be processed in a matter of seconds. The coach can then use this facility as a visual aid to support the detailed analysis. Franks (1988) devised a more detailed model of the feedback process that could be possible with this type of technology. It is only 15 years later that the top professional clubs in sports, and some National Governing Bodies, are implementing these ideas fully.

As these systems are used more and more, and larger databases are created, a clearer understanding of each sport will follow. The mathematical approach, typified by Eom (1988) and McGarry and Franks (1994 and 1995), will make these systems more and more accurate in their predictions. At the moment the main functions of the systems are analysis, diagnosis and feedback – few sports have gathered enough data to allow prediction of optimum tactics in set situations. Where large databases have been collected (e.g. soccer and squash), models of the games have been created and this has enabled predictive assertions of winning tactics. This has led to some controversy, particularly in soccer, due to the lack of understanding of the statistics involved and their range of application. Nevertheless, the function of the systems could well change, particularly as the financial rewards in certain sports are providing such large incentives for success. The following glimpse (Franks, 1996b) into future integrated match analyses should help illustrate this point:

> The analysis from the match has been established and after reviewing a brief summary of the game statistics the coaching staff are concerned that late in the game crosses from the right side of the team's attack were being delivered behind the defenders and close to the opposing team's goalkeeper. The result being that the front strikers were not able to contact the ball despite making the correct approach runs (information also gained from the match summary). The coaching staff call for videodisc (immediate recovery) excerpts of each crossing opportunity from the right side of the field in the last 15 minutes of play. Along with this visual information, the computer retrieves other on-line information that is presented in the inset of the large projected video image. This information relates to the physiological condition of the player(s) under review leading up to the crossing opportunity. In addition a 3-D analysis of the crossing technique is presented as each cross is viewed. One player had been responsible for these crosses. Upon advice from the consulting exercise physiologist the coaching staff have concerns about the telemetered respiration and heart rate of the player. A time–motion analysis of the player's movements in the second half of the game is called for, as well as a profile of the player's fitness level and physiotherapy report prior to the game. These are also retrieved from the same videodisc. After considering the information the coaching staff record their recommendations for team and individual improvement and move on to the next problem provided by a comparison of the predicted data and real data. A computer program running in the background is busy compiling instances of good performance (successful crosses) and poor performance that will make up an educational modelling programme for the individual player to view. Also the expert system of coaching practice is being queried about the most appropriate practice for remedial treatment of crossing in this specific setting. An individual fitness programme is prescribed when another expert system is queried. The final question that is asked of the mathematical model is 'given these changes are implemented, what is the likelihood that the number of crosses in the final fifteen minutes from the right side of the field will be more successful against our next opponent and what is their expected effect on match outcome?'

All aspects of the above scenario are either in place or under investigation in notational analysis laboratories throughout the world.

Technological advances aside, the real future of notational analysis lies in the growing awareness by coaches, athletes and sports scientists of its potential applications to all sports. Whether the most sophisticated and expensive of systems is being used, or a simple pen and paper analysis, as long as it produces accurate results that are easy to understand, then coaches, athletes and sports scientists will gain objective, reliable data that will increase their insights into sport performance.

5 Sports analysis

Mike Hughes and Ian M. Franks

The aim of this chapter is to provide an insight into how different sports can be broken down into a series of decisions represented by a limited number of actions and their possible outcomes. These logical progressions provide the inherent structure within each sport. The construction of flowcharts of different sports is examined, together with the definition of key events in these respective sports. The next step is to design a data collection and data processing system, so anyone interested in designing a notation system should read this chapter first.

5.1 Introduction

Before discussing the work and research done in the field of notational analysis, including both manual and computerised systems, it is necessary to explore methods of applying analysis to sport in general. As stated in previous chapters, the very essence of coaching athletes is to instigate an observable change in behaviour. Methods of analysis used to measure these changes form the central focus of the remaining sections of this chapter. Objective performance measures should serve as the basis for future planning in any coaching process. While it is clear that both the quantification of performance and the assessment of qualitative aspects of performance are required, it would seem from the current research in these fields (see sections 2.2, 2.3), that the former has been largely ignored, and the latter has many inherent weaknesses. This section, therefore, focuses on measures of performance that can be collected in order to analyse quantitatively the performance of an athletic event. Firstly analysis systems will be discussed with a view to applying them generally to either team sports or individual sports. In later chapters these systems are extended into data recording systems. Current research work, both pure and applied, is reviewed and assessed. Finally, the recent extension of these systems by the development of fast and inexpensive microcomputers will form the nucleus of the final sections of the book.

5.2 Creating flowcharts

The information that is available during a game is diverse and extensive. Continuous action and a dynamic environment make objective data collection difficult. Any quantitative analysis must therefore be structured. As there are so many ways in which to collect information about any sport, two very important points should be considered:

1   consult with the best technical expert (i.e. coach) of the game to be analysed
2   the potential use of the information should guide how the system will be designed – i.e. make sure that what is required from the analysis system has been completely determined before starting anything else.

The first step is to create a 'flowchart' or logical structure of the game itself. This means defining the possible actions in the game and linking these actions with the possible outcomes, thus describing the sequential path the game can take. This is more easily explained by example. In a team sport, field hockey, Franks and Goodman (1984) described the game very simply by a two-state model: either 'our' team has possession or the opposing team has possession of the ball. This would be the top of what Franks and Goodman termed 'the hierarchy'. They then proposed that the next level of questions in the hierarchy would be:

1   Where on the field did our team gain and lose possession?
2   Can these areas be easily identified? (e.g. field divided into six areas)
3   Who on the team gained or lost possession?
4   How was possession gained and lost? (e.g. was it from a tackle, an interception, foul, etc.)

These questions can be included in the hierarchical structure as indicated in Figure 5.1. (Note: For those interested in reading around the subject further, Franks *et al.* (1986b) developed a series of detailed and more complex structures in which they modelled the decision-making processes of athletes engaged in team games. This work is very interesting from a modelling point of view, but as it approaches the problem from a perceptual point of view on the part of the player, rather than an analytical view from the coach, it is not directly applicable here. However, it does provide a basis for a more thorough understanding of how to build up hierarchical structures.)

The questions posed in Figure 5.1 can yield extremely useful information, although this level of analysis is obviously very simple. It is best to anticipate the form in which you wish to look at your data. Simple tabulated records are often the easiest to produce, and are easily translated to pictorial representations which are always easier to assimilate. More detailed analyses might be concerned with the techniques individuals used during performance. They might also include physiological and psychological parameters that are mapped along a time axis during the performance. No matter how simple or complicated your intended analysis, always start as simply as possible and gradually add other actions and their outcomes bit by bit: in computing terminology this would be termed the addition of more sub-routines.

Figure 5.1 Hierarchical structure of a model for representing events that take place in a team game such as field hockey, soccer, basketball, water polo.

Franks and Goodman (1984) go on to suggest a simple series of steps or tasks in the evaluation of performance. The first one is based on the above analysis:

TASK 1: *Describe your sport from a general level to a specific focus.*

The next step outlined by Franks and Goodman is fundamental in forming any evaluative analysis system:

TASK 2: *Prioritise key factors of performance.*

The final step in the process is:

TASK 3: *Devise a recording method that is efficient and easy to learn.*

The first two steps are discussed further with more examples in this chapter; the third task is given separate consideration in Chapter 6.

Consider our simple analysis of the team sport in Figure 5.1. This can be made more sophisticated by considering in more detail the possible actions and their respective outcomes (Table 5.1). These actions and outcomes can then be incorporated into a model for the events taking place in this team game, which happens to be soccer, but which could easily be transposed to any team sport. This is shown in Figure 5.2.

The natural sequential logic of the game can be followed. As possession is gained by one of the players, a number of choices of action are presented to the

Table 5.1 Some actions, and their respective outcomes, for soccer

Action	Outcome	Effect on possession
Pass	Good	Retained
	Bad	Lost
Shot	Wide	Lost
	High	Lost
	Blocked	Retained or lost
	Saved	Lost
	Goal	Lost
Cross	Good	Retained
	Bad	Lost
Corner kick	Good	Retained
	Bad	Lost
Goal kick	Good	Retained
	Bad	Lost
Throw-in	Good	Retained
	Bad	Lost
Goalkeeper's throw	Good	Retained
	Bad	Lost
Goalkeeper's kick	Good	Retained
	Bad	Lost

Free kick – pass, shot, etc. and their subsequent routines
Penalty – shot (subsequent routines)

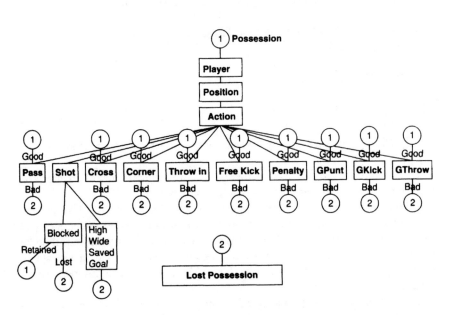

Figure 5.2 Simple schematic flowchart for soccer.

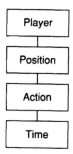

Figure 5.3 Core elements of any analysis system of performance.

player. The choice, and the outcome of the action, determines whether this side retains possession, scores a goal, gives away a free kick, etc. Inevitably this system can be made more sophisticated still: that is always possible with any system. For example, the dribble, run, tackle, foul, etc. have not been included, nor have any actions when not in possession. The difficult decision to make in designing this type of model is knowing when the limitations of the model are acceptable within the terms of reference of the desired data.

The core elements – 'player', 'position', 'action' – in Figure 5.3 can be seen to be fundamental to analysis systems. If 'time' is also included then this will represent the most complex of systems. These elements are rarely included in all systems: for example, if we were analysing the attacking patterns of a hockey team, we would not need to record the players' identities – only the position on the pitch, the action and outcomes (if any). If we were examining the workrate of a player then all we would be recording would be the position, the action (stand, walk, jog, run, etc.) and possibly the time. These basic elements form the heart of any analysis of a sport.

Consider the game of squash as another example. This is a field-invasive individual racket sport. Other than the definition of the playing area, the logic of this game could as easily be applied to tennis or to badminton, which are non-field invasive. The system in Figure 5.4 shows the simple logic needed to record and analyse the key elements of the performance. To include the scoring system would require considerable additions to this flowchart. The basis of the 'English' scoring (a similar system is used in badminton) is that the server receives a point if he/she wins the rally. If the non-server, 'hand-out' wins the rally, he/she does not receive a point. The winner of the rally serves for the start of the next rally. This simple logic to the game of squash is complicated a little by the concept of 'lets' and 'strokes'. A 'let' is when one player impedes the other in the process of his/her shot; this results in the rally being played again, no change in score, same server. A 'stroke' is given against a player when he/she prevents the opponent from hitting the front wall with a direct shot

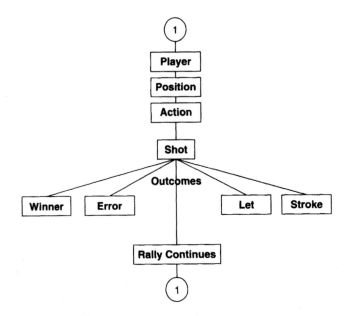

Figure 5.4 Simple flowchart for squash.

or prevents a winner. (The concept is a little more complicated than this, as all squash players will testify, but this explanation should suffice for non-combatants.) So a 'stroke' given against a player is equivalent to the player conceding an error.

Creating the model for the logic of the sequence of the shot production and respective positions is relatively straightforward (see Figure 5.4). If the shot is a winner then that player serves the next rally. Whoever hits an error, or receives a 'stroke' adjudged against him/her, does not serve the next rally. The 'let' ball decision results in the rally starting again. If none of these conditions apply then the ball is still in play and the other player strikes his/her shot from the notated court position. In most simple systems for racket sports, analysts will start with a 'winner/error' analysis – recording the type of shots that were winners or errors and where on the court they were played.

One way of incorporating the logic of the scoring, and who serves, into the model of the action is to keep the definition of the server and non-server throughout the rally. This helps clarify whether the score is increased at the end of the rally or not, depending on who won. The selection of actions or, in this case, shots to be inserted into these models, as in the previous examples, is determined by the detail of complexity required by the data collection. Sanderson and Way (1979) used a relatively complex menu of shots, which included:

Straight drive	Cross-court drive
Straight drop	Cross-court drop
Volley drive	Volley cross drive
Volley drop	Volley cross drop
Boast	Volley boast
Lob	Cross-court lob
Others	

Included in 'others' were infrequent shots: cross-angles, corkscrew lobs, skid boasts, back-wall boasts, shots behind the player's back, etc. Perhaps this selection of shots does not look too complex at first sight, but consider these facts. Sanderson and Way divided the court into 28 cells for definition of position. In the course of one match they would record in the region of 4,500 items of information. Processing these data would take another 40 person-hours of work. In addition, the learning time to use the system 'in-match' was five to eight hours. This was a complex system despite its apparent simplicity; it produced the data that its designers required. But it is only too easy to gather too much data: be sure that your system gathers only the data needed. The recording system is discussed in detail in Chapter 6.

Franks and Goodman (1986b), working with David Hart and John MacMaster, both of the Canadian Water Polo Association, developed a flow diagram of water polo. The design was attack-based, whereby the events, the player responsible, and the reason are recorded. By using this flow diagram, a computer program was constructed so that the whole history of the game was stored and produced for analysis. This system is further discussed later in this chapter, and also in Chapter 7.

5.3 Levels of analysis – the team, subsidiary units and individuals

Although there are many facets of the team's performance that could be described, there are only a limited set of priority elements that serve a useful function with a view to improving performance. In deciding on which information is useful, Franks *et al.* (1983a) suggested that the coach should be guided by three elements:

1   coaching philosophy
2   primary objectives of the game
3   database of past games.

For example, if a game objective has roots in the principle of possession then the important questions to be answered should relate to possession (i.e. total number of possessions; where on the playing surface possession was lost and won; who was responsible for winning and losing possession; etc.). Coaching philosophy may also dictate certain defensive or offensive strategies to implement at critical time periods during a game. If this is the case, then the analysis should be directed towards objective counts of defensive or offensive behaviours during these periods of play. It should be noted that Franks *et al.* contend that: 'The most important of these three elements is the formation of a database of past games. With such a database it is possible to fomulate a predictive model.'

If one knew how, where and when goals or points were scored in past games, a probabilistic model could be constructed to aid future training and performance. Technical and tactical training could then be directed towards the high probablility events. Coaching could be directed at gradually modelling a team to more fully fitting a winning profile.

After all of the significant game-related questions have been defined by the technical expert, it is necessary to decide on the level of analysis that is needed. Figure 5.5 illustrates a primary level of team analysis. The example extends the soccer model already used, but it must again be emphasised that this can be

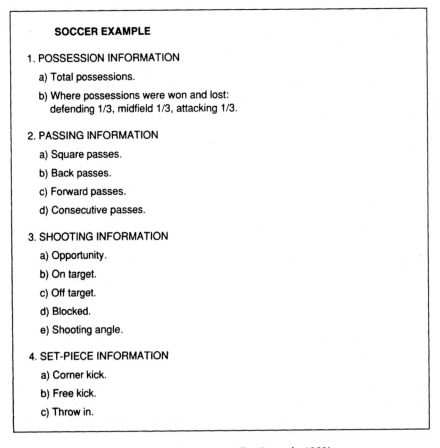

SOCCER EXAMPLE

1. POSSESSION INFORMATION
    a) Total possessions.
    b) Where possessions were won and lost:
       defending 1/3, midfield 1/3, attacking 1/3.

2. PASSING INFORMATION
    a) Square passes.
    b) Back passes.
    c) Forward passes.
    d) Consecutive passes.

3. SHOOTING INFORMATION
    a) Opportunity.
    b) On target.
    c) Off target.
    d) Blocked.
    e) Shooting angle.

4. SET-PIECE INFORMATION
    a) Corner kick.
    b) Free kick.
    c) Throw in.

Figure 5.5 Primary level game analysis – team (Franks *et al.*, 1983).

equally be applied to other team games. Four areas are considered for information gathering: possession, passing, shooting, and set-pieces. However, within each of these categories more detail is available. For example, when a shot is taken, this analysis should not only reveal if the shot was on or off target, but also, if it was on target, whether it was saved or was a goal. Further information about the off-target shooting could also be gathered – was it high, wide or high and wide? This type of information is extremely important and should greatly influence subsequent coaching practices.

Franks *et al.* (1983b) stated that 'The information gained from set pieces (i.e. corner kicks, throw-ins and free-kicks) should be relative to some prescribed definition of success or failure.' Coaches should have expectations of performance at set-pieces in a game such as soccer. Other games will have similar structured phases where similar definitions of performance should be met, e.g. American football (yardage on a running play); field hockey (percentage of short corners converted to goals); rugby league (number of tackles made by specific positions). The definition of performance in each case will depend on the personal philosophy of the coach in relation to her/his sport. These expectations should be made clear to the players and should be practised. For example, a free kick that is awarded in the defending third of the field should be delivered in fewer than three moves to the attacking third of the field, whereas a free kick that is awarded in the attacking third of the field should result in a strike on goal in fewer than three moves. If these expectations are not met then the set-piece is registered as a failure. Franks *et al.* (1983b) go on to say:

> It is important to note that these definitions of success and failure should be continually upgraded to correspond to the level of performance and realistic expectations of the coach. If the definitions are unrealistic then the evaluation will not be sensitive to the performance changes.

A detailed analysis of an individual player is illustrated in Figure 5.6. It would take a very detailed and comprehensive recording system, involving a battery of experts, to gather the data for this sort of analysis. Franks *et al.* have, however, provided a very complete example of the way to go about defining the type of data required for an individual analysis. The player has two distinct categories of performance that can be evaluated, these are on-the-ball and off-the-ball behaviour. These behaviours could be recorded in a cumulative fashion, e.g. number of defensive recovery runs, or given a success/failure rating, e.g. 20 successful square short passes and 10 unsuccessful short passes gives a success/failure ratio of 2:1. The area of the field in which events occur could, and should, be included in these computations to give the necessary spatial dimensions to the analysis. The division of the area of the pitch is again subject to the detail required: a simple division of the pitch into six equal areas would give a definition of the attacking, midfield and defending one-thirds of the pitch. Other studies have used finer definition overall, and then a finer definition yet again in the penalty area (Church and Hughes, 1986; Hughes *et al.*, 1988),

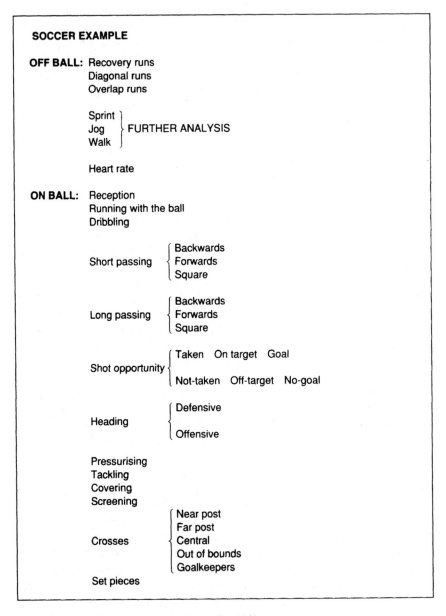

Figure 5.6 Individual analysis (Franks *et al.*, 1983).

so that these areas of specific interest have a finer degree of detail to them. Finally, further data relative to physiological requirements can be accessed in methods of measuring heart rate and blood lactates during and/or after game action. These measures can be correlated to technical data and then inferences can be made about the complete performance of individuals within a team game.

The way of applying these analyses, demonstrated in this example, should be applied to units in a team as well as the whole team or individuals. The efficiency of attacking, midfield or defensive groups of players within a team can be assessed. This is one objective way of selecting the best combinations of players within the tactical sub-groupings within a team, and monitoring their continued performance.

For sports such as tennis, golf and martial arts, individual levels of analysis can be applied, using similar logical analyses to those shown in Figure 5.6.

5.4 Summary

Logical analysis of the form and function of the events taking place in a sport is necessary before further analysis can take place. Franks and Goodman (1984) outlined three steps in forming any analysis sytem:

TASK 1: *Describe your sport from a general level to a specific focus.*
TASK 2: *Prioritise key factors of performance.*
TASK 3: *Devise a recording method that is efficient and easy to learn.*

By elucidating tasks 1 and 2, the creation of a notation system becomes an easy and logical progression. Practising these logical definitions is not difficult but it is a skill that becomes easier and easier with practice.

The more complex the sport (team games like soccer or American football, for example), the more care must be taken in deciding exactly what is required of the system: which units of the team, or individuals, are to be analysed, which actions and events have the most relevance, and so on.

The next step in analysis logic is to decide the level at which the analysis will take place. If it is a team game, what units of the team are going to be analysed? Or are individuals to be monitored? Or the whole team? This type of decision does not apply in individual sports, but the level or degree of detail of output must be decided – and it is vital that these decisions are made early in the analytical process.

6 How to develop a notation system

Mike Hughes and Ian M. Franks

6.1 Introduction

The aim of this chapter is to enable you to develop your own hand notation system. No matter how simple or complicated you wish to make it, the same underlying principles apply. If you are hoping to develop a computerised system, the same logical process must be followed, so this chapter is a vital part of that developmental process too. To gain the most benefit from this chapter, Chapters 4 and 5 should have also been read.

6.2 Examples of data collection systems

There are several types of data collection system, which can be roughly divided into three categories:

1 scatter diagrams
2 frequency tables
3 sequential systems.

6.2.1 Scatter diagrams

Scatter diagrams are usually simple and are most often used to gather data in-event and enable immediate feedback for the coach and athlete. Usually, a scatter diagram involves drawing a schematic representation of the playing surface of the sport in which you are interested on a sheet of paper, and then notating on this the actions of interest, at the position at which they took place (player number too?). For example, consider a soccer coach wanting to know where his football team lose possession: a simple plan of the pitch enables the recording of these positions (Figure 6.1).

What else does the coach need to know – which of the players is offending most? The system can be made a little more sophisticated by adding the number of the player who lost possession (Figure 6.2).

What else might we need to know about our problem of loss of possession? Perhaps the actions that the players are executing might give us more insight

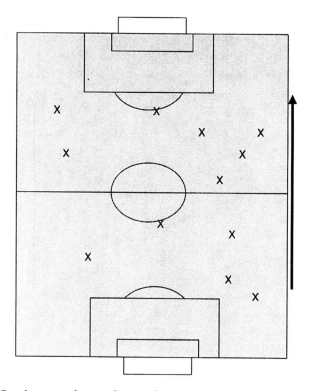

Figure 6.1 Simple scatter diagram for recording position of loss of possession for soccer.

into the relative merits of their performance. To record the actions involved, we will need a simple definition of the most common actions and some symbols:

- P – pass
- D – dribble
- C – cross
- S – shot
- K – clear

Figure 6.3 shows an example of this form of data gathering. Because it is more complicated, to be able to do this at match speed might take a little practice.

Scatter diagrams have a number of immediate advantages and disadvantages:

- simple and quick
- can be quite accurate if you practise a lot
- usually 'in-event'
- immediate feedback

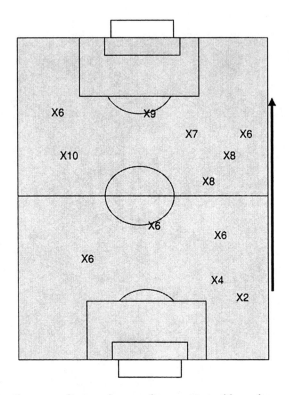

Figure 6.2 Simple scatter diagram for recording position of loss of possession, and the player involved, for soccer.

- usually no need to process data
- do not know the order of events – no 'sequentiality'.

But it must be noted that there are dangers in interpretation of these simple forms of data, not only because usually their accuracy is not very high, but also because the simple data can only yield simple analyses. Attempts at further depth of analysis will only lead to problems.

6.2.2 *Frequency tables*

Frequency tables are a commonly used form of data gathering that enables quick, simple analyses of performance of athletes and teams. Let us consider an example of a basketball coach wanting to know which players have made which actions during a game. By using a frequency table like that shown in Table 6.1, the analyst can easily record the frequency of each of the actions by the players in the squad.

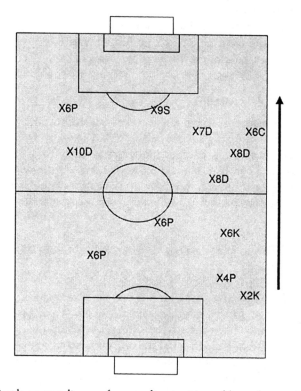

Figure 6.3 Simple scatter diagram for recording position of loss of possession, and the player, and the action involved, for soccer.

Table 6.1 A simple frequency table for basketball

Actions	1	2	3	4	5	6 ...
Pass	☆☆☆☆☆☆		☆☆☆	☆☆☆☆		
Dribble	☆☆☆		☆	☆☆		
2-pt shot	☆☆☆☆		☆☆☆☆	☆☆		
3-pt shot	☆☆			☆		
Assist	☆☆☆☆		☆☆☆☆	☆		
Lost possession	☆		☆☆			

Like scatter diagrams, frequency tables have some obvious advantages and disadvantages:

• simple and quick
• can be accurate with practice
• usually 'in-event'

- immediate feedback
- need to process data – usually not too bad
- do not know the order of events – no 'sequentiality'
- dangers in interpretation of these simple forms of data.

6.2.3 Sequential data systems

Recording the sequence in which events occur enables the analyst to go to far greater depths in interpreting a performance. Now critical events, such as a shot at goal or a winning shot in a racket sport, can be analysed so that the events that led up to them can be examined for repetitions of patterns. These can be very informative for the coach, not only on their own players, but also on the opposition. These patterns can also help the sports scientist understand different sports.

> FIRST STEP: You must decide what you want from your system before you design the system.

This sounds a little odd: the reason for it is that notation systems provide masses of data. Unless you have a crystal-clear idea about what data you wish to collect, you will find that your system will collect confusing, and sometimes irrelevant, information. Keep in mind the old adage about not seeing the wood for the trees. Time spent working on what form(s) your output might take can save a great deal of frustration later. Most importantly, it also simplifies the job of defining input. Having decided what you want, the process of designing your data collection system is simple and straightforward. Often the most difficult part is making sense of the mass of data – this is true for all analysis systems.

The simplest way of starting is to consider a basic example. A field-hockey coach may wish to have more information about the shooting patterns, or lack of them, of her/his team. The coach will need an output from this system consisting of:

1   position of the pass preceding the shot (the assist)
2   player who made the pass
3   type of pass
4   position from which the shot was taken
5   which player made the shot
6   outcome of the shot (i.e. goal, save, block, miss (wide), miss (high), corner, etc.)

(Note: If field hockey is not a game with which you are familiar, this method will as easily apply to any field-invasive team sport such as basketball, soccer, water polo or lacrosse.)

The data needed to be notated in this example is relatively simple. The next step is to assign notation symbols for each of the above variables. First divide

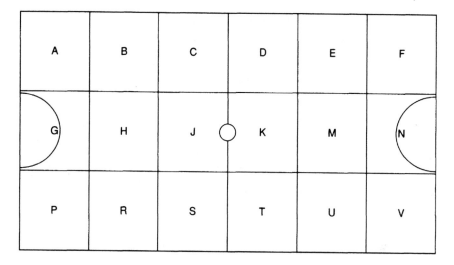

Figure 6.4 Definition of position on a representation of a field hockey pitch.

the pitch into segments or cells and give each one a code: this could be either a number or a letter, but there are usually advantages in using specifically one or the other. Deciding on how the playing surface should be divided is not always as simple as it might appear. Using small cells enables fine definition of the positions at which actions take place, but the more cells you have, the more data you have to collect in order to have significant numbers of actions in each cell. If in doubt, err on the side of simplicity – the most influential research on soccer was done with the pitch divided into three (the defending third, the middle third and the attacking third). The hockey pitch in Figure 6.4 is at the other extreme of definition, with a large number of position cells.

As position, player, action, and so on are notated, it is often useful to have the codes entered in the system alternating from letter to number to letter: this makes interpretation of the data much simpler. Any saving that can be made in the number of items entered can also mean a large saving in time – often the difference between being able to notate 'in-match' and not. It is easy to identify players by their shirt number (if they have one, of course), but if there are more than nine in a team or squad then you have to note two digits instead of one. Some systems in the past have employed letters for players '10' and '11'. In Figure 6.4, letters rather than numbers have been used to differentiate between areas of the pitch. The significance of this is that, for each of the areas above, only a single item of information needs to be written down for area. This may sound trivial, but when systems are recording thousands of items of data, each small saving in design at the developmental stage will increase the effectiveness of the system many times over.

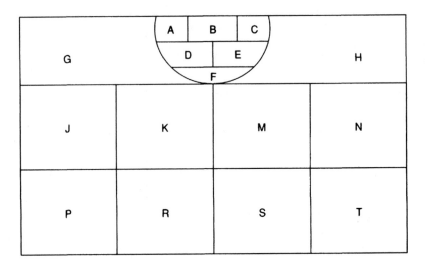

Figure 6.5 Definition of position on a representation of a field hockey pitch oriented to analysing attacking moves.

Let us assume that the coach has decided to use letters for pitch cell divisions and numbers for the players of the team. Does the coding of position cells in Figure 6.4 seem a reasonable layout? There are a number of potential problems. The use of letters 'I', 'L' and 'O' could present some translational problems later. Most notation is done at speed, 'I' and 'L' can easily be confused both with each other and the number '1', and of course the letters 'O' and 'Q' with zero.

The main problem with the representation in Figure 6.4 is one of definition. Will these pitch divisions give the coach sufficient information on the significant areas of the pitch from which his team are shooting well or poorly? It would seem unlikely. In this situation previous researchers have used unequal divisions of the playing areas, making the definition finer in the areas of most interest. In this example this will be around the goal. There are a number of ways of doing this. Figure 6.5 shows a simple way using a representation of just half the playing area – this does, however, negate the possibility of notating shots at goal from the player's own half.

Another way of doing this would be to use lines radiating from the goal as shown in Figure 6.6. This has been used in a number of systems, in both basketball and soccer, to good effect. In both games there is an optimum area from which to shoot, which is more easily defined in this way.

For our example let us assume that the coach is using the area representation shown in Figure 6.5, and that players are identified by their shirt numbers. The two actions that we are notating are the pass and the shot. Our coach has defined four different types of pass:

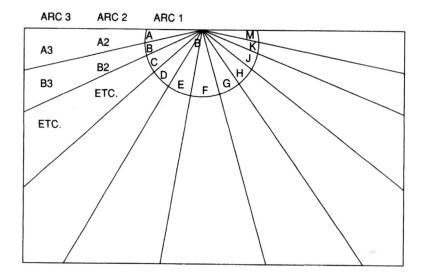

Figure 6.6 Alternative definition of position on a representation of a field hockey pitch oriented to analysing attacking moves.

- Flick – F
- Push – P
- Aerial – A
- Hit – H

Now we only have to decide on the possible outcomes of the other action variable, the shot, and we will have a notation system. The coach has decided at this stage not to differentiate between types of shot, so it is the outcome of the shots that need coding. As we are writing letter and then number as we notate position and player, let us use a letter code for the action outcome. A number of systems involve specifically invented symbols but, for the sake of keeping this example simple, let us stick to recognised alphanumeric symbols. A simple code would be:

- Goal – G
- Saved – S
- Wide – W
- High – H
- Blocked – B
- Rebound – R

The coach is now able to start notating a match. An example of the type of data obtained is shown in the table.

Position assist	Player	Pass type	Position shot	Player	Outcome
M	7	F	D	8	S
M	6	P	E	7	G
J	5	F	B	9	G
K	9	H	D	11	W

In this way the coach, or any other operator, can record the position from which the shot was made, who made it and the outcome. Because of the way that the data have been entered – a number, a letter, another number, and a separate line for each shot – interpretation of the data is relatively easy.

Remember that the codes in this example were chosen for simplicity. A number of systems utilise invented symbols that represent actions or outcomes. This is a decision that can only be made by the individual designing the system. Use whatever you are most comfortable and familiar with. Above all, keep it as simple and as easy as possible.

The only problem facing the coach now is processing the data. Firstly enough data will need to be collected to make it significant, then the distribution of the shots and their assists, with respect to players or position, together with their outcome, can be explored. This form of data processing is very important in most forms of analysis and feedback. Data analysis is a difficult part of notational analysis, to which a separate section is devoted later in this chapter.

The table above makes it easy to record the above data: there is less chance of becoming confused, and it is easier to interpret the data once recorded. It also makes it easier for someone else to understand the data collection system, should that be desirable. Decide who is likely to use your system: if it is only for your own use, spend only as much time 'dressing it up' as is necessary.

NB: Always remember that when other people either use your system or are presented with the data from your system, they will tend to judge the whole system by its appearance.

6.3 Data collection systems in general

What can we learn in general terms about notational analysis from our example? In the most general form of notation, the following parameters are being recorded:

1   position
2   player
3   action – and the subsequent outcome(s)
4   time.

This is the most general situation possible in any match analysis: in most notation systems only two or three of these variables will be necessary. In individual sports, such as squash, tennis or gymnastics, the notation of which player is involved is easier. In team sports it is more difficult, depending on the analysis and the form of the output. In certain situations, perhaps where the movements of a particular player are being recorded, it will be unnecessary to record that player's identity. The time variable is not used as frequently as the other variables in notation systems: it increases the complexity considerably, but some analyses will require it. Analyses where velocities, accelerations and/or rates of work are the desired output from the data will use a time base. Reilly and Thomas (1976) completed what can now be regarded as a classical study of motion analysis in soccer by using a combination of hand notation with stopwatches and audio tape recorders. Position and action are nearly always involved in notation systems, although there are examples of systems not using one of these. Most systems will use two or three of the above variables: there are very few instances where it is necessary to use all four.

In our example we recorded position, player and then the outcome of the action (shot). The beginning and end of each sequence were indicated by using a new line for each event.

Position – The way in which the position was defined in the example was as good a way as any in going about recording positional data. The needs of the system often dictate the definition required within the system. Obviously, the finer the definition, the more accurate the information; BUT the finer the definition, the more data will need to be collected to make it significant. Be careful not to submerge yourself in too much data or too much data collection – notation is not an end in itself; the end-product has to justify the time spent on it. Notating position is always a compromise between accuracy and having manageable data.

Player – Recording which player executed the action cannot be very different in more sophisticated systems. In individual sports the system may only be notating one player at a time, so differentiation will not be necessary.

Action – What made our example a relatively simple one was that we were considering only two actions – the assist and the shot. However, the system still required four different types of pass (assist) and six possible outcomes of the shot to be notated. These again could have been more complicated, since it may be useful to know whether possession was regained after the save or the block. Consider then the complexity of the situation when defining all the possible actions, and their respective outcomes, in a game such as soccer or hockey or basketball. It is this logical and structured analysis, coupled with a clear idea of the salient information that is required from the game, that forms the nucleus of any notation system. A sound system, that will produce consistent and meaningful data, must be based on a careful analysis of the sport to be notated. It is most important to be able to understand the logic of the game structure of the sport under study – a separate section is devoted to sport analysis (see Chapter 5, section 5.2).

The most important aspect of defining any action, or outcome, is to ensure that the 'operational definition' of this term is clear and unambiguous. The operational definition of the action and outcomes enable you, and others, to interpret events consistently in the same way. We have found, with experience, that any problem with reliability (repeatability) of data gathering is nearly always associated with the clarity of the operational definitions.

Before we consider a few more examples, here are a few notes to remember.

1   You must have a clear idea what information you want from the system.
2   Make the data collection, and the data processing, as simple as possible to start with. Build the complexity of your system in easy stages, adding on to what you know works and to what you can handle.
3   Test your system on a small part of a match or event using video. In this way you can practise and improve your notation skills, and also find out how accurate you are. Then practise some more: after that, my advice is to practise some more. There is nothing worse than notating for half an hour, getting in a muddle and then realising you have made a mess of the whole thing (always after you have promised a detailed analysis to someone important).
4   Having tested the system, does it collect the data you wanted? It is easy to be carried away with the design stage, adding on little bits here and collecting a little more information there, until the whole structure has assumed gargantuan proportions, and does not fulfil the aims defined at the start.
5   The more complex your system, the longer it will take to learn. In addition the amount of output increases immensely, which means considerably more work in processing the data. For example, the notation system developed by Sanderson and Way (1979) involved 5–8 hours' learning time and also required 40 hours of work to process the data of a single match. Remember:

KEEP IT SIMPLE

You can always add to your system and build up its complexity as you grow in experience, confidence and speed, and, most importantly, you have fully processed the data output and have decided on additional forms of output.
6   Once you have arrived at the final version of your system, you find this out by continually testing the system to examine whether the data that you can gather provides the answers to the questions that you have about your sport; then you must test its reliability. This is not necessarily a complicated process, but it is very important to know the accuracy of your system. We have devoted a whole chapter to this subject (Chapter 9).

6.4 Examples

6.4.1 A cricket notation system

Cricket is a game that has used notational analysis of one form or another for a long time. The main analyses and scoring systems only incorporate data on the batsmen's run-gathering and bowlers' wicket-taking performances. There are a number of sophisticated systems that record very detailed data for player analysis: this example is a simple way of obtaining more detailed information about a player's performance. A complete understanding of cricket is not necessary to be able to follow the logic involved in setting up the system. When one analyses a batsman's performance in more detail, his strengths and weaknesses become apparent, either for rescheduling his training and practising or for the opponents to reshape their tactics when playing against him.

In this simple example, which could easily be modified for rounders or baseball, it has been decided that the position of the player is not important. The data to be recorded are the player, the action and the outcome.

In cricket, batsmen play off either the front foot or the rear foot; this leads to two sets of symbols to represent the possible strokes made by the batsman. The following symbols were invented:

Front foot strokes
- Forward defensive – F\
- Straight drive – FSD
- Off drive – FOD
- Cover drive – FCD
- Square drive – FSQD
- On drive – FOND
- Leg glance – FG

Note: For non-aficionados of this strange and wonderful game, the terms 'off', 'cover', 'square' and 'on' refer to areas of the pitch. The term 'leg glance' means playing the ball off the legs with a glancing shot; for a right-hander the ball will travel in the direction of 7 o'clock if the batsman is facing noon.

Back foot strokes
- Backward defensive – B\
- Square cut – BSQC
- Cover drive – BCD
- Off drive – BOD
- Pull shot – BP
- Hook shot – BH
- Leg glance – BG

Note: The 'pull', 'hook' and 'cut' are different techniques of striking the ball. The important point here, for the sake of understanding the principles behind the example, is to recognise to which area the ball has been directed.

The number of runs scored by the batsmen is shown at the end of the sequence. For example:

BCD3

shows that the batsman scored three runs playing the cover drive off the back foot.

Additional symbols are:

- 0 – The batsman played the ball, but scored no runs.
- M – The batsman played at the ball, but missed.
- L – The batsman left the ball.
- E – The batsman edged the ball (he did not hit it with the full face of the bat).

6.4.2 Examples of analysis of cricket data

Batsman: **BOYCOTT**	Score: **27 (not out)**
Number of balls played	47
Number of times played and missed	1
Most frequent shot	Forward defensive – 14
Number of scoring shots	13
Most frequent scoring shot	Square cut – 5
Shot which scored the most runs in total	Square cut – 10
Shot which scored the second most runs in total	Square drive – 9
Percentage front foot strokes	60%
Percentage back foot strokes	40%
Percentage of runs scored on the onside	22%
Percentage of runs scored on the offside	78%

Batsman: **MOXON**	Score: **21**
Number of balls played	25
Number of times played and missed	5
Most frequent shot	Backward defensive – 6
Number of scoring shots	10
Most frequent scoring shot	Cover drive – 3
Shot which scored the most runs in total:	Cover and straight drive, leg glance, back defensive – 4
Shot which scored the second most runs in total	As above – 4
Percentage front foot strokes	61%
Percentage back foot strokes	39%
Percentage of runs scored on the onside	23.5%
Percentage of runs scored on the offside	76.5%

Batsman: **BLAKEY**	Score: **41**
Number of balls played	29
Number of times played and missed	1
Most frequent shot	Forward defensive – 6
Number of scoring shots	13
Most frequent scoring shot	Pull shot/hook – 5
Shot which scored the most runs in total	Hook shot – 14
Shot which scored the second most runs in total	Pull shot – 9
Percentage front foot strokes	46%
Percentage back foot strokes	54%
Percentage of runs scored on the onside	100%
Percentage of runs scored on the offside	0%

This system, although quite simple, provides batsmen or opposing bowlers with very pertinent details about their most frequent shots, most effective shots and least effective shots. For example, a good tactic for a team fielding against batsman Blakey would be to put the majority of their fielders on the legside, leaving perhaps two or three of their best catchers on the offside, to tempt him to play that side. Firstly this would cut down the run rate on the legside, but he would be bound to try to play on the offside, his weaker side, where hopefully he might make a mistake, perhaps giving a catching opportunity. A similar analysis could be completed for the bowlers, showing their weaknesses and strengths. Because cricket is such a slow game, this type of analysis can easily be done in-match, and the results processed during the game, enabling better tactical evaluations of the game situation. Keeping the data, i.e. building up a database, enables planned practices specific to opponents before they are played, and a clear understanding by all the players in the team of the tactics to be employed in beating those opponents.

These data could be further detailed by drawing an overview of the directions in which the scoring shots were made. This type of analysis has been used extensively in cricket, detailing where batsmen are most, and least, successful. This is very useful information in placing field settings against these batsmen and planning the tactics of the direction of the bowlers' aim.

There are many ways in which these data could be examined in more detail, becoming more and more specific. The question that must always be answered before proceeding to the next level of analysis is, 'will the information provided by this further analysis be worth the time spent in processing it?'. It is very easy to become involved in analysis for the sake of analysis – questions such as 'will the players find it of use?' or 'does the coach need this much information?' could help to keep your work in perspective.

6.5 General steps in analysis

There are a number of steps in analysis that this cricket example highlights very well.

1   Always start with general overview, or summary data, of the main variables, actions and outcomes that were notated.
2   Where there are large differences in sets of data, or discrepancies from expected levels of performance, perform a more detailed analysis of the data, attempting to show areas or events that explain or contrast these data.

In this example of the cricket match, the analyses of the performances of the batsmen show one or two interesting pieces of information. For example, Blakey scored runs on only one side of the pitch, Moxon played and missed the ball five times as opposed to the other batsmen's once, Boycott's 'score per ball faced' was much lower than those of the other two batsmen. Each set of data asks another question in turn. Analysing the patterns of the bowlers and linking these to the batsmen's data would certainly go a long way to answering these questions.

3   Before going on to another analysis of this data, perhaps proceeding to a finer level of definition, always refer back to the general overview in case there is another problem that merits further analysis first.

In examining the data for Blakey above, it would be tempting to immediately complete a chart of the direction in which all his shots were hit. But in examining the overall data it would seem that perhaps the most productive way ahead would be to analyse the patterns of the bowlers. This could explain this anomaly, as well as providing further descriptive data about the relative performances of the other batsmen with respect to the particular bowlers involved. It will also give a detailed analysis of the bowlers' performance which could be presented in much the same way as the data of the batsmen.

4   Be very critical of the time to be spent on any analysis: be sure it is worth the effort. Do not smother important facts with a multitude of other data – keep the analysis simple.
5   Be aware of to whom the data will be presented – this may limit the level of analysis you undertake; it will certainly limit the way in which you can present your data. If 10 per cent of your presented information is not understood, the players and/or coaches will reject 100 per cent of your analysis.

Remember – your whole system will be judged on its output.

- Is it clear?
- Is it well laid out?
- Can the presentation be simplified?

Compare the following ways of presenting the same data.

Presentation 1

Batsman: Blakey Score: 41
Number of balls played: 29
Number of times played and missed: 1
Most frequent shot: Forward defensive 6
Number of scoring shots:13
Most frequent scoring shot: Pull shot/Hook 5
Shot which scored the most runs
in total: Hook shot 14
Shot which scored the second most
runs in total: Pull shot 9
Percentage front foot strokes: 46
Percentage back foot strokes: 54
Percentage of runs scored on the onside: 100
Percentage of runs scored on the offside: 0

Note how much more difficult it is to extract meaningful information from the
data. Compare this with the presentation used above.

Presentation 2

Batsman: **BLAKEY**	Score: **41**
Number of balls played	29
Number of times played and missed	1
Most frequent shot	Forward defensive – 6
Number of scoring shots	13
Most frequent scoring shot	Pull shot/hook – 5
Shot which scored the most runs in total	Hook shot – 14
Shot which scored the second most runs in total	Pull shot – 9
Percentage front foot strokes	46%
Percentage back foot strokes	54%
Percentage of runs scored on the onside	100%
Percentage of runs scored on the offside	0%

There are probably a number of ways in which this presentation could be
improved and made easier to interpret. This is inevitable – production of output,
and its interpretation, is very much a matter of individual perception. Try to
keep it as simple as possible – always remember that your output will seem easy
and obvious to you, because you have been handling this data for some time:
two or three weeks is not unusual. Think of the person who is seeing it for the
first time. The use of colours in the text always helps definition of important

data. Of course, wherever possible, graphs, figures, histograms and pie-charts should be used. Your system will usually be designed to meet the specific needs or demands of the coaches, players or work involved, but it is even more important that your output, and its format, should be specifically tailored to your clientele. As you gather more and more detailed data, this part of the notation task becomes correspondingly more difficult.

The data occurs in a limited number of forms. The easiest way of building ideas of how data can be presented is to familiarise yourself completely with all the other types of data presentation already in use in the field of notational analysis. A great deal of imagination has been applied to this part of the analysis problem, but even so, it is still the least developed area. Although some research tackles these problems of feedback directly (Franks and Nagelkerke, 1988; Hughes and McGarry, 1989), most work has struggled to keep pace with the technological advances of computerised graphics and/or interactive video.

One of the main reasons for gathering data, forming a database, is for purposes of comparison. To test whether a comparison of performances is significantly different, and not just a chance occurrence, statistical methods are used. Statistics will not only indicate whether sets of data are different or not, but will also determine how much data has to be collected before the comparisons can be made. If you are unfamiliar with the use of these types of procedure, consult an expert: help can usually be found at the nearest college or university. If you are going to use statistics on your data:

Decide on your statistical methods at the design stage of your system.

6.6 Different types of data

The different forms in which data can fall are discussed below. The terminology is not standard and is defined in each section.

6.6.1 *General or summary data*

This tends to be in the form of totals of variables, usually actions, for a team or an individual. Handling this form of data is usually done by tables, although graphs or figures may sometimes be used. The usual statistical test for significant differences with this form of data is a paired t-test. Examples of these data are shown below in Tables 6.2, 6.3 and 6.4 (squash data, Hughes, 1986; soccer data, Partridge and Franks, 1989a, 1989b). All data listed have difference levels of $P < 0.05$ unless * indicates $P < 0.01$.

6.6.2 *Frequency distributions*

Output design begins to become a little more difficult with the problems posed by enabling a clear understanding of the presentation of frequency distributions.

Table 6.2 Comparison of descriptive match data for different levels of competitive players (Hughes, 1986)

	Recreational players	County players	Nationally ranked players
Mean number of shots per match	686	830	1651
Mean number of rallies per match	113.2	94.6	89.2
Mean number of shots per rally	6.03	8.80	18.48
Mean number of winning shots per match	28.55	22.4	19.83
Mean number of errors per match	26.0	21.1	16.83
Winner/error ratio	1.096	1.07	1.18

Table 6.3 Comparison of nationally ranked players to county players: shot patterns that have differences in frequency ($P < 0.05$) (Xi-square analysis) (Hughes, 1986)

	Shot	Pattern	Longitudinal presentation	Lateral presentation
1	Drive	Total distribution	9.52*	6.93
2	Cross-court drives	Total distribution	1.68	3.64
3	X-court volley (short)	Total distribution	9.75*	8.26*
4	X-court volley (long)	Total distribution	3.76	4.02
5	Boast	Errors	10.02*	4.43
6	Drop-shot		2.49	5.00
7	X-court volley (short)		5.20	5.60
8	Drives	Winners	5.62	5.61
9	Boasts	($n - 1$) to winner (by opponent)	6.10	2.44
10	X-court	($n - 1$) to winner (by opponent)	4.21	4.21
11	X-court	($n - 2$) shot to an error	4.21	4.20
12	Services	($n - 2$) shot to an error	5.15	2.86
13	Services	Shot to a winner	4.23	4.19

All data listed have difference levels of $P < 0.05$ except that * indicates $P < 0.01$.

Two-dimensional distributions are not difficult. A graph, a histogram, etc. will demonstrate clearly any important data. See, for example, Figures 6.7 and 6.8, which show the distribution of an action variable, the shot, with another variable, the players. Both demonstrate the main point of the data: that certain players are not shooting as often as others.

The presentation becomes more difficult once more variables become involved, or the distribution across a playing area is examined. The playing area is usually

Table 6.4 Shooting data from the 1990 soccer World Cup

	Group A				Group B			
	Argentina	Italy	Bulgaria	S. Korea	Mexico	Paraguay	Belgium	Iraq
Total opportunities	53	48	43	48	36	46	42	39
Taken	38	32	30	40	31	40	36	33
Not taken	15	16	13	8	5	6	6	6
Off target	16	13	10	17	11	22	12	20
Off target of shots taken	42%	41%	33%	42.5%	35.5%	55%	60%	61%
Blocked	7	7	12	12	4	5	2	5
Blocked of shots taken	18%	21.5%	40%	30%	13%	12.5%	3%	15%
Goals	6	5	2	4	3	4	3	1

Source: Partridge and Franks (1990).

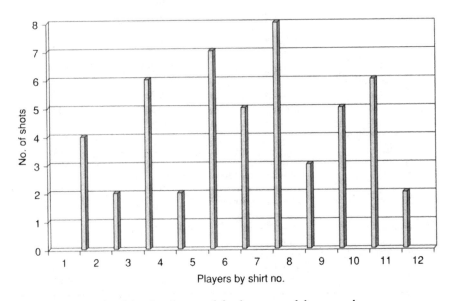

Figure 6.7 Example of the distribution of the frequency of shots per player.

a two-dimensional space, or regarded as such, so a frequency distribution of an action with respect to position will require three dimensions: one for the variable, another two for the playing area. A number of ways of tackling this problem have been attempted. The straightforward approach is of the type shown in Figures 6.9 and 6.10, which is data taken from a field-hockey match (Hughes and Cunliffe, 1986). The value of the variable is inserted in the corresponding area of the pitch representation. This is in effect, little more than a

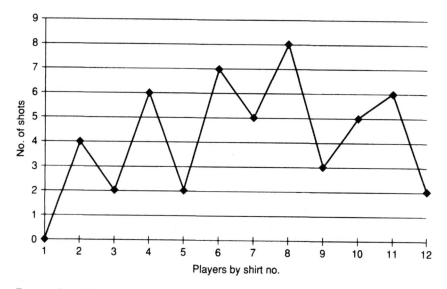

Figure 6.8 A different way of presenting the same data of the distribution of the frequency of shots per player as in Figure 6.7.

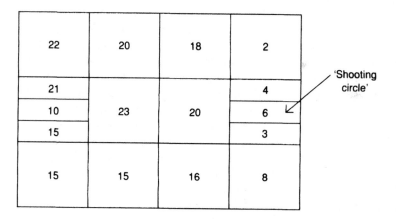

Figure 6.9 Example of a frequency distribution of actions in a field hockey match, showing number of passes, runs, etc. in each area of the pitch (Hughes and Cunliffe,
1986).

table of data but it does relate to how the frequency of the action variable is
distributed across the playing area. Ideally, to gain a clear pictorial impression of
the distribution of the action variable with respect to its position on the playing
area, a three-dimensional graphic display should be used. This should make
the data easier to understand, as long as the presentation is good enough. It
does have two associated problems, however: firstly, the creation of clear and

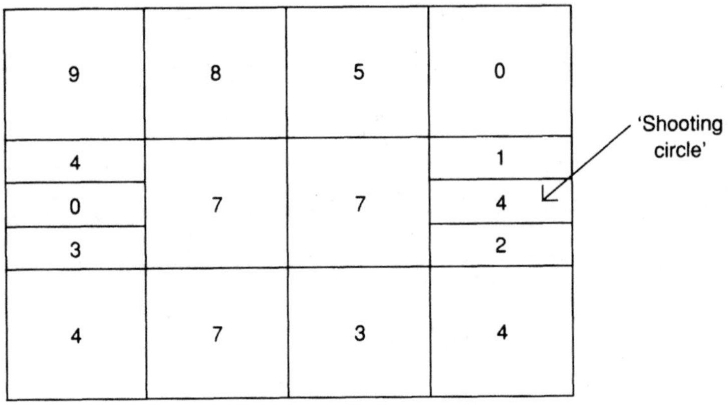

9	8	5	0
4			1
0	7	7	4
3			2
4	7	3	4

'Shooting circle'

Figure 6.10 Example of a frequency distribution of errors in a field hockey match, showing number of errors made in each area of the pitch (Hughes and Cunliffe,
1986).

understandable three-dimensional graphics is very difficult. Secondly, this
degree of difficulty is considerably increased when one considers that any low-
frequency data occurring 'behind' high-frequency data will be hidden.

Sanderson and Way (1979) tackled this problem in an ingenious way by
using what they termed longitudinal and latitudinal summations across the
playing surface, in their case a squash court. For example, the distribution of
shots shown in Figure 6.11 were summed across the court cell by cell (a lateral
summation) to give the longitudinal profile of shots. Similarly, the distribution
of shots was summed along the length of the court (a longitudinal summation)
to yield a lateral profile of shots. In this way a presentation of two graphs
enabled a two-dimensional representation of the three-dimensional distribution
of shots across the playing surface. Hughes adopted this form of presentation in
his work on squash, but this was mainly for purposes of comparison of his data
to that of Sanderson and Way. While some people had no problems in handling
this spatial transposition, it was found that a large number of coaches and
athletes found it very confusing. Consequently, Hughes and McGarry (1989)
went on to seek a solution to this form of data presentation using computer
graphics. Nowadays most databases and spreadsheets have three-dimensional
graphics integrated so that a similar form of presentation is possible without all
the hard work that these researchers had to undertake. The important point is,
and will always remain, that the presentation of the data should be as simple
and as clear as possible.

6.6.3 Sequentially dependent data

In sequentially dependent data the sequence forms a set pattern with respect to
position, player or, most frequently, time. An example of this type of data might

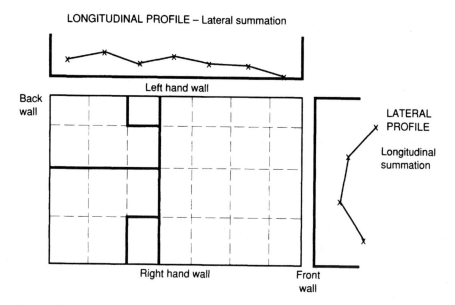

LONGITUDINAL PROFILE – Lateral summation

Figure 6.11 Representation of three-dimensional data distribution using two two-dimensional graphs (Sanderson and Way, 1979).

be the passing patterns of the ball in producing tries in rugby union. Comparing two international sides such as France and England in 1988 would produce very different approaches in their route to scoring tries. France at this time were a very fluid running side that could pass and run with the ball anywhere on the field of play. England at this time were a very stilted side tactically, preferring to kick, either under instructions from their coaches or from fear of making an error, and very rarely running with the ball despite possessing some of the best threequarters at the time. To compare sets of this type of data, correlation methods would be used to test for significance.

Presenting this form of data again benefits from a pictorial approach. Figure 6.12 shows the paths of passes, runs and dribbles shots taken in field hockey (Hughes and Cunliffe, 1986). This is a very simple graphic picture of what would otherwise be tabular data, but is nonetheless effective.

Reilly and Thomas (1976) developed a notation system that combined hand notation and dictation into a portable audio tape recorder. They used the system to study work rates of players in the game of soccer. They would follow the movement patterns of an individual player, recording ambulatory motions (i.e. standing, walking, trotting, running, sprinting), the position on the field of these motions and the time-span involved. This enabled them to calculate distances travelled, and the overall work-rate of different positions in the team.

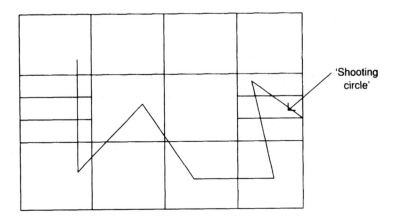

Figure 6.12 Example of sequential data – path to a shot on goal in field hockey (Hughes and Cunliffe, 1986).

6.7 Summary

Remember these guidelines in developing and using a notation system.

- Make sure that you have a clear idea of what it is you are trying to analyse before you start. If possible, you should also know what your output is going to be and the form it will take. Being able to do this, of course, requires a great deal of experience of notation within that particular sport. In any case, the more planning done beforehand, the more fruitless hours will be saved.
- Keep the data collection system as simple as possible for as long as possible. If it does need to become more complex, then add an extra routine at a time. Before adding another, make sure that the new system works fully.
- If you are going to use statistics to test your data for significant differences etc., again, be sure of the procedures that you are going to use before you start collecting the data. Most statistical tests will require minimum amounts of data, so this will determine how many matches etc. you must notate.
- If your data are to be presented to others, as is usually the case, take great care to fit the format and style of presentation to the people to whom you are attempting to communicate. Always remember that because you have been wrestling with this type of data for some time now, what seems simple and obvious to you, can be very confusing to others. If in doubt, always err on the side of simplicity.

7 Examples of notation systems

Mike Hughes and Ian M. Franks

7.1 Introduction

The best way to appreciate the intricacies of notational analysis is to examine systems for the sport(s) in which you are interested, or sports that are similar. Presented here are a number of examples of different systems for different sports. They have been devised by students of notational analysis and are therefore of differing levels of complexity and sophistication, but there are always lessons to be learnt, even from the simplest of systems. The explanations and analyses are completed by beginners at notational analysis; coaches of these sports should not therefore be irritated at some of the simplistic levels of analysis for the respective sports. The encouraging aspect of these examples is the amount of information that even the simplest systems provide. Examples 7.2.1–7.2.2 are for individual sports, while examples 7.3.1–7.3.3 are for team games. More examples can be found in the first version of this book, *Notational Analysis of Sport*, by Hughes and Franks (1997).

7.2 Individual sports

7.2.1 A notation system for tennis

This system for the notation and analysis of data for tennis was designed to gather basic information on winners and errors. The court was divided up into sections as shown in Figure 7.1. Six sections were chosen in order to keep the recording of position, and its subsequent analysis, as simple as possible. A singles match was to be notated, which reduced the court size, removing the need for the tramlines and thus simplifying the system.

Symbols were allocated for the basic shots to be recorded, as follows:

- S = serve
- F = forehand drive
- B = backhand drive
- V = forehand volley
- <u>V</u> = backhand volley

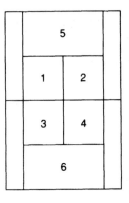

Figure 7.1 Division of the court into six cells for analysis of tennis.

- L = forehand lob
- <u>L</u> = backhand lob
- Sm = smash

Having established shot symbols, it was then necessary to devise 'result of shot' symbols, i.e. whether the shot was a winner or whether a mistake was made. These were as follows.

- A dot (.) following a shot symbol indicates that the shot was played into the net.
- An arrow (→) following a shot symbol indicates that the ball was played out of court.
- A shot symbol followed by 'W' indicates either that the shot was an outright winner or that the opponent's shot following this one was a mistake.
- A single line indicates the end of a point.
- A double line indicates the end of a game.
- A triple line indicates the end of a set.

For the actual notation purposes, the construction of simple columns was used, with one vertical column for each player. The play was notated by entering data alternately in each column as the shots were played, until the conclusion of the point. A single line was then drawn across both columns and the winning player's last shot ringed. An example of a game notated using this system is shown in Figure 7.2.

Description of point

Smith served the ball wide and Jones returned the serve with a forehand that landed short. Smith moved in to play a deep cross-court backhand, causing

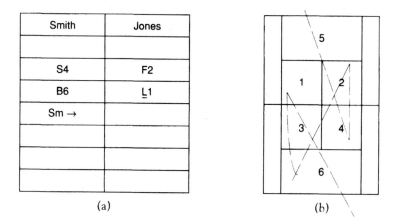

Smith	Jones
S4	F2
B6	L1
Sm →	

(a)

(b)

Figure 7.2 (a) Notation of data using the system for tennis; (b) schematic representation of data used in example in (a).

Jones to play a defensive backhand lob. This lob was not a good one, and Smith had the chance to smash the ball, but he hit the ball out of court. Jones won the point and the score was 0–15.

The match chosen for analysis was the 1989 Ladies' Wimbledon Final between Steffi Graf and Martina Navratilova. This selection was made to incorporate a wide variety of shots while at the same time displaying constructive rallies to analyse, but which did not continue for too long as is the case with some women's matches, i.e. making notation strenuous.

Also, the choice of a grass court surface would produce an exciting game without creating very short rallies as displayed in a men's game, with one player hitting a fast serve which results in either a mistake or an outright winner from his opponent.

The aim of the notation was to devise a system which was simple enough to notate a match live without the use of video cameras. Therefore, although this match was viewed from video, it was notated continuously without pausing or rewinding the tape. An example of part of the notation is shown in Figure 7.3.

Results

A simple analysis of the data from this match is presented: more information could have been obtained from the data given more time.

WIMBLEDON LADIES' FINAL 1989
Steffi Graf v. Martina Navratilova

First set (Graf won, 6–2)

STEFFI	MARTINA		STEFFI	MARTINA
	S4			S3
B2	V3		B.	
F1 W	V →			S4
	S3		B.	
B2	V4			S3
B2 W			B →	
	S4		1–0	
F5	V4		S4	B →
F2	V3 W		S3	B5
	S3		F6	F2
B.			F6	B5
	S4		F4 W	
B2 W	V.		S4 W	
	S3		S3	F5
F5	V6 W		F4	B5
	S4		L	Sm2 W
F5	L6 W		S4	B.
XF →			1–1	
	S3			S1
F1	V4		F3 W	
F2 W			ETC.	
	S4 →			
	S3 W			
B.				

Figure 7.3 Example of the tennis data-gathering system.

STEFFI GRAF

Mistakes	NET =	1 FOREHAND
		4 BACKHANDS
	OUT =	2 FOREHANDS
		3 BACKHANDS
		2 BACKHAND LOBS

Outright winners =   5 FOREHANDS
                      4 BACKHANDS
                      1 SERVE
                      1 LOB

Points lost:

Unforced errors   Navratilova winners
     12   12

MARTINA NAVRATILOVA

Mistakes   NET =   3 FOREHANDS
                     5 BACKHANDS
                     4 VOLLEYS
                     1 DOUBLE FAULT
            OUT =   4 FOREHANDS
                     4 BACKHANDS
                     1 VOLLEY
Outright winners =   1 FOREHAND
                     8 VOLLEYS
                     2 SMASHES
                     1 SERVE

Points lost:

Unforced errors   Graf winners
     23   11

Summary of results

If a performance indicator is defined as:

$$\text{Tennis ratio} = \frac{\text{Number of errors}}{\text{Number of winners}}$$

GRAF tennis ratio = 12/11 (or nearly 1:1)
NAVRATILOVA tennis ratio = 23/12 (or nearly 2:1)

Discussion and conclusions

Analysis of the results showed that in this particular match, the loser (Navratilova) had a ratio of nearly 2:1 for unforced errors to winners. The players analysed were of the highest playing standard currently competing and therefore made relatively few unforced errors. Also, the fast grass court made rallies shorter than usual with many more winners played, in contrast to the 'waiting game' played on slow clay courts. Another reason for Navratilova's results could be related to the nature of her game. She plays a high-powered attacking game, aiming to control play from the net position as soon as possible. Consequently her mistakes occurred in trying to get to that position but once there, very few unforced errors occurred and points were won by outright volley winners or by passing shots played by Graf.

7.2.2 A *notation system for boxing*

Firstly, the types of punches have to be identified, together with other behaviour variables considered to be important in defining a boxing match. These were considered to be:

1 jabs
2 hooks
3 uppercuts
4 misses (complete)
5 front body punches
6 side body punches
7 holding
8 hit guard (partial miss)
9 foul punching
10 ducking
11 on ropes
12 knockdown
13 knock-out
14 technical KO
15 points decision.

As can be seen, there are numerous actions which constitute:

• offensive information
• defensive information
• positional information
• fight outcome.

These provided too many variables to notate using a hand system, as many or all could be occurring simultaneously. It is suggested that, if both boxers are to be notated, only offensive actions and specific key features could be recorded. These could be identified as:

• jabs
• misses
• knockdowns
• hooks
• body shots
• uppercuts
• holding.

Table 7.1 Symbols used in the data-gathering system for boxing

Left	Right	Punch
-]	[-	Jab
(	)	Hook
UL	UR	Uppercut
m	m	Miss
B	B	Body punch
<	>	Holding
v	v	Knockdown

The system was now progressed to separating these factors into left and right sides depending on which side the punch was thrown from. (Knockdowns remained universal, as the final punch would be recorded.) The symbol denoting the jab aims to represent the jab itself, i.e. a straight punch. Hence the symbol used was a straight line. The dash was placed either side depending on where it was thrown from, the left or right. This reasoning was then followed for the construction of the other symbols. Thus the notation shown in Table 7.1 was devised.

For example, a boxer while holding his opponent with his left arm produces an uppercut which misses with his right; it would be notated as:

<URm

A chart (see Table 7.2) was then devised to record a fight on which the punches of each boxer could be notated in sequential order.

This format of a vertical linear layout remains common in hand systems, as it enables quickly translated and stored records. One line of the chart corresponds to one punch from each boxer. In situations where punches were thrown simultaneously, both were recorded on the same line to indicate that they occurred within the time space of one punch.

It was decided that characteristics of a fight that might ease the notation task were:

1 a heavyweight match in which the 'punch rate' is considerably slower than lower weight categories
2 a fight which is relatively short in duration, so massive amounts of raw data are not produced.

The chosen match was Mike Tyson vs Frank Bruno, held in 1989 at the Hilton International, Las Vegas. This was a five-round fight between two heavyweight boxers.

Notating the fight involved first watching the fight through completely, to get a 'feeling' of punch speed and of any anomolies which may exist in their

Table 7.2 Sample data from the Tyson–Bruno fight (1989) using the data-gathering system for boxing

Tyson	Bruno	Tyson	Bruno	Tyson	Bruno
-]			<		<URm
	-]		<UR		<URm
(	)		<UR		<URm
)			<)m		<)m
	)		<UR		)
	)		<)	-]	
	)		<)m	(	
(			<)		<UR
BUR	<)		)		<UR
	<)		<)		<UR
(		(	<)	(m	
-]			<)		<(
)					)m
(m		-]			-]
URm		)			-]
	V		<>	(	
(	<		UR	)m	
	<		)		-]
	)		-]	(m	
<)	<)	)	<)		-]
<)	<)		<)	)m	
	(		<)		)
)		(	<)	(	

boxing style. Then the fight was notated using the pause function on the video; at instances when numerous punches were thrown within a very short period, a frame-by-frame analysis was used. The raw data were then collated by frequency tallies (see Figures 7.4 and 7.5). Summary totals could be calculated and represented graphically.

Results

From the results we can see that Bruno threw 55 per cent of the punches; however, if these are broken down round by round, we see that in the first three rounds he threw more than Tyson, and in Rounds 4 and 5 Tyson threw more than Bruno (Table 7.3). This suggests that Bruno was tiring and was failing to counter-punch. So the fight was essentially lost in rounds 4 and 5.

The two boxers had almost identical punch compositions (see Table 7.4), with Bruno missing one percentage point more than Tyson. However, during the fight Bruno was cautioned for holding. This is illustrated by Table 7.5, which shows the number of punches made while holding. Bruno made 41 per cent of his punches while holding, compared with Tyson's 4 per cent. This is probably

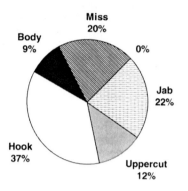

Figure 7.4 Distribution of the types of punches thrown by Tyson in the Bruno–Tyson match (1989).

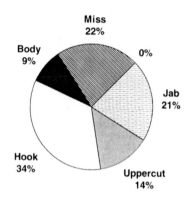

Figure 7.5 Distribution of the types of punches thrown by Bruno in the Bruno–Tyson match (1989).

Table 7.3 Collated data of total punches thrown

	Tyson	*Bruno*
Round 1	38	68
Round 2	36	54
Round 3	27	47
Round 4	32	24
Round 5	48	23
Total	181	216

a reflection of Bruno trying to punch 'inside' Tyson, i.e. by staying close you have less chance of being knocked out with one punch, which was characteristic of Tyson's fights. This was therefore intentional and probably not due to fatigue alone.

Table 7.4 Analysis of the number of types of punches thrown by both boxers

Punch	Tyson		Bruno	
	Number	% of total	Number	% of total
Jab	40	22	45	21
Uppercut	22	12	29	13
Hook	66	37	72	36
Body	16	9	19	9
Miss	37	20	46	21

Table 7.5 The number of punches thrown while holding

Tyson	Bruno
8	89

Table 7.6 The number of jabs thrown in each round

Round	Tyson	Bruno
1	5	9
2	8	21
3	8	20
4	15	7
5	6	5
Total	42	62

Bruno had a reputation for his jabs, which intimidated his opponents. In the first three rounds his jabs were more than double those of Tyson (see Table 7.6). However, from then on the number of his jabs decreased dramatically and Tyson's increased (Figure 7.6). The final round contained roughly the same number of jabs thrown by each opponent. This was probably due to Bruno having only the strength to produce jabs and Tyson trying to finish the fight off with hooks and uppercuts, which are more powerful punches. All the statistics tend to suggest that the fight was won in rounds 4 and 5.

Conclusions

1   This simple system enables the notation of a boxing match by a post-event analysis of video. While acknowledging that the results describe the basic

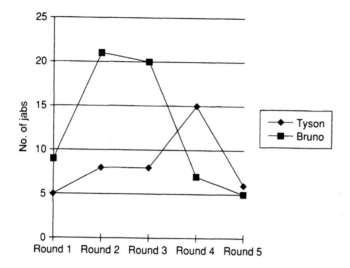

Figure 7.6 Distribution of jabs by both fighters on a round-by-round analysis (Bruno–Tyson, 1989).

techniques employed by a boxer during a match, one must recognise that the notation in itself was very simplified and somewhat crude, and did not address many essential aspects of a fight, namely positional information, defensive information and subjective measures of power and accuracy (which may require the knowledge of a skilled coach).

2 Considering the speed of boxing matches, it was almost impossible to notate a fight live. The use of video and playback was therefore essential. However, some very simple and basic information clearly maps the progress of the fight and gives a quantitative analysis of the progress of the two boxers during the bout.

7.3 Team sports

7.3.1 A notation system for basketball

The schematic representation of a basketball court in Figure 7.7 shows the court positions used in the notation. In basketball a team squad has ten members, five of whom are on the court at any one time. For the purpose of this notation the players were assigned numbers in the range 4 to 14 (1, 2 and 3 were not used to avoid confusion with the letters I, Z and B), although some teams, and all American ones, often use numbers such 33 and 42.

The actions under consideration in this hand notation and the symbols used to represent them are listed as follows:

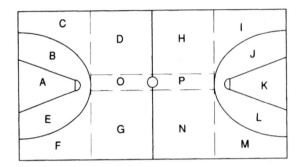

Figure 7.7 Schematic representation of the basketball court in order to define position cells for a data-gathering system.

Action	Symbol	
Tip off	TO	
Dribble	D	
Drive	V	
Shot	S	B or M (basket good – B)
Lay-up	L	B or M (basket missed – M)
Rebound	R	
Pass	P	
Fastbreak	F	
Foul	FL	
Free throws	FT	
Turnover	T	The time the action occurred should be recorded
Substitution	SB	
Out of court	O	
Sideline ball	SL	
Baseline ball	BL	

These symbols, together with the player number and his position on the court, are written down in columns in a table in the following manner.

6   G   P

i.e. player No. 6, in position cell G, passed the ball.

The following is an explanation of the events notated in Table 7.7.

Line	Comment
1	The tip-off was won by 6, who passed.
2	No. 7 received the ball in H and dribbled
3	to I, where the ball was passed
4	to No. 13 in K, who shot and missed.

Table 7.7 A demonstration of how the notation system works

Team A	Time	Team B
TO 6 P		
H 7 D		
I 7 P		
K 13 S M		
		K 4 R
		K 4 D
		L 4 P
	2:20	N 13 FL (5)
		SL-N 13 P
		N 10 P
	2:59	T
C 6 P		
I 13 L B	3:01	
2–0		
		BL-K 4 P
		I O
	3:05	SB-4/6
		SL-I 6 P
	etc.	

5	Team B: No. 4 rebounded in K
6	dribbled from K
7	to L where the ball was passed
8	to 13 in N who was fouled by No. 5.
9	No. 13 took a sideline ball in N passing
10	to No. 10 in N who dribbled
11	to O where the ball was passed
12	Turnover – after 2 min 59 s.
13	No. 6 intercepted the ball in C and passed
14	to No. 13 in I who scored a lay-up.
15	The running score is 2–0, time 3 min 01 s.
16	Baseline ball in K is passed by No. 4,
17	the ball goes out of court in I.
18	Substitution: No. 6 comes on for No. 4.
19	Sideline ball in I is passed by No. 6.

Conclusion and discussion

A coach or analyst can use this very simple notation system to gather performance data on individual players or the whole team. It can be used to analyse
from which side of the court the most successful attacks come; what success rate
the team and individuals achieve at rebounds (do they win more than they
lose?); how successful they are in the majority of free throws; whether there is
any increase in success rate/performance after a time-out, etc. The coach can

then assess the strengths and weaknesses of the individuals and the team, or their opponents, and make an attempt at correcting them.

This type of system is very easily changed to suit any team sport, redefining the playing surface, the number of players and the actions, and their outcomes accordingly.

7.3.2 A notation system for soccer

The aim of this notation system was to notate the distribution ability of a right full back in soccer.

Method

Notation occurred each time the subject, the right full back of Brook House FC, appeared to play or distribute the ball. The following symbols and meanings were used in order for the system to function.

Passes/Clearances/Shots	Distances	Symbols
By foot	<10 yards	F1
	10–30 yards	F2
	>30 yards	F3
By head	<10 yards	H1
	10–30 yards	H2
	>30 yards	H3
By hand	<10 yards	T1
(i.e. throw-in)	10–30 yards	T2
	>30 yards	T3

- Clearances – above symbols preceded by 'C', e.g. CF2 is a clearance by foot of 10–30 yards (it should be noted that clearances were counted neither as completed nor as uncompleted passes).
- Shots-above symbols for feet or head followed by '!' (i.e. F, !) for a goal and 'X' for a miss.
- Completed passes-above symbols for feet, head or hand.
- Uncompleted passes-above symbols for feet, head or hand, *circled*.
- The time elapsed of the half was also recorded at the end of each piece of information.

Therefore, an example of notated data is:

CH3 12,37

This refers to a clearance by head of a distance of 30 yards or more, that occurred after 12 min 37 s of the half. These data were then recorded in columns on a prepared data collection sheet.

Results

The data was collected over 45 minutes (one half) of a 'local Sunday football league' match.

Match Information   Date = 29/10/89   Start = 12.09 pm

1st half of Bow and Arrow FC   vs   Brook House FC
(Black and white stripes)   (Royal blue and navy stripes)

Half-time score: 1–3

The data was obtained by notating the first half of the above match and processing the data in a very simple way. From these results the following analysis was carried out.

Analysis

1   Number of touches of the ball = 29
2   Number of touches of the ball by each method:
    (i)   Number of foot contacts = 21
    (ii) Number of headed contacts = 3
    (iii) Number of throw-ins = 5
3   Percentage of touches by each method:
    (i)   Feet = 21/29 = 72.4%
    (ii) Head = 3/29 = 10.4%
    (iii) Throw-ins = 5/29 = 17.2%
4   Number of uncomplete a passes (i.e. errors), signified by circled symbol = 9
5   Number of errors by each method:
    (i)   Feet = 8
    (ii) Head = 0
    (iii) Throw-ins = 1
6   Percentage of errors by each method:
    (i)   Feet = 8/9 = 88.9%
    (ii) Head = 0/9 = 0%
    (iii) Throw-ins = 11.1%
7   Distribution at the various distances:
    (A) Total analysis
        (i)   Total <10 yards = 14 (by foot = 12, by head = 1, throw-in = 1)
        (ii) Total 10–30 yards = 11 (by foot = 5, by head = 2, throw-in = 4)
        (iii) Total >30 yards = 4 (by foot = 4, by head = 0, throw-in = 0)

    TOTAL: 29

    Percentages of this total analysis, A(i)–(iii):
    <10 yards = 48.3% (by foot = 85.7%, by head = 7.1%, throw-in = 7.1%)

10–30 yards = 37.9% (by foot = 45.5%, by head = 18.2%, throw-in = 37.4%)

>30 yards = 13.8% (by foot = 100%)

(B) Completed pass analysis (not including clearances):

    (i)   Total <10 yards = 3 (by foot = 2, by head = 0, throw-in = 1)

    (ii) Total 10–30 yards = 6 (by foot = 3, by head = 0, throw-in = 3)

    (iii) Total >30 yards = 2 (by foot = 2, by head = 0, throw-in = 0)

TOTAL: 11

*includes one successful attempt at goal

Percentages of completed pass analysis, B(i)–(iii):

Total <10 yards = 27.3% (by foot = 66.7%, throw-in = 33.3%)

Total 10–30 yards = 54.6% (by foot = 50%, throw-in = 50%)

Total >30 yards = 18.2% (by foot = 100%)

(C) Uncompleted pass analysis (not including clearances):

    (i)   Total <10 yards = 6 (by foot = 6)

    (ii) Total 10–30 yards = 2 (by foot = 1, throw-in = 1)

    (iii) Total >30 yards = 1 (by foot = 1)

TOTAL: 9

Percentages of uncompleted pass analysis, C(i)–(iii):

Total <10 yards = 66.7% (by foot = 100%)

Total 10–30 yards = 22.2% (by foot = 50%, throw-in = 50%)

Total >30 yards = 11.1% (by foot = 100%)

8   Ratio: completed passes to total number of passes = 11/20 = 0.55

Ratio: uncompleted passes to total number of passes = 9/20 = 0.45

(NB, doesn't include clearances)

9   Clearance study:

(A) Total number of clearances = 9

(B) Total number of clearances at each distance:

    (i)   Total <10 yards = 5 (by foot = 4, by head = 1)

    (ii) Total 10–30 yards = 3 (by foot = 1, by head = 2)

    (iii) Total >30 yards = 1 (by foot = 1)

Percentages of B(i)–(iii):

Total <10 yards = 55.6% (by foot = 80%, by head = 20%)

Total 10–30 yards = 33.3% (by foot = 33.3%, by head = 66.7%)

Total >30 yards = 11.1% (by foot = 100%)

10 Outline of the subjects' activity:

Section	No. of touches	Successful	Unsuccessful	Clears
(i) 0–5 min	2	1	1	0
(ii) 5–10 min	2	0	1	0
(iii) 10–15 min	4	1	2	1
(iv) 15–20 min	4	1	1	2

(v) 20–25 min	3	3	0	0
(vi) 25–30 min	3	1	2	0
(vii) 30–35 min	1	0	0	1
(viii) 35–40 min	3	1	0	2
(ix) 40–45 min	4	3*	1	0
(x) 45–50 min	3	0	1	2

*Including one successful attempt at goal.

See Figures 7.8–7.11 for visual representation of some of the data.

Discussion

Just one half of a soccer match does not produce anything like a significant amount of data about which conclusions can be drawn, but this example does give ideas about analysing and presenting data. A few statements can be made

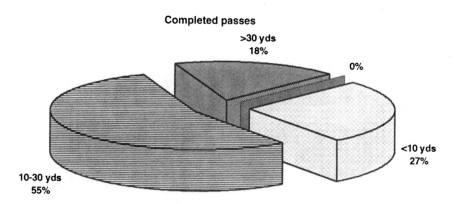

Figure 7.8 Representation of the number of completed passes.

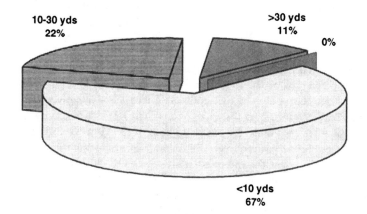

Figure 7.9 Representation of the number of uncompleted passes.

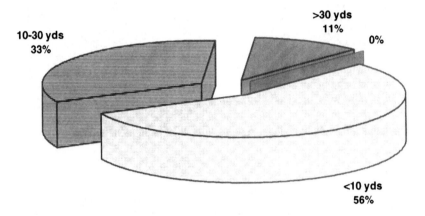

Figure 7.10 Representation of the number of clearances.

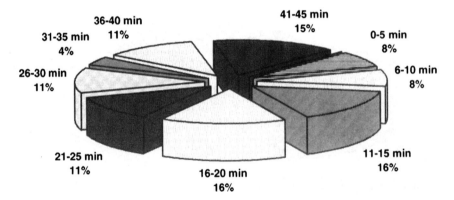

Figure 7.11 Representation of the percentage of activities throughout the first half.

about these interpretations. The majority of the full-back touches, 72.4 per cent, were performed by the foot. But this percentage led to a larger amount of errors, 88.9 per cent, being by foot contact. There was a roughly equal distribution of passes performed over distances of less than 10 yards and between 10 and 30 yards, 48.3 per cent and 37.9 per cent respectively. However, the subject was twice as successful at passing over 10–30 yards as at passing over less than 10 yards. This success over the intermediate distance (10–30 yards) is mirrored by the fact that the subject committed only 1/5 of the total errors committed over the distance. From the analysis it was found that the subject performed 10 per cent more completed passes (not including clearances) than uncompleted passes (not including clearances).

Analysis of the clearances the subject performed shows that the majority were carried out over the short distance of less than 10 yards. As the 'direction of distribution' was not recorded (see 'Adjustments' below), this aspect of clearance distance is difficult to interpret, but a part explanation could be that the full back plays near the touchline and so a safe clearance will be over this touchline, which in many situations will be less than 10 yards from the point of play. The subject's intense periods of involvement were evenly spread throughout the half, with no one 'five minute section' having no activity. A more general observation is of the small contribution that heading made to the subject's play, but this could be explained by the opposition employing two small forwards and subsequently not playing the ball to them in the air.

It would be interesting to see if these statements still held true with six to eight matches of data. Many of these points are somewhat subjective as they are made on the basis of only one short data collection session. It could be that all of the points made came about due to the context of the game, and a completely different set of remarks could have occurred if a different game had been notated.

The exercise did, however, produce some recommendations to improve the system.

Adjustments to the system

1   Divide foot passes into left-foot and right-foot passes. Therefore the present symbol would be followed by 'L' or 'R' (e.g. F1L = a left-foot pass of less than 10 yards).
2   Notate fouls and indiscretions (i.e. bookings or sendings-off).
3   Notate attempts on goal with a separate symbol = 'S' e.g. SF1L, ! = a successful attempt at goal with the left foot less than 10 yards from goal; SH1, X = an unsuccessful attempt at goal with the head less than 10 yards from goal.
4   Notation of tackles could be introduced, but this is moving away from the aim of notating the 'distribution ability' of a full back.
5   Notation with the aid of a grid. The grid could be designed by measuring the length and width of a pitch and dividing it into nine equal areas (see Figure 7.12). Notation of positional data from where the full back passes, and where the passes go, then becomes possible.

This grid adjustment could lead to either of the following methods of notating.

1   Produce printed sheets of the grid, and for each piece of notation draw a line from the origin of the pass (i.e. position of full back) to its destination. On the same sheet, include the appropriate symbol and time as before.
2   Similar to the original system of notating in columns, the following type of codes could be used:

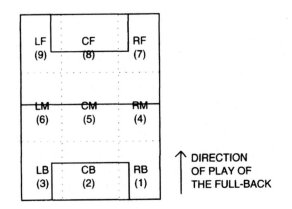

Figure 7.12 Schematic diagram of a soccer pitch showing suggested divisions of the playing area into a grid for notation.

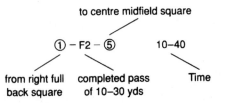

Method 1 would be more accurate, as the exact position and not just the square would be notated. But it would require one sheet for each piece of information notated. Also, learning time would be much longer and 'logging time' for each action would be longer and more complicated.

7.3.3 A notation system for netball

A netball team consists of seven players. Each player has a limited area within which to operate. Every player is allocated a specific role in the game which corresponds to the area in which they operate. The object of the game is to attempt to score as many goals as possible. To achieve this requires team cohesion, cooperation and understanding between all the team members. A skilful game of netball relies on effective passing to maintain possession of the ball.

Method

Before outlining the system, it is necessary to ensure that you understand the basic rules of the game.

Like any other team game, netball has its own specific set of rules which must be adhered to throughout the match. Before a system of notational analysis can be designed, it is important to be familiar with these rules.

1   There is a three-second limit on the time it takes a team member to pass the ball or attempt a shot at goal.
2   The ball must be caught or touched in each third of the court during play.
3   The centre pass must be caught or touched by a player allowed in the centre third of the court.
4   When a ball goes out of court it can only be thrown-in by a player allowed in that particular area.
5   Only the goal-shooter or goal-attack can score a goal. The ball must also have been wholly caught within the goal circle.
6   A player must keep within the limits of area prescribed by her position.

Notation symbols

The symbols to be used will record the following.

1   The team member in possession of the ball and the position on the court where they received the ball.
2   What happens at the end of the passing sequence before reverting to the centre pass or change of possession.
3   Out-of-court shots where the ball has been passed outside the sideline.

Each player wears a vest with letters representing their roles (each one is self-explanatory):

*   GK = goalkeeper
*   GD = goal defence
*   WD = wing defence
*   C = centre
*   WA = wing attack
*   GA = goal attack
*   GS = goal shooter

The court was divided into five areas so that a simple view of the path of the ball can be deduced (Figure 7.13)

*   1 = goal circle
*   2 = goal third
*   3 = centre third
*   4 = goal third
*   5 = goal circle

Each player has a prescribed playing area (Table 7.8).

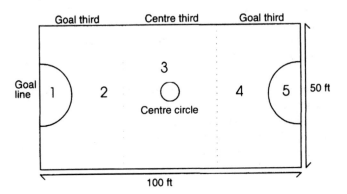

Figure 7.13 Schematic representation of the netball court for divisions of the playing surface.

Table 7.8 Each player has designated areas within which she must play

Player	Areas for team playing from area 1 towards area 5			
GK	1	2		
GD	1	2	3	
WD	2	3		
C	2	3	4	
WA		3	4	
GA	3	4	5	
GS		4	5	

Actions:

- V = goal scored (should be followed by a centre pass).
- X = goal attempted but missed.
- O = out-of-court shot (the appropriate team is given a free throw from the sideline where the ball went out).
- C = centre pass (no court position number is added since it is always taken from within the centre circle).

Continued notation within the column implies a successful pass.

The record sheet

It is necessary for the recording sheet to contain descriptive details of the match or practice session so that the information obtained is available for analysis, and future reference if required.

1   Match or practice session?
2   Venue.
3   Date.
4   Names of players (if possible).

The recording sheet consists of vertical columns under the headings of red and blue (referring to the team colours). Play is recorded in the appropriate column according to the team in possession of the ball. Play is recorded from the top to the bottom of the column. The score is shown at the left side of each column.

Recording a sequence

Each sequence begins with the centre pass represented by the symbol 'C'. The centre pass is always taken from within the centre circle. Play continues and the player and position are notated. The sequence is completed when a goal is scored and represented by the symbol V. An example of a record sheet is shown in Table 7.9.

Results

The results (see Table 7.10) showed that the red team were more successful at retaining possession once they had got it. The red team averaged three passes per possession and had only two passing errors. Both passing errors were caused by the red centre player passing the ball out-of-court.

The blue team had more possessions but that did not compensate for their passing errors, since they managed only 1.6 passes per possession and committed more passing errors. From this short example of data few conclusions can be

Table 7.9 Example of a record sheet for simple data-gathering for notation of netball

Score	Red	Blue	Score	Red	Blue
		C		O	
		WA 3		GD 4	
		GA 4		WD 3	
		GS 5		C 3	
		X		O	GK 2
		GS 5			O
0–1		V		WA 3	
	C			C 3	
	WA 3			GA 2	
	C 2			GS 1	
	GS 1		2–1	V	
1–1	V				
	C			etc.	

Table 7.10 Data processed from a notated netball match (part only)

	Red	Blue
No. of possessions	7	10
No. of passes	21	16
Average sequence	21/7 = 3	16/10 = 1.6
No. of passing errors	2	4

drawn about the play – much more data is needed. But the notation exercise enabled an assessment of the notation system. By examining the record sheet, several factors can be analysed without a great deal of effort.

1   The number of possessions by each team. A possession is defined as a single player or sequence of players following each other simultaneously in the team's column on the record sheet.

2   Related to the number of possessions is the number of passing errors by a team and the frequency of passing errors by a particular player. To obtain a percentage of passing errors it would be necessary to evaluate the number of touches by that player. It is then also possible for the coach to assess whether the team is making good use of all the players in the team, although this is somewhat dependent on their accessibility at the time. The latter information would need to be combined with the coach's own subjective observations.

   A passing error would be defined as the ball changing possession or going out of court. A touch would be defined as the ball actually being caught and passed, or being touched as it travelled through the air.

3   It is possible to calculate the average number of passes in a sequence. This is important when assessing the path of the ball, particularly from the centre pass to an attempt at goal. A common strategy outlined in books is a three-pass attack down the centre, although a two pass attack is possible. The greater the number of passes, the greater the opportunity for defenders to break the attack.

4   A percentage success rate of goals by the goal shooter and goal attack can be calculated. It allows the coach to assess whether one or both players need goal-shooting practice.

5   When analysing who attempted the most shots at goal it could be beneficial to work backwards and see the shots leading to the attempt. With sufficient data it may be possible to outline a common attacking strategy.

Although the record sheet appears simplistic, a great deal of information can be gleaned from it. It is possible to assemble a quick summary after the match. Given more time, more detailed information may be extracted. Once the notation is sufficiently rehearsed it is easy to modify the system to consider a number of other factors.

Possible improvements

1   The court could be subdivided into smaller sections to outline a more accurate path of the ball which can then be transferred to plans of play. For example, this would be useful when tracing the path of the ball from centre pass – a common strategy advocated in coaching books is an attack down the centre. By recording the team's patterns with their centre pass, the coach can conclude whether the centre-line attacking strategy is successful for them or whether the team tends to play more down one side than the other. On the other hand, having more position cells will mean that more matches will have to be analysed to produce significant amounts of data in all the cells.

2   Players can be penalised for foot-faults, but this is not common in experienced players, so it would only be relevant when notating novices.

3   A throw-up is called for when a player of each team gains possession of the ball equally at the same time. The success of a particular team at gaining possession in throw-ups could be notated.

8 The use of performance indicators in performance analysis

Mike Hughes and Roger Bartlett

8.1 Summary

The aims of this chapter are to examine the application of performance indicators in different sports and, using the different structural definitions of games, to make general recommendations about the use and application of these indicators. Formal games are classified into three categories: net and wall games, invasion games, and striking and fielding games. The different types of sports are also subcategorised by the rules of scoring and of ending the respective matches. These classes are analysed further to enable definition of useful performance indicators and to examine similarities and differences in the analysis of the different categories of game. The indices of performance are subcategorised into general match indicators, tactical indicators, technical indicators and biomechanical indicators. Different research examples and the accuracy of their presentation are discussed. We conclude that, to enable a full and objective interpretation of the data from the analysis of a performance, comparisons of data are vital. In addition, any analysis of the distribution of actions across the playing surface should also be presented normalised, or non-dimensionalised, to the total distribution of actions across the area. Other normalisations of performance indicators should also be used more widely in conjunction with the accepted forms of data analysis.

8.2 Introduction

Notational analysts and sport biomechanists are concerned with the analysis and improvement of sports performance. The practitioners of both make extensive use of video analysis and video-based technology. Recently, those involved in these two sub-disciplines of sport science have recognised some other commonalities, which suggest that the two should grow closer together, collaborate more and share ideas, theories and methods. The formation of the British Olympic Association's Performance Analysis Steering Group, which brings together biomechanists and notational analysts, is an example of this convergence. The issues that are common to biomechanists and notational analysts include optimising feedback to the performer and coach to improve performance (see

Liebermann *et al.*, 2002a; Smith and Loschner, 2002). Other common issues include the management of information complexity, addressing the reliability and validity of their data, and exploitation of the approaches and methods of artificial intelligence (see Lapham and Bartlett, 1995). The investigators from both disciplines study patterns of play involving the individual or 'constellations of individuals' (Shephard, 1999). One approach to theoretical grounding that is common to these elements of 'performance analysis' is the derivation of performance indicators (also called performance parameters by sport biomechanists) from flowcharts for notational analysis (see e.g. Hughes and Franks, 1997) or hierarchical technique models for biomechanics (see e.g. Hay and Reid, 1988).

A performance indicator is a selection, or combination, of action variables that aims to define some or all aspects of a performance. Clearly, to be useful, performance indicators should relate to successful performance or outcome. Biomechanical performance indicators are often linked to the outcome through hierarchical technique models, such as Figure 8.1, in which clear biomechanical relationships exist between the levels of the model (see also Lees, 2002). Mathematical modelling can often serve to reinforce this relationship, particularly in closed skills, as in Figure 8.2. In this figure, an optimal combination of two javelin release parameters (performance indicators), here release angle of attack and release angle, produces a maximum throw; departures from that optimum result in a decrement in distance thrown. Such modelling techniques have not yet been applied to team games.

Analysts and coaches use performance indicators to assess the performance of an individual, a team, or elements of a team. They are sometimes used in a comparative way, with opponents, other athletes or peer groups of athletes or

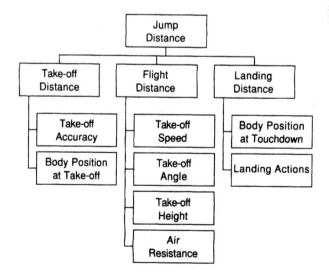

Figure 8.1 Hierarchical technique model of the long jump (adapted from Hay and Reid, 1988).

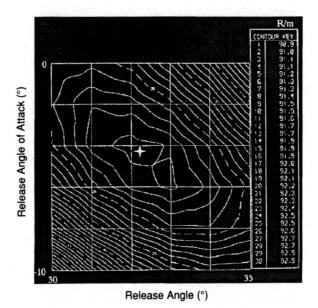

Release Angle (°)

Figure 8.2 Contour map of the distance a javelin travels (R) as a function of two release parameters, with all others held constant. Release angle is the angle between the direction in which the javelin's centre of mass is travelling (the javelin's velocity vector) and the horizontal; release angle of attack is the angle from the javelin's long axis to its velocity vector at release. Contour lines (every fifth one numbered) are lines of constant R; the cross marks the maximal value of R (92.9 m). Any departure from that optimum results in a reduction in R (adapted from Best *et al.*, 1995).

teams; often they are used in isolation as a measure of the performance of a team or individual alone.

Sport biomechanists have generally concentrated their analyses of performance on sports in which the movement technique is critical. Such sports involve predominantly closed skills and are classified as acrobatic (including gymnastics, trampolining, diving, freestyle skiing), athletic (including jumping and throwing) and cyclic (including running, swimming, skating and wheelchair racing) (Yeadon and Challis, 1992). The performance goal, or primary performance parameter (such as the distance jumped in the long jump), is initially partitioned into secondary performance parameters (such as the take-off, flight and landing distances in the long jump): these are sometimes based on phase analysis of the technique (e.g. Bartlett, 1999). In this example, these partial distances can be normalised by expressing them as ratios of the distance jumped – a similar approach is often used in the triple jump and sometimes in gymnastic vaults. The use of hierarchical technique models then allows these performance parameters to be related to the movements of the athlete that contribute to successful execution of the skill. All these parameters and movement variables can be considered as performance indicators provided that they do meaningfully contribute to the performance. These performance indicators are usually kinematic variables or parameters, such as body segment speeds or angles. When trying to relate such indicators to the mechanisms of the movement, net joint reaction forces and moments and electromyographic (EMG) descriptors of muscle activation patterns are also used.

Sport biomechanists have paid far less attention to team sports, perhaps because of the perception that biomechanical interventions are less important in those sports than fitness training, psychological preparation and tactics. There are some exceptions to this. They include analyses of fast bowling in cricket (see Bartlett *et al.*, 1996), some studies of soccer skills (see Lees and Nolan, 1998) and limited studies of other games such as rugby and racket sports. Even then, however, the focus is predominantly on isolated individual closed skills within the game. The lack of biomechanical analyses of team sports is regrettable, given that the most important requirement for success for any games player is *skill* – which is what most biomechanists try to understand and measure. The result is insufficient attention to the interaction of skill and successful play, clearly an important contribution to successful outcomes of games (Bartlett, 2000).

Notational analysis, on the other hand, has focused traditionally on team and match play sports, studying the interactions between players and the movements and behaviours of individual team members – mostly open skills. Few studies of acrobatic, athletic and cyclic sports exist from a notational analysis perspective, despite the widespread use of dance notation systems. Clearly, however, notational analysis is far less relevant, if at all, to these sports than to team and match play sports. Notational analysts have focused on general match indicators, tactical indicators and technical indicators and have contributed to our understanding of the physiological, psychological, technical and tactical demands of many types of sports. For example, in tennis, performance of a player may be assessed by the distribution of winners and errors around the court. In soccer, one aspect of a team's performance may be appraised by the ratio of goals scored to shots attempted by the team. Other examples, taken from published research, are shown in Table 8.1.

These indicators can be categorised as either scoring indicators or indicators of the quality of the performance. Examples of scoring indicators are goals,

Table 8.1 Published performance indicators used in notational analysis

Soccer	Shots, passes, passing accuracy (see e.g. Hughes *et al.*, 1988; Winkler, 1996)
Rugby	Turnovers, tackles, passes/possession (see e.g. Carter, 1996)
Tennis	Winners to errors ratio, shots/rally, quality – service/return (see e.g. Taylor and Hughes, 1998)
Cricket	Strike rate, dismissal rate, fielding efficiency (see e.g. Hughes and Bell, 2001)

baskets, winners, errors, the ratios of winners to errors and goals to shots, and dismissal rates. Examples of quality indicators are turnovers, tackles, passes/possession, shots per rally, and strike rate. Both types of indicator have been used as a measure of positive or negative aspects of performance in the analysis of a particular sport.

If presented in isolation, a single set of data (indicators for a performance of an individual or a team) can give a distorted impression of a performance, by ignoring other, more or less important, variables. From our reviews of recent research and the work of many consultants, it is clear that many analysts do not give sufficient data from a performance to represent fully the significant events of that performance. Presenting data from both sets of performers is often not enough to inform on the performance. For example, in a rugby match, if team A have had 12 turnovers (handling errors that led to a change in possession) and team B have had eight turnovers, it would be tempting to assume that team B were having the better of the game. However, if team A had 48 possessions and team B 24 possessions, then their relative turnovers with respect to possessions (turnovers/possessions, T/P) would be:

$$(T/P)_A = 1/4; \quad (T/P)_B = 1/3$$

Now team A could be said to be performing better than team B because, although they have conceded more turnovers, they are making these errors once in four possessions whereas team B are making them once in every three possessions.

The comparison of performances between teams, team members and within individuals is often facilitated if the performance indicators are expressed as ratios, as in the example above, such as winners to errors and goals to shots and the ratios of jump phases to overall jump distance. These proportions represent a binomial response variable (see Nevill et al. (2002) for appropriate analytical methods). These examples are clearly non-dimensional as they divide a measure (e.g. number of goals or phase jump distance) by a similar measure (number of shots or total jump distance). Similar non-dimensional ratios are formed by sports biomechanists by expressing forces acting on the performer as ratios to body weight, and by normalising EMG descriptors to the magnitude of that descriptor in a maximum voluntary contraction (MVC). More attention should be paid to this normalising, or non-dimensional, approach. For example, Stockill (1994) found a difference in the magnitudes and times of occurrence of peak segment speeds in senior and junior cricket fast bowlers. However, when the times were normalised to the time from the start of delivery to release, these ratio times of peak speeds were the same; the ratio speeds were also comparable. Therefore, the difference between the groups was not in timing or in different segmental significance but simply in speed of execution, a finding that is consistent with existing motor control literature (see e.g. Newell and Corcos, 1993).

The wider scientific context

There are parallels with the use of non-dimensional analysis elsewhere; for example, indices such as the ratio of specific heats in high-speed flows, or non-dimensional groups such as Reynolds number in low-speed fluid mechanics. When flow conditions are very complex, so that the equations of motion cannot easily be solved, fluid mechanists use dimensional analysis to predict how one variable may depend on several others. This is then used to direct the course of an experiment or the analysis of experimental results. Sport science has not reached this degree of sophistication in the application of analysis of performance, but there are certain empirical recommendations that can be explored. Few of the non-dimensional ratios in performance analysis relate to the importance of various forces, with the exception of expressing ratios of forces to body weight. Many of the important non-dimensional groups in fluid dynamics are force ratios, and some of these are important for biomechanical analysis. The Reynolds number is the ratio of inertia to viscous forces; it is important in any sport in which drag forces are significant or in which lift forces are used to generate propulsion or improve performance. These sports include swimming, ski jumping, skiing, throws of an aerodynamic object – such as the discus or javelin – and ball games in which the ball spins quickly (such as golf and tennis). The Froude number is the square root of the ratio of inertia to gravity forces; it is important in sports in which the body moving through the water makes waves, for example fast front crawl swimming, sailing and canoeing.

As we have noted above, biomechanists use measured forces, performance distances and segmental peak speeds to compare performances. However, far more meaningful comparisons may be obtained by using simple ratios of force to body weight, partial distances or speed ratios. We need to be careful to avoid information being lost by normalisation, which should be used to aid the evaluation of the measured results by adding relevant information. The most appropriate analysis of the results is best determined case by case, and non-dimensionalising is not always appropriate. An illustration of the last statement was provided by Fleissig (2001), who proposed comparing ground reaction forces between baseball pitchers of widely varying ages by normalising forces (F) to body weight (W), to assess injury risk. However, tissue injury is related to the tissue stress (force/cross-sectional area), which is proportional to F/l^2, where l is an appropriate tissue dimension such as radius, whereas F/W is proportional to F/l^3. Such incorrect use of normalisation shows that performance analysts have much to learn from allometric scaling (see e.g. Schmidt-Nielsen, 1984).

Notational analysts use simple measures such as the number of shots per game in soccer. However, far more meaningful information is obtained from *ratios* such as number of shots per game to number of shooting opportunities, number of shots per game on goal to number of shots per game, number of goals per game to number of shots per game (see Nevill *et al.* (2002) for appropriate analytical methods for binomial response variables). In tennis, the winner and error distributions on their own are used to show relative strengths and weaknesses on the forehand and backhand; for example, 60 per cent errors on backhand and 40 per cent on forehand. However, such measures are meaningless unless expressed relative to the total shot distribution – the opponent could have been overloading the backhand (as is often the case) by 75 per cent to 25 per cent forehand: this dramatically changes the analysis. These simple examples demonstrate how misleading it can be to use only measured data to evaluate and analyse the complex factors that make for successful sports performance.

Performance indicators are also used in different ways. They have become increasingly popular in media coverage of sport; for example, possession, tackling and passing statistics in rugby and shot distribution patterns in cricket. They are also used in judging contests, in coaching and in other applications in sport science, such as monitoring team performance against that of rivals over a season in soccer (Olsen and Larsen, 1997). An interesting example of the usefulness of performance analysis is in ice hockey, where players are given a score after each game based on, for example, whether they scored or assisted and if the team scored or conceded when they were on the ice. These indicators are used both by the media and by the management when negotiating contracts. None of these applications is explicitly the focus of this chapter. The aims are rather to examine the application of performance indicators in different sports and, using the different structural definitions of games, to make general recommendations about the use and application of these indicators.

8.3 Analysis of game structures

Read and Edwards (1992) classified formal games into three categories: net and wall games, invasion games, and striking and fielding games (see Figure 8.3). This classification will be used in this chapter as a starting point. The different types of sports are also subcategorised by the rules of scoring or ending the respective matches. These classes will be examined further, to enable analysis of useful performance indicators and as a means of examining similarities and differences in the analysis of the different categories of game.

8.3.1 Net–wall games

Net games can be subcategorised into no-volley, bounce-and-volley and no-bounce games. Some examples of the more common sports that fall into these classes are shown in Figure 8.4. The common wall games in Britain, squash and fives, are bounce and volley games. There are many wall games from different

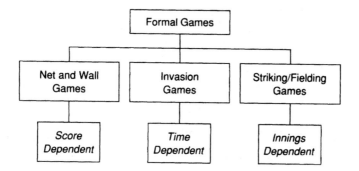

Figure 8.3 Game classification (after Read and Edwards, 1992).

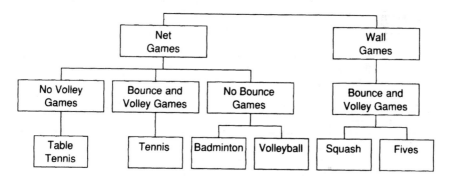

Figure 8.4 Subcategorisation of net and wall games, with some common examples.

parts of the world, each with its own rules, that may well fall into the same subcategories of the net games.

Despite the differences in the rules of these games, the performance indic-ators that have been used by different analysts are very similar. Figure 8.5 shows some of the different variables that contribute to success in all of these net and wall games.

The types of performance indicator that have been used in previous research further exemplify these variables; some are shown in Table 8.2. These general indicators have been classified as match descriptors, data that define the nature of the overall match, as well as biomechanical, technical and tactical. In some cases these categories are similar, somewhat inevitably, since match descriptors and tactics will depend on technical strengths and weaknesses, but we feel that keeping the distinction between the two will be useful.

All these indicators have been used as ways of indexing performances, without reference to other normative data (such as previous performances or aggregated performances of peer opponents) and, in some cases, without reference to the opponents' data. The use of any of these variables in isolation is misleading.

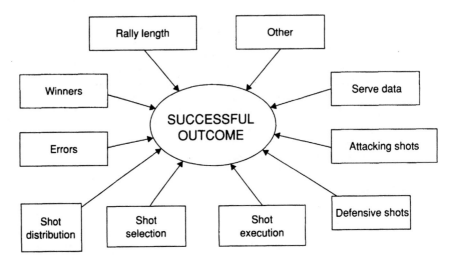

Figure 8.5 Some factors that contribute to success or improved performance in net and wall games.

Table 8.2 Categorisation of different performance indicators that have been used in analyses of net or wall games

Match classification	Biomechanical	Technical	Tactical
No. of shots	Ball projection (release) velocity	Winners (W)	Shots/second
No. of rallies	Racket, bat or hand speed at impact	Errors (E)	Shots/rally
Scores	Kinematics of throwing or striking arm:	Winning shot distribution	Shot types – distribution
Serve data:	Pronation/supination	Error shot distribution	Length of shot
1st serve winner	Elbow extension	Serve data, etc.	Winning shot distribution
2nd serve winner	Sequence of segment movements		Error shot distribution
			Opponent's:
	Weight transfer into shot or stroke		Winning shot distribution
			Error shot distribution
For a review, see Hughes (1998). See also O'Donoghue and Liddle (1998), Taylor and Hughes (1998).	See e.g. Bartlett *et al.* (1995), Tang *et al.* (1995), Kasai and Mori (1998), Bahamonde (2000), Marshall and Elliott (2000).	For a review, see Hughes (1998). See also McGarry and Franks (1994), Hughes and Robertson (1998).	For a review, see Hughes (1998). See also Furlong (1995), Hughes and Clarke (1995).

8.3.1.1 Match classification indicators

Consider the example of a squash match that had 250 shots in 50 rallies. What can be said about the match other than that the ratio of shots per rally was 5? This, as a performance indicator, is meaningless without some other reference point. If elite players, for whom the average equivalent data was approximately 1000 shots and 100 rallies, had played this match, then these figures would suggest that something unusual had taken place. It would seem that one player had beaten the other player very easily. If, however, the match had been played by recreational players, then the figures would suggest that the match was closely contested as the values are close to the averages for that class of player. So the same data can give two totally different messages. Providing comparative data from samples of the same playing standard allows the best assessment of the important features of any performances.

The effectiveness of a serve in tennis will always depend on the returning skills of the opponent; even aces will vary with the positioning, reflexes and skill of the other player. Consequently, presenting serve data without the opponents' complementary data can be misleading. It is equally important to present the data with a frame of reference, as discussed with the previous match classification data. If Goran Ivanisevich has made 14 aces in a match, compared to eight by his opponent, André Agassi, then this would seem to be a good performance for Ivanisevich and not so good for Agassi. If the average number of aces for elite players is six per match, then, by this standard, Ivanisevich is having a good performance and Agassi is also playing relatively well. This is true with the aggregate of elite players as a standard of comparison, and this contrast is a sound way of assessing players' strengths and weaknesses. Another way of assessing a particular performance of an individual or team is to compare that performance with the aggregated profile of previous performances at this standard of play. Ivanisevich averages 16 aces per match; Agassi averages 10 aces per match. Comparing the aces for this match to their individual averages of previous performances changes the interpretation of the data, with both underachieving in this part of the game. These data have been presented in three ways: relative to each other, relative to players of the same standard, and relative to their own profiles of previous performance. Each can give valuable comparisons, but it is important to remember that each of these comparisons elicits different interpretations of the quality of a performance. Consequently, to enable efficient interpretation of data, when using match classification indicators, it is very important to have comparative data from previous performances and also from peer group previous performances. Profiles of players will vary depending on whom they are playing; this too must be borne in mind when presenting information, ensuring that enough data are collected to present a normative profile (see Chapter 10).

The above comparisons could be made even more meaningful by incorporating biomechanical indicators, such as hitting speeds and segmental velocities. More important information could be provided if biomechanists developed qualitative analyses, which enabled the key features that contribute to a successful stroke to be recognised from direct observation. This happens, after all, in judging gymnastics and diving. Biomechanists have, to date, paid far too little attention to qualitative biomechanical analysis in their research, notwithstanding several well-known texts on the topic (e.g. Kreighbaum and Barthels, 1990; Knudsen and Morrison, 1997). These comments apply equally to the technical and tactical indicators in racket sports, as well as to the other categories of games. The reliability and objectivity of measures based on human perceptions and judgements is clearly an issue. This needs to be addressed by validating such performance indicators against valid and reliable quantitative measures to which they are clearly related.

8.3.1.2 Technical indicators

Winners and errors are powerful indicators of technical competence and have often been used in research in notational analysis of net–wall games (Sanderson, 1983; Hughes, 1986; Brown and Hughes, 1995). However, there are dangers of misinterpreting a performance if they are used in isolation. Sanderson (1983) used a winner–error ratio as a performance indicator. He found that, for all standards of play in squash, if the winner–error ratio for a particular player in a match was greater than 1, then that player usually won. (This was achieved with English scoring and a 19-inch tin and when players were using wooden rackets.) Although this ratio is a good index of technique, it would be better used with data for both players, and the ratios should not be simplified nor decimalised. Winner–error ratios of 0.9 and 1.1 respectively tell that the first player is losing but little else about the match. However, if the ratios had been presented as 9/10 and 44/40, then it is clear that this is a long hard match for players of this standard (103 rallies). The first player is playing defensively, making few errors but few winners. The second player is playing more aggressively, hitting many winners but also many errors. Perhaps the better way to present the processed data is as a combination of both forms, the former for an overview and the latter for more detail.

Rally end distributions, i.e. the frequencies of winners and errors in the different position cells across the court, have often been used to define technical strengths and weaknesses (O'Donoghue and Liddle, 1998; Hughes et al., 2000d). The use of these distributions as indicators is valid as long as the overall distribution of shots across the court is evenly balanced on both sides of the court. However, this even distribution of shots across all the cells in a court rarely occurs in any net or wall game. For example, it could be that in a badminton match, player A has 20 drops from the backhand side of the court and 15 drops from the forehand. This would suggest that the backhand side of player A is the stronger and more aggressive flank. If, however, the overall total of shots on the backhand side was 120, and the equivalent total on the forehand was 60 shots, then the respective 'drops to total shots' ratios for each side are 20/120 (1 drop in 6 shots, or 0.167) and 15/60 (1 drop in 4 shots, or 0.25). Again, it can be seen how this normalisation changes the interpretation of these data. Dispersions of winners and errors should be normalised to the totals of shots from those cells. It would be more accurate to represent the winner, or error, frequency from particular position cells as a ratio to the total number of shots from those cells.

Often rally end distributions are shot-specific (Hughes, 1986; O'Donoghue and Liddle, 1998), for example a distribution of volley winners in different position cells of a tennis court. The distribution of these volleys will reflect the respective volleying skills of the player and will indicate the areas of the court where the strengths and weaknesses lie. However, the pattern of winners will also depend heavily on the overall distribution of shots and the total distribution of volleys. So, by the same argument that was used to explain the need for normalising the total shot distributions, the frequencies in this case should be standardised to the total distribution of volleys in each cell position and presented in both forms to give the complete picture.

8.3.1.3 Tactical indicators

Tactical performance indicators seek to reflect the relative importance of the use of pace, space, fitness and movement, and how players use these aspects of performance, of themselves and their opponents, targeting the technical strengths and weaknesses of the respective performers. These will be reflected in the ways that individuals and teams attack and defend, how they use the spaces in the playing surface and the variety of playing actions. The examples shown in Table 8.1 are representative of indicators used to identify these types of tactical play (Sanderson, 1983; McGarry and Franks, 1994).

The identification of the use of pace in net or wall games is not common; researchers have rarely used time bases to enable definition of the speed of play (Hughes and Clarke, 1995). When they are used, comparisons should be made to means of groups of peer performers. When players are trying to use perceived superior fitness in net or wall games, it will usually be reflected in the shots-per-rally indicators and the respective winner to error ratios. The latter will indicate which team or player is trying to sustain rallies in the hope of wearing down their opponents. Often the serve will be linked with control of the rally; sometimes this is through the scoring rules of the game. Therefore, linking the shots per rally to the respective serves is an additional way of using this indicator, which gives greater depth to the analysis and enables deeper insight into the tactics employed in the game. Comparing these values to means of groups of peer performers will yield greater insight into the respective performances. The importance of technical strengths and weaknesses is assessed using similar indicators to those discussed in the previous section – and the same provisos to their use apply.

8.3.1.4 Biomechanical indicators

The biomechanics of racket sports has received much less attention than other aspects of these games. For example, the proceedings of the first two Congresses of Science and Racket Sports (Reilly et al., 1995; Lees et al., 1998) contain, respectively, five out of 44 and four out of 40 biomechanics papers. Five of these papers focused on tennis – one was a review; of the others, two were studies of the serve, one reported results on grip strength and one studied the effects of ball flight on several strokes. The emphasis on the serve reflects the closed nature of that skill compared with other skills – a trend that we shall see again for the other two categories of games discussed below. As we note below, biomechanical studies of the variability in stroke movement patterns and how these relate to the influence of opponents – and, in volleyball, the rest of the team – have received scant attention. Such studies in the future should afford great opportunities for collaboration between biomechanists and notational analysts.

Table 8.2 summarises some of the biomechanical performance indicators most often measured in net or wall games. These range from the descriptive – such as bat or hand speed at impact – to variables that relate more to mechanisms. The importance of segmental sequencing is more complex for racket arm movements than for kicking movements of the leg (see below). This is because of the supination–pronation of the radio-ulnar joints and the external–internal rotation of the humerus. Although the relevance of these long axis rotations was recognised more than two decades ago (e.g. Waddell and Gowitzke, 1977), it is only recently that their role in the proximal-to-distal sequence has been established (see Marshall and Elliott (2000) for an overview). Their speed and timing could become important biomechanical performance indicators, although considerable scope remains for establishing the precise mechanisms that control and coordinate such strokes.

In all segmental analyses, the timing and speed of the segments should be normalised to the overall time of the stroke and the impact speed, so that we can ascertain whether differences between, for example, good, average and poor shots are due to timing differences or simply to speed.

Making detailed three-dimensional biomechanical measurements in racket sports – and many other games – is difficult and often impossible. It may also be unnecessary. If complex sports – such as gymnastics and diving – can be scored by judges in real time (perhaps not *always* validly or reliably), then why cannot biomechanists develop and validate qualitative indicators of successful stroke production in tennis, other racket sports and other games? Coaches already use similar indicators when they coach technique. This is an area that demands far more attention by performance analysts, interacting with coaches and players, to develop sets of valid and reliable skill-related performance indicators that can be assessed qualitatively in a game, or from video, along with other performance indicators.

8.3.2 Invasion games

Invasion games can be subcategorised into goal-throwing games, try-scoring games and goal-striking games. Figure 8.6 shows these and some examples of

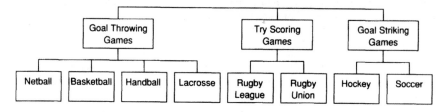

Figure 8.6 Subcategorisation of invasive games, with some common examples.

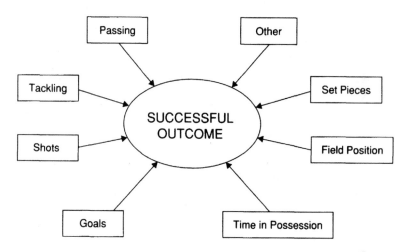

Figure 8.7 Some factors that contribute to success or improved performance in invasive games.

common sports that fall into these categories. Despite the differences in the rules of these games, the performance indicators that have been used by different analysts are very similar.

As with net or wall games, we shall consider the different variables that contribute to an improved performance. Figure 8.7 shows some of the factors that contribute to success in soccer. Although the different invasion games have very similar types of performance indicators, the specific terms in each game, such as goal, try, basket, make a general list impracticable. Consequently we have used soccer as an example, but the same types of indicators have been used in all the other invasion games, and are easily translated to other sports.

Some of the performance indicators that have been used in previous research in soccer are shown in Table 8.3. All these indicators have been, and are still, used as ways of indexing performances, without reference to other normative data and, in some cases, without reference to the opponents' data. As in the analysis of the net or wall games, the indicators can be classified as match descriptors, and indices of biomechanical, technical and tactical performances.

Table 8.3 Categorisation of different performance indicators that have been used in analyses of soccer, an example of invasion games

Match classification	Biomechanical	Technical	Tactical
Scores	Kicking	Passes to	Passes/Possession
No. of shots on	Ball projection	opposition	Pace of attack
target	velocity and spin	Tackles won and	
		lost	
No. of shots off	Kinematics and	Shots off target	Shots
target	kinetics of kicking leg:		
	Energy transfers	Dribbles	Tackles won and
Corners etc.			lost
	Sequencing of joint	Lost control	Passing
Crosses etc.	actions		distribution
	Net joint forces and	On target crosses	Length of passes
	moments		
	Throw in	Off target crosses	Dribbles
	Ball release velocity	etc.	etc.
	Kinematics of arms,		
	including sequence		
	of peak segment		
	speeds.		
	For a review, see Lees	For a review see	For a review see
For a review see	and Nolan (1998); see	Hughes (1993);	Hughes (1993);
Hughes (1993).	also Putnam (1993).	see also Pettit and	see also Pettit and
		Hughes (2001).	Hughes (2001).

8.3.2.1 *Match indicators*

Match indicators for invasion games give simple information to describe and define that particular performance. Such information differs from sport to sport but, inevitably, there are similarities – in soccer we have used examples such as scores, shots on and off target, corners and crosses. These can easily be translated to other sports. In rugby union, the equivalent indicators could be scores, penalties and drop goals (successful and otherwise), line-outs, incursions into the opponents' '22'. Similar examples could be inventoried for other invasion sports. The indicators for any of the invasion games can be seen to follow very similar rules of application to those of the net or wall games. Knowing the scores of the game will tell who won the match but, without knowing the average goals scored per match at this standard of play, it would not be possible to decide whether this was a high or low scoring performance. Similarly, the other match indicators can be seen to be potentially misleading without both the data of the opponents and the means of previous performances at this standard.

8.3.2.2 *Technical indicators*

Analysing and listing tactical indicators for invasion games such as shots on goal (soccer), missed shots at the basket (basketball), short corner conversions (field hockey), and so on, again reflects the similarities in the definition of these indicators. The differences in analyses will usually depend on the questions the coaches have about their players, or the research question being posed.

Accuracy in passing is a common technical indicator in all invasion games (Hughes *et al.*, 1988; Carter, 1996). Any error or success frequencies of a player, unit or team should be normalised to the total number of passes made by that player, unit or team. Although it is a good index of technique for these sports, it should be used for both sets of players and, as explained above, the ratios could be presented firstly as simplified ratios or decimals and then as non-simplified, or non-decimalised, data. This will prevent any loss of information.

Loss of possession through any other action variables is another common way of assessing technical weaknesses in an invasion team, whether the action variable is catching (netball), free hits (field hockey), line-outs (rugby union), tackles (rugby league) and so on. These should all be linked to totals of actions involved so that they represent indices of the error frequency of the particular action with respect to that action's total frequency.

Other indices of technical success or failure – shots on goal (soccer), missed shots at the basket (basketball), short corner conversions (field hockey), and so on – should also be normalised to these particular action totals. The total of this particular action variable could then be standardised by the overall number of possessions. This can also be seen to apply to all the indicators listed as examples used in research in soccer, and this rule should be applied to all technical indicators of invasion games.

8.3.2.3 Tactical indicators

Tactical performance indicators in invasion games seek to reflect the relative importance of teamwork, pace, fitness and movement, and targeting the technical strengths and weaknesses of the respective performers – very similar to those of the net or wall games. The examples shown in Table 8.3 are representative of indicators used in recent research to identify these types of tactical play; examples in soccer include Reep and Benjamin (1968), Hughes *et al.* (1988), Partridge and Franks (1989a, 1989b), Olsen and Larsen (1997), Garganta *et al.* (1997), Pettit and Hughes (2001). Similar examples in other invasion games could be cited for their respective tactical indicators.

The nature of these tactical indicators can be seen to be the same as those in Table 8.3, and the rules for their use follow the same logic. If two players, A and B, have four and six shots on goal respectively, it is not appropriate to report that player B is having the better performance. What are the respective totals of shot attempts? Player A could have had four shot attempts, while player B had 12 shot attempts, thus resulting in shooting indices of 4/4 and 6/12 shots on target per attempt respectively. Even this could be further analysed – how many shooting opportunities did each player have? Player A could have had a total of 12 opportunities but decided to pass eight times instead of shooting; player B could have shot on all 12 of the possible opportunities that were presented. Does this now indicate that player B was having the better game? Analysis of the errors could show that the passing options adopted by player A were deemed better tactically for the team. This would lead to further analysis, and so on. As noted above, simple analysis of the data induces simple interpretation, which is not always appropriate in sport. The indicators in Table 8.3 should all be normalised to the respective action totals.

8.3.2.4 Biomechanical indicators

In soccer, biomechanists have focused almost exclusively on kicking. Other invasive sports have received far less attention, except for basketball, where most studies are of shooting skills (e.g. Miller and Bartlett, 1993, 1996). Soccer kicks occur in set pieces, such as penalties and free kicks, as well as in passing and shooting. Almost all of the reported studies are of maximum speed instep kicks of a stationary ball (Lees and Nolan, 1998). The many other kicks have been studied in far less detail, including passing – a crucial interaction between players, as noted above in the section on tactical performance indicators. The biomechanical performance indicators reported by researchers are summarised in Table 8.3. These vary – as with net or wall games – from the descriptive, such as ball projection velocity and spin, to those that cause the movements, such as net joint forces and moments. The sequencing of joint actions has also been studied, showing a clear proximal-to-distal kinematic sequence, unlike that for arm movements. This has led to the magnitudes and timings of segment peak speeds becoming recognised biomechanical performance indicators; their non-dimensionalising, i.e. normalising to ball speed or total duration of a phase of the movement (see below for cricket) has not yet been explored. Overall, the contribution of biomechanists to our understanding of various information-processing aspects of the game, including the control and coordination of movements, remains limited. One factor is the complexity of multi-segmental movements. This has led, *inter alia*, to different interpretations of the causes of segmental deceleration in kicks (see e.g. Putnam, 1993), calling into question fundamental biomechanical tenets about proximal-to-distal sequencing and momentum transfer along segment chains. Marshall and Elliott (2000) have recently demonstrated the lack of a clear proximal-to-distal sequence in the tennis serve.

There has been far less research into other skills in the sport. Studies of heading have concentrated exclusively on injury risk factors rather than performance variables (see e.g. Shephard, 1999). The throw-in has received some attention; the main biomechanical performance indicators for this skill are summarised in Table 8.3. Goalkeeping skills, crucial to successful outcome, have been largely neglected by biomechanists.

Soccer is a team game in which individual skills have to fit within the tactical demands of the game. It is unfortunate – although understandable – that biomechanists have, to date, concentrated on the more closed skills, such as kicking a stationary ball and the throw-in. Considerable light might be shed on interactive aspects of the game if performance analysts could agree on, and then measure and validate, the important skill-related performance indicators in passing movements, tackling and dribbling. This could add rich skill descriptions to the other outcome-focused performance measures. Although in a cross, for example, the outcome might relate primarily to the positions of the ball, attackers and defenders, the execution of the crossing technique is hardly irrelevant. David Beckham is a supreme exponent of this skill mainly because he reproduces the skill consistently under pressure. Clearly, a cross is more difficult to analyse biomechanically than a kick or throw-in, but that should not prevent us from trying; after all, science does not progress by avoiding difficulties. As we have argued above, these measures should be qualitative so that they can be recognised in the game or from video by trained observers. They might include balance, in all these movements, minimising the foot-to-ball distance and its variability in dribbling and so on. Knudsen and Morrison (1997) advocated a 'critical factors' approach to qualitative skill analysis of soccer kicking (and other skills), each associated with observable clues. This approach might serve as a starting point for developing valid sets of qualitative skill indicators.

8.3.3 Striking and fielding games

These games can be subcategorised into wicket games and base running games; Figure 8.8 shows these and some examples of common sports that fall within these categories. Despite the differences in the rules of these games, the performance indicators that have been used by different analysts are very similar. As with the approach to net or wall games, we consider the different variables that contribute to an improved performance. Figure 8.9 shows some of the factors that contribute to success in cricket, as an example of such games.

The types of performance indicators that have been used in previous research in cricket can also further exemplify these factors; some are shown in Table 8.4. All these indicators can be categorised by the same process used for the net or wall and invasion games.

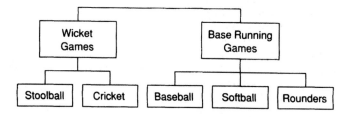

Figure 8.8 Subcategorisation of striking and fielding games, with some common examples.

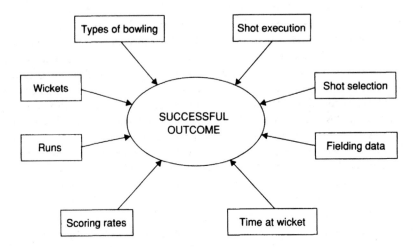

Figure 8.9 Some factors that contribute to success or improved performance in striking and fielding games.

Table 8.4 Categorisation of different performance indicators that have been used in analyses of cricket, an example of striking and fielding games

Match classification	Biomechanics	Technical	Tactical
Runs	Batting	Types of shot	(Types of ball)$_{Shot}$
Wickets	Timing of phases of stroke	Types of ball	(Types of shot)$_{Ball}$
Overs	Front foot movement, front knee angle and weight transfer in stroke	Types of dismissal	Field placing (Shots)$_{Field-Posn/Ball}$ etc.
Batting – individual data	Arm kinematics and grip force	Shot – position etc.	
Bowling – individual data	Pre- and post-impact bat and ball speed		
etc.	Kinetic variability		
	Bowling		
	Run-up speed and ball release speed		
	Class of technique (side-on, front-on, mixed) and shoulder counter-rotation in delivery stride		
See Hughes and Bell (2001).	See reviews by Bartlett *et al.* (1995), Stretch *et al.* (2000); see also Cook and Strike (2000) for a rare study of throwing in cricket.	See Hughes and Bell (2001).	See Hughes and Bell (2001).

8.3.3.1 Match indicators

The indicators to be discussed here for cricket can be seen to follow very similar rules of application to those of the net or wall games and invasion games. The interaction of the bowlers and the batters is the crux of the relative performances, a bowler having an outstanding performance can make an excellent batter appear ordinary and vice versa. Consequently, the match classification indicators can be seen to be potentially misleading without the opponents' data. As with all other sports, it is essential to place a team or individual performance in the context of previous performances; it is necessary then to compare each performance with the means of previous performances at this standard.

8.3.3.2 Technical indicators

These indicators for the example of cricket can be readily translated to other sports. They reflect the interactive nature of these sports – a batting performance is difficult to contextualise without some analysis of the bowling performance (and the fielding). Consequently it can be seen that these variables are similar to the technical indicators discussed in the previous sections. The indices of technical success or failure, types of shot, type of ball, and so on, should also be normalised to either the particular action totals or the overall number of actions. This can also be seen to apply to all the indicators listed as examples used in research in striking and fielding games.

8.3.3.3 Tactical indicators

Some of the variables listed are a shorthand representation of the way actions have been analysed in cricket to interpret tactical decisions made by the players. The variables reflect the interaction of the batter and the bowler. For example, (Types of ball)$_{Shot}$ indicates the frequency of the different types of ball bowled that produced a particular shot made by a batsman. Similarly, (Types of shot)$_{Ball}$ indicates the frequency of the different types of shot made by a batsman from a particular ball bowled. These could be subdivided into the areas of the pitch into which the batter hit the ball – depending on the analyses.

These tactical indicators can be seen to be similar to those in Tables 8.2 and 8.3, and the rules for their use follow the same logic. The indicators shown in Table 8.4 should, as above, all be normalised to the respective action totals.

8.3.3.4 Biomechanical indicators

The two striking and fielding games that have attracted most attention from biomechanists are baseball and cricket, with pitching and bowling respectively being the most studied skills. This skill selection reflects the importance of these skills to the two games and their closed nature compared with batting and fielding skills. The latter of these presents far greater problems in data acquisition and the analysis of the former relies not only on the skills of the batter but also those of the bowler. The selection also reflects an interest in the causes of the overuse injuries that often affect fast bowlers and baseball pitchers. The incidence of low back injuries in cricket, for example, has been shown to be far more prevalent in mixed technique bowlers than in front-on or side-on bowlers (see Elliott et al., 1996; Elliott, 2000).

Ball release speed is crucial to successful fast bowling performance. Biomechanical analysis of fast bowling has identified various indicators that contribute to ball release speed. These include run-up speed and delivery stride length. The technique used (side-on, front-on or mixed) is mainly used in identifying injury risk; counter-rotation of the shoulders also affects the acceleration path of the ball and, possibly, its release speed (see also Table 8.4 and Bartlett et al., 1996).

The sequence of segment peak speeds has received some attention, although it is more constrained than in many sports by the rule that prohibits the extension of the delivery arm before release. Few studies have non-dimensionalised the peak speeds and their timing although, as noted in the introduction, this helps to identify whether differences between bowlers of different ages are due to speed or segmental coordination (Stockill, 1994).

There are far fewer studies of batting techniques in cricket; all of them do, however, focus on performance indicators rather than injury risk factors (see Stretch et al. (2000) for a review). This research has concentrated on only a few of the many cricket strokes – the forward defensive and the front foot drives. The identified performance indicators are mostly kinematic, including the body position in the stance, the height of the backlift, the movements of the front foot and knee, and weight transfer. The kinematics of the arms and bat have been measured, including pre- and post-impact bat (and ball) speeds. The grip force has also received some attention (Stretch et al., 1998).

Many of these performance indicators have been shown to substantiate recognised coaching tips for the skill, but none has yet been shown to correlate with successful batting performance; more research into batting skill will be needed before such associations emerge. No non-dimensional indicators have been studied to date; this type of analysis could help to identify whether differences between similar strokes are due to different segmental recruitment patterns or simply faster execution. Although Stretch et al. (1998) did measure variability in grip force, no attempt has been made to 'establish the role of compensatory variability in the skill of striking a moving cricket ball with a moving cricket bat' (Stretch et al., 2000). This would mark an important step forward for biomechanists involved in performance analysis, as it would begin to identify interactions between the bowler and the batsman.

Such interactions are a key feature of games. For example, if a batter intends to play a cover drive to the boundary but instead hits the ball directly to extra cover or edges a catch to the slips, was the ball too good, could the batter not read cues or is there a technique defect? If the last of these, what is the problem? This approach could be developed to include the effects of field placement on the selection and successful execution of batting strokes and to evaluate fielding and catching skills.

8.4 Conclusions

Through an analysis of game structures and the performance indicators used in recent research in performance analysis, basic rules emerge in the application of performance indicators to any sport. In every case, success or failure in a performance is relative, either to the opposition or to previous performances of the team or individual. To enable a full and objective interpretation of the data from the analysis of a performance, it is necessary to compare the collected data to aggregated data of a peer group of teams, or individuals, which compete at an appropriate standard. In addition, any analysis of the distribution of actions across the playing surface must be normalised with respect to the total distribution of actions across the area.

Performance indicators, expressed as non-dimensional ratios, *can* have the advantage of being independent of any units that are used; furthermore, they are implicitly independent of any one variable. Mathematics, fluid dynamics and physics in general have shown the benefits of using these types of parameters to define particular environments. They also enable, as in the example of bowling in cricket, an insight into differences between performers that can be obscure in the raw data. The particular applications of non-dimensional analysis are common in fluid dynamics, which offers empirical clues to the solution of multivariate problems that cannot easily be solved mathematically. Sport is even more complex, the result of interacting human behaviours; to apply simplistic analyses of raw sports data can be highly misleading. Further research could examine how normative profiles are established – how much data is required to define reliably a profile and how this varies with the different types of data involved in any analysis profile. Hughes *et al.* (2001) have completed an empirical study but this area needs more exploration and understanding.

Many of the most important aspects of team performance cannot be 'teased out' by biomechanists or match analysts working alone – a combined research approach is needed. This is particularly important for information processing – both in movement control and decision-making. We should move rapidly to incorporate into such analyses qualitative biomechanical indicators that contribute to a successful movement. These should be identified interactively by biomechanists, notational analysts and coaches, sport by sport and movement by movement, and validated against detailed biomechanical measurements in controlled conditions. Biomechanists and notational analysts, along with experts in other sports science disciplines – particularly motor control – should also seek to agree on, and measure, those performance indicators that are important from this perspective.

For the different types of game considered, it has become clear that the classification of the different action variables being used as performance indicators follows rules that transcend the sports. The selection and use of these performance indicators depend on the research questions being posed, but it is clear that certain guidelines will ensure a clearer and more accurate interpretation of these data. These are summarised below.

Match classification

Always compare with opponents' data and, where possible, with aggregated data from peer performances.

Biomechanical

Compare with previous performances and with team members, opponents and those of a similar standard. As well as presenting the original data analysis, consider presenting normalised data when a maximum or overall value both exists and is important or when inter-individual or intra-individual across-time comparisons are to be made.

Technical/tactical

The technical and tactical variables should be treated in the same way. Always normalise the action variables with the total frequency of that action variable or, in some instances, the total frequency of all actions, and present this data with the raw frequency or processed data.

Most of the research community in performance analysis have not followed these simple guidelines to date. We feel that the utility of performance analysis could be considerably enhanced if its practitioners agreed and implemented such conventions in the future.

9 Analysis of notation data: reliability

M. Hughes, S.M. Cooper and A. Nevill

9.1 Introduction

The key factor in any research that uses new equipment is the repeatability and accuracy of this equipment. In most performance analysis papers the researchers are presenting systems that have been specifically designed for that experiment. It is the exception (Hughes *et al.*, 1989; Wilson and Barnes, 1998) rather than the rule that papers presenting new systems produce evidence of systematised testing of the reliability of these new systems. A survey of papers presented in performance analysis at the first three world conferences on Science and Football (Reilly *et al.*, 1988, 1993, 1997), the first two conferences on Science and Racket Sports (Reilly *et al.*, 1995; Lees *et al.*, 1998) and the first two world conferences on the Science of Notational Analysis of Sport (Hughes, 1996a) produced 67 papers that were experimental studies with notation systems. Seventy per cent of these did not mention reliability studies (see Table 9.1). A further 15 per cent used correlations to provide evidence of the consistency of the repeatability of the data produced from the systems. Bland and Altman (1986) have demonstrated that correlations alone are often an incomplete process for confirming reliability.

The subsequent data analyses (see Table 9.2) used a multiplicity of techniques, but there were a large number of studies that did not present any statistics to compare sets of data. Those labelled 'not specific' did cite probability values, but

Table 9.1 An analysis of the different statistical processes used in reliability studies in some randomly selected performance analysis research papers

Statistical processes for reliability	No.	%
None	47	70
Correlation	10	15
Method of errors (%)	5	8
Chi-square	2	3
t-test	2	3
Cronbach's alpha	1	2
Total	67	100

Table 9.2 An analysis of the different statistical processes used in subsequent data analyses in some randomly selected performance analysis research papers

Statistical processes for data analysis	No.	%
Chi-square	21	29
None	19	26
Not specific	12	17
t-test	8	11
ANOVA	5	7
Factor analysis	2	3
ANCOVA	1	1
Mann Whitney	1	1
Hotelling T^2 test	1	1
Wilcoxon	1	1
Bivariate analysis	1	1
Total	72	100

did not mention which statistical process had been used. In a number of studies, parametric techniques were used with data that were non-parametric; although, in some cases, the means of the data sets appeared ordinal, they were often means of nominal data and therefore the use of a parametric test put the conclusions at risk.

There are many similarities in the nature of the data generated by experiments in performance analysis of sport. Although Atkinson and Nevill (1998) have produced a definitive summary of reliability techniques in sports medicine, there has been no similar attempt to make recommendations in the use of techniques in performance analysis for solving some of the common problems associated with these types of data. Some of the issues that are perceived as causes for uncertainty are explained below.

- It is vital that the reliability of a system is demonstrated clearly and in a way that is compatible with the intended analyses of the data. The data must be tested in the same way and to the same depth in which it will be processed in the subsequent analyses. In some cases the reliability studies were executed on summary data, and the system was then assumed to be reliable for all the other types of more detailed data analyses that were produced.
- In general, the work of Bland and Altman (1986) has transformed the attitude of sport scientists to testing reliability; can similar techniques be applied to non-parametric data?
- The most common form of data analysis in notation studies is to record frequencies of actions and their respective positions on the performance area; these are then presented as sums or totals in each respective area. What are the effects of cumulative errors nullifying each other, so that the overall totals appear less incorrect than they actually are?

- The application of parametric statistical techniques is often misused in performance analysis – how does this affect the confidence of the conclusions to say something about the data, with respect to more appropriate non-parametric tests?

By using practical examples from research, this chapter aims to investigate these issues associated with reliability studies and subsequent analyses in performance analysis.

9.2 The nature of the data, the depth of analysis

9.2.1 Sample data

As a test of inter-operator reliability, a squash match was notated in-event by two experienced analysts. A computerised system was used. The match was analysed live, rather than from videotape. It was a match in the team World Cup, played in Holland, July 1999. Both analysts had already gathered data for four matches that day and were therefore tired; errors could be expected. Both recorded the match from similar positions from behind the court, both using similar laptop computers with which they were very familiar. The data input system required the number of shots in each rally, the outcome, which player made the rally ending shot, the type of shot and from which position on the court this shot was struck (the court was divided into 16 position cells, coded by number). The system stored the data of each rally sequentially in the 'Access' database and, as part of the system, there was specifically written software to process the data into graphical output for feedback to coaches and athletes. The 'raw' data in the database was used, rather than the processed output, as this enabled certain questions to be posed that could not otherwise be answered from the processed data, which no longer retained the sequential nature of the data.

Analysing the total shots in each analysis of the match indicates a 100 per cent accuracy between the two operators (Table 9.3). The analysis of the different totals of shots in each game demonstrates how adding frequency data from two or more sources can hide differences. The different totals now indicate that there are errors, but they are all less than 1 per cent. This is a very simple example, and more complex data analyses are demonstrated below; adding data

Table 9.3 The total shots per game

	Analyst 1	Analyst 2	% Difference
Game 1	789	792	0.38
Game 2	439	435	0.91
Game 3	457	458	0.21
Total	1685	1685	0

together in this way will lead to masking of 'true' error figures. The results will always depend on the relative depth of analysis that is applied to the sequentiality of the data and also the definition of the terms involved in percentage error. Let us examine different ways of analysing these types of data.

9.2.2 *The sequential nature of data*

It is becoming more and more clear that the first step in a reliability test should always be to compare the raw data of the study, if this is possible, in their original form. Sometimes, in the case of pre-programmed computer systems, this is not possible. The raw data sets in this example from squash – two sets of columns – were scanned and it was seen that they were of different lengths. One of the sets of data had a series of null data that occupied a row of data. This could have been a software error, an operator error or a combination of the two. This row was deleted and the two sets of data were of equal length. To test for any further problems, differences in one of the variables, the number of shots in a rally, were plotted against time (Figure 9.1).

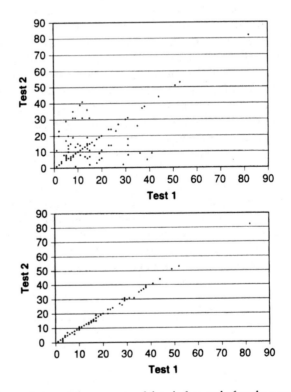

Figure 9.1 A correlation of the two sets of data before and after the extra lines of data were deleted.

The data approximately followed a straight line, until there was a sudden dispersion of data indicating another mismatch – either another 'software' error or one of the operators 'missed' a rally. Subjective interpretations were made to enter or delete data rows as appropriate. When the data differences were re-plotted, the 'straight line' extended further but there was another fan of data indicating another mismatch of lines of data. This process was repeated four times until the differences in the data were within the expected range from operator errors (see Figure 9.1). So the data had five errors in non-matching lines of data due to either operator or software error. The two data sets then appeared to match in length and content. The respective shot and/or error totals had not indicated these errors.

9.3 Consistency of percentage difference calculations

Consider now the simple concept of calculating the percentage difference in the repeatability of counting the number of shots in each rally. We have already seen the different values obtained by using the game totals and the match total. Let us examine some of the different possible interpretations of 'percentage difference'.

- There were 20 lines of data in which there were differences between the data sets – errors made – in counting the lengths of the rallies. There was an (adjusted) total of 105 rallies in the match, so the percentage error, based on the number of lines with differences in them, and the five mismatches, could be stated as 24.1 per cent of the number of rallies.
- The differences of the 20 error measurements totalled 37 shots, 1.85 shots/line. The average rally length was 16.2 shots, so the average percentage error per average rally length was 1.85/16.2 = 11.4 per cent.
- When each error was calculated as a percentage of the length of that particular rally, then the error on the length of the rally (1.85/9.25) averaged a 20.0 per cent error of the length of the respective rally.
- However, taking into account all the rallies, then by calculating:

$$[\Sigma(\text{mod}(V_1 - V_2))/V_{\text{TOTmean}}] \times 100\%$$

where mod is the modulus and Σ indicates the sum of; the overall percentage error figure for rally length comes out as 2.1 per cent, and V_{TOTmean} is the mean of the total variables measured.

By examining the data at different levels, and using different definitions for the calculations involved, very different values for the percentage error of the rally length have been obtained. There are no right and/or wrong answers in these scenarios, but it does emphasise the necessity for analysts to be very explicit when presenting these types of data analysis, so that their audience can clearly understand what is meant by the definition of 'percentage error' presented.

9.4 Processing data

Let us consider another example from these data. It would be expected, from experience of previous work in performance analysis, that a notation of position would result in the largest source of errors in this process. The positions were defined in a 16-cell distribution across the court (see Figure 9.2). Figures 9.3 and 9.4 show the data; a correlation was performed on the two adjusted sets of data ($R = 0.998$; adjusted $R = 0.987$), indicating strong reliability.

Comparing each pair of positions in each data line (Table 9.4) tallied the differences in position. The total number of differences is 34 in 104 measurements, which would seem to support Bland and Altman's (1986) statement that correlation alone is not sufficient to test reliability. The value of the differences was noted to examine how many were perceptual errors and how many were

Front Wall

1	2	3	4
5	6	7	8
9	10	11	12
13	14	15	16

Back Wall

Figure 9.2 Definition of positional cells across the squash court area.

Front Wall

13	4	3	17
4	5	3	3
21	2	2	9
8	1	1	8

Back Wall

Front Wall

16	0	3	17
8	3	2	4
23	2	0	11
6	0	3	7

Back Wall

Figure 9.3 The data added by column to give the positional frequency of rally ending shots in the example squash match data.

Table 9.4 The arithmetic differences in the positions recorded by the two analysts

Value of the difference	Frequency
-11	1
-8	1
-4	7
-3	2
-1	4
0	70
1	7
4	10
5	1
11	1
Total	104

likely to be typographical errors. The data in the shaded areas of Table 9.2 are attributed to typographical errors, as differences of 1, 3, 4 or 5 can be attributed to perceptual differences of the two analysts. There were 34 differences in 104 rallies in total, i.e. percentage error of 32.7 per cent, of which 31 were perceptual (29.8 per cent) and three were typographical (2.9 per cent).

By summing each column, the number of rally-ending shots played in each position in the court gives the totals shown in Figure 9.3. This is the way an analyst will usually add up the data to present patterns of play across a playing surface. Between these two sets of data there are 27 (26 per cent error) differences; from the data checked sequentially there were 34 (32.7 per cent error). The seven errors were missed due to the process of adding the data effectively eliminating some mistakes from the sum. Adding frequencies has masked errors again: this is a very dangerous contaminant of reliability tests of data of this nature, particularly where there are large amounts of data; compare the percentage errors of the total numbers of shots per game and per match.

A chi-square test of independence was used and a value of X = 11.16 (d.f. = 15) was obtained.

9.5 Visual interpretation of the data (Bland and Altman plot)

A Bland and Altman plot was constructed for the variable – number of shots in a rally (Figure 9.4). But what does this plot mean with this type of data? The range of errors across the mean (16.2) was found to be ±2, i.e. percentage error of 12 per cent. The normal process is to include on the graph an indication of the range of ±1.96 × SD to demonstrate how the data varied about the mean. The mean of the data is 16.2 shots with a standard deviation of 12.88; to plot these data as a Bland and Altman range is meaningless. The range is ±1.96 × SD = ±25.2 shots, but a range of ±25.2 is obviously unacceptable.

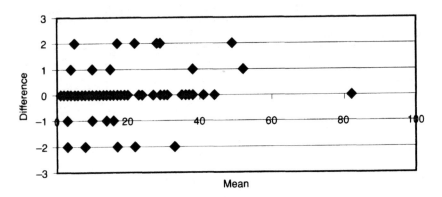

Figure 9.4   A Bland and Altman plot of the differences in rally length plotted against the
mean of the rally length from the two tests.

Confidence levels can be calculated (Bland and Altman, 1986), but perhaps, in notation studies with non-parametric data, we have to reconsider the logic behind the idea of these plots. The abscissa, with non-parametric data such as these, is different. This is not a continuous scale: each of the items (in this case the length of rally) is different; they are not related in any simple way. It is better to modify the graph to meet the same ideas of Bland and Altman – how much of the data falls within the range of accuracy set by the researcher (usually less than 5 per cent error)?

Instead of plotting the differences in measurements on the same subjects against their means (a continuous scale), let us consider summing the differences found and non-dimensionalising them with the sum of all the readings taken. Multiplying this by 100 will then, in effect, give a plot of percentage errors. Hence, by calculating and plotting

$$(\Sigma(\text{mod}[V_1 - V_2])/V_{\text{TOTmean}}) \times 100\%$$

against each variable reading, the data should fall within the range of percentage error already indicated as acceptable by the researcher. Let us examine a more complex reliability study.

9.5.1 *Sample data*

Consider an example from rugby union. Five analysts were to undertake an analysis of the 1999 World Cup and all five notated the same match twice each, so that data was available for intra- and inter-operator reliability studies. The data for the frequencies of the simple variable actions of tackle, pass, ruck, kick, scrum and line are shown in Table 9.5. An accepted way of testing these operators would be to use X-square and percentage differences for the

Table 9.5 Data from a rugby match notated twice by five different operators and presented as an intra-operator reliability analysis

Operators	L		S		I		G		O	
	V_1	V_2	V_1	V_2	V_1	V_2	V_1	V_2	V_1	V_2
Tackle	51	53	53	55	54	49	53	56	53	55
Pass	102	108	97	99	94	97	98	99	99	97
Kick	39	40	38	39	39	38	39	41	37	39
Ruck	49	49	50	51	49	46	51	49	44	49
Scrum	6	6	6	6	6	6	6	6	6	6
Lineout	14	15	14	14	14	15	14	15	14	15
$\Sigma \text{Mod}[V_1 - V_2]$	10		6		13		9		12	
$\Sigma [V_1 + V_2]/2$	264.5		261		258.5		263.5		260	
% error overall	3.8		2.3		5.0		3.4		4.6	

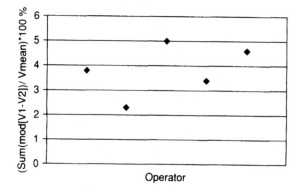

Figure 9.5 The overall data from the reliability study, the intra-operator test, presented as a function of the accuracy of each operator.

intra-operator tests, and to use Kruskal-Wallis and percentage differences for the inter-operator tests. The X-square and Kruskal-Wallis tests reflect the shape of the data sets rather than the actual differences, so there is a need for a second simple difference test. However, care must be taken with the percentage differ-ence test, in both its definition and its application.

The overall percentage differences in Table 9.5 show a satisfactory analysis, all of the operators scoring 5 per cent or less. They are presented in Figure 9.5 as a plot of $(\Sigma(\text{mod}[V_1 - V_2])/V\text{mean}) \times 100\%$ for each operator. As the ex-pected limits of agreement in this study were 5 per cent, all the data should fall below this line. There is a similarity in presenting the data in this way with that

Table 9.6 Data from a rugby match notated twice by five different operators and the differences for each operator expressed as a percentage of the respective mean

	L	S	I	G	O
Tackle	3.8	3.7	9.7	5.5	3.7
Pass	5.7	2.0	3.1	1.0	2.0
Kick	2.5	2.6	2.6	2.5	5.3
Ruck	0	2.0	4.0	4.0	10.8
Scrum	0	0	0	0	0
Lineout	6.9	0	6.9	6.9	6.9

of the Bland and Altman plot; the visual power of the chart is its ability to identify immediately those measurements that are in danger of transgressing the limits of agreements.

The processed data in Table 9.6 is the intra-operator test for reliability of each of the separate variables, with the difference between tests 1 and 2 shown as a percentage of the respective operators' mean for that particular variable. The error percentages for each of the variables vary much more, as would be expected, depending on the degree of difficulty of recognition of the defined action. This variation may depend on the accuracy of the operational definition of that action by the operators, the quantity of training of the operators, or it may be that there are accepted difficulties in observation of that particular variable.

Some observations are more difficult to make than others: for example, deciding when a maul becomes a ruck in rugby union or, using the previous example, the identification of position in a squash match. It is logical then to have different levels of expected accuracy for different variables. Some research papers have argued for different levels of accuracy to be acceptable, because of the nature of the data they were measuring (Hughes and Franks, 1991; Wilson and Barnes, 1998).

These data were then plotted as percentages against each of the actions in Figure 9.6 (left-hand plot). They can also be plotted against each of the operators (see Figure 9.6, right-hand plot) to test which of the operators are more, or less, reliable and by how much. These charts are very useful, highlighting which variables are contributing most to violations of the levels of expected reliability.

Table 9.7 shows this data expressed as an inter-operator test: now the mean value for each variable, for each operator, is expressed as a difference from the common mean, and calculated as a percentage of the respective common mean, i.e.

$$\% \text{ error} = [(V_M - V_m)/V_M] \times 100$$

where V_M is the common mean of all the operators, and V_m is the mean of the readings for each operator. This, however, must decrease the possible values

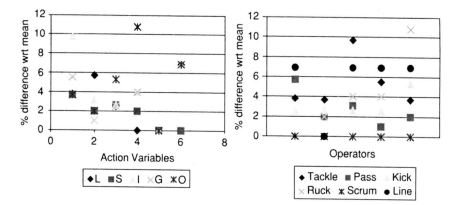

Figure 9.6 The data from the reliability study, the intra-operator test, presented as a function of the action variables and the operators.

Table 9.7 Data from a rugby match notated twice by five different operators and the mean for each operator expressed as a difference from the overall respective mean and then calculated as a percentage of the overall mean for each respective variable

	Mean	L	S	I	G	O
Tackle	53.2	2.3	1.5	0.9	2.4	1.5
Pass	99	6.1	1.0	3.5	0.5	1.0
Kick	38.9	1.5	1.0	1.0	3.3	2.3
Ruck	48.7	0.6	3.7	2.5	2.7	4.5
Scrum	6	0	0	0	0	0
Line-out	14.4	6.9	0	6.9	6.9	6.9

of error, as can be seen in comparing Table 9.6 and Table 9.7. It is less conservative to express these percentage errors as the difference in the variables for each operator as a percentage of the respective common means (Table 9.8 and Figure 9.7), i.e.

$$\% \text{ error} = [(V_1 - V_2)/V_M] \times 100$$

where V_1 and V_2 are the individual readings for each operator. It would be more conservative to examine the data for the largest differences between operators for each variable, and then examine whether these are acceptable. There are only small changes in the data from Table 9.6 to Table 9.8, which is unusual. The inter-operator reliability data in performance analysis almost always shows greater differences than intra-operator tests. From these figures it can be seen that the operator 'O' has three of the six variables with a percentage difference greater than 5 per cent; there is then a strong suggestion by the data that this operator should undergo more training.

Table 9.8 Data from a rugby match notated twice by five different operators and the differences for each operator expressed as a percentage of the overall mean for each respective variable

	Mean	L	S	I	G	O
Tackle	53.2	3.8	3.8	9.4	5.6	3.8
Pass	99	6.1	2.0	3.0	1.0	2.0
Kick	38.9	2.6	2.6	2.6	5.1	5.1
Ruck	48.7	0	2.1	6.1	4.1	10.3
Scrum	6	0	0	0	0	0
Lineout	14.4	6.9	0	6.9	6.9	6.9

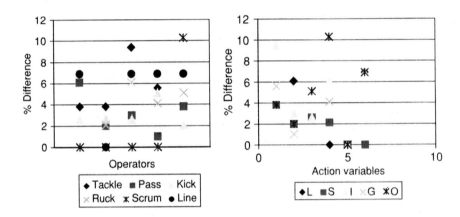

Figure 9.7 The data from the reliability study, the inter-operator test, presented as a function of the action variables and the operators.

The variables' distribution indicates that there is a consistent problem with the line-out – this was re-analysed, and most of the operators had notated an extra line-out that formed but did not actually take place. Because there were only 14 line-outs, this error was over 5 per cent (6.9 per cent) – an implicit problem, and common in notation, with sets of data that include small amounts of one or more variable. There would also seem to be a problem with the tackle variable: perhaps a more rigid operational definition is needed and more training of those operators who were inaccurate.

These observations are clear because of the power of these data presentations. Like the Bland and Altman Plot, this is a simple way of analysing the data, yet the visual impact of the data is powerful, immediate and easy to interpret. It should also be noted that, as the analysis has moved through this section, a number of different interpretations on the accuracy of these reliability studies have emerged, depending on the processes used and the definitions therein.

9.6 Statistical processes and reliability

Parametric statistical techniques are often applied to notational analysis data, either through ignorance, or lack of availability of software to provide appropriate non-parametric processes. Correlation was the most common technique used in confirming reliability, when a technique was used (Table 9.1). To test the sensitivity of correlation, and other techniques, more tests were applied to this data in Table 9.3, with the intent of assessing the threat to interpretation of reliability using these types of method. More correctly (Vincent, 1999), a X^2 analysis should be applied to data of this nature. As a means of comparison, these analyses are presented in Table 9.9. It is disturbing, given the percentage error calculations on the different variables above, that these tests indicate little sensitivity to the differences in the sets of data. It seems puzzling that these tests are so insensitive to differences as large as 5 per cent. This is a recurring prob-lem in analysis of elite sport, where margins between success and failure are considerably less than 5 per cent difference of a performance – the difference in the gold medal in a 400 m race and coming eighth is less than 2 per cent. How does a $P < 0.05$ relate to 'real' differences in performance? What size of differ-ences indicates a significant difference? To examine further the sensitivity of these tests to differences in data sets, the data for operator 'L' (Table 9.8) was manipulated with increments of 10 per cent changes in values.

When these differences were calculated all in the same direction, then the correlation coefficient, and the equivalent for X^2 analysis, was always perfect ($r = 1$). Consequently the increments were alternately added and subtracted from the items in descending order in the column of data (Table 9.10). The

Table 9.9 Correlation and X^2 analysis applied to the intra-operator data from Table 9.8.

	L	S	I	G	O
R	1.000	1.000	0.996	0.999	0.998
P value	0.000	0.000	0.000	0.000	0.000
X^2	0.069	0.005	0.383	0.165	0.289
P value	1.000	1.000	0.996	0.999	0.998

Table 9.10 Testing and comparing the efficacy of correlation and X^2 analysis in testing reliability of non-parametric data

% Differences	Correlation	P-values for X-square
10	0.989	0.94
20	0.948	0.416
30	0.866	0.036
40	0.744	0.001
50	0.595	0

Table 9.11 Kruskal-Wallis and ANOVA applied to the different variables for the five operators for inter-operator reliability

Variables	Kruskal-Wallis		ANOVA	
	H-value	P-value	F-value	P-value
Tackle	2.89	0.576	0.79	0.577
Pass	6.65	0.156	4.68	0.061
Kick	4.34	0.361	1.23	0.405
Ruck	6.03	0.197	1.45	0.342
Lineout	1.50	0.827	0.25	0.898

correlation data dropped below the $P > 0.05$ ($r_{crit} = 0.811$) level when differences of 40 per cent were added and subtracted to the original data, i.e. data sets over 30 per cent different would be indicated to be the same ($P < 0.05$) using correlation. The X^2 analysis data showed significant difference ($P < 0.05$) between 20 per cent and 30 per cent differences in the data.

The expected process to analyse the inter-operator data, non-parametric data across five different medians, would be to apply a Kruskal-Wallis on the medians of the operator for each variable. A number of the research papers examined used ANOVA, which is not the correct method for non-parametric data. The textbooks (Vincent, 1999) explain that this is a threat to the validity of the testing process, but by how much? There is little in the literature to help with this difficulty. Because of this a comparison of the Kruskal-Wallis analysis and ANOVA is presented in Table 9.11.

The surprising fact in the analysis is that neither test indicates that there are any significant differences at the $P < 0.05$ level. Both tests indicate that the biggest differences are in the 'pass' variable, while the tackle and the ruck had the largest differences (9.4 per cent and 10.3 per cent respectively) when calculated by percentage measurements. This is because these tests measure the overall variance about the median and mean – and may therefore miss one relatively large error measurement if all the others are close to the mean or median. It is interesting to manipulate the data, as before, to examine what levels of errors will cause these tests to indicate a violation of the accepted levels of reliability (Table 9.12).

The F value is a ratio of between-group variances to those within the groups. Consequently, although the means of the data are moving further apart, because the variation within each group varies as much, more in some cases, the F values do not approach any closer to the critical values. Consequently using these tests does not appear to be practical for reliability studies. Another common problem in notation studies is with the amounts of data collected for the reliability study – have enough repetitions been completed? How many are required? Perhaps the small amounts of data here contribute to the poor performance of these tests.

Table 9.12 Manipulation of some sample data to test the sensitivity of Kruskal-Wallis and ANOVA for inter-operator reliability

% changes	Kruskal-Wallis		ANOVA	
	H-value	P-value	F-value	P-value
5	2.89	0.576	2.84	0.118
10	6.65	0.156	0.86	0.551
15	4.34	0.361	1.57	0.297
20	6.03	0.197	0.97	0.503

The problem is exacerbated when the analyst starts to divide the data into further subcategories of actions or with respect to position. This is a recurring problem with performance analysis, not only in reliability studies but also in establishing 'performance profiles' (aggregated means of performance variables from a number of performances). How does an analyst know that enough performances have been analysed to stabilise these means? It is not enough to analyse an arbitrary number of matches – many research papers set the figure at six, or eight; some suggested that ten matches should be enough. But this will again depend on the nature of the data being analysed, and how it is being analysed. Surely investigating passes (about 300 per team per match) in soccer, using ten matches, will give stable means of passing patterns? But this will depend on how the playing surface is divided for the analysis. If the pitch is divided into 48 cells, then many of the cells will have non-significant totals and means. How many matches would be required to analyse shooting patterns in soccer (approximately 30 shots per team per match) or short corners in hockey (approximately ten corners per team per match)?

9.7 Conclusions

It was found that many research papers in performance analysis present no reliability tests whatsoever and, when they do, they apply inappropriate statistical processes for these tests, and the subsequent data processing. Many research papers have used parametric tests in the past – these were found to be slightly less sensitive than the non-parametric tests, and they did not respond to large differences within the data. Further, the generally accepted tests for comparing sets of non-parametric data, X^2 analysis and Kruskal-Wallis, were found to be insensitive to relatively large changes within the data. It would seem that a simple percentage calculation gives the best indicator of reliability, but it was demonstrated that these tests can also lead to errors and confusion. The following conditions should be applied.

- The data should initially retain its sequentiality and be cross-checked item against item.

- Any data processing should be carefully examined as these processes can mask original observation errors.
- The reliability test should be examined to the same depth of analysis as the subsequent data processing, rather than being performed on just some of the summary data.
- Careful definition of the variables involved in the percentage calculation is necessary to avoid confusion in the mind of the reader, and also to prevent any compromise of the reliability study.
- It is recommended that a calculation based on

$$(\Sigma(\text{mod}[V_1 - V_2])/V_{mean}) \times 100\%$$

(where V_1 and V_2 are variables, V_{mean} their mean, mod is short for modulus and Σ means 'sum of') be used to calculate percentage error for each variable involved in the observation system, and these be plotted against each variable, and each operator. This will give a powerful and immediate visual image of the reliability tests.

It is recommended that further work examine the problems of sufficiency of data first, to ensure that the data for reliability is significant, and also confirming that the data present in a 'performance profile' has reached stable means.

10 Establishing normative profiles in performance analysis

Mike Hughes, Steve Evans and Julia Wells

10.1 Introduction

A perennial question raised by analysts is how many matches, or how many performances, do I need to gather to ensure that the analyses of my team's (or athletes') performance really represent their average performance, i.e. is it truly their normative profile? In previous notation research there has been little statistical basis to quantify the number of matches analysed in providing a performance profile. The essential question is whether a consistent state of performance per match has been reached to classify the data as a profile. Large variations in the frequencies of the individual variables between matches can often occur, and this gives no credibility to the presentation of these data as a performance profile. In one soccer match a striker may have ten or 12 shots; the following week the same striker has none. McGarry and Franks (1994) suggested that players exhibit greater consistency in play when matched against the same opponent than against a different opponent. The authors concluded that invariant athletic behaviour is dependent to a certain degree on the level of analysis used. It is an implicit assumption in notational analysis that in presenting a performance profile of a team or an individual a 'normative profile' has been achieved. Inherently this implies that all the means of the variables that are to be analysed and compared have all stabilised. Most researchers assume that this will have happened if they analyse enough performances. But how many is enough? In the literature there are large differences in sample sizes. Just trawling through some of the analyses in a variety of sports shows the differences (Table 10.1).

If the data have not stabilised then any conclusions drawn by researchers must be questioned. Just analysing a large number of performances cannot guarantee that the profile is normative: instinct suggests that there must be ways of testing the data so that this can be confirmed or otherwise. These problems have very serious direct outcomes for the analyst working with coaches and athletes, both in practical and theoretical applications. It is vital when analysts are presenting profiles of performance about specific teams or athletes that they are definitely stable; otherwise any statement about that performance is spurious.

Table 10.1 Some examples of sample sizes for profiling in sport

Research	Sport	N (matches for profile)
Reep and Benjamin (1968)	Soccer	3,216
Eniseler et al. (2000)	Soccer	4
Larsen et al. (2000)	Soccer	4
Hughes et al. (1988)	Soccer	8 (16 teams)
Tiryaki et al. (2000)	Soccer	4 and 3 (2 groups)
Hughes (1986)	Squash	12, 9 and 6 – 3 groups
Hughes and Knight (1995)	Squash	400 rallies
Hughes and Williams (1987)	Rugby union	5
Smyth et al. (2001)	Rugby union	5 and 5
Blomqvist et al. (1998)	Badminton	5
O'Donoghue (2001)	Badminton	16, 17, 17, 16, 15
Hughes and Clarke (1995)	Tennis	400 rallies
O'Donoghue and Ingram (2001)	Tennis	1328 < rallies < 4300 (8 groups)

The whole process of analysis and feedback of performance has many practical difficulties. Let us consider some examples. In badminton the National Governing Bodies control player entry into international tournaments. At these international events the English national coaches are often in charge of large numbers of players (up to 20), playing in any of five disciplines spread throughout the day. A 12 hour day of match play is not uncommon, especially during the first three days of an event. Players expect to play twice or three times in one day, particularly if they have entered more than one discipline. Under these conditions it is impossible for the practising notational analyst to provide detailed performance analysis support for every player between matches or even overnight. The emphasis has to be to help the coaches have a more effective impact on developing optimal performance in certain key players. Due to the nature of the sport and its tournament structure, it is preferable that most of the analysis support is prepared before the event. Even so, the national coaches are well advised to prioritise and use the services of the performance analyst in the most effective way to achieve the goals set for that tournament and in the long term.

The performance analyst working in this applied environment will experience strict deadlines and acute time pressures defined by the date of the next tournament, the schedule and the draw. It is usual for the Badminton Association of England to receive a copy of the draw just one week before the tournament start: in squash there is not quite the same time restriction, but it can be worse in other cases. In soccer opponents are known for varying amounts of time – all season in the domestic leagues, two to three weeks in cup competitions, three to seven days in tournaments (such as European or World Cups). The need then is to provide coaches with accurate information on as many of the likely opposition players, or teams, in the amount of time available. This may be achieved by the instigation of a library of team and/or player analysis files, which can be extended over time and updated frequently. There should be a regular assessment of the effectiveness and efficiency of the notation and analysis procedures.

One method of improving the efficiency of the notation and analysis procedures is to notate the minimum number of matches necessary to provide an accurate, reliable performance profile for the team and/or player data library. At present this required number of matches is not known and may even be different for individual players, player groups, gender groups, playing standards and the different sport disciplines. Player files must be regularly updated by adding analyses from recent matches to the database held on each player.

Potter and Hughes (2001) reinforced the theory that the greater the database, the more accurate is the model against which to compare future performances. However, even this safeguard will have inherent disadvantages: it can be argued that as a database increases in size, it will become less sensitive to changes of playing patterns. Mosteller (1979) advised the use of match weighting in performance modelling, with recent games weighted much more heavily than earlier games. If the amount of data is known to establish statistically a player template, then as additional matches are added to the database the oldest dated matches may be dropped from the model. This will enable the model to respond to any long-term changes in a player's game.

There must be some way of assessing how data within a study are stabilising. The nature of the data itself will also affect how many performances are required – five matches may be enough to analyse passing in field hockey; would you need ten matches to analyse crossing or perhaps 30 for shooting? The way in which the data are analysed will affect the stabilisation of performance means – data that is analysed across a multi-cell representation of the playing area will require far more performances to stabilise than data that is analysed on overall performance descriptors (e.g. shots per match). Further, it is misleading to test data of the latter variety and then go on to analyse the data in further detail.

This chapter aims to explore strategies in addressing these problems in depth in two sports, drawing on recent research in squash and badminton, and then present further examples from other sports. The main thrust came from three studies: the first, in squash, raised the problem, a study in badminton explored the methodology, and then another study in squash applied it as part of the overall aims.

10.2 Development of the method

Data were used from a large number of sources for examples in this study, but the main sources of data came from three studies that examined some of these problems as a part of their overall aims. One was a study in badminton (Evans,

1999) and the others were in squash (Hughes *et al.*, 2000d; Wells and Hughes, 2001).

10.2.1 Patterns of play in women's squash

The same computerised notation system (Brown and Hughes, 1995) was used to record and analyse play, post-event, for both the squash studies. The first study was an analysis of women's patterns of play, so matches of elite ($N = 20$), county ($N = 20$) and recreational ($N = 20$) players were examined. A reliability study was completed by both operators notating the same match twice, comparing their own results (intra-observer reliability) and then comparing with each other (inter-observer reliability). The data was found not to differ significantly ($P < 0.01$) for both the summary data (shots per rally, winners per game, etc.) and analyses of distribution of particular shots across the court. (NB: The match notated for inter- and intra-observer reliability was a county standard match. It was found that notating the different standards of players required more skill as the level increased. Due to the different playing abilities and the different types of game it could be necessary, therefore, to notate a match from each standard of play. This would show that the operator notating the match was used to notating various standards of play; in this instance, elite, county and recreational women's matches. If this were done successfully then the results would be more valid and reliable than the results already shown in this study.)

The general data analyses in this study were preceded by an attempt to establish whether or not the profiles were stabilising. As a first attempt (since Hughes and McGarry, 1989), standard methods of comparing groups were used. Comparisons were made between means of sets of data after N matches and then compared with the means after ($N + 1$) matches, and then ($N + 2$); ANOVA was used to make these comparisons. Although the data was not parametric, it was felt, at the time, that the test was robust enough to withstand this fault. An example of the tests on data from eight, nine and ten matches is shown for each of the respective standards (Table 10.2). Table 10.2 shows that

Table 10.2 Levels of confidence between numbers of matches and playing standards

	P-Values			
	N	Elite	County	Recreational
No. of shots per match	8v9	0.86	0.72	0.67
	9v10	0.98	0.84	0.76
No. of rallies per match	8v9	0.92	0.99	0.88
	9v10	0.94	0.98	0.89
No. of shots per rally	8v9	0.98	0.84	0.99
	9v10	0.99	0.95	0.87

the elite players and county players did establish a playing pattern that could be said to be reproduced reasonably consistently. The recreational players failed to show any real significance at a suitable level, therefore a normal playing pattern was not established.

It must be understood that squash matches, even at the same level, can differ from one another. A question that arises from this is, how much can they differ before it is suspected that the difference is caused by something other than chance? Especially for the recreational playing standards, the differences were not caused by chance but by the fact that they have no fixed pattern of play. As players work their way up the different standards of play, set patterns emerge. The county players' data showed a set pattern forming, but this will not be fully achieved until the standard reaches the top level of squash, elite level. The elite players are at a level where a fixed pattern can be established. Although the average 'profiles' of the recreational players are relatively meaningless, they were included in the analyses to indicate comparative levels only.

These methods could be criticised on two levels. The use of ANOVA is not strictly appropriate, as the data are not parametric, but the test is a robust one that has been used in a number of studies analysing similar data. More importantly, ANOVA was designed to detect differences in sets of data and not really to indicate degrees of similarity – what do the differences signify in physical terms of performance? The P values do not relate directly to any performance values, and so it is difficult to interpret what the test is really indicating. The other problem with these analyses is that the levels at which these data were analysed were the most general – shots per rally, rallies per match, and so on – and could be expected to stabilise quite quickly, but what would be the effect of comparing the number of drop-shot winners from a particular area of the court? Would this deeper stratum of data require the same number of matches to stabilise, or more, or fewer matches? The final criticism is that the test is clumsy. Where do we start – after four matches or after ten matches? But in raising these questions with this piece of research we have at least brought into the open this real methodological problem of performance profiling. This led us to attempt to find a more direct and simpler way of testing these types of data.

10.2.2 Rally-end conditions in badminton

To explore the ideas that we had, we needed some accurate, real and reliable data. We decided to use some data gathered from the English national badminton squads playing in international competitions.

A notation system designed to record rally-end variables in badminton was known to be both valid and reliable. Inter- and intra-operator reliability ranged from 98.6 per cent (rally length) to 91.3 per cent (position). An English male player was selected for this study after consultation with the Performance Director of the Badminton Association of England. The badminton notation system was used to examine the cumulative means of selected variables over a series of 11 matches of this player.

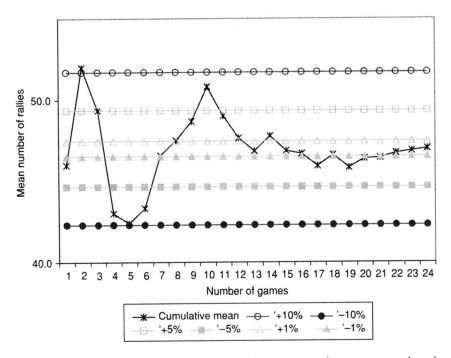

Figure 10.1 Example of the variation of the cumulative mean with increasing number of games analysed: mean number of rallies per game.

To examine whether a true performance profile had reached stable means, we felt that calculations of percentage differences could be a simple and direct way to estimate the stabilisation of the means. Percentage difference calculations have been found to be useful to evaluate the reliability of systems, for intra- and inter-operator observations, producing similar graphs to those of Bland and Altman (1986): see Hughes *et al.* (2002a). It was the shape of the Bland and Altman graphs that gave the idea of plotting a graph of the cumulative means of variables, with increase of the number of matches, hopefully showing a decreasing variation of the mean until it dips below a defined limit of error. Figure 10.1 shows an example where the variable is stable within a 10 per cent limit of error after five games, within a 5 per cent limit of error after 11 games and within a 1 per cent limit of error after 21 games. Unusual (outlier data) games, or matches, are shown clearly on the graph, and adjustments can be made if necessary.

Let n be the variable 'number of matches', g be the variable 'number of games', $N_{(E)}$ be the value of n to reach limits of error, and $N_{(T)}$ be the total number of matches.

Table 10.3 Description information of the matches analysed

Match number	Total no. of rallies	Total no. of shots	Mean no. of shots per rally	Standard deviation shots per rally	Maximum rally length (shots)
1	104	968	9.3	8.0	39
2	68	607	8.9	5.8	33
3	88	702	8.0	5.0	24
4	120	952	7.9	5.7	26
5	118	1196	10.1	7.1	35
6	64	545	8.5	6.5	31
7	97	789	8.1	5.6	28
8	78	576	7.4	4.9	27
9	124	896	7.2	5.4	33
10	104	713	6.9	4.1	19
11	153	1252	8.2	6.3	49
Range	89	707	3.2	n/a	30
Median	104	789	8.1	n/a	31
Mean	101.6	836.0	8.2	5.9	31.3
St. Dev.	21.4	229.8	0.9	1.1	5.1
SD/mean %	21.0	27.5	10.7	18.3	16.2

Cumulative mean = (sum of the frequencies of defined variable of 'n')/n

Limits of error (10%) = mean $N_{(T)}$ ± (mean $N_{(T)}$ × 0.1)

Limits of error (5%) = mean $N_{(T)}$ ± (mean $N_{(T)}$ × 0.05)

Limits of error (1%) = mean $N_{(T)}$ ± (mean $N_{(T)}$ × 0.01)

% difference = (no. of differing observations/total no. of observations) × 100

The frequencies of each variable per match were summated and the mean and standard deviation of the data set calculated (Table 10.3). Evaluating the relative size of the standard deviation to the mean (SD/mean%) enabled comparison of the variability of the data between different variables.

SD/mean% = (standard deviation/mean) × 100

The original purpose of gathering the badminton data was to analyse variable differences between matches/games won by Player A and lost by Player A in order to identify the existence of a winning and losing templates. t-tests were used to evaluate the significance of differences between these independent means. A significance level of $P = 0.01$ was set as some assumptions of the t-test were not met (non-parametric data).

Table 10.4 The means and limits of error of shots by game (Figure 10.5)

Game	Shots	Cum. Mean	Mean (24)	10%	10%	5%	5%	1%	1%
1	428	428.0	383.2	421.5	344.9	402.3	364.0	387.0	379.3
2	540	484.0	383.2	421.5	344.9	402.3	364.0	387.0	379.3
3	373	447.0	383.2	421.5	344.9	402.3	364.0	387.0	379.3
4	234	393.8	383.2	421.5	344.9	402.3	364.0	387.0	379.3
5	350	385.0	383.2	421.5	344.9	402.3	364.0	387.0	379.3
6	352	379.5	383.2	421.5	344.9	402.3	364.0	387.0	379.3
7	507	397.7	383.2	421.5	344.9	402.3	364.0	387.0	379.3
8	445	403.6	383.2	421.5	344.9	402.3	364.0	387.0	379.3
9	476	411.7	383.2	421.5	344.9	402.3	364.0	387.0	379.3
10	720	442.5	383.2	421.5	344.9	402.3	364.0	387.0	379.3
11	299	429.5	383.2	421.5	344.9	402.3	364.0	387.0	379.3
12	246	**414.2**	383.2	**421.5**	**344.9**	402.3	364.0	387.0	379.3
13	292	404.8	383.2	421.5	344.9	402.3	364.0	387.0	379.3
14	497	411.4	383.2	421.5	344.9	402.3	364.0	387.0	379.3
15	210	**397.9**	383.2	421.5	344.9	**402.3**	**364.0**	387.0	379.3
16	366	395.9	383.2	421.5	344.9	402.3	364.0	387.0	379.3
17	268	388.4	383.2	421.5	344.9	402.3	364.0	387.0	379.3
18	416	389.9	383.2	421.5	344.9	402.3	364.0	387.0	379.3
19	212	380.6	383.2	421.5	344.9	402.3	364.0	387.0	379.3
20	401	381.6	383.2	421.5	344.9	402.3	364.0	387.0	379.3
21	312	378.3	383.2	421.5	344.9	402.3	364.0	387.0	379.3
22	456	**381.8**	383.2	421.5	344.9	402.3	364.0	**387.0**	**379.3**
23	414	383.2	383.2	421.5	344.9	402.3	364.0	387.0	379.3
24	382	383.2	383.2	421.5	344.9	402.3	364.0	387.0	379.3
Sum	9196								
Mean	383.2								
St. Dev.	118.9								
SD/ave. %	31.0								

Frequency data were normalised to allow for true comparison of data from matches and games of differing lengths.

$$\text{Normalised match frequency} = (\text{match frequency/no. of rallies in match}) \times 100$$

$$\text{Normalised game frequency} = (\text{game frequency/no. of rallies in game}) \times 50$$

Bland and Altman (1986) compared the agreements between two sets of data with a simple plot of one test measurement against the other. A further plot of the differences between the test measurements against their means, the Bland and Altman plot, may be more informative (Atkinson and Nevill, 1998) in the assessment of agreement. The plot of cumulative means over a number of matches, with reference to the methods of agreement comparison described by Bland and Altman (1986), stimulated this application of statistical methods to establish performance templates. An example plot of the frequency of shots per game is shown in Table 10.4.

The number of games and/or matches, $N_{(E)}$, for each performance variable required to attain a stable cumulative mean within the set limits of error is summarised in Table 10.5. These values of $N_{(E)}$ (shaded areas) were calculated from the cumulative mean tables. The figures based on these tables provided visual evidence of the stability of the cumulative means (Figures 10.2–10.6). Also, the visual impact of the figures leads to recommendations for adjustment on $N_{(E)}$ values due to extreme frequency counts. For example, $N_{(E)} = 12$ for 'shots per game' at the 80 per cent confidence level. When compared with the other values of $N_{(E)}$ games for similar variables, this figure was not in keeping with the data type; it was too high. Examining the graph in Figure 10.2, it can be seen that the tenth game takes the data from within the limits of error to way outside. Looking at Table 10.4, it can be seen that the number of shots played in the tenth notated game was unusually high (freq.$_{(10)}$ = 720, mean$_{(24)}$ = 383), which took the cumulative mean temporarily out of the limits of error. Recommendations for amendment of the $N_{(E)}$ value are shown as bracketed values in Table 10.5.

The examination of the cumulative means by games and by matches for rallies, shots and shots per rally provided for verification of $N_{(E)}$. However, the game $N_{(E)}$ values (Table 10.5) were all less than the equivalent $N_{(E)}$ matches previously established, if the 'shots per game' amendment above is accepted. Direct comparison between games and matches will always be estimation as there are possibly two or three games in a match. This may be because there is less within-game variation of play than within-match variation. If a game template is established with less data than for a match, then it is more efficient for the performance analyst to examine data in this way, frequencies permitting. Investigation of other data is necessary to confirm or deny these conclusions.

10.2.3 *Movement patterns in elite women's squash*

As a direct application of this methodology developed in the badminton study, it was decided to use it in a study of movement in elite women's squash. Ten elite women squash players were selected for a detailed notational analysis of their movement patterns. The elite women's matches were previously recorded during the 1997 and 1999 British Open, the 1999 Test match and the 1999 World Championships. The squash matches were notated using a computerised system on Microsoft Access. Intra-observer and inter-observer reliability tests were carried out to test the reliability of the data input. To carry out intra-observer reliability, 100 movements were notated twice by the operators and the data compared. Unacceptable differences were found between the two sets of data. The operational definitions of those variables highlighted by the data plots – 'modified Bland and Altman plots' (Figure 10.7) – were redefined and the operators underwent further training. The third analysis of the same data produced acceptable differences (also in Figure 10.7); no significant differences (95 per cent level of confidence) were found between the sets of data (Tables 10.6 and 10.7).

Type of Variable	Combo. Variable	Player	Game/ Match	Match outcome	10% Limits of error	5% Limits of error	1% Limits of error
Rallies		Both	Match	Any	4	x (10)	x
Shots		Both	Match	Any	2	6	x
Shots/rally		Both	Match	Any	3	8	x
Rallies		Both	Game	Any	3	11	22
Shots		Both	Game	Any	12 (4)	15	22
Shots/rally		Both	Game	Any	6	15	21
Winners		A	Game (N)	A	5	5	10
Errors		A	Game (N)	A	10	11	12
Winners		Opp.	Game (N)	A	4	10 (4)	11
Errors		Opp.	Game (N)	A	9	10	12
Winners		A	Game (N)	Opp.	8	x	x
Errors		A	Game (N)	Opp.	4	9 (6)	x
Winners		Opp.	Game (N)	Opp.	4	x (4)	x
Errors		Opp.	Game (N)	Opp.	8	9	x
Smash	Winners	A	Match (N)	Any	6	8 (6)	0
Smash	Errors	A	Match (N)	Any	6	8	0
Smash	Winners	Opp.	Match (N)	Any	4	7	0
Smash	Errors	Opp.	Match (N)	Any	x	x	0
Position 3	Winners	A	Match (N)	Any	6	10	0
Position 3	Errors	A	Match (N)	Any	6	10	0
Position 3	Winners	Opp.	Match (N)	Any	7	10 (8)	0
Position 3	Errors	Opp.	Match (N)	Any	6	x	0

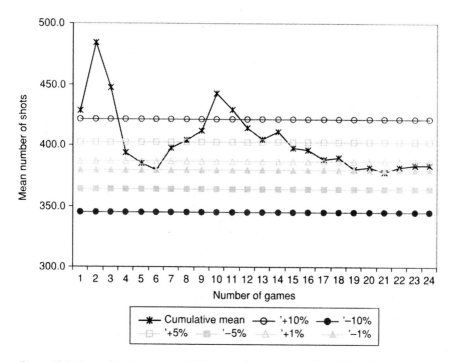

Figure 10.2 Example of percentage difference plot: mean number of shots per game.

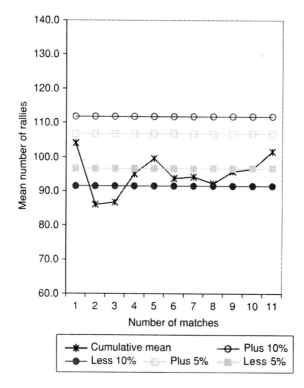

Figure 10.3 Example of percentage difference plot: mean number of rallies per match.

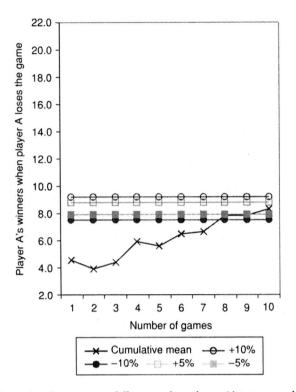

Figure 10.4 Example of percentage difference plot: player A's winners when player A loses the game.

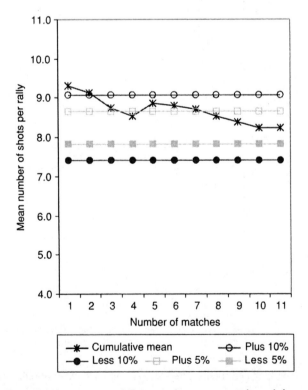

Figure 10.5 Example of percentage difference plot: mean number of shots per rally by match.

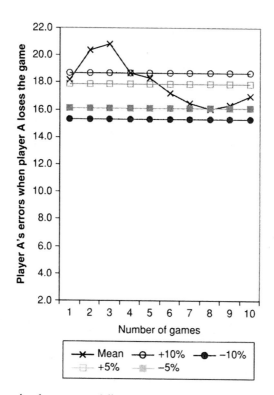

Figure 10.6 Example of percentage difference plot: player A's errors when player A loses the game.

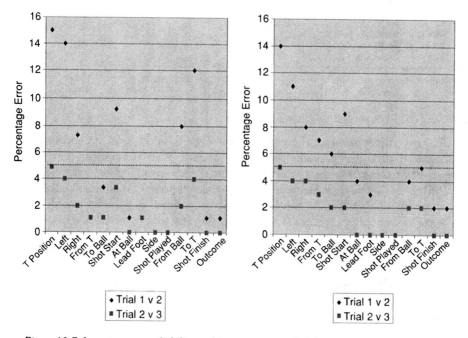

Figure 10.7 Inter-operator reliability and intra-operator reliability, using a modified Bland and Altman plot to demonstrate the percentage differences (Nevill *et al.*, 2002)

Table 10.6 Analysis of the stability of the profiles of winning shots and errors

Smash	80%	90%	98%	
Constable's winners	6	6	>11	matches
Constable's errors	8	>11	>11	matches
Opponent's winners	6	10	>11	matches
Opponent's errors	9	10	>11	matches
All winners	6	10	>11	matches
All errors	9	>11	>11	matches

Table 10.7 Games that player A wins – player A data

Winners/ 50 shots	Game	Sum	Cumulative	Mean (24)	10%	10%	5%	5%	1%	1%
14.1	1	14.1	14.1	14.2	15.6	12.7	14.9	13.4	14.3	14.0
13.8	2	27.9	14.0	14.2	15.6	12.7	14.9	13.4	14.3	14.0
18.2	3	46.1	15.4	14.2	15.6	12.7	14.9	13.4	14.3	14.0
17.7	4	63.8	16.0	14.2	15.6	12.7	14.9	13.4	14.3	14.0
10.3	5	74.1	14.8	14.2	15.6	12.7	14.9	13.4	14.3	14.0
11.8	6	85.9	14.3	14.2	15.6	12.7	14.9	13.4	14.3	14.0
14.9	7	100.8	14.4	14.2	15.6	12.7	14.9	13.4	14.3	14.0
8.5	8	109.3	13.7	14.2	15.6	12.7	14.9	13.4	14.3	14.0
14.7	9	124	13.8	14.2	15.6	12.7	14.9	13.4	14.3	14.0
16.7	10	140.7	14.1	14.2	15.6	12.7	14.9	13.4	14.3	14.0
14.8	11	155.5	14.1	14.2	15.6	12.7	14.9	13.4	14.3	14.0
16.4	12	171.9	14.3	14.2	15.6	12.7	14.9	13.4	14.3	14.0
11.4	13	183.3	14.1	14.2	15.6	12.7	14.9	13.4	14.3	14.0
14.9	14	198.2	14.2	14.2	15.6	12.7	14.9	13.4	14.3	14.0
198.2	Sum									
14.2	Mean									
2.8	St. dev.									
19.8	SD/ave. %									

10.2.3.1 The analysis procedures employed

Using analyses based on the work of Evans (1999) – the work on badminton summarised in the previous part of this chapter – an attempt was made to establish a true representation of a 'normal' movement profile, creating an accurate movement profile for elite women squash players. The critical research question was: what is the appropriate number of matches required in order to establish movement sequences that are stable? The tests involved investigating the mean values of different variables between each match (player) analysed. The variation, or lack of it, would test when a normal movement sequence would be established.

Table 10.8 summarises the different variables being analysed in order to establish movement profiles. Each variable has its own individual representation for where and when the profile is appearing (examples are shown in Figure

Table 10.8 Number of matches required to establish movement profiles of elite women squash players using percentage errors of between 5% and 10%

Variable	% Error		Variable	% Error	
1. 'T' position	Below 10%	Below 5%	7. Lead foot	Below 10%	Below 5%
NN	7	7	Correct	5	7
NO	8	–	Incorrect	8	–
OO	8	9	Two-footed	3	9
2. Foot position			8. Side		
1,1	7	8	Forehand	6	6
8,1	5	7	Backhand	5	6
1,2	8	9			
3. From the 'T'			9. From the ball		
Split-jump	6	7	Rotate	7	8
Side-step	9	9	Push	6	6
Forward	5	6	Stand	9	9
Movement through	7	7	Movement through	7	–
4. To the ball			10. Back to the 'T'		
Chassis-step	9	9	Chassis-step	8	–
Forward	6	8	Backward	8	9
Side-step	5	9	Forward	7	8
Side-step forward	5	9	Chassis-step forward	9	–
5. Shot start			11. Shot finish		
Cell 13	3	9	Cell 5	5	6
Cell 12	6	7	Cell 12	7	9
Cell 16	8	8	Cell 16	6	7
Cell 5	6	6	Cell 13	6	7
6. At the ball			12. Outcome		
Step	5	6	Rally continues	5	6
Stride	7	8	Winner	2	5
Stand	7	7	Error	7	9
Lunge	6	8			

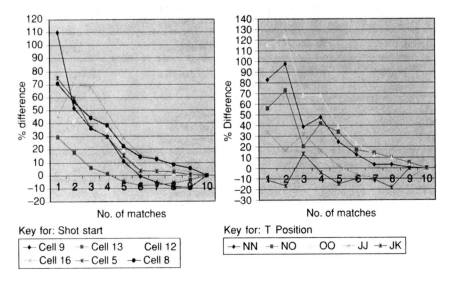

Figure 10.8 Using percentage difference distribution to display the pattern for the number of matches required to establish elite player movement profiles for the shot start position and for the different positions at the 'T'.

10.8). This clearly demonstrated the pattern of stabilisation towards the mean. The danger with using this percentage error method is that the data will naturally move towards the mean. However, extreme numbers cannot be hidden, as displayed in the results. For example, Figure 10.10 demonstrated for 'T' position, 'JK' (these are two of the data cells for court position) stabilisation occurring around five to seven matches, but was increased to eight due to an extreme value. This is why it is important to try to understand the nature of the data. The results clearly showed similarities and differences of variability between the different types of data. The percentage error distribution for 'T' position and foot position displayed similarities due to the fine detail required to analyse these positions. An overall average was calculated for a percentage error of below 10 (6.4). This showed that for the collection and analysis of movement data, an average of seven players' matches would be sufficient to reach a profile for elite women squash players.

10.2.4 *Other examples*

10.2.4.1 *Soccer*

In a study analysing passing patterns in soccer, the variable that was defined as most difficult to replicate was the position on the pitch of the action. Before the variation of passing sequences and duration were analysed with respect to pitch position, the reliability of the process was tested in the appropriate methods

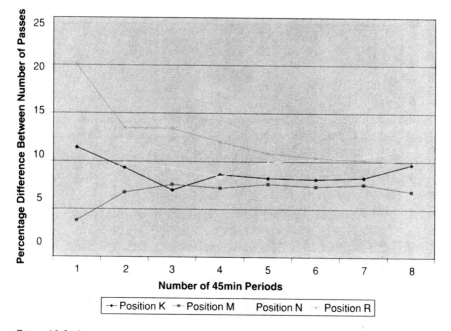

Figure 10.9 Aggregate percentage of passes completed in or from each of the selected pitch positions for unsuccessful teams.

already demonstrated. It was shown to be accurate within 10 per cent error, which was deemed acceptable in this study, given the camera angles etc. More importantly for this example, a modified Bland and Altman test was completed on four random pitch positions to investigate how quickly the data would stabilise with respect to pitch position. Because different parts of the pitch see different amounts of action, the plots were made for four positions on the pitch. As shown in Figures 10.9 and 10.10, the percentage of passing actions in all four pitch positions begin to stabilise around the fifth 45-minute period, suggesting the data collected is valid to utilise and apply to larger samples. Therefore, it is deemed that all pitch positions would be valid to analyse for passing patterns for unsuccessful teams.

10.2.4.2 Rugby union

Hughes and White (1997) established the validity of the computer notation system utilised in this study. Statistical tests reported no significant differences ($r < 0.98$) when the results produced by the computer system were compared to the results of a hand notation system. Further, the inter-observer reliability test found differences of 1.69 per cent and 3.51 per cent. The intra-observer reliability tests found differences of 3.44 per cent and 3.16 per cent in the data collected. The accepted level of error was 5 per cent. All reliability test results fell

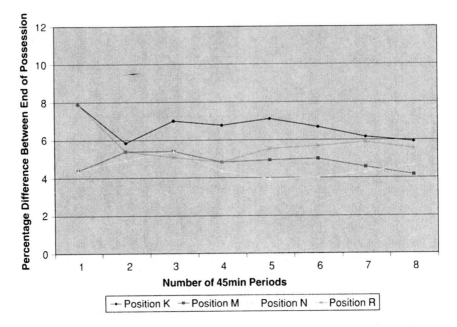

Figure 10.10 Aggregate comparison of the percentage of possession that is lost either in or from each of the four positions of the pitch for unsuccessful teams.

Table 10.9 Number of matches that need to be analysed to achieve a true average that represents the population

Variable	Number of matches	Averages per team, per half
Tackles (Fig. 4.1)	5	25–26
Passes (Fig. 4.2)	5	48–49
Kicks (Fig. 4.3)	4	11–12
Rucks (Fig. 4.4)	5	21–22
Mauls (Fig. 4.5)	7	5–6
Scrums (Fig. 4.6)	3	6–7

inside this boundary, thus no significant differences were found between analysts and the test–re-test procedure.

The normative profiles (Marshall and Hughes, 2002) demonstrated that a sufficient number of games were analysed to provide averages for the main actions that were representative of the population. Research by Hughes *et al.* (1996) notated only five matches. The normative profiles illustrated that at least seven matches needed to be analysed for the results of the maul to be representative of the population. Therefore, all results containing information on the maul in 1994 may not be a true representation of elite-level women's rugby (see Table 10.9 and Figures 10.11–10.13).

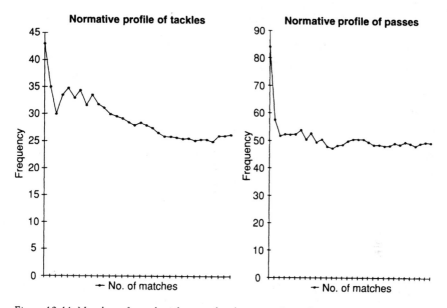

Figure 10.11 Number of matches that need to be notated to achieve a critical number of tackles and passes representative of elite-level women's rugby.

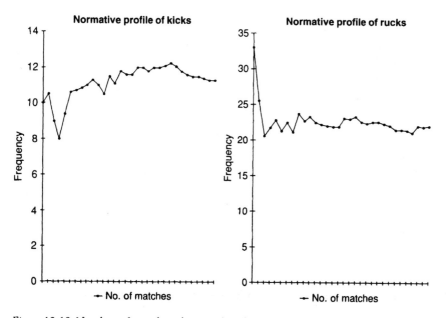

Figure 10.12 Number of matches that need to be notated to achieve stability in the number of kicks and rucks representative of elite-level women's rugby.

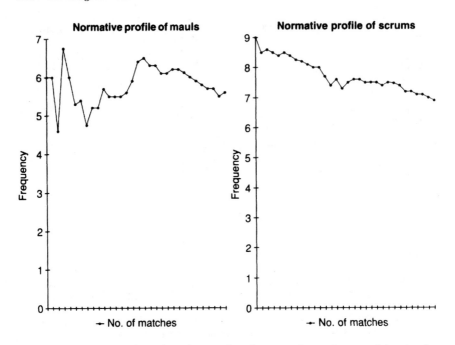

Figure 10.13 Number of matches that need to be notated to achieve stability in the number of mauls and scrums representative of elite-level women's rugby.

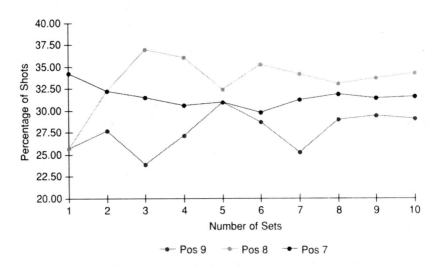

Figure 10.14 Accumulated means of attacking positions of elite volleyball teams.

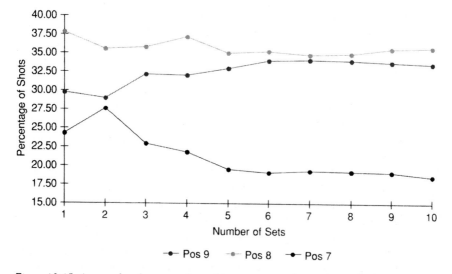

Figure 10.15 Accumulated means of attacking positions of non-elite volleyball teams.

10.2.4.3 Volleyball

The research of Daniel and Hughes (2001) employed similar reliability tests and also the same methods to establish performance profiles. However, the data in this study showed up something unusual. The line charts (Figures 10.14 and 10.15) test the stability of the profile data. The lines for elite teams' attacking position stabilised to 5 per cent after eight sets; data for non-elite teams stabilised much sooner, after only five sets. Previously, in other sports, the elite performers' patterns of play stabilised earlier than the lower standards of player. This discrepancy must be a function of the types of skill specific to volleyball.

10.3 Conclusions

From the studies summarised and discussed in this chapter, the following conclusions can be drawn.

- This method clearly demonstrates that those studies assuming that four, six or eight matches or performances are enough for a normative profile, without resorting to this sort of test, are clearly subject to possible flaws. The number of matches required for a normal profile of a subject population to be reached is dependent on the nature of the data and, in particular, the nature of the performers.
- Previous literature declared profiles of performance without adequately tackling the problem of quantifying the data required in creating a normative template. The badminton notation system was used to examine the cumulative means of selected variables over a series of 11 matches of a

player. A template, at match $N_{(E)}$, was established when these means became stable within set limits of error (LE). *T*-tests on the variable means in games won and games lost established the existence of winning and losing templates for winners and errors. Match descriptors (rallies, shots and shots per rally) were independent of match outcome. General values of $N_{(E)}$ established for data types (10 per cent LE) were three matches (descriptive variables), four (winners/errors (w/e)), six (smash + w/e), seven (position + w/e). Respective values at 5 per cent LE were 7, 5, 8 and 10. There was little difference in the values of $N_{(E)}$ when variable means were analysed by game than by match.

- The number of matches required to establish a profile of elite women's movement was dependent on the nature of the data. For elite women, profiles were achieved within three to nine matches (under 10 per cent error) depending on the variables being analysed.
- The main problems associated with any primary study aiming at establishing previously unrecorded 'normal' profiles remains reliability and accuracy. Any future studies that proclaim data as a performance profile should provide supportive evidence that the variable means are stabilising. A percentage error plot, showing the mean variation as each match/player is analysed, is one such technique. This can be adapted to different sports when analysing profiles/templates of performance.

For the working performance analyst the results provide an estimate of the minimum number of matches to profile a performance. While the results may be limited, the methodology of using graphical plots of cumulative means in attempting to establish templates of performance has been served.

11 Models of sports contests

Markov processes, dynamical systems and neural networks

Tim McGarry and Jürgen Perl

11.1 Introduction

Science is a formal method of enquiry through which knowledge is generated in successive fashion using the processes of description, explanation and prediction (i.e. description → explanation → prediction → description etc.). In this chapter, we consider the analysis of sports behaviours within this scientific framework. From this viewpoint, we report on contemporary research that has sought to analyse sports contests using various models of sports performance. The incompleteness of the various models developed to date, however, indicates the difficulties presented in identifying a formal description for sports contests.

The outline for this chapter is as follows. The first section introduces the notion that the behaviours and outcomes in sports contests can be analysed on the basis of chance. This idea led us (McGarry and Franks, 1994) to analyse the shot selection patterns of squash players as a random process. The section that follows therefore details the main results from this line of research. These findings in turn led to our consideration of sports contests in terms of a dynamical system (McGarry *et al.*, 1999), a brief account of which is offered in the subsequent section. The last section also considers sports contests as dynamical processes, but this time from the standpoint of neural networks. We finish by suggesting that the various types of model presented herein need not be considered as exclusive. Instead, a hybrid type of system description (or model) for sports contests may well be appropriate in the future, as we seek to fuse the various contributions to knowledge that each line of research enquiry has yielded to date.

11.2 Sport and chance

Sports behaviours are uncertain rather than certain and, as such, can be approximated on the basis of chance, or probability. For example, the frequency distribution of passing sequences in soccer follows a well-defined structure that is known as the negative binomial distribution (Reep and Benjamin, 1968). Simply put, the frequencies of passing sequences decrease as the length of the passing sequences increases in a lawful way. The finding that longer passing sequences yielded lower frequencies is expected, on account that the likelihood of the sequence being broken would be predicted to increase as the length of the sequence increases. Notwithstanding, the stability of these binomial patterns in time, together with the reported 1/9–1/10 goal/shot ratio, led Reep and Benjamin to the following statistical interpretation – that chance has an important influence on the behaviours and outcomes of a soccer match. Subsequent studies have confirmed repeatedly the general finding that sports behaviours in various sports contests can be described on the basis of chance.

Reep and Benjamin analysed a technical action in terms of its outcome. For example, the outcome of a pass to a team-mate was recorded in terms of whether it was successful or unsuccessful. In this way the sequences of successful passes were recorded for later analysis. The outcome of a shot on goal was similarly recorded in terms of whether it was successful or unsuccessful, i.e. whether a goal was scored or not. The findings of Reep and Benjamin were interpreted by some soccer practitioners as a template for soccer success, on which the 'long-ball' or 'direct-play' strategy was formulated. While the particulars of this interpretation remain a point of contention among some, there is little argument regarding Reep and Benjamin's thesis that soccer behaviours can be described (and prescribed) on the basis of chance, or probability. The issue at hand, therefore, is one of managing chance so as to maximise the upsides (rewards) and minimise the downsides (risks). With this intention of improved decision-making in mind, we (McGarry and Franks) undertook a series of studies that analysed the shot selection behaviours of players in squash contests as a random process. First, the types of shots were recorded in sequence for each rally of a squash contest. These shot sequences were subsequently analysed in terms of their probabilities of occurrence. For example, if Player A produced a serve, then what is the probability that Player B responded with a drive, drop, volley, etc.? Similarly, if Player B made a drop shot, what is the probability that Player A replied with a drive, drop, lob etc.? In this way a stochastic process, or model, was developed that sought to describe the sequence of shot behaviours as a probability structure. The term 'stochastic' means 'random'. The behaviours of the stochastic model were investigated using simulation procedures.

11.2.1 Stochastic (Markov) processes, shot selections and outcomes in squash contests

Imagine a system of many units (e.g. A, B, C, D, etc.) whose behaviour is characterized by the random switching from one unit to another unit (e.g. A → C → D → A → B etc.). If the probabilities of switching between the various units are known, then the probabilities of any sequence of switches within the system is also known (using appropriate calculations). The behaviour of the system can therefore be thought of and analysed as a stochastic process. Furthermore, if the switching from one unit to another unit depends only on where the system is at present (i.e. in which unit the system currently resides), then the stochastic process is said to possess Markov properties. In other words, there is sufficient information in the present unit, or state, to predict the immediate future of the system without regard for the past. The path that the system took to get to the present is therefore of no consequence as to where the system will switch to next. For example, in a system whose behaviour switches from A → C → D → A → B etc., the system is characterised as a Markov process if the switch from D to A is dependent only on D, and independent of the sequence of steps that the system took to get to D (i.e. A → C → D). The same condition applies for any of the other units in which the system may reside (e.g. A, B, C, D, etc.) We analysed the shot selection behaviours in squash contests as a Markov process.

The shot data, including the player, the type of shot selected, and where on court the shot was initiated, was collected from videotape records of international squash contests (see McGarry and Franks (1996a, 1996b) for further details). Subsequent analysis of these data yielded a playing matrix for each individual. The playing matrix contained two distinct sets of data, a *shot–response* matrix (for an example, see Table 11.1) and a *winner–error* matrix (for an example, see Table 11.2). The shot–response matrix contained the frequency distribution of shots selected by an individual in reply to each type of antecedent shot produced by the opponent. The winner–error matrix contained the frequency distribution of the outcomes that were associated with each type of shot produced by the individual, as yielded from the shot–response matrix.

Table 11.1 contains the frequencies of the various shots selected by a player in response to the various antecedent shots selected by the opponent. The frequency distribution of a given shot by the player is presented in rows, and the array of shot responses to each type of antecedent shot from the opponent is presented in columns. The shot code that references each column is found in parentheses in the shot listings that reference each row. The data in Table 11.1 therefore can be read by row or by column, as required. For example, in reply to the serve (S) from the opponent, the player produced one drive (A), two cross-court boasts (D), nine long volleys (I) and 12 long cross-court volleys (J) (see column S, Table 11.1). Thus, the shot probabilities in reply to the serve obtained from these data are 0.042, 0.083, 0.375, and 0.500, respectively. Similarly, Table 11.2 contains the frequencies of the various outcomes that were associated with the shots produced by the player. The column data indicate that the serve (S) yielded no outcomes whatsoever, as expected. In contrast, the drive produced one unconditional winner, four conditional winners, two unforced errors, zero forced errors and three lets (see column A, Table 11.2). In other words, the drive shot for this player won five points (winners), lost two points (errors) and produced three neutral (let) outcomes. The outcome frequencies for the other shot types from the same player are listed in their respective columns. Once again, the outcome probabilities for each shot type are easily obtained from the frequency data, as required.

The sequence of shots in a squash rally were analysed as a stochastic (Markov) process as presented in schematic form in Figure 11.1. The system begins in an initial state (shot, i.e. serve) before switching in random fashion to the next

Table 11.1 Shot–response profile for an individual player

Shot response (player)	Antecedent shot (opponent)															Total
	S	A	B	C	D	E	F	G	H	I	J	K	L	M	N	
Serve (S)	1	–	–	–	–	–	–	–	–	–	–	–	–	–	–	–
Drive (A)	–	56	24	1	6	2	3	1	1	17	7	–	–	1	6	126
XC-drive (B)	–	34	11	2	5	–	4	–	–	13	4	1	–	–	3	77
Boast (C)	–	–	–	–	2	1	–	–	–	–	2	–	–	–	1	6
XC-boast (D)	2	19	9	–	4	4	–	–	–	4	4	–	–	–	–	46
Drop (E)	–	6	2	–	18	11	6	3	2	–	–	–	–	–	2	50
XC-drop (F)	–	2	–	2	4	–	1	1	1	1	1	–	–	–	–	13
Volley (short) (G)	–	14	7	–	–	–	–	–	–	1	4	–	–	–	5	31
XC-volley (short) (H)	–	6	–	–	–	–	–	–	–	1	1	–	–	–	–	8
Volley (long) (I)	9	1	2	–	–	–	–	–	–	–	–	–	–	2	12	26
XC-volley (long) (J)	12	10	2	–	–	–	–	–	–	2	3	–	–	–	2	31
Volley-boast (K)	–	–	1	–	–	–	–	–	–	–	–	–	–	–	–	1
XC-volley-boast (L)	–	5	–	–	–	–	–	–	–	–	–	–	–	–	–	5
Lob (M)	–	–	–	–	–	–	–	1	–	–	–	–	–	–	–	1
XC-lob (N)	–	–	–	1	1	–	3	1	–	–	–	1	–	1	2	9
Total	24	153	58	5	40	18	17	7	4	39	26	2	–	4	33	430

Note: The shot codes for the opponent are given in parentheses in the list of shots for the player.

Table 11.2 Winner–error profile for an individual player

Outcome	Current shot (player)															Total
	S	A	B	C	D	E	F	G	H	I	J	K	L	M	N	
Unconditional winner	–	1	1	–	–	4	4	3	–	–	–	–	–	–	–	13
Conditional winner	–	4	–	3	1	10	1	2	2	2	1	–	–	–	–	26
Unforced error	–	2	1	–	2	4	–	2	–	–	–	–	1	–	–	12
Forced error	–	–	–	1	1	1	–	–	–	–	–	–	–	–	–	3
Let	–	3	1	–	–	2	–	1	–	4	–	–	–	–	–	11
Total	–	10	3	4	4	21	5	8	2	6	1	–	1	–	–	65

Note: See Table 11.1 for a list of shot codes.

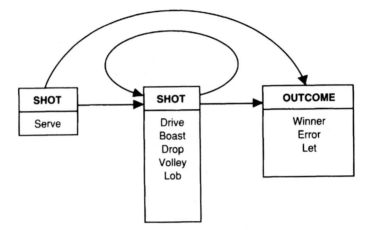

Figure 11.1 Stochastic (Markov) processes for the sequence of shots and outcomes produced in a squash rally.

state (shot). The system likewise switches at random to the next state, and so on, until the end state (outcome) is reached. The path that the system takes, known as a random walk, is of unspecified length and is thus represented using a recursive loop (see Figure 11.1). To provide an example of how the stochastic (Markov) process works, we will now take a short random walk through the system.

The system begins in its starting state which necessarily is the serve, as this type of shot is used to begin each rally. From there, the system passes to the next state in the sequence on the basis of probability. Keep in mind that the probabilities for switching between states when analysing a sports contest are obtained from the recorded data of two players. In our example, we take the data in Tables 11.1 and 11.2 as representing the probabilities of shot selection and outcome for the player that serves. The decision to be made on the basis of probability is which next state the system is to switch to, an outcome state or a shot state. First, the winner–error profile is inspected for the player that made the serve, and an outcome is assigned, or not, based on probability. From Tables 11.1 and 11.2, we see that zero outcomes were assigned to 24 serves, indicating that the serve did not result in an outcome for this player on any instance. The system therefore passes from the serve state to the next shot in the sequence. The next shot will be decided on a random basis as informed from the opponent's data (not shown). We therefore suppose that the next shot by the opponent is a short volley. From this state an outcome is assigned, or not, as indicated earlier (once again the data are not shown). In this example, we imagine that the system once more passes to the next shot in the sequence. From Table 11.1, we see that the server responded to a short volley with probabilities of 1/7, 1/7, 3/7, 1/7 and 1/7, for the drive, cross-court boast, drop, cross-court drop and cross-court lob, respectively. On this occasion, we suppose that the server responds with a drop shot, and furthermore that an outcome is assigned. Of 50 drop shots played by the server (see row E, Table 11.1), 21 shots resulted in an outcome (see column E, Table 11.2). Furthermore, of the 21 drop shots that produced an outcome, 14 shots yielded some type of winner, five shots resulted in some type of error and two shots finished in a let. In this example, we assign a winner to the drop shot played by the server and the rally ends.

The above example presents a random walk through the system for a single squash rally. Of course the system can take many different paths, of many different lengths, with various outcomes, as determined on the basis of chance in each instance. This random (Markov) process repeats for each rally within a contest. Since the outcome of each rally is known, a score is kept and the contest ends when one player reaches a winning score. Since the outcome for a squash contest will vary, the squash contest is repeated a number of times using simulation procedures until a predicted outcome is settled upon. In simulation procedures the stability of the final prediction is an important consideration. In our studies of squash contests, we selected to contest the playing profiles 1,000 times. We reasoned that this number of contests provided an acceptable degree of stability in the final prediction (standard error ≈ 0.016 for $P = q = 0.5$).

11.2.2 Identification of optimal decision-making strategies

The above section details how a squash contest might be described in terms of a stochastic process. The same type of description might be applied equally well to other types of sports contests. In this section, we address some of the possible benefits of using this type of approach for sports analysis.

The valid construction of a stochastic model for sports contests has a twofold application: firstly as a descriptor of sports behaviours, and secondly as a predictor of future sports performance. The ability to predict the future on the basis of the past, if possible, gives the sports practitioner (not to mention the sports gambler) an immense advantage. If sports performances can be predicted with accuracy, then those strategies that maximise or minimise the desired behaviours and outcomes can be identified and planned for in advance. For example, a player's shot–response and/or winner–error profile might be changed in systematic fashion and the predicted effects on the final outcome analysed. In this way a shot–response profile might be 'tweaked' towards maximising a predicted winning outcome. In principle, this information could be used in future practice settings by the coach and/or athlete to help shape the shot-selection responses towards a winning profile. We present an example of how such a strategy might be identified from the recorded data.

Inspection of Table 11.2 indicates that the player's winner–error profile is influenced strongly by that player's short game (shots C–H). In particular, we see that the drop shot yielded 21 of 65 outcomes (32.3 per cent), including 14 winners (66.7 per cent), five errors (23.8 per cent) and two lets (9.5 per cent). In other words, the player benefited from playing a strong short game against his (her) opponent with high usage of the drop shot. On this information, a subsequent opponent might determine it a good idea not to get drawn into a short game against this player, if possible. This strategy would require the opponent to minimise those conditions from which the player might instigate a short game in order to make use of the drop shot. On viewing the player's shot–response profile, we find that of the 50 drop shots selected by the player, 18 (36 per cent) and 11 (22 per cent) were made in response to the cross-court boast (D) and drop shot (E), respectively (see row E, Table 11.1). One strategy for the future opponent therefore might be to minimise his (her) frequency of cross-court boasts and drop shots, on the supposition that this tactic might be expected to reduce the frequency of drop shots that the player will select to reply with. In general terms, this would mean the opponent using a percentage strategy that is aimed towards a long game, and refusing when possible to get drawn into a short game. This strategy can be used in practice sessions when preparing for specific future matches. The use of gaming simulations, where the shot selection patterns, and strategies, for a future contest can be practised using video-like type of games, offers a striking example of this type of possible application for sports practice.

11.2.3 Interactions between winner–error profiles

Unfortunately, there are some limitations on the types of optimal decision-making strategies outlined above. One such limitation is found in the interactions between the two players. For example, the game profiles for one player are influenced somewhat by the game profiles of the other player, and vice versa. Thus, a strong playing profile might be attributed to a player after competing against a weak opponent. Similarly, a weak playing profile might be assigned to the same player when competing against a strong opponent. This issue becomes important when, as desired, the profile of a player obtained against one opponent is to be used to predict future behaviours against other opponents. The stochastic model must therefore account somehow for a player's profile while, at the same time, accounting for the opponent's profile. For example, if a player is simulated to play many winners against an opponent, then the question arises as to whether his (her) opponent permits many winners against him (her). Similarly, if a player is simulated to commit many errors against an opponent, the question is asked as to whether the opponent induces many errors in his (her) opponents. We tried to account for these types of interactions among the players' winner–error profiles by separating unconditional winners from conditional winners, and forced errors from unforced errors. See McGarry and Franks (1996a) for further specifics on the interactions between the winner–error profiles beyond those details provided below.

In brief, unconditional winners and unforced errors were defined as winners and errors that were awarded without regard for the opponent, whereas conditional winners and forced errors were defined as arising as a direct result of the interaction with that same opponent. The aim of this distinction was to document in some way the dependency of the conditional winners and forced errors on the player–opponent interaction, a dependency that changes as the player–opponent interaction changes (i.e. as the player and/or opponent changes). The idea, then, is that a conditional winner, or a forced error, assigned to a player when competing against a given opponent might be rejected in some instances when competing against a different opponent. While these attempts go some way to recognising the interactions among the assignments of winners and errors, the complexities of these interactions are still not well understood at present.

One other limitation on the winner–error interactions described above lies in the strong dependency of the predicted winners and errors on the existing data. This dependency means that more winners or errors (in terms of probabilities) cannot be awarded for a player beyond those that occurred in the contest from which the profiles were obtained. The stochastic model reported above, for example, generates a winner for a player from his (her) profile which, if it is a conditional winner, is then analysed further by looking at the opponent's profile and determining whether or not a conditional winner will be awarded on that instance. For further details on the mechanism of this player–opponent interaction in the awarding of conditional winners and forced errors, see McGarry and Franks (1996a). However, the winner for the player, if awarded, is always generated from his (her) profile and not from his (her) opponent's profile. This arrangement poses a problem when the player competes against a weaker opponent than when his (her) profile was first obtained. The reason for this is that it is reasonable to expect the player to make more winners, and conditional winners in particular, when playing against a weaker opponent. For example, if Player A hits conditional winners against Player B with a probability of 0.25, and Player A is simulated to play against Player C, then the stochastic model will award conditional winners to Player A against Player C with a probability of 0.25 on the basis of existing data. These probabilities might furthermore be reduced depending on the characteristics contained in the winner–error profile of Player C. If Player C should have a weaker profile than Player B, however, it would not be unreasonable to suppose that Player A would hit conditional winners against Player C with an increased probability over that obtained against Player B. The stochastic model, as developed, does not contain this feature. Similar considerations for the awarding of forced errors likewise applies when competing against stronger or weaker opponents. The fact that an outcome is initiated on the existing data contained in the player's profile, and not perhaps also from the opponent's profile, is considered a limitation of the present model. Specifically, some accounting of the opponent's previous outcomes when generating outcomes for a given player might yield better predictions of the contest outcome. Further research on this issue is required.

11.2.4 Interactions between shot–response profiles

We reported above that the interactions of the winner–error profiles are important considerations when trying to predict future outcomes. In turn, the interaction of the shot–response profiles is similarly an important consideration for predicting the shot selection behaviours that lead to the outcomes described in the winner–error profiles. We reported mixed findings from a series of statistical analyses designed to investigate whether the shot selection patterns for a given player varied as a function of the particular opponent (see McGarry and Franks (1996b) for further details). Speaking generally, the patterns of shot selections contained in the shot–response profiles varied sufficiently from contest to contest to shed doubt on the validity of the stochastic model for predicting future shot selections from past behaviours. This said, a player's shot selection patterns became more reliable when the context of the antecedent shot selected by the opponent was further specified, for example, where on court a selected shot type was played from. However, the specific contexts that yielded the most stable patterns varied between players. These results were taken to suggest that the context of the antecedent shot is an important consideration when analysing the shot selection patterns of squash players.

The general findings of inconsistent shot selection patterns when a player competes against different opponents might be attributed to a number of factors. First, there might be too little data produced from a single contest on which to generalise to a shot–response profile (see Hughes *et al.* (2001) for further research on this particular point). This consideration of too few data is analogous to sampling error in a random sample. Secondly, it is possible that the antecedent shot is a naive predictor of the next shot to be selected. For example, important qualifiers of the preceding shot such as pace, proximity of the ball to a wall, as well as the court location of the player and opponent, would each be expected to have an influence on the shot response. Thirdly, the memory-limiting nature of stochastic (Markov) processes, where the future is predicted only from the present, might be an insufficient descriptor of sports behaviours. For instance, a common idea is that a player will look to create openings in a rally on which to base an attack, using approach shots that displace the opponent, or that capitalise on a weak shot by the opponent. The use of shot sequences may therefore be a better predictor of shot selections than the antecedent shot. Finally, there might be more inconsistency (or variablity) in the selection of shot behaviours than first thought. Further research is required to discriminate further between these alternatives.

11.3 From Markov processes to dynamical systems

Sports analysts have tended to record all the data from a sports contest and to search that data for patterns. Implicit in this method of analysis are two assumptions. The first assumption is that the data are of equal importance, at least in the long run. The second assumption is that if the data are to have information value then they are likely to be repeated under similar future circumstances. Our analyses of squash contests as a stochastic (Markov) process led us to question both of these assumptions (McGarry and Franks, 1996b). We subsequently reconsidered the behaviours of squash contests as a dynamic (changing) system in which some behaviours assume more importance than other behaviours. For example, a well-placed shot that creates an opening on which to attack might be considered a key behaviour among other behaviours of lesser importance. Subsequent research using visual inspections of sports contests confirmed the identification of key behaviours in both squash (see McGarry *et al.* 1999) and soccer (see Hughes *et al.*, 1998). These findings suggest the possibility of a different type of description for sports contests. One such description for sports contests is of a system whose behaviours subscribe to self-organising principles of dynamical systems.

11.3.1 *Dynamical systems*

The aim of this section is to report in brief on some research of sports contests as a dynamical system. 'Dynamical system' is a special term that is used to refer to a system whose behaviours are the result of self-organising properties, which is to say that regularity is held to result from changes within the system rather than having the changes prescribed on the system as a result of outside influences. The principles of dynamical systems (see Haken, 1983) have been applied extensively to some features of human (see Haken *et al.* 1985) and animal coordination, specifically to those types of actions that make use of rhythmic behaviours in their function (walking, cycling, swimming, etc.). Of interest for our purposes is that these coordination tendencies can be described in mathematical terms as a dynamical 'model', whose behaviours are the result of couplings between individual limbs. These couplings give rise to signature features of dynamical systems, one of the most important being the tendency of the system to reorganise itself when the system becomes destabilised. Thus, as the system becomes increasingly unstable the system reorganises and a new pattern of behavioural relations is formed. These new relations yield more stability for the system than those relations that the system changed from. The various gait patterns in quadrupeds (i.e. walk, trot and gallop) that are produced in response to varying speeds of locomotion offers an interesting example of a possible dynamical system. From the dynamical point of view, the gait patterns switch without design as a simple result of the changing physical demands that are placed on the animal. This same type of reasoning has been used to explain (with data) some of the rhythmic patterns that describe some forms of human coordination, including those of inter-person coordination (see e.g. Schmidt *et al.*, 1999; and Foo and Kelso, 2000). We began to analyse squash contests as a dynamical system, first by investigating whether the system can be detected as switching between periods of stability and instability from visual inspections (McGarry *et al.*, 1999). Independent observers were able to identify those behavioural transitions, or perturbations, that were held as switching the system from and to regions of stability and instability. The identification of perturbations from visual inspections of soccer behaviours was likewise reported by Hughes *et al.* (1998). Further considerations on this new line of enquiry for sports contests as dynamical systems are detailed in McGarry *et al.* (2002).

11.3.2 Dynamical processes

The term 'dynamic' or 'dynamical' in wider usage refers to systems that change in time. We have outlined above two different considerations for sports (squash) contests as a system that changes in time. In the context of stochastic processes, the changes within the system are described in the language of transitions between the various states of the system. In the context of dynamical processes, these changes are thought of in terms of the relations between the units that are used to describe the system. In the next section, we consider dynamical processes within the context of neural networks. Following a brief description of neural networks, we reflect on how these types of model might inform our understanding of sports behaviours.

11.3.3 Neural networks

The term 'neural networks' refers to a specific type of computational model, whose origins are found in the properties of neurons (i.e. nerve cells) and their interactions. Simply put, neurons receive inputs and send outputs in relay fashion, i.e. the outputs serve as inputs to other neurons in the network. Neural networks are used for two main tasks, and these two tasks lend the specific characteristics to the two types of network that service these tasks. The first task that neural networks can be used for is to recognise patterns, such as pictures, situations, processes, or any other types of structured objects. For this task, a special type of neural network is used which is called a Kohonen feature map (KFM). The characteristic of a KFM is that these networks are able to learn by forming clusters in response to a set of training patterns. These learning features allow the network to later identify other arbitrary patterns by associating these patterns to one of the already learned clusters within the network.

The second task that neural networks can be used for is in the selection of actions, in particular those actions that are identified as being optimal for given situations. One application of these tasks is the ability to make behavioural decisions in the context of sports games. For this task of selecting actions, a different type of network is used that often makes use of the attributes of 'feed forward' and 'back propagation'. In brief, the reason for the use of these attributes is as follows. In the first phase of learning, the correct (or desired) correlations between the inputs and outputs are fed to the network (feed forward), whereas in the second phase the network is trained to recognise the correct answers (i.e. outputs), by feeding back information and using rewards when the network is successful (back propagation). This approach for neural networks could be very helpful for identifying and assisting the decision-making processes in sports games. However, the present situation must first be recognised before such decision-making processes can be identified. We therefore restrict further considerations on neural networks to the use of KFMs and how their up-to-date derivations might help to recognise situations and analyse processes.

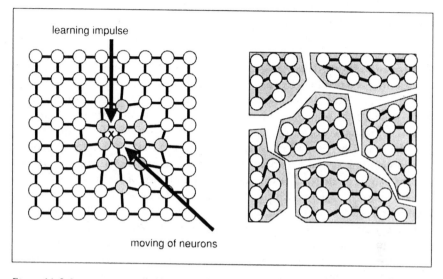

Figure 11.2 Learning step (left) and information clusters on a Kohonen feature map (right).

Finally, we address briefly some possible contributions of KFMs to the learning of techniques or tactics in sports contests.

11.3.3.1 *Pattern learning with Kohonen feature maps*

Each neuron of a KFM contains an information structure that stands for the representation of a pattern. For example, this information structure can consist of a pair of coordinates. The pattern, then, is of a two-dimensional position, which is represented by its *x*- and *y*-coordinates. As sketched in Figure 11.2 (left graphic), a learning impulse, which itself represents a two-dimensional pattern (i.e. position), can be applied to the network. The result of the stimulus is to bring about local changes within the network. This process of change is usually controlled by a set of rules and parameters that determine how the network adapts to a specific learning situation. Of course, different stimulus patterns will bring about different changes in the network. Once the learning process is finished, the neural network, as sketched in Figure 11.2 (right graphic), forms clusters that represent the structure, or distribution, of the inputs that have been 'learned'. In the second phase, the network can be used to recognise other inputs, or patterns – i.e. the network is given the pattern and then indicates the cluster of neurons that the pattern belongs to. From a higher point of view, the clusters can each be thought of as representing a certain set of properties or attributes, and the new inputs are assigned to these properties in order for them to be recognised or identified.

While this example of learning within the neural network is straightforward, much more complex applications such as picture recognition use the same learning principles. The digital representaton of a picture consists of a matrix of coloured dots (pixels), where each dot is represented as a k-dimensional vector that contains the attributes of position and colour. Thus, the only difference for the learning of a two-dimensional vector and that of a multi-dimensional vector (e.g. a picture) is that the number of attribute values is much greater in the latter instance. In principle, the same reasoning holds for pattern recognition within neural networks for a series of pictures. It follows from this point of view that the processes that take place in a sports contest can be subjected to pattern detections using neural networks. For example, the processes within a squash contest can be modelled as a time-dependent sequence of positions (of the ball or of a player), together with other semantic attributes such as techniques, tactics and success. (The stochastic model described earlier also considered squash contests as a time-dependent sequence of states, i.e. shots and outcomes.) In the simplest case, the processes for a sports game can be represented within the neural network as an n-dimensional vector of positions (see Figure 11.3, top). The clusters of a network trained with a set of patterned inputs from one, or many, contest(s) might then be used to recognise similar input patterns from other contests. In Figure 11.3 (bottom), an example of a neural network trained on data from squash contests is presented. The dots stand for types

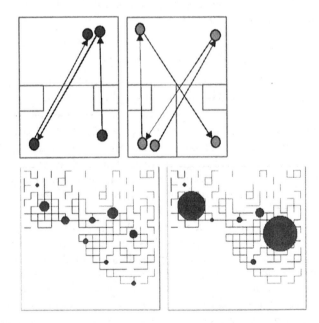

Figure 11.3 Squash processes on the court (top) and process clusters on a squash network (bottom).

of processes, or inputs, and the diameters of the dots indicate the frequency, or strength, of the types of inputs that occurred during the game. Once a sports contest is represented in terms of network and process information, as in Figure 11.1, a lot of game analysis concerning the frequencies, distributions, and the success of actions, as well as tactical structures and the success of action sequences, can be undertaken.

11.3.3.2 Learning within dynamical neural networks

One problem of the conventional KFM approach described above is that the learning behaviour of a network is fixed by the starting rules and the parameters that are used. This means that a KFM network, once trained, cannot be used thereafter for continued learning, as would be necessary if the input patterns themselves change over time. These input patterns might vary, for example as a result of a change in the players and/or their tactical behaviours. For the network to meet this task of continuous learning, the network itself must be able to adapt by rearranging its cluster structures in reactions to new learning stimuli. The ability of each neuron to control its own learning within a KFM structure was therefore introduced using the concept of a dynamically controlled network (DyCoN) (Perl, 2002a). The first point to make is that DyCoN is able to learn in continuous fashion, as intended, and so can adapt to changing process structures as required. Secondly, DyCoN can learn in separate phases and so the learning information need not be presented to the network as one data set. This feature of DyCoN is particularly useful when the amount of available information to the network is very small. In this case the training can be done in stepwise fashion over time as new information materialises. Finally, the changes that occur within the network processes as a result of continuous learning can themselves become the subject of analysis (Perl, 2002b). This means that the learning behaviours that take place within a dynamical neural network can themselves be investigated using simulation procedures. The information gathered on the learning of dynamical neural networks might be useful for complementing our understanding of the processes that take place in the learning of cognitive and/or motor skills in humans. (Recall that neural networks are based on the properties of neurons.) The learning processes of skilled behaviours might then be analysed using DyCoN. For example, one mechanism for learning might be to add the new technique to be learned to the old technique that is already learned, thus shaping a new skill on the basis of an existing skill set. Or, alternatively, the old technique may get replaced in time with the new technique, thereby requiring the forgetting (or unlearning) of an existing skill as the new skill is being learned. These possibilities for learning can be analysed using dynamical neural networks (DyCoN) within the wider context of the extant literature on motor learning, which seeks to inform on those processes that are responsible for the acquisition, retention and production of motor skills.

11.4 Summary

In this chapter we have considered various models of sports contests in various states of development. The analysis of sports behaviours using stochastic processes would seem to represent the most complete type of model for sports contests to date. This observation is unsurprising given the widespread uses of statistics based on probabilities in many different fields (actuarial tables, insurance statistics, stock market forecasts, sports betting, etc.). Indeed, the behaviours in sports contests would seem to be good candidates for this type of analysis, not least since the strategies for sports contests are often designed on the basis of future expectations (e.g. the use of strategies based on 'percentage play'). This said, some limitations of this type of analysis for squash contests were reported, indicating that any such type of system description on the basis of probability is not as straightforward as might otherwise be imagined. These results led in time to the consideration of a new type of description for sports contests. However, the data required to pursue the description of sports contests as a dynamical system remains sparse at the time of writing. Finally, we briefly considered the use of neural networks for recognising structures, or processes, within sports contests. Each of these system descriptions, while incomplete, may assist in our understanding of the behaviours that form sports contests. Furthermore, these descriptions for sports contests need not be exclusive of each other, and a hybrid type of description (or model) may be appropriate in the future: a suggestion that remains only a point of conjecture at this time. For these reasons, further research on sports contests using various types of system descriptions is warranted. The use of simulation procedures in the modelling of sports contests will continue to be a useful technique in the pursuit of these objectives.

12 Measuring coaching effectiveness

Ken More and Ian M. Franks

Research into coaching effectiveness has increased over the past decade, and now planning, management, instruction and monitoring skills are being analysed (Segrave and Ciancio, 1990). To direct this research, coaching effectiveness has drawn its theoretical framework from the teacher effectiveness domain where, in recent years, evaluation and analysis of teaching skills in the sport environment have steadily gained favour. Indeed, it is now suggested that teaching skills are a science and, therefore, amenable to systematic evaluation (Siedentop, 1991). Therefore this chapter will examine the research on both coaching and teaching effectiveness.

12.1 Instruction

Effective instruction is crucial to the pursuit of optimal sporting performance. The more effective the instruction, the more fully the instructor's role will benefit athlete performance. Such instruction requires the application of skills that range from the planning and organisation of learning experiences to the presentation of instructional and feedback information. Quantitative analysis of the instructional process promotes the objective assessment of instructional behaviour and provides information on variables deemed important in determining effectiveness. Systematic observation is an analytic process that can provide valid and reliable information on the key elements of effective instruction, and 'systematic observation instruments' can accurately describe instruction within the unique physical education and sport setting. Computer technology has enhanced the observation and analysis process as it allows for immediate summary and display of data which offers the potential for the timely return of meaningful feedback on the observed teaching/coaching performance. The utility of systematic observation instruments as an intervention strategy has application to those in supervisory positions within education and sport organisations.

While it is not yet possible to assess completely the full range of skills needed for effective instruction, we should endeavour to assess specific skills where and when we can (Siedentop, 1991). To this end, research into the verbal behaviour of teachers and coaches in the act of instruction is widespread and has used student achievement as the criterion variable and a variety of teaching activities as the predictor variable. Studies using event recording have identified the percentage of contact time effective coaches give different verbal information (Tharp and Gallimore, 1976; Miller, 1992), and have assessed certain rates and ratios of verbal behaviours by effective coaches (Lacy and Darst, 1985; Claxton, 1988; Segrave and Ciancio, 1990). As a result there is considerable pedagogic and motor learning literature available to direct the skills of effective verbal behaviour (e.g. Siedentop, 1991; Schmidt and Lee, 1999).

12.2 Teaching and coaching effectiveness

In the 1950s the American Educational Research Association stated that after 40 years of research into teacher effectiveness, during which a vast number of studies were carried out, few outcomes could be acknowledged that would advance teacher assessments or that could be employed in planning or improving teacher education programmes. The collection of teacher effectiveness data was described by Dunkin and Biddle (1974) as 'dust-bowl empiricism' as there appeared to be no rationale for what aspects of teacher behaviour were to be examined. Rink (1993) declared it 'a blind search for the universal qualities of good teaching'.

After years of fruitless search for effective teaching methodologies (Medley, 1979), the late 1950s saw a major shift in teacher effectiveness research and the study of teaching was then organised to investigate the relationships between presage, context, process and product variables. By the 1960s and early 1970s, the process of teaching (those variables concerned with the actual activities of classroom teaching) became the focus of attention, and actual instances of instruction were observed. Researchers began to study what teachers did in the act of teaching, because teacher process variables (e.g. the skills of giving instruction, strategies for organisation and provision of feedback) were shown to relate directly to teacher performance (Siedentop, 1991). For these skills to improve, Siedentop (1991) stated that teachers should have their teaching observed, receive regular feedback based on these observations, have goals to reach, and be provided with the opportunity to improve.

The quality and accuracy of feedback given to the teacher is central to efforts to modify their instructional behaviour. A substantial body of evidence suggests that this feedback should be based on information gathered by systematic observation, because intuitive observation is unlikely to be a powerful enough tool to account for improvement (Siedentop, 1991). Therefore systematic observation, which is the foundation on which modern research on teaching has been built, should also be the foundation on which teaching skills are developed.

12.3 Systematic observation

Observation is a key element in efforts to improve teaching skills, and the turning point for teaching research was the development of strategies for observing teachers as they taught. However, the observation and data collection process had to be sufficiently objective to give a reliable account of teacher behaviour, and not be susceptible to the distortion of suggestion and perception (Siedentop, 1991). This process was labelled 'the systematic observation of classroom behaviour', and it provided researchers with a method of obtaining objective, reliable and valid measures of instructional behaviour (Rink, 1993). Only through systematic observation will sufficiently reliable, accurate and consistent information be obtained to assess teacher effectiveness (Siedentop, 1991; Metzler, 1979).

Systematic observation permits a trained observer to use a set of guidelines and procedures to observe, record and analyse observable events and behaviours, with the assumption that other observers, using the same observation instrument, and viewing the same sequence of events, would agree with the recorded data. This process results in higher degrees of observer objectivity, and is not susceptible to the shortcomings of 'eyeballing', anecdotal recordings and rating scales (Metzler, 1981). While originally developed for use in traditional educational settings, these instruments have been adapted to study instructional behaviour in the sport environment (Tharp and Gallimore, 1976; Lacy and Darst, 1985; Markland and Martinek, 1988; Claxton, 1988; Segrave and Ciancio, 1990; Miller, 1992). To ease the process of data collection and analysis, researchers have used microcomputers as the data collection tool (Carlson and McKenzie, 1984; Hawkins and Wiegand, 1989; Johnson and Franks, 1991).

The data obtained from systematic observation and recording can serve as information by which teaching skills can be improved. For example, classroom management and discipline are teaching skills deemed important and they have become a main focus for research (Luke, 1989). Through systematic observation, successful management techniques have been identified and these are now changing how physical education lessons are taught (Siedentop, 1991). Systematic observation has also produced valuable information on the concept of 'academic learning time–physical education' (ALT-PE, Metzler (1979)). ALT-PE is a unit of time in which a student is engaged in physical education content suitable to their stage of development. Studies have denounced many teachers' use of class time, particularly the lack of time they afford to productive student participation (Metzler, 1989).

Observation systems are designed to produce information on specific teacher and student variables, and the specific system chosen should be tailored to the goals of the particular observation. For example, event recording, which gathers information relating to the frequency of event occurrence, may, in certain instances, be more informative than assessment by duration recording. Once the technique(s) best suited to achieve the observational goals is identified, a means and format for data collection must be chosen. Depending on the teacher behaviour being observed and the resources available to assist data collection, collection can occur in real time or post-event (providing the session has been recorded on either audio-tape or videotape), and can be achieved through hand notation or computer-assisted coding.

One of the first instruments used to observe instructional behaviour was the Flanders Interaction Analysis System (FIAS) (Flanders, 1960). It was designed to analyse verbal teaching behaviour under three major headings: teacher talk, student talk and silence/confusion. Following this lead within educational research, interactions in the physical education environment were analysed using similar methods. Such were the strengths of FIAS that several of the instruments developed for use in physical education were modifications of it (Dougherty, 1970; Cheffers, 1972). Since the inception of systematic observation in physical education, numerous instruments have been designed to record information on different aspects of teacher behaviour. Darst et al. (1989) provided a compilation of observer systems specific to the physical education and sport environment.

Tharp and Gallimore (1976) were among the first to report observational data on coaching behaviour. They devised a ten-category system to observe UCLA basketball coach, John Wooden. This pioneer study sparked a host of similar studies designed to challenge and compare their findings (Lacy and Darst, 1985; Claxton, 1988; Segrave and Ciancio, 1990). Other instruments were developed to report information on varying areas of coaching effectiveness (Rushall, 1977; Sinclair, 1989; Franks et al., 1986b; Markland and Martinek, 1988).

Franks et al. (1988) undertook the task of extending and improving upon the existing techniques and procedures of systematic observation in a sporting environment. Specific attention was directed towards the recording of coaching and athlete behaviours during team sport practices. A hierarchical model of Team Sport Practice Components was formulated and used as the basis on which a triad of observation instruments were developed. These instruments collected data on the individual comments made by the coach (CAI), the technical success of athletes during practice situations (AAI), and the time management skills of the coach (ATEI).

There are several differences between the Computerized Coaching Analysis System (CCAS) and its predecessors. Firstly, when using the CCAS the coach is required to outline the key factors of performance, the categories under which the factors will be classified, and the criteria for successful and unsuccessful performance. Some researchers have argued that knowledge of such information before the observation period may produce observer bias (Rosenthal, 1963) or reactivity in the coach (Smith et al., 1977). However, Franks et al. believed that the observer needed to know the coach's objectives before the coaching practice in order to determine whether or not the behaviour that was observed was relevant to the intended task. In addition, coaching education programmes now outline a generic model of coaching behaviour which includes the use of a coaching practice plan. Finally, it seemed likely that the coach would react more positively to any feedback process if the basis for that feedback included input from the coach.

The second notable difference between the CCAS and existing systems was in the methods used to collect data. The existing systematic observation instruments were relatively slow and inefficient. Although researchers have attempted to computerise their instruments (McKenzie and Carlson, 1984;

Metzler, 1984), the majority have used a pencil and paper method, whereby observations are coded on a recording sheet and later entered into a computer for processing. The CCAS was developed to be an on-site real-time computer-driven system. A trained observer coded the coach and athlete behaviours using the keyboard of a portable computer and a touch-sensitive digitisation board that interfaced with the parallel port of the computer. This type of input device allowed flexibility when designing the digitisation board's overlay. Following the coding session, the data were tabulated, analysed and printed to screen or hard copy. These results could then be available immediately or stored for later analysis and used to create a database of recorded behaviours.

An important feature of the CCAS is its ability to recall the audiovisual representation of the previously recorded behaviour. In order to accomplish this a computer–video interactive system was developed that augmented the previously described observation instruments. Application of this technology allowed the computer to control the functions of the VCR. Moreover, it offers a significant potential for the efficient retrieval of audiovisual images that depict previously recorded behaviours (Franks *et al.*, 1989). The observed behaviour is recorded and stored along with the corresponding time of the event. At the same time, a video recording is made of the observation session and a computer-produced time code is dubbed onto the second audio channel of the videotape, giving the computer data and the video data a common time frame. At the commencement of the observation period the analyst can not only access, via the computer, a digital and graphical summary of behavioural data, but can also view the video scene that corresponds to one of a classified group of specified behaviours.

The purpose of a study by Johnson and Franks (1991) was to determine the reliability of data collected by observers trained in the use of the Coaching Analysis Instrument (CAI) of the CCAS. In addition, the validity of the instrument was considered at all stages of its development and testing. During the development of the CCAS and the Model of Team Sport Practice Components on which it was based, consideration was given to content validity. A draft of the model, the CCAS categories and their definitions was presented to and discussed with a panel of observational analysis experts, members of the Coaching Association of Canada, master coaches and other members of the coaching fraternity. These people were asked to comment on how well the model and system described the total range of possible behaviours to be coded. Based on their comments and suggestions, revisions were made to both the model and system before the final draft was completed. Further, a follow-up questionnaire was presented to the coaches who participated as subjects in this study. The questionnaire included questions about the completeness of the model and the system as well as their perceptions on the utility of the data collected by the instrument. After having direct contact with the model and one component of the CCAS system (CAI), all coaches suggested that they felt the model appeared complete in their minds and felt that the information collected would be useful in terms of professional development.

12.4 Systematic observation and the modification of behaviour

> Having the opportunity to practice relevant skills with the provision for systematic feedback is the quickest way to develop skills in teaching. For a long time we have known this to be true for sport skills. It also appears to be true for teaching skills.
>
> (Siedentop, 1991)

Can instructional behaviour be modified? A review of the pertinent literature would suggest that it can, given the appropriate contingencies. For example, Rink (1993) stated that change can be expedited if attention is on one process variable, and only a few teaching behaviours are selected for change at any one time. Siedentop (1984) found that enhancement in teaching performance can occur if the attention of the supervisor/educator is reinforcing to the trainee/coach. Counsel is given by Rink (1993), however, that changing behaviour is not easy, even when teachers are aware of both their behaviour and the changes they want to make.

Pedagogic literature of specific intervention studies provides evidence that behaviour can be modified/changed through systematic analysis (Borg, 1972; Werner and Rink, 1989; Grant et al., 1990). Initial study of pre-service training indicated that traditional supervisory methods could effect change in students' stress levels, ethics, appearance and confidence, but hardly any in the development of pedagogical skills (Paese, 1984). However, subsequent work carried out at Ohio State University (cited by Paese, 1984) showed that when their supervisors utilised systematic observation and goal-setting, those students not only could attain modification goals set by their supervisors, but were able to maintain them at approximately 75 per cent of the level achieved during intervention. Mancini et al. (1985) also reported that, based on observations of 201 pre-service teachers, teaching behaviour could be altered if supervisory feedback included the systematic analysis of their behaviour.

As those participating in this study had coached for several years, it was important to ascertain the success of intervention strategies designed to change the behaviour of experienced teachers/coaches. A review of intervention studies dealing with those experienced in instruction was undertaken but failed to find any studies relating specifically to the coaching environment, or to physical education teachers, after 1990. Nevertheless, the studies to be reported generally support the contention that behaviour can be modified.

Whaley (1980) reported feedback on teaching performance to be successful in improving a variety of behaviours, and proposed that it may be an unobtrusive method of increasing ALT-PE. Graphic feedback on ALT-PE categories was given to four high school physical education teachers with the expectation of improving their behaviour. Whaley (1980) concluded that, within the limitations of the study, no effect was found on the amount of content time, engaged time of students, or motor responses of students. The changes reported in ALT-

PE were associated with changes in activity rather than with intervention. It would appear that an intervention strategy that is solely graphic in nature is insufficient to create an increase in ALT-PE.

Event and duration recording was used by Ewens (1981) to assess the verbal behaviour of eight matched pairs of experienced elementary teachers. Following a baseline phase, where no significant differences between control and experimental groups were reported, planned intervention packages of self-assessment and goal-setting strategies were designed to increase positive specific feedback, corrective specific feedback, and the acceptance of student ideas in the experimental group. Results showed partial success as a significant difference was found between groups in all but the acceptance of student ideas. Similarly, only partial success was reported by O'Sullivan (1984) when assessing the effects of an in-service model of supervision on activity time, positive learning environment, and student involvement. Feedback to teachers was provided in a series of conferences where strengths and weaknesses were discussed and strategies for improvement examined. O'Sullivan (1984) concluded that improvement in teacher performance could only occur when the environmental context within which teachers teach becomes supportive of their efforts towards instructional improvement. She implied that the intervention model would remain somewhat ineffective until teachers in service, had incentive to improve and those at managerial level were held accountable for student learning. Clearly, this has implications for the context in which any intervention package or strategy is given, and the importance the participating teachers/coaches attach to the results of their behaviour.

Grant *et al.* (1990) conducted a study on the on-task behaviour exhibited by the students of three experienced physical education teachers. Feedback was given to two of these teachers in the form of data generated by the Ohio State ALT-PE observation system. The findings were that the intervention teachers were able to respond to feedback and modify their lessons so that the amount of student participation was increased. The results showed that these teachers increased the motor on-task behaviour of their students by 15 per cent, while the third teacher, not receiving feedback, showed no substantive differences in behaviour. An interesting feature of their methodology was the inclusion of interviews with the teachers to gain an insight into their perceptions of trying to modify behaviour. These interviews clearly revealed that the teachers were unaware of their initial levels of behaviour, and therefore insensitive to a need for change.

In conducting a single-subject analysis on the verbal behaviour of an experienced physical education teacher, McKenzie (1981) analysed three distinct and independent verbal behaviours: the use of 'OK', the use of first names, and the use of positive specific feedback. Direct information feedback and goal-setting were the intervention components designed to modify and maintain improvement in these behaviours. Substantial positive change in the rates of all three behaviours was shown during intervention: OKs were reduced by 93 per cent, the use of first names increased by 478 per cent and the use of positive specific feedback increased by 1,144 per cent. Moreover, in a 12 month follow-up test, the use of OKs reduced further and, while decreasing slightly, the use of first names and positive specific feedback remained above baseline. While the behaviours targeted for change may appear rather cosmetic, and be somewhat independent of one another, the results suggest that behaviour modification is possible.

In our own lab we (More et al., 1992; More and Franks, 1996) modified the CAI (Coach Analysis Instrument II) to provide a more complete description of the verbal comments of coaches. We then used this instrument to analyse the coaches' verbal behaviour and to modify aspects of their ineffective behaviour. Four coaches were observed and analysed across 12 soccer practice sessions. Coaches A, B and C received intervention feedback through CAI (II) data, where selected behaviours were highlighted for discussion, and videotape evidence was used to illustrate discussion points. However, Coach D was provided with videotapes of his own performance, and told to formulate and implement any of his own recommendations. The CAI (II) data is primarily quantitative, so target values were created for the different dimensions of verbal behaviour. This benefited the coaches in interpreting their effectiveness and provided a reference to evaluate the magnitude of change. Written journals and audio-tape recordings were also utilised to promote insight into the complexity of verbal behaviour and the 'human factors' (e.g. relationship with players, attitude to researcher) that affect behaviour modification.

Change was quantified according to the 'organisational' and 'instructional' components of the CAI (II). Interpretation of cumulative values for organisational effectiveness revealed marked improvements in Coaches A and B's behaviour following intervention, and marginal improvement in the clarity and conciseness of Coach C. Marginal change was also reported in the organisational behaviour of Coach D, although this was not maintained. Instructional effectiveness was assessed by time-series analysis, according to recognised criteria (Grant et al., 1990; Kazdin, 1978). There was evidence from each behaviour dimension that change can occur and be maintained as a result of exposure to the CAI (II) intervention strategy. However, this was clearly contingent on the coach understanding what was asked of him, and remaining focused and committed to changing these particular behaviours. The analysis of Coach D's behavioural change suggested that there were limitations to the sensitivity of discretionary viewing, as only two dimensions of behaviour were identified for, and resulted in, positive change. The results of this study provided support for Locke's (1984) contention that behaviour modification can occur by using data as direct feedback, as reinforcement, and as information in the form of recommendations. However, the study also illuminated several factors that could negate the modification and maintenance of verbal coaching behaviour.

It does appear therefore that the modification of instructional behaviour requires the systematic collection of valid and reliable information (Siedentop, 1991). Systematic observation instruments have been presented in this section as the means by which sufficiently reliable data can be gathered to assess behaviour. The modification (or learning) of behaviour can then occur by using the data as direct feedback on teaching performance, as reinforcement of appropriate performance and as information in the form of directions and/or recommendations (Locke, 1984). This feedback process can oversee the 'fine-tuning' of existing instructional skills, as well as the understanding and acquisition of new skills.

Ocansey (1988) proposed a five-component guide to effectively oversee the modification of behaviour. The components were as follows.

1   Establish a baseline of teaching performance. Three observations are sufficient to establish a baseline, unless the data fail to show stability.
2   Select behaviours that need remediation or maintenance based on the baseline data.
3   Specify strategies to facilitate the remediation or maintenance of targeted behaviour(s).
4   Establish a criteria for evaluating performance of each targeted behaviour.
5   Indicate commencement and completion dates for the specified targeted behaviour(s).

These components provide an excellent framework to monitor the modification of behaviour – a framework that is to be adopted in this study.

12.5 Identification of effective verbal coaching strategies

McKenzie *et al.* (1984) stated that 'an instructional strategy can be viewed as a particular arrangement of antecedents and consequences designed and implemented by a teacher to develop and control the behaviour of learners'. However, there are no stereotypical coaching strategies that will lead to success in all coaching environments; rather, effective coaching behaviour is flexible and dependent on many aspects of the coaching environment (Cratty, 1983). The following section reviews literature on behaviours that can be analysed through the Coaching Analysis Instrument (CAI) developed by More and Franks (1996), citing literature on effective verbal strategies from a range of learning contexts and identifying those coaching behaviours acknowledged as most effective.

Performance-related feedback is interactions directed at the athletic performance of the learners, while behavioural feedback is interactions directed at the organisation and social behaviour of the learners. 'More effective' physical education teachers spend more time instructing the proposed content of the lesson and providing performance-related feedback than do 'less effective' teachers (Phillips and Carlisle, 1983). Intuitively, this suggests that more effective teachers spend less time organising the class and providing behavioural feedback. In respect to these findings, Mustain (1990) suggested that a necessity for increased amounts of behavioural feedback may reflect a lack of effective planning or result from poor organisation and instruction. The implication for coaches is that they must seek a solution to the origin of the problem, rather than increase behavioural feedback to maintain the learning environment. Doing so will allow them to spend a greater proportion of time giving performance-related instruction and feedback.

Schmidt (1988) stated that most researchers agree that feedback about the proficiency of an individual's response is the most important variable (except for practice itself) for motor learning. As coaches, by the nature of their roles, are responsible for much of the augmented feedback received by athletes as they perform, it is crucial that the feedback they give reflect effective strategies identified in the literature. Current motor learning literature states that augmented feedback produces learning not by the reward or punishment of responses, but by the provision of information about actions from a previous trial, and by suggestion of how to change subsequent trials (see Schmidt, 1988). Augmented feedback should, therefore, have informational content to direct the learner's attention to specific aspects of performance, as the allocation of attentional capacity is an important feature of skill acquisition (Magill, 1989).

Coaches, therefore, should ensure that their instructional feedback goes beyond simple reward or punishment (e.g. 'Nice job' or 'Not that way') and includes some informational content (e.g. 'Nice job, but get more pace on the ball'). The information should reinforce the specific aspect(s) of performance that are 'correct', or should identify discrepancies between actual and desired response, so that 'incorrect' aspect(s) of performance can be modified. Thus, regardless of the quality of athlete performance, feedback should be enhanced by the inclusion of informational content, and comments that have no informational content, i.e. general and non-specific comments, should be limited.

While it is widely accepted that inclusion of information will provide for effective feedback comments, studies concerning the nature of this information are inconclusive. Markland and Martinek (1988) analysed the behaviour of high school varsity coaches and noted that most of the feedback given by more successful coaches was 'corrective' in nature, given in reference to some error in performance. Tharp and Gallimore (1976) studied UCLA's highly successful basketball coach, John Wooden, and found that 'corrective' feedback, in the form of 'scold/reinstructions', outweighed 'praise' in the ratio of 2:1. Claxton (1988) compiled data on nine more or less successful high school tennis coaches and found that the more successful coaches indulged in less praise than less successful coaches. These studies would indicate, therefore, that effective coaches (as measured by their winning records) direct a large proportion of their feedback information towards aspects of performance that are performed incorrectly or inadequately.

Conversely, Miller (1992) analysed the behaviours of youth soccer coaches and noted that the 'praise' to 'scold' ratio was 6.7:1.5, indicating that these coaches spent a much higher proportion of time reinforcing correct behaviour than scolding incorrect behaviour. Lacy and Darst (1985), when analysing winning high school football coaches, observed that, across the entire season, praise was used over twice as much as scold. Segrave and Ciancio (1990) compared the profile of a successful football coach with that of John Wooden (discussed earlier) and found that the former, Beau Kilmer, used twice as much praise as did Wooden.

The data from these selected studies suggest a differential use of feedback strategies commensurate with the age and ability of the athletes involved. In explaining Wooden's sparing use of praise, Tharp and Gallimore (1976) stated that 'with players who are highly motivated towards specific goals, John Wooden did not need to hand out quick rewards on the practice court'. With athletes at the elite collegiate level, praise on the floor becomes virtually unnecessary. Interestingly, Tharp and Gallimore (1976) noted that 'for students less motivated than Wooden's players social reward may be necessary as incentive to keep them in reach of instruction, modelling, feedback, and other activities that do produce learning'. Thus, for those involved in this study, an effective feedback strategy would be to concentrate on feedback that will reinforce correct performance, rather than use negative behaviours to stimulate the athletes. This is not to suggest that coaches eliminate feedback on incorrect performance, but rather that they develop a feedback strategy that favours providing information to reinforce correct actions (Sinclair, 1989).

The need for coaching comments to include informational content seems conclusive. Further, it would seem appropriate that the information given should pertain specifically to the skills and concepts that the drill is designed to improve. Information should specifically relate to the focus of the movement tasks being attempted (Mustain, 1990). For example, in a soccer drill designed to improve the skill of crossing, the coaching information should concentrate on the player's ability to gain the required pace, direction and flight of ball. The information should concentrate on the skill's mechanical and decision-making requirements and not dwell on information regarding ball reception or dribbling technique prior to cross delivery. While other aspects of performance will, instinctively, be commented upon, it is clearly desirable that the majority of skill-related comments concentrate on the key factors of the drill. To this end the decision to concentrate on specific 'key factors' should occur prior to the practice, to help ensure that the coach's, and consequently the learner's, attention is focused on them.

In addition to being informational, skill-related feedback must be accurate, yet not all teachers possess the ability to discriminate between actual and desired performance (Siedentop, 1991). Inaccurate evaluation of performance would clearly be inappropriate, and damaging to skill acquisition, so coaches must develop sufficient knowledge to diagnose athletic performance accurately.

If the skill being attempted has low attentional demands that can be handled within capacity limits, then the information-processing system can effectively attend to other tasks and stimuli at the same time. This, however, is not true if the task requires full allocation of our attention (see Magill (1989) for attention capacity theories). This feature of attentional capacity has clear implications for the coach. Firstly, consideration must be given to different approaches of coaching high- and low-complexity skills. That is, should the skill be practised in its entirety or should parts of it be practised? Secondly, consideration must be given to the amount and timing of verbal instruction or feedback given. Because learners can only effectively process a limited amount of information at once, little benefit can be derived from coaching information if the task demand itself consumes most or all of the learner's attentional capacity. Markland and Martinek (1988) noted that successful high school volleyball coaches gave more immediate, terminal feedback than did less successful coaches, the inference being that successful coaches provide most of their feedback once the learner is free from the immediate attentional demands of performance. 'Immediate terminal' feedback was defined as 'feedback provided after the completed motor skill attempt and before participation in one or more intervening motor skill attempts'. This temporal location of feedback is supported in the motor learning literature. Schmidt (1988) stated that during the delay between the learner's response and the provision of feedback, the active learner is engaged in processing information about the response. The learner's perception of the movement is thus retained so that when augmented feedback is received the two can be associated.

The frequency with which the athletes receive feedback is also an important feature in determining the effectiveness of verbal behaviour. Practice with the athletes receiving feedback after every performance (a schedule referred to as 100 per cent relative frequency) has been shown to aid performance during acquisition, but to degrade learning relative to other feedback schedules (Swinnen et al., 1990; Winstein and Schmidt, 1990). These findings provide empirical support for the Guidance Hypothesis, which suggests that immediate performance is facilitated because the subject is guided towards the target performance by the feedback, but that long-term retention (i.e. learning) is degraded because the athlete will rely on these guidance properties to perform correctly. The findings also provide support for Schmidt's (1988) contention that relative frequency should be large in initial practice to guide the athlete to enhanced performance, but systematically smaller as practice continues, and so force the learner to engage in other processes to aid retention (e.g. detect one's own errors, attend to sensory feedback).

In the unique and dynamic setting of a team-sport practice, it is unrealistic to expect coaches to monitor the frequency with which they give feedback to individual athletes. A manageable schedule, therefore, would see the coach give many instances of individual feedback early in the practice drill but, thereafter, reduce the number of individual feedback comments and provide feedback judiciously to the whole group.

In teaching skills, particularly new skills, often the best way of communicating information is through a demonstration. Demonstrations (commonly referred to as modelling) can aid the learning of skills by accurately and skilfully portraying the critical features of the skill being taught (Magill, 1989). These demonstrations can occur before practice, to give the learners 'the idea of the movement' (Gentile, 1972), or during practice, to confirm and extend the learner's understanding of the task. McCullagh (1987) noted that provided the person is skilled in the act of demonstration, the athletes will learn from their coach or from one of their peers.

Demonstrations benefit learning by creating a representation of performance that can be copied. Cognitive mediation theory (Carroll and Bandura, 1987) suggests that the information conveyed in the demonstration is extracted via selective attention to the critical features of performance. This information is then transformed into symbolic codes that are stored in memory as internal models for action. This internal model is then, after rehearsal and organisation, turned into a physical action, provided that the required motivation and physical abilities are present. The cognitive representation not only guides the learner's response production, it also provides the standard against which feedback is compared.

By creating a representation of physical relationships (e.g. body parts, forces, speeds), demonstrations enhance the learner's understanding of the skill to be learned. Both slow motion and real-time demonstrations are useful, although real-time demonstrations are more important in later stages to help the learner acquire the speed and flow characteristics of the movement (Scully, 1988). The demonstration should be accompanied by succinct verbal instructions, aimed at ensuring that the learner's attention is directed to aspects of performance that will yield benefit (Mawer, 1990).

The theoretical literature stresses the importance of demonstrations being skilfully performed, but does not indicate the extent to which demonstrations should focus on 'correct' or 'incorrect' performance. Studies of coaching behaviour, however, have shown that successful coaches tend to give more demonstrations of correct performance than of incorrect performance (Lacy and Darst, 1985; Claxton, 1988; Segrave and Ciancio, 1990). Results suggest that demonstrations account for between 3.4 per cent and 6.1 per cent of all coaching behaviours, and that demonstrations of correct performance outnumber those of incorrect performance by approximately 3:1. The studies by Lacy and Darst (1985), and Segrave and Ciancio (1990), also showed that the use of demonstration decreased as the season progressed (3.3 per cent to 1.8 per cent, and 7.4 per cent to 2.7 per cent of all behaviours respectively), while Miller (1992), working with youth soccer coaches, found no such drop-off. This latter study could perhaps indicate that with younger athletes, there is a greater need for demonstrations to enhance the coaching process.

This section has focused on the effectiveness of comments considered to be skill-related. However, those comments considered non-skill-related, i.e. organisational, behavioural, effort or non-specific, also contribute to the quality of the learning environment. With the exception of organisational comments, all non-skill comments should carry a measure of intent to motivate the learner towards the coach's demands. For example, the coach may use an enthusiastic tone to generate more effort, or a forceful tone to deal with an incident of misbehaviour. Both of these strategies increase the likelihood of the learner becoming more productive.

The coach is the individual responsible for establishing the climate of the learning environment. While there is no empirical support that a positive climate (i.e. friendly, reinforcing) enhances student learning, it is clear that a negative climate is detrimental to learning (Soar and Soar, 1979). It is therefore apparent that when the coach is maintaining productive behaviour, demanding effort or providing motivation, the majority of comments should be positive in nature (i.e. constructive, reinforcing) to increase the effectiveness of the learning environment.

12.6 Summary

Research into coaching has been able to draw on the physical education pedagogy literature in much the same way as research in teaching physical education has drawn on the findings of mainstream educational research (Hastie, 1992). As a result, all instructors within the sport environment have available to them an extensive and growing knowledge base from which to make decisions about their practice. However, despite research identifying practices of effective instruction that are clearly linked to indices of student achievement, and studies producing an optimistic database for the modification of behaviour, little effort has been made to make behaviour modification the central issue in most teacher and coach education programmes. Siedentop (1984) contended that this is because 'the old argument between education and training is currently being decided in favour of education', despite there being little evidence to support the cognitivist position that education provides a deeper, broader and more lasting teaching ability.

13 From analysis to coaching

Mike Hughes and Ian M. Franks

13.1 Examples of the applications of analysis systems to coaching practice

The ultimate problem facing the coach and the analyst now is the transformation of these oceans of data into meaningful interpretations with respect to their sport. There is no set paradigm for this process, so examples will be presented in different types of sport to highlight good practice.

13.1.1 Soccer – crossing and shooting in the 1986 and 1998 World Cups

Having analysed the best in the world it should be possible to apply some general principles to coaching to emulate these skills in practice, and to try to reproduce them in a game situation. After analysing the 1986 World Cup for soccer, Partridge and Franks (1989a, 1989b) reported that all but one of the crosses that led to goals were played into the area behind the defence. Coaches can then plan training sessions around the results, to create better chances when the ball is crossed. This would lead to more shots on goal in a game, creating more excitement for the spectator.

By analysing all the 1998 World Cup matches, it was hoped to see if there is a trend in the way that a certain type of cross from a certain area creates more shooting opportunities than other types of crosses from different areas. Shooting opportunities will also be analysed to see if a certain type of shot is more successful than others, such as shooting across the face of the goalkeeper, as well as shots from different areas. A comparison will then be made with the study carried out by Franks and Partridge on the crossing and shooting opportunities of the 1986 World Cup. A template of best practice can then be drawn up.

13.1.1.1 Data collection

The study was conducted using a system designed to analyse crossing and shooting, with the use of a database to which the data was inputted. A reliability study using the test–retest method (conducted one week later) was carried out on the semi-final of Euro 96 between England and Spain. All 64 matches from the 1998 World Cup were notated post-event over a period of 90 minutes plus injury time; extra time and penalty shootouts were omitted from the analysis. The time the cross occurred, event leading, team, area crossed from, area crossed to, type of cross, in front or behind the defence, result of cross, if applicable; whether or not a pass was made, number of passes in sequence, shot type, height of shot, direction in relation to goalkeeper, speed and intent of shot, contact, directional position of shot in goal, outcome and possession, were analysed, which enabled the frequency of the actions to be recorded. A chi-square test was used as a statistical process to determine whether differences occurred between the 1986 and 1998 World Cup Finals.

13.1.1.2 Results

The study was found to be very accurate, producing low percentage reliability scores, but an 11 per cent error was found with crosses played in front of and behind the defence: this is addressed in the discussion. The results are presented below.

13.1.1.3 Discussion

RELIABILITY

No errors were found with most of the variables, and the errors that were found were low percentages, except for crosses played in front of and behind defenders, which produced 11 per cent errors. The reason for this was that in the reliability study a number of crosses were played directly to defenders, making it hard to decipher whether the ball was in front or behind. The reason why the percentage error seems high is due to there being a low number of crosses that were clipped and driven, hence one mistake between the tests increases the mean considerably.

COMPARISONS BETWEEN THE TWO WORLD CUPS

A larger number of crosses were played in front of defenders during the 1998 World Cup: 30.5 per cent in comparison with 24.9 per cent in 1986. Although crosses played in front of defenders do not produce as good chances to score as crosses played behind defenders, strikes on goal are still created and, as there were more crosses in front of defenders in 1998, there were a greater number of strikes on goal (34 per cent; 29 per cent in 1986). Significant differences ($P < 0.05$) were found not only in the number of crosses played behind defenders between the two World Cups' but also in the strikes on goal created from crosses behind the defence: in 1998 10 per cent led to goals being scored, whereas in 1986 only 1 per cent led to goals (see Table 13.1).

A significant difference ($P < 0.05$) was found in the number of crosses that were blocked or with which no contact was made between the two World Cups.

Table 13.1 Comparison of crosses played in front of and behind defences in the 1986 and 1998 World Cups with respect to strikes on goal and goals scored

	Total		% of total		Strikes on goal		Goals scored	
	1986	1998	1986	1998	1986	1998	1986	1998
In front	356	625	24.9	30.5	85 (29%)	116 (34%)	1	12
Behind	769	1,231	53.9	60.0	213 (71%)	227 (66%)	37	41
No contact/ blocked	302	194	21.2	9.5	0	0	0	0

Table 13.2 Comparison of types of crosses in the 1986 and 1998 World Cups with respect to strikes on goal and goals scored

Type	Total number of crosses		% of crosses		Strikes on goal		Goals	
	1986	1998	1986	1998	1986	1998	1986	1998
Bent round	310	478	21.8	23.3	92	125	14	19
Chipped	157	298	10.9	14.5	43	53	3	6
Clipped	153	166	10.9	9.1	34	8	3	1
Driven	60	29	4.3	1.4	16	6	1	2
High lofted	278	331	19.6	16.1	54	72	4	6
Lobbed	22	9	1.6	0.4	8	1	0	0
Passed	61	228	4.3	12.0	25	50	9	12
Pulled back	83	123	5.8	6.0	29	27	4	7
Blocked/no contact	302	388	21.0	19.0	0	0	0	0

In 1998, 9.5 per cent of crosses were blocked or no contact was made; in 1986, 21.2 per cent of crosses were blocked or no contact was made. The reason for this could be that a greater number of crosses were played from deep in 1998, and defenders do not always close the gap on players who are deeper as they believe there is less danger than when the attacker is closer. A significant difference ($P < 0.05$) was found with respect to the number of crosses played behind the defence between the two World Cups: this could be because more crosses were played from deep in 1998; crosses from deep are normally bent round behind the defence and fewer crosses were blocked in 1998. However, although there were more crosses behind the defence in 1998, there were similar results between the two World Cups as in 1986, 71 per cent of the crosses behind defenders led to strikes on goal, with 17 per cent of the shots leading to goals. In 1998, 66 per cent of the crosses led to strikes, with 18 per cent of the strikes resulting in goals being scored (see Table 13.2).

As Partridge and Franks (1989a, 1989b) suggested, crosses should not be taken from areas close to the corner flags. Similar results were found in the 1998 World Cup, as from 215 crosses from wide areas, only 30 led to strikes on goal, with a total of three goals being scored. As Partridge and Franks (1989b) mention,

Figure 13.1 The prime target area to where the ball should be crossed.

a number of factors could account for this low ratio, as the very nature of the position of the crosser makes it difficult to deliver the ball in front of rather than behind the defence.

PRIME TARGET AREA FOR CROSSES

When a team attacks, the opposing defence tends to be concentrated in the central area in order to deflect attacks down the wings away from the danger area. This is why it is important that teams can effectively attack down the wings. When crossing from the wings the ball should be played to the prime target area, which is the area that consists of the length of the six-yard box, and is from the penalty spot to within two yards inside the six-yard box (Figure 13.1). This is the ideal place to cross the ball: Hughes (1996a) stated that about four goals in every five scored from crosses are hit from the prime target area. When crossing to this area the ball should be bent round behind the defence with enough swerve that it is just out of reach of the goalkeeper. This forces defenders to attempt a clearance from a position where they are under challenge and facing their own goal. The cross behind the defence should be below head height with pace, as this gives the defence little time to recover to get into a position to deal with the cross. This is important as the data show that most crosses are dealt with by the defence: a total of 796 in the 1998 World Cup, with only 344 crosses leading to strikes on goal.

If possible the ball should be played to the prime target area, but this is not always possible and sometimes attackers are forced into positions where the ball cannot be bent round or played behind the defence. Hence players with the ball must select the right type of cross to use: for example, when the player is on the touchline the ball should be pulled back (if possible towards the penalty spot), driven into prime target area or high-lofted towards the far post. The nearer the ball is to the touchline, the more likely it is that the goalkeeper will be covering the back half of the goal, so the cross should be aimed towards the near half of the prime target area. The nearer the ball is to the penalty spot, the greater the possibility of a direct shot and the more likely the goalkeeper is to be positioned in the front half of the goal. The cross should then be aimed for the far half of the prime target area. A cross should always be played as early as possible to give defenders as little time as possible to get into a position to clear the ball. However, there is no point in playing a cross early if there are not attackers in the area; in this case the ball should be held up until attackers are in position.

The overall findings on crossing the ball were very similar to the data of Partridge and Franks (1989a, 1989b). They concluded their work by considering what they termed 'key factors'. These were as follows:

1 Take the opportunity to cross the ball if (a) a target player can contact the cross, (b) you have the chance to play the ball behind defenders and eliminate the goalkeeper.
2 The cross should be played (a) first time, where possible, (b) behind defenders, (c) past the near post, (d) without loft and hang time.
3 Target players should be in position to contact the cross by (a) individual moves to get goal-side of the marking defender, (b) being as direct as possible, (c) not running past the near post to contact the ball, (d) always making an attempt to contact the ball.
4 Supporting players should position themselves to (a) seal off the top of the penalty area, (b) seal off the back-post area (not allow any ball to go through the back-post area).
5 Crosses should not be taken from areas close to the corner flag. Instead, the crosser should dribble towards the goal and either win a corner or get into the penalty area and cross to a particular player.

In conclusion, the authors related their results to the design of practices to aid players understand their roles in the successful performance of crossing in soccer.

13.1.1.4 Shooting

As Hughes (1973) stated, shooting is not only the most exciting part of association football, it is also the most important part of attacking play. Too often we are satisfied with having created scoring opportunities and not sufficiently dissatisfied with our inability to convert chances into goals.

Partridge and Franks (1989a, 1989b) reported that in the 1986 World Cup Finals, 22 goals (58 per cent) were as a result of crosses contacted by the feet and 16 goals (42 per cent) were scored with headers; all but one of the goals were from crosses played behind the defence. Similar results were found during the 1998 World Cup Finals, with 32 goals (60 per cent) scored with the feet and 21 with the head (40 per cent) (see Table 13.3). Although more shots, which are taken with the feet, are blocked, the goalkeeper saves fewer shots than headers. This is because more power can be achieved with a strike using the foot, and also it is easier to place a shot with the foot than the head, leading

Table 13.3 Analysis of shot types from crosses for the 1998 World Cup

Shot type	Total	Blocked	Goal	Off target	Saved
Head	206	2	21	114	69
Foot	237	46	32	107	52
Height					
Below waist	147	32	21	52	42
Waist – head	131	13	22	42	54
Head+	164	1	10	126	27
Contact					
From the ground	141	32	19	61	29
Half volley	51	9	6	19	17
Volley	44	4	7	27	6
Direction goalpost					
Near	188	7	27	104	50
Middle	81	3	10	29	39
Far	140	2	16	88	34
Direction goalkeeper					
Across	76	1	6	46	23
At	40	3	0	0	0
Over	73	0	2	60	11
Side of	220	8	45	115	52
Speed and intent					
Chipped	20	6	2	9	3
Driven	163	32	16	84	31
Lobbed	58	0	1	41	16
Passed	5	0	1	1	3
Placed	197	7	33	87	70

to fewer shots off target. This suggests that crosses should be low to enable shots to be made with the feet. This is supported by the results, as in 1986 from 61 'passed' crosses 25 strikes on goal were created resulting in nine goals, and from 83 crosses that were pulled back there were 29 strikes on goal creating four goals (see Table 13.2). In 1998, 12 goals were scored from passed crosses and seven goals were created from crosses that were pulled back.

The type of shot that produces the best chance for a goal is with the foot striking the ball while it is on the ground, as it is easier to control it on the ground as compared with a volley or half-volley. The ball should be struck low to one the side of the goalkeeper towards one of the posts, as this makes it harder for the goalkeeper to save it. Often it is easier and more effective to shoot towards the near post; however, if the near post is covered, for example during corners or free kicks, then a strike across the face of the goal is often the next best option. If a strike across the goalkeeper does not cross the goal line then it is possible that a rebound may occur and a team member may take the opportunity to score, or the ball may even deflect off a defender into the net. If possible the shot should be placed or driven: a placed shot is more accurate but a driven shot can be harder to save due to the pace of the ball. In the 1998 World Cup, 16.7 per cent of the strikes on goal that were placed resulted in goals; 9.8 per cent of the driven strikes resulted in goals. (Note: The data for this example is from Pettit and Hughes (2001), which holds a great deal more data for those who are interested).

13.2 Tactical performance profiling in elite level senior squash

In this example, the analyses are used to create templates of performance to advise players on their own strengths and weaknesses, so that the coaches, in conjunction with the players, can best plan their training and practising. In addition, templates of the top opposition are created so that tactical plans will be ready when the players within the client squads meet these players.

13.2.1 Introduction

In conjunction with analysis of your own performance, it is essential to have an understanding of your opposition's tactical strengths and weaknesses. By modelling opposition's performance it is possible to predict certain outcomes and patterns, and therefore intervene or change tactics before the critical incident has occurred. The modelling of competitive sport is an informative analytic technique because it directs the attention of the modeller to the critical aspects of data that delineate successful performance (McGarry and Franks, 1996a). By using tactical performance profiles to pull out and visualise these critical aspects of performance, players can build justified and sophisticated tactical plans.

Recent research in squash (Hughes *et al.*, 2000d) outlined the need to calculate the number of matches required to reach a normative profile of data. This research suggested that the optimum number of matches or performances required relied heavily on the nature of the data and, in particular, the nature of the performers. By using statistical methods and comparing sets of data from differing numbers of matches it was shown that unless a normative profile had been reached (with supporting statistical data), the subsequent analyses could be subject to significant flaws. However, the research suggested that five to six elite-level squash matches provide sufficient data for the normative profile to be reached.

The aim of this example is to outline and review the development, methodology and application of tactical performance profiles used with elite-level male and female English squash players. The aim of the methodology (tactical performance profiles) outlined in this chapter is to provide the performers with quantitative analyses, highlighting their own, or an opponent's, comparative strengths and weaknesses. By modelling performance in this way, tactical plans can be based on empirical evidence as well as the usual subjective observations of the coaches. These profiles are used in conjunction with high-quality edited videotapes, providing the elite performers with both statistical and visual feedforward; the tapes lend visual evidence of these sets of data and heighten the user-friendliness of the analyses. By describing the development of these processes it is hoped that there may be practical ideas that can be used in other sports by analysts and other sports science support operators. Defining some of the experiences and processes could start the process of delineating the generic functions of a performance analyst.

13.2.2 Method

SUBJECTS

Five matches for each profile were selected from the top opposition (non-English) male players and the top opposition female players in the world. Only matches of a competitive nature (i.e. international governing body ranking events) were selected for the purpose of this study. The score outcome of the matches was deemed irrelevant, as research has shown that elite squash players retain the same patterns regardless of winning or losing the match (Hughes, 1985; Murray *et al.*, 1998), although heavily one-sided matches were avoided.

DATA COLLECTION

Two computerised notational analysis systems (Brown and Hughes, 1995; Murray *et al.*, 1998), one real-time (in-event) and the other lapsed-time (post-event) were used to collect the data from the five matches. Due to the amount of data being collected, the data capture was done from digital video recordings. This allowed the analyst to rest when needed during data collection, thereby minimising any user error. The systems were validated (Brown and Hughes, 1995; Murray *et al.*, 1998) and deemed reliable (Murray *et al.*, 1998; Hughes *et al.*, 2000). The court was divided into 16 cells for the purpose of data collection, as shown in Figure 13.2.

The data position of the shot played was placed in the cell where the racket face struck the ball. In order to increase the accuracy of this figure, frame-by-frame motion analysis, with freeze frame and jog shuttle, was used.

1	2	3	4
5	6	7	8
9	10	11	12
13	14	15	16

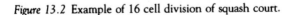

Figure 13.2 Example of 16 cell division of squash court.

REAL-TIME ANALYSIS SYSTEM

The real-time system (SWEAT – Simple Winner and Error Analysis Technology) was based on a hand notation system designed by Hughes and Robertson (1998) and later computerised to speed up both data collection and processing. This system analyses the distribution, frequency, and type of the rally-ending shot. If more than the rally ending shot is analysed then the lapsed-time system is needed. The data is entered using a QWERTY keyboard and mouse. The data is gathered into a Microsoft Access database using a Visual Basic interface (Figure 13.8). The data is processed real time and available for viewing between game sets of data. The data is processed into 3-D graphs, with the ability to filter by game, shots per rally, players, outcome and shot.

LAPSED-TIME ANALYSIS SYSTEM

The lapsed-time analysis system (Brown and Hughes, 1995) collects much more complex performance data than the real-time system. The position on the court, the time and type of shot are entered for every shot in the match. The data collection for this system has around a 1:4 real:notation time ratio for a trained user (i.e. 30 minute match = two hours' data collection).

13.2.3 Results and discussion

The data from these matches are processed and analysed. Analyses ranging from simple winner and error ratios to complex rally-ending patterns were produced from the computerised systems.

The full analysis system firstly provides simple winner and error ratios and average rally length data. The next set of data (Figure 13.3) produced analyses of the shot options taken (therefore patterns used) by both players. These two sets of data provide the coach and the player with the patterns used in a specific match, a simple thumbprint of the players' patterns – a combination of five or more matches was used. The final four lines of the above data further processes the shot type into straight, cross-court, short and long: this simplifies the data further for easier understanding by the players. Figure 13.4 shows the distribution graphs produced by the full system. The three examples below demonstrate the possible combinations (around 300) that the system produces.

As a result of initial feedback from the coaches and players, and years of experience in interpreting these figures at the top level of squash, these sets of data were then further analysed and summarised into a briefer format (about 16 sides of A4) outlining the major strengths and weaknesses of the player. The coaches and players asked us to condense these data into bullet-point form in order to simplify the information, and therefore avoid overload and confusion. Further, these bullet points were then used as a storyboard for the accompanying edited videos assembled to support the performance data. The feedback

■ Squash Match Shot Summary Details	Player A	Player B
Serve	56	66
Drive	126	116
X - Drive	82	56
Drop	30	44
X - Drop	11	14
Boast	31	52
Lob	0	1
X - Lob	20	7
Volley - Short	11	22
Volley - Long	18	23
X - Volley - Short	2	8

	Player A	Player B
Straight Long	144	140
Cross Court Long	144	104
Straight Short	41	66
Cross Court Short	47	74

Print Screen   /   ▷   Exit

Figure 13.3 Example of shot frequency summary data.

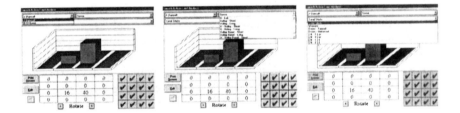

Figure 13.4 Examples of various screens of data available.

from the players and coaches was positive about this summary form of data, which coupled with the edited video made a very powerful tool.

As a result of some more feedback from the players, it was decided to combine the data from the five matches into one figure, again reducing the complexity level of the data. Also the data was normalised, and put into percentage form. Areas of the court that had unusual data in the analysis were further examined with respect to the shot types. The court was split into forehand/backhand, front/back and the four quarters of the court. These more simple sets of data can more easily be put into tactical plans.

Additional depth was given to the profiles by analysing the distribution across the court of not only the winners and errors, but also the shots that preceded the end shot, $(N - 1)$W and $(N - 1)$E. The full analysis system (see Figure 13.4 – right hand screen) also enables the analyses of the shot that preceded these

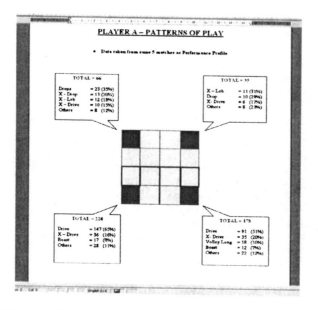

Figure 13.5 Example of shot option analysis.

shots – (N – 2)W and (N – 2)E. Using these we could present the positive profiles of shot distributions from winners (W), (N – 1)E, (N – 2)W (see Murray and Hughes (2001) for detailed examples), and negative profiles from errors (E), (N – 1)W and (N – 2)E. These overall distributions were further analysed to examine which shot types were contributing most to the frequencies in the important areas of the court.

These profiles were given to the players at a national squad: again the feedback was positive and ideas from the players were often very perceptive and always very practical. The British champion at the time suggested that we go one layer deeper in the analysis and analyse the shot selection of the top players from the four corners of the court (Figure 13.5). This form of analysis assists the players in building a constructive rally and anticipating the opposition's next shot.

A further analysis produced by the real-time system is the rally length analysis. This provides information on varying winner/error (W/E) ratios over varying rally lengths. Players were especially receptive to this data as it often provided a focus for the mental approach to the tactics; for example, a major very highly ranked opposition player showed a 1/3 W/E ratio in rallies over 15 shots. The next English player to play this opponent counted to 16 shots in his head before playing the ball to the front of the court. He won 3/1, beating this player for the first time in his career.

A discussion with the SRA psychologist highlighted her interest in extremes of body language and the resultant outcomes of the next three or four rallies. We realised that we had the outcome data in the computer from the SWEAT

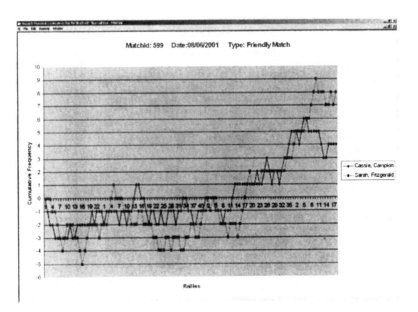

Figure 13.6 Example of 'momentum analysis' graph.

analyses. By writing another analysis program we calculated a running score (momentum) for a player during a game. We gave a winning shot by a player a '+1' score, an error a '–1' score, and if the opponent hit the rally-end shot, or it was a let, the running score stayed the same (Figure 13.6). This would also show any swings in momentum during the match, then the video could be used to analyse the body language and try to understand the reason for these swings.

When the physiologist saw these graphs he asked if we could incorporate the rally length into the graphs. He was interested to see if these swings might be related to fitness aspects. By analysing the rally in relation to the momentum this could be observed.

We are still discovering the potential of the 'momentum graphs' as they have only recently been developed. They seem a strong indicator of the mental strength of a player during the different stages of a match, and it is felt that there could be more that can be explored with these analyses. The exciting part is how the analyses are pulling together all the different parts of the sports science support team.

13.2.4 Conclusions

It is very difficult to quantify the effect that these profiles may have on the performance of the athletes, and to attribute transition of performance to the implementation of these profiles may be somewhat naive. However, considering that the world of elite sport (especially when on the playing field or court) is such a multivariate situation, any singular attribution would be very difficult to achieve. The verbal feedback from the players and coaches was both constructive and positive and has raised several issues around how we, as sports scientists, give our information to elite performers. Nevertheless, the process alone made the players more analytical and focused in their approach to matches and tournaments, which, arguably, is a positive effect in itself. In June 2001, the then world number 1 changed allegiances from Scotland to England, citing, among other reasons, that 'to remain number 1 he needed the video analysis being provided for the England squad at that time' (Kervin, 2001).

The process is one of analysis and, more importantly, of self-analysis and change. These experiences are presented as an exemplar of performance analysis, not because we think that they should be imitated, but because there are aspects of the processes that can be analysed and improved. Perhaps from these we can then define some generic indicators of process for the performance analyst. (Note: The data in this squash section is based on the presentation made at pass.com in July 2001 (Murray and Hughes, 2001), which contains many more examples and data.)

13.3 Rugby union – a game of change

Rugby union uses notation in the ways demonstrated in examples 1 and 2, i.e. using team profiling based on predefined performance indicators, and also analysis of individual skill sets again based on predetermined, but different, performance indicators. In addition, it demonstrates how notation can be used to analyse a technical aspect of the game and then apply the lessons learnt from these analyses to the game. It is the only sport, at the moment, to use analysis to monitor how its rule changes actually affect the game and, further, now utilises the skills of the analysts in examining rule changes before putting them into practice.

Table 13.4 Evolution of international rugby union, 1971–2000

	Scotland v. Wales, 1971	Australia v. New Zealand, 2000
Ball in play	24 m in 34 s (31%)	34 m in 17 s (43%)
Stoppages	151	68 (down 55%)
Line-outs	71	18 (down 75%)
Scrums	39	14 (down 64%)
Kicks	85	36 (down 58%)
Passes	145	325 (up 124%)
Errors	30	22
Pass:error ratio	5:1	15:1
Turnovers	12	3
Ruck/Maul	37	170
Turnover:R/M ratio	1:3	1:56
Activity cycles (>30 s)	3	27

Rugby has changed radically over 30 years, when it was owned as a 'players' game, not a game for spectators'. It has changed radically in its appeal, and has become an athletic performance by very big men and women. It used to be a game of rugby 'FOOTball', now it has become a game of rugby 'HANDball'. The continuity skills in retaining possession in open play have grown out of all proportion with any change in any other sport, transforming the game. The International Rugby Board actually employs a team of analysts, based at the CPA at UWIC in Cardiff, who analyse every important game and monitor a host of pertinent performance indicators – thus mapping the world game (Thomas et al., 2001).

13.3.1 Technical issues

We can use some data on the scrum to highlight how notation analysis can be used to understand one of the technical problems of the game. In 18 games in the 1999 season prior to the Rugby World Cup there were 585 scrums; the game average was 33.

- The highest incidence was 38 (South Africa v. Australia).
- The lowest incidence was 15 (Australia v. Ireland).

If we take a particular game at random from these data, we can probe further into how the scrum impacts on the game as a whole.

- Total number of scrums – 35
- Total time taken – 18 m in 56 s
- Percentage of game – 23%
- Average duration – 32.5 s
- Front row engagements – 51
- Penalties and free kicks – 7

But when we compare similar data of 5 m scrums it can be seen that there are problems with this area of the game.

- Total 5 m scrums – 10
- Total time taken – 7 m in 6 s
- Average time per scrum – 43 s
- Clean scrums – 1
- Number of engagements – 18
- Collapses – 6
- Penalties – 4

This is a critical area of the game and it is essential for the coaches to work out strategies for both eventualities: when the team is defending and when they are attacking at a 5 m scrum. This will consist of technical applications of front-row decision-making, as well as the other units in the team – the second row, the back row and the half-backs. While this is a fascinating challenge for the coach in these two diverse problem areas, it poses real problems for the game itself. If the scrummage is an essential and non-negotiable feature of the game, what can be done about 5 m scrums in terms of risk management? In clean scrums the average time from engagement to put-in is 3.5 s and put-in to exit 3.5 s. There are other contests going on within this competition within the game – at what point must the rule-makers intervene for the sake of safety and/or the majority of spectators? If the importance of the scrummage is lessened, then the game will approach other sports, and cater less to the original ethos of providing positions for all shapes and sizes. (Note: The data used in this rugby presentation was kindly donated by Kevin Bowring, lecturer at UWIC, former National Coach to Wales Rugby Union.)

13.4 Summary

The use of systematic observation instruments provides researchers with a method of collecting behavioural data on both the coach and the athlete. These data can be analysed and processed in a variety of ways to provide a descriptive profile that can be used for giving both the athlete and the coach feedback about their actions. Advances in computer and video technology can make this observation process more efficient and also provide the coach with audiovisual feedback about their interactions with athletes. The next phase of solving these problems in their entirety is translating the use of these objective observation systems into practice. The presentation here attempts to exemplify some of the better practical uses of analysis by elite coaches and athletes. The next step is to be able to describe in generic terms the whole process of performance analyses and their applications to the coaching process, so that it can be applied to any type of sport.

Glossary

Inevitably any technical discipline develops its own jargon, particularly those involving computers. This glossary is included to help readers that may be unfamiliar with some of the terms used.

algorithms   A process of rules for calculating something, especially by machine.

arrays   A function capable of storing columns of data, or even rows and columns (i.e. in two-dimensional arrays) of data, under one variable name.

BASIC   A computer language (Beginners All-purpose Symbolic Instruction Code).

bit of memory   The fundamental unit of a computer's memory.

buffer   A software buffer is an area of memory set aside for data in the process of being transferred from one device, or piece of software, to another. A hardware buffer is put into a signal line to increase the line's drive capability.

byte of memory   Eight bits of memory. Data is normally transferred between devices one byte at a time over the data bus.

concept keyboard   A touch-sensitive digitisation pad permitting alternative, and often easier, methods of data input into a computer.

flowchart   Diagrammatic representation of the logical processes involved in solving a problem.

hardware   Computer and other peripheral machinery.

machine code   Programs produced in a computer's assembler.

peripheral   Any device connected to the central processing unit, such as the analog port and printer port, but not including the memory.

RAM	Random access memory – the main memory in the microcomputer.
software	The computer program.
string	Computer terminology denoting a function capable of storing any character or group of characters, for example words.
VDU	Visual display unit.

Summary

The main function of this book is to act as a manual for the sports scientist, coach, athlete or any interested reader. It is probably impossible to write sections of a book such as this that would be readable and appealing to all this cross-section of intended clientele. Consequently, the various chapters in the book should be regarded as the different sections of a manual – many can be used as stand-alone units without reference to others; some, on the other hand, have recommended prior reading. Each chapter explains the prerequisites, if there are any.

Notational analysis is a developing subject area, attractive to many sports scientists and coaches because of the applied nature of any material developed or data gathered. For anyone who wishes to understand their own sport, and thereby the structure and tactics of most other sports, there is no better way of understanding the real logic behind the structure of the game. The more coaches and players that come to understand that notation systems are going to improve the players' performance, their team's performance and, especially, the coaches' performance, the better it will be for sport in general.

References and Bibliography

Adolphe, R.M., Vickers, J.N. and Laplante G. (1997) The effects of training visual attention on gaze behaviour and accuracy: A pilot study. *International Journal of Sports Vision*, **4**(1), 28–33.

Al-Abood, S.A., Davids, K. and Bennett, S.J. (2001) Specificity of task constraints and effects of visual demonstrations and verbal instructions in directing learner's search during skill acquisition. *Journal of Motor Behavior*, 33, 295–305.

Alderson, J., Fuller, N. and Treadwell, P. (1990) *Match Analysis in Sport: A 'State of Art' Review*. National Coaching Foundation: Leeds.

Alexander McNeill, R. (1992) Simple models in human movement. *Human Movement Science*, **11**, 3–9.

Alexander McNeill, R. (1999) Simple models of muscle action in human movement. *Book of Abstracts of the XVIIth Congress of the of Biomechanics*, Calgary, Alberta, Canada, Aug. 8–13, p. 14.

Alexander, M. (1976) 'The relationship of somatotype and selected anthropometric measures to Basketball performance in highly skilled females'. In, *Research Quarterly*, 47, 4: 575–85.

Ali, A.H. (1988) A statistical analysis of tactical movement patterns in soccer. In T. Reilly, A. Lees, K. Davids and W. Murphy (eds), *Science and Football*. London: E & F Spon.

Ali, A.H. (1992) Analysis of patterns of play of an international soccer team. In T. Reilly (ed.), *Science and Football II*. London: E & F Spon.

Allen, P., Wells, J. and Hughes, M. (2001) Performance profiles of elite under 17 and under 19 male juniors. In (eds M. Hughes and I.M. Franks) *pass.com*. Cardiff: CPA, UWIC, pp. 203–212.

Alexander, D., McClements, K. and Simmons, J. (1988) Calculating to win. *New Scientist*. 10 December, 30–33.

Andrews, K. (1985) A match analysis of attacking circle play: *Hockey Field*, 72, April, 199–201.

Annett, J. (1993) The learning of motor skills: Sports science and ergonomics perspectives. *Ergonomics*, 37, 5–16.

Armstrong, C.W. and Hoffman, S.J. (1979) Effects of teaching experience, knowledge of performer competence, and knowledge of performance outcome on performance error identification. *Research Quarterly*, 50, 318–327.

Asami, T., Togari, H. and Oshashi, J. (1988) Analysis of movement patterns of referees during soccer matches. In T. Reilly, A. Lees, K. Davids and W.J. Murphy (eds) *Science and Football*. London: E & FN Spon, pp. 341–345.

Atkinson, G. and Nevill, A. (1998) Statistical methods for assessing measurement error (reliability) in variables relevant to sports medicine. *Sports Med.*, **26**, 217–238.

Ay, M. and Kubo, Y. (1999) A biomechanical approach to the improvement and optimisation of sports techniques. In *Proceedings of the '99 Seoul International Sport Science Congress*, pp. 865–887. Seoul: Korean Alliance for Health, Physical Education, Recreation and Dance.

Baacke, H. (1982) Statistical match analysis for evaluation of players and teams performances. *Volleyball Technical Journal*, VII, 45–56.

Bahamonde, R.E. (2000) Changes in angular momentum during the tennis serve. *Journal of Sports Sciences*, **18**, 579–592.

Bale, P. (1986) 'A review of the physique and performance qualities characteristics of games players in specific positions and field of play'. In, *J. Sports Med.*, 26, 2, 109–122.

Bale, P. (1991) 'Anthropometric, body composition and performance variables of young elite female basketball players'. In, *J. Sports Medi. and Phys. Fitness*, 31, 173–7.

Barham, P.J. (1980) A systematic analysis of play in netball. *Sports Coach*. Vol. 4, No. 2, 27–31.

Bartlett, R.M. (1999) *Sports Biomechanics: Reducing Injury and Improving Performance*. London: E & FN Spon.

Bartlett, R.M. (2000) Performance analysis: Is it the bringing together of biomechanics and notational analysis or an illusion? In *Proceedings of Oral Sessions, XIX International Symposium on Biomechanics in Sports* (edited by J.R. Blackwell), pp. 328–331. San Francisco: University of San Francisco.

Bartlett, R.M., Pillar, J. and Miller, S.A. (1995) A three-dimensional analysis of the tennis serves of National (British) and County standard male players. In *Science and Racket Sports* (edited by T. Reilly, M.D. Hughes and A. Lees), pp. 99–102. London: E & FN Spon.

Bartlett, R.M., Stockill, N.P., Elliott, B.C. and Burnett, A.F. (1996) The biomechanics of fast bowling in men's cricket: A review. *Journal of Sports Sciences*, **14**, 403–424.

Bate, R. (1988) Football chance: tactics and strategy. In T. Reilly, A. Lees, K. Davids and W. Murphy (eds), *Science and Football*. London: E & F Spon.

Beilock, S.L., Carr, T.H., MacMahon, C. and Starkes, J.L. (2002) When paying attention becomes counterproductive: Impact of divided versus skill-focused attention on novice and experienced performance of sensorimotor skills. *Journal of Experimental Psychology: Applied*, 8, 6–16.

Bekkering, H., Wohlschläger, A. and Gattis, M. (1996) Motor imitation: What is imitated? *Corpus, Psyche et Societas*, 3, 68–74.

Benesh, J. and Benesh, R. (1956) *Reading Dance – The Birth of Choreology*. London: Souvenir Press.

Best, R.J., Bartlett, R.M. and Sawyer, R.A. (1995) Optimal javelin release. *Journal Of Applied Biomechanics*, 11, 371–394.

Beukers, M.J.A., Magill, R.A. and Hall, K.G. (1992) The effect of erroneous knowledge of results on skill acquisition when augmented information is redundant. *Quarterly Journal of Experimental Psychology*, 44, 105–117.

Beynon, S. (1995) A computerised analysis of field hockey. Unpublished Dissertation, Cardiff Institute.

Bilodeau, E.A. and Bilodeau, I.M. (1961) Motor skills learning. *Annual Review of Psychology*, 12, 243–280.

Bland, J.M. and Altman, D.G. (1986) Statistical methods for assessing agreement between two methods of clinical measurement. *The Lancet*, 1, 307–310.

Blandin, Y. and Proteau, L. (2000) On the cognitive basis of observational learning: Development of mechanisms for the detection and correction of errors. *The Quarterly Journal of Experimental Psychology*, 53A, 846–867.

Blandin, Y., Lhuisset, L. and Proteau, L. (1999) Cognitive processes underlying observational learning of motor skills. *The Quarterly Journal of Experimental Psychology*, 52A, 957–979.

Blomqvist, M., Luhtanen, P. and Laakso, L. (1998) Game performance and game understanding in badminton of Finnish primary schoolchildren. In A. Lees, I. Maynard, M. Hughes and T. Reilly (eds), *Science and Racket Sports II*. London: E & FN Spon, pp. 269–274.

Boddington, M., Lambert, M., St Clair Gibson, A. and Noakes., T. (2001) Time-motion study of female field hockey. In (eds M. Hughes and I.M. Franks) *pass.com*, Cardiff: CPA, UWIC, pp. 333–335.

Borg, W.R. (1972) The minicourse as a vehicle for changing teacher behavior: A three-year follow-up. *Journal of Educational Psychology*, 63(6), 572–579.

Borrie, A., Mullan., M., Palmer, C. and Hughes, M. (1994) Requirements in netball: an example of the benefits of an inter-disciplinary approach to sports science support. *Journal of Sports Sciences*, 12, 2, 81.

Bouthier,D., Barthed, D., David, B. and Grehaigne, J.F. (1997) Tactical analysis of play combinations in rugby union with video-computer technology – rationalising French 'flair'. In M.D. Hughes (ed.) *Notational Analysis of Sport – I & II*, Cardiff: UWIC, pp. 135–145.

Brackenridge, L. and Alderson, G.J.K. (1985) *Match Analysis*. Leeds:National Coaching Foundation. White Line Press, pp. 1–7.

Brandão, E. (1995) 'A performance em Basquetebol: um estudo multivariado no escalão de cadetes masculinos'. Dissertação apresentada às provas de Mestrado. FCDEF – UP.

Brisson, T.A. and Alain, C. (1997) A comparison of two references for using knowledge of performance in learning a motor task. *Journal of Motor Behavior*, 29, 339–350.

Broker, J.P., Gregor, R.J. and Schmidt, R.A. (1993) Extrinsic feedback and the learning of kinetic patterns in cycling. *Journal of Applied Biomechanics*, 9, 111–123.

Brooke, J.D. and Knowles, J.E. (1974) A movement analysis of player behaviour in soccer match performance. *British Proceedings of Sport Psychology*, 246–256.

Brown, D. and Hughes, M.D. (1995) The effectiveness of quantitative and qualitative feedback on performance in squash. In *Science and Racket Sports* (edited by T. Reilly, M.D. Hughes and A. Lees), pp. 232–237, London: E & FN Spon.

Buekers, M.J.A., Magill, R.A. and Hall, K.G. (1992) The effect of erroneous knowledge of results on skill acquisition when augmented information is redundant. *Quarterly Journal of Experimental Psychology*, 44, 105–117.

Byra, M. and Scott, A. (1983) A method for recording team statistics in volleyball. *Volleyball Technical Journal*, VII, 39–44.

Cadopi, M., Chatillon, J.F. and Baldy, R. (1995) Representation and performance: Reproduction of form and quality of movement in dance by eight and eleven-year-old novices. *British Journal of Psychology*, 86, 217–225.

Carlson, B.R. and McKenzie, T.L. (1984) Computer technology for recording, storing, and analyzing temporal data in physical activity settings. *Journal of Teaching in Physical Education*, 4(1), 24–29.

Carroll, W.R. and Bandura, A. (1982) The role of visual monitoring in observational learning of action patterns: Making the unobservable observable. *Journal of Motor Behavior*, 14, 153–167.

Carroll, W.R. and Bandura, A. (1985) Role of timing of visual monitoring and motor rehearsal in observational learning of action patterns. *Journal of Motor Behavior, 17,* 269–281.

Carroll, W.R. and Bandura, A. (1987) Translating cognition into action: the role of visual guidance in observational learning. *Journal of Motor Behavior, 19,* 385–398.

Carroll, W.R. and Bandura, A. (1987) Translating cognition into action: The role of visual guidance in observational learning. *Journal of Motor Behavior, 19(3),* 385–398.

Carroll, W.R. and Bandura, A. (1990) Representational guidance of action production in observational learning: A causal analysis. *Journal of Motor Behavior, 22,* 85–97.

Carter, A. (1996) Time and motion analysis and heart rate monitoring of a back-row forward in first class rugby union football. In *Notational Analysis of Sport – I & II* (edited by M. Hughes), pp. 145–160. Cardiff: UWIC.

Carter, A. and Potter, G. (2001a) Where does all the time go? In M.D. Hughes (ed.) *Notational Analysis of Sport – III,* Cardiff: UWIC, pp. 220–223.

Carter, A. and Potter, G. (2001b) 207 tries. In M.D. Hughes (ed.) *Notational Analysis of Sport – III,* Cardiff: UWIC, pp. 224–228.

Cattterall, C., Reilly, T. Atkinso, G. and Coldwells, A. (1993) Analysis of the work rates and heart rates of association football referees. *British Journal of Sports Medecine, 27,* 193–196.

Chapman, A.E. and Sanderson, D.J. (1990) Muscular Coordination in Sporting Skills. In *Multiple Muscle Systems: Biomechanics and Movement Organization* (edited by J.M. Winters and S.L.-Y. Woo), N.Y.: Springer-Verlag: pp. 608–620.

Cheffers, J.T.F. (1972) The validation of an instrument designed to expand the Flanders system of interaction analysis to describe non-verbal interaction, different varieties of teacher behaviour and pupil response. Unpublished doctoral dissertation, Temple University.

Chervenjakov, M. and Dimitrov, G. (1988) Assessment of the playing effectiveness of soccer players. In T. Reilly, A. Lees, K. Davids and W. Murphy (eds), *Science and Football.* London: E & F Spon.

Church, S. and Hughes, M.D. (1986) Patterns of Play in Association Football – A computerised Analysis. *Communication to First World Congress of Science and Football,* Liverpool, 13th–17th April.

Claxton, B. (1988) A systematic observation of more and less successful high school tennis coaches. *Journal of Teaching in Physical Education, 7,* 302–310.

Clifford, B. and Hollin, C. (1980) Effects of type of incident and the number of perpetrators on eyewitness memory. *Journal of Applied Psychology, 65,* 364–370.

Colli, R. and Faina, M. (1985) 'Pallacanestro: ricerca sulla prestazione'. *Sds, 2,* 22–29.

Colli, R. and Faina, M. (1987) 'Investigation sobre el rendimiento en basket' In *Revista de entrenamiento Deportivo, 1,* Nº 2, 3–10.

Collier, G.L. and Wright, C.E. (1995) Temporal rescaling of simple and complex ratios in rhythmic tapping. *Journal of Experimental Psychology: Human Perception and Performance, 21,* 602–627.

Cook, D.P. and Strike, S.C. (2000) Throwing in cricket. *Journal of Sports Sciences, 18,* 965–973.

Craik, F.I.M. and Lockhart, R.S. (1972) Levels of processing: A framework for memory research. *Journal of Verbal Learning and Verbal Behaviour, 11,* 671–684.

Cratty, B.J. (1983) *Psychology in Contemporary Sport.* Englewood Cliffs, NJ: Prentice-Hall.

Croucher, J.S. (1997) The use of notational analysis in determining optimal strategies in sports. In M. Hughes (ed.) *Notational Analysis of Sport – 1 & II*, Cardiff: UWIC, pp. 3–21.

Crowley, J.S. (1987) Simulator sickness: a problem for army aviation. *Aviation, Space and Env. Med.*, **58**, 355–357.

Cruz, J. and Tavares, F. (2001) Notational analysis of the offensive patterns in cadet basketball teams. In Hughes, M.D. and Tavares, F. (eds) (2001) *Notational Analysis of Sport – IV*, Cardiff: UWIC, pp. 112–119.

Dagget, A. and Davies, B. (1982) Physical Fitness: a prerequisite for the game of hockey. *Hockey Field*, **70**, 12–15.

Dal Monte, A. and Komar, A. (1988) Rowing and sculling mechanics. In *Biomechanics of Sport* (edited by C.L. Vaughan), pp. 53–119, Boca Raton, SC: CRC Press.

Daniel, R. and Hughes, M. (2001) Playing Patterns of Elite and Non-Elite Volleyball Teams. In (eds M. Hughes and I.M. Franks) *pass.com*, Cardiff: CPA, UWIC, pp. 337–346.

Darst, P.W. (ed.) (1983) *Systematic Observation and Instrumentation for Physical Education*. New York: Leisure Press.

Darst, P.W., Zakrajsek, D.B. and Mancini, V.H. (1989) *Analyzing Physical Education and Sport Instruction (2nd ed.)* Champaign, IL: Human Kinetics.

Davis, J.W. and Bobick, A.F. (1998) Virtual PAT: A virtual personal aerobics trainer. In *Workshop on Perceptual User Interfaces*. In: vismod.www.media.mit.edu/~jdavis/Publications/publications.html#interactive

Dobrov, I. and Liebermann, D.G. (1993) Implementation of kinematic (rhythmical) optimization criteria in long distance running. Communication presented at the *International Conference of Biomechanics in Honor of N. Bernstein*, held in Moscow, October 23–26, 1993.

Dobson, K. (2001) Playing patterns of ladies elite and non-elite badminton players. Undergraduate dissertation, B.Sc. Coaching Science, Cardiff: UWIC.

Docherty, D., Wenger, H.A. and Neary, P. (1988) Time-Motion Analysis related to the Physiological demands of Rugby. *Journal of Human Movement Studies*, **14**, 269–277.

Dodds, P. and Rife, F. (1981) A descriptive-analytic study of the practice field behaviour of a winning female coach. Master's Thesis: Iowa State, USA.

Dougherty, N.J. (1970) A comparison of command, task and individual program styles of teaching in the development of physical fitness and motor skills. Unpublished doctoral dissertation, Temple University.

Downey, J.C. (1973) The Singles Game. London: E.P. Publications.

Dowrick, P.W. (1991) *Practical Guide to Using Video in the Behavioural Sciences*. New York: John Wiley.

Duckenfield, K. and Hughes, M. (2002) Notational analysis of elite level 400 m runners. In (eds M. Hughes and I.M. Franks) *pass.com*, Cardiff: CPA, UWIC, pp. 384–392.

Dufour, W. (1993) Observation techniques of human behaviour. In T. Reilly (ed.), *Science and Football II*. London: E & F Spon.

Dunkin, M.J. and Biddle, B.J. (1974) *The Study of Teaching*. New York: Holt, Reinhart & Wilson.

Elliott, B.C. (2000) Back injuries and the fast bowler in cricket. *Journal of Sports Sciences*, **18**, 983–991.

Elliott, B.C. and Smith, J.R. (1983) Netball shooting – a statitical analysis. *Sports Coach*, **7**, No. 1, 29–36.

Elliott, B.C., Burnett, A., Stockill, N.P. and Bartlett, R.M. (1996) The fast bowler in cricket: A sports medicine perspective. *Sports Exercise and Injury*, 1, 201–206.

Ellis, H. (1984) Practical aspects of face memory. In *Eyewitness testimony – psychological perspectives* (eds G. Wells and E. Loftus) Cambridge: Cambridge University Press.

Embrey, L. (1978) Analysing netball matches. *Sports Coach*. 2, 35–38.

Eniseler, N., Doðan, B., Aydin, S., Üstün, S.V. and Taþkiran, Y. (2000) Area and time analysis of duels in matches of the Turkish football team in elimination stages of the European Cup. In (ed. M. Hughes) *Notational Analysis of Sport III*. Cardiff: CPA, UWIC, pp. 121–132.

Eom, H.J. (1988) A mathematical analysis of team performance in volleyball. *Canadian Journal of Sports Sciences*, 13, 55–56.

Evans, G. (1997) *Notational analysis of elite level male 800 m runners*. UWIC Unpublished.

Evans, S. (1998a) Notation analysis with the national squads. *The Badminton Association of England Limited: Coaches Bulletin*, 105, 7–8.

Evans, S. (1998b) Winners and errors. *The Badminton Association of England Limited: Coaches Bulletin 'Courtside'*, 108, 8–9.

Evans, S. (1999) *Establishing normative templates in performance analysis of badminton*. Unpublished Masters of Science dissertation, University of Wales, Institute, Cardiff.

Ewens, B.L. (1981) Effects of self-assessment and goal setting on verbal behavior of elementary physical education teachers. *Dissertation Abstracts International*, 42, 2559–A.

Feiner, S.K. (2002) Augmented reality: a new way of seeing. *Scientific American*, **April**, 50–55.

Fitts and Posner (1967) *Human Performance*, California, Brooke/Cole.

Flanders, N. (1960) Interaction Analysis in the Classroom: A manual for Observers. University of Minnesota Press, Minneapolis, MU.

Fleissig, G. (2001) The biomechanics of throwing. In *Proceedings of Oral Sessions, XIX International Symposium on Biomechanics in Sports* (edited by J.R. Blackwell), pp. 61–64. San Francisco: University of San Francisco.

Foo. P. and Kelso, J.A.S. (2000) The nature of social coordination in stabilizing unstable systems: Two brains versus one. S39. *Journal of Sport and Exercise Psychology*, 22, Supplement, S39.

Fowler, N. (1989) *The development of a computerised notation system for the analysis of velocity in middle distance track athletics*. Liverpool Polytechnic: Unpublished thesis.

Franks, I.M. (1988) Analysis of Association Football. *Soccer Journal*, September/October, 35–43.

Franks, I.M. (1992) Computer technology and the education of soccer coaches. In T. Reilly (ed.), *Science and Football II*. London: E & F Spon.

Franks, I.M. (1993) The effects of experience on the detection and location of performance differences in a gymnastic technique. *Research Quarterly for Exercise and Sport*, 64, 2, 227–231.

Franks, I.M. (1993) The effects of experience on the detection and location of performance differences in a gymnastic technique. *Research Quarterly for Exercise and Sport*, 64, 2, 227–231.

Franks, I.M. (1996) Use of feedback by coaches and players. In T. Reilly, J. Bangsbo and M. Hughes (eds) *Science and Football III*. London: E & FN Spon.

Franks, I.M. (1996b) The science of match analysis. In T. Reilly (ed.) *Science and Soccer*, London: E & FN Spon.

Franks, I.M. (2000) The structure of sport and the collection of relevant data. In *Computer Science in Sport* (edited by A. Baca), pp. 226–240. Vienna, Austria: OBV and HPT publishers.

Franks, I.M. and Goodman, D. (1984) A hierarchical approach to performance analysis. *SPORTS*, June.

Franks, I.M. and Goodman, D. (1986a) A systematic approach to analyzing sports performance. *Journal of Sports Sciences*, 4, 49–59.

Franks, I.M. and Goodman, D. (1986b) Computer-assisted technical analysis of sport. *Coaching Review*, May/June. 58–64.

Franks, I.M. and Hanvey, T. (1997) Cues for goalkeepers. *Soccer Journal*, May–June, 30–38.

Franks, I.M. and Maile, L.J. (1991) The Use of Video in Sport Skill Acquisition. In P.W. Dowrick ed. (1991) *Practical Guide to Using Video in the Behavioural Sciences*. New York: John Wiley.

Franks, I.M. and Miller, G. (1986) Eyewitness testimony in sport. *Journal of Sport Behavior*, 9, 39–45.

Franks, I.M. and Miller, G. (1991) 'Training coaches to observe and remember.' *Journal of Sports Sciences*, 9, 285–297.

Franks, I.M. and Nagelkerke, P. (1988) The Use of Computer Interactive Video Technology in Sport Analysis. *Ergonomics*, 31, 99, 1593–1603.

Franks, I.M., Elliot, M. and Johnson, R. (1985) Paper presented at the Canadian Psychomotor Conference, Montreal, October.

Franks, I.M., Goodman, D. and Miller, G. (1983) Analysis of performance: Qualitative or Quantitative? *SPORTS*, March.

Franks, I.M., Goodman, D. and Miller, G. (1983a) Analysis of performance: Qualitative or Quantitative. *SPORTS*, March.

Franks, I.M., Goodman, D. and Miller, G. (1983b) Human factors in sport systems: An empirical investigation of events in team games. *Proceedings of the Human Factors Society-27th Annual meeting*, 383–386.

Franks, I.M., Goodman, D. and Paterson, D. (1986) The real time analysis of sport: an overview. *Canadian Journal of Sports Sciences*, Vol. 11, 55–57.

Franks, I.M., Johnson, R. and Sinclair, G.D. (1988) The development of a computerised coaching analysis system for recording behaviour in sporting environments. *Journal of Teaching Physical Education*, 8, 23–32.

Franks, I.M., Nagelkerke, P. and Goodman, D. (1989) Computer controlled video: an inexpensive IBM based system. *Computers in Education*, 13, No. 1, 33–44.

Franks, I.M., Wilson, G.E. and Goodman, D. (1987) Analyzing a team sport with the aid of computers. *Canadian Journal of Sports Sciences*, 12, 120–125.

Franks, I.M., Sinclair, G.D., Thomson, W. and Goodman, D. (1986) Analysis of the coaching process. *SPORTS*, January.

Fronske, H., Blakemore, C. and Abendroth-Smith, J. (1997) The effect of critical cues on over-hand throwing efficiency of elementary school children. *Physical Educator*, 54, 88–95.

Fuller, N. (1990) Computerised performance analysis in netball. In *Match Analysis in Sport: A 'State of Art' Review* (eds J. Alderson, N. Fuller and P. Treadwell), Leeds: National Coaching Foundation.

Fullerton, H.S. (1912) The inside game: the science of baseball. *The American Magazine*, LXX, 2–13.

Furlong, J.D.G. (1995) The service in lawn tennis: how important is it? In *Science and Racket Sports* (edited by T. Reilly, M.D. Hughes and A. Lees), pp. 266–271, London: E & FN Spon.

Gardiner, G. (1984) *Beaten by statistics:possible problems with the Canadian Olympic team selection guidelines*. Unpublished M.Sc. degree thesis, University of British Columbia, BC, Canada.

Garganta, J. and Goncalves, G. (1996) Comparison of successful attacking play in male and female Portuguese national soccer teams. In M.D. Hughes (ed.) *Notational Analysis of Sport – I & II*, Cardiff: UWIC, pp. 79–85.

Garganta, J., Maia, J. and Basto, F. (1997) Analysis of goal scoring patterns of European top level soccer teams. In *Science and Football III* (edited by T. Reilly, Bangsbo, J. and Hughes, M.D.), pp. 246–250. London: E & FN Spon.

Gentile, A.M. (1972) A working model of skill acquisition to teaching. *Quest, 17,* 3–23.

Gerber, H., Jenny, J., Sudan, J. and Stussi, E. (1985) Biomechanical performance analysis in rowing with a new measuring system. Communication to the 10th Congress of the International Society of Biomechanics, Umea, Sweden, June.

Gerisch, G. and Reichelt, M. (1993) Computer- and video-aided analysis of football games. In T. Reilly, J. Clarys and A. Stibbe (eds) *Science and Football II*. London: E & FN Spon, pp. 167–173.

Gibson, J.J. (1979) *The Ecological Approach to Visual Perception*. Boston, MA: Houghton Mifflin.

Goodman, D. and Franks, I.M. (1994) The computer and the hockey coach. *Proceedings of the International Ice Hockey Coaching Symposium*, Cavalese, Italy, May.

Goodwin, J.E. and Meeuwsen, H.J. (1995) Using bandwidth knowledge of results to alter relative frequencies during motor skill acquisition. *Research Quarterly for Exercise and Sport*, 66, 99–104.

Grant, B.C., Ballard, K.D. and Glynn, T.L. (1990) Teacher feedback intervention, motor-on-task behavior, and successful task performance. *Journal of Teaching in Physical Education*, 9, 123–139.

Grehaigne, J.-F. (2001) Computerised analysis of soccer. e*IJPAS (International Journal of Performance Analysis of Sport, electronic)*, 1, 48–57.

Grehaigne, J.-F., Bouthier, D. and David, B. (1996) Soccer: the players' action zone in a team. In M.D. Hughes (ed.) *Notational Analysis of Sport – I & II*, Cardiff: CPA, UWIC, pp. 27–38.

Haken, H. (1983) *Advanced synergetics: instability hierarchies of self-organizing systems and devices*. New York: Springer-Verlag.

Haken, H., Kelso, J.A.S. and Bunz, H.A. (1985) Theoretical model of phase transitions in human hand movements. *Biological Cybernetics*, 51, 347–356.

Hall, C., Moore, J., Annett, J. and Rodgers, W. (1997) Recalling demonstrated and guided movements using imaginary and verbal rehearsal strategies. *Research Quarterly for Exercise and Sport*, 68, 136–144.

Handford, C. and Smith, N.C. (1996) Three touches and it's over: addressing the problems of performance analysis in volleyball. In M.D. Hughes (ed.) *Notational Analysis of Sport – I & II*, Cardiff: UWIC, pp. 205–212.

Harris, S. and Reilly, T. (1988) Space, teamwork and attacking success in soccer. In T. Reilly, A. Lees, K. Davids and W. Murphy (eds), *Science and Football*. London: E & F Spon.

Harris-Jenkins, E. and Hughes, M.D. (1996) Computerised analysis of female coaching behaviour in tennis with male and female athletes. In M.D. Hughes (ed.) *Notational Analysis of Sport – I & II*, Cardiff: UWIC, pp. 273–280.

Hastie, P.A. (1992) Models of videotape use in sports settings. *Physical Education Review*, 13(2), 101–108.

Hawkins, A.H. and Wiegand, R.L. (1989) West Virginia University teaching evaluation system and feedback taxonomy. In P.W. Darst, D.B. Zakrajsek, V.H. Mancini (eds), *Analyzing Physical Education and Sport Instruction*, Champaign, IL: Human Kinetics. pp. 277–293.

Hay, J.G. and Reid, J.G. (1988) *Anatomy, Mechanics and Human Motion*. Englewood Cliffs, NJ: Prentice Hall.

Hayes, S.J., Scott, M.A., Hodges, N.J., Horn, R.R., Smeeton, N.J. and Williams, A.M. (2003) *How do children extract and use information from point-lights when performing unfamiliar movements: Effects of perceptual training and task constraints*. Paper to be presented at the North American Society of Sport Psychology and Physical Activity Conference in Savannah, Georgia.

Herbert, P. and Tong, R. (1996) A comparison of the positional demands of wingers and back row forwards using movement analysis and heart rate telemetry. In M.D. Hughes (ed.) *Notational Analysis of Sport – I & II*, Cardiff: UWIC, pp. 177–182.

Herborn, R. (1989) *Video Analysis of Association Football: the long ball theory*. Cardiff Institute of Higher Education. Unpublished undergraduate dissertation.

Hodges, N.J. and Franks, I.M. (2000) Focus of attention and coordination bias: Implications for learning a novel bimanual task. *Human Movement Science*, 19, 843–867.

Hodges, N.J. and Franks, I.M. (2001) Learning a coordination skill: Interactive effects of instruction and feedback. *Research Quarterly for Exercise and Sport*, 72, 132–142.

Hodges, N.J. and Franks, I.M. (2002a) Learning as a function of coordination bias: Building upon pre-practice behaviours. *Human Movement Science*, 21, 231–258.

Hodges, N.J. and Franks, I.M. (2002b) Modelling coaching practice: The role of instruction and demonstration. *Journal of Sports Sciences*, 20, 1–19.

Hodges, N.J. and Franks, I.M. (2003, in press) Instructions, demonstrations and the learning process: creating or constraining movement options. In A.M. Williams, N.J. Hodges and M.A. Scott (eds), *Skill Acquisition in Sport: Research, Theory and Practice*. London, UK: Routledge.

Hodges, N.J. and Lee, T.D. (1999) The role of augmented information prior to learning a bimanual visual-motor coordination task: Do instructions of the movement pattern facilitate learning relative to discovery learning. *British Journal of Psychology*, 90, 389–403.

Hodges, N.J. and Chua, R., Franks, I.M (2003, in press) The role of video in facilitating perception and action of a novel coordination movement. *Journal of Motor Behavior*.

Hodges, N.J., Hayes, S.J., Eaves, D., Horn, R. and Williams, A.M. (2003, April) *Teaching soccer skills through ball-trajectory matching strategies*. Paper presented at the Fifth World Congress for Science and Soccer, Lisbon, Portugal.

Hogan, J.C. and Yanowitz, B.A. (1978) The role of verbal estimates of movement error in ballistic skill acquisition. *Journal of Motor Behavior*, 10, 133–138.

Hong, Y. and Tong, Y.M. (2000) The playing pattern of the world's top single badminton players in competition – a notation analysis. *Journal of Human Movement Studies*, 38, 185–200.

Hong, Y., Chi-Ming Chang, T. and Wan-ka Chan, D. (1996) A comparison of the game strategies employed by national and international squash players in competitive situation by notational analysis. *Journal of Human Movement Studies*, 31(2), 89–104.

Hong, Y., Robinson, P.D., Chan, W.K., Clark, C.R. and Choi, T. (1996) Notational analysis on game strategy used by the world's top male squash players in international competition. *The Australian Journal of Sciences and Medicine in Sport*, 28(1), 17–22.

Horn, R., Williams, A.M., Scott, M.A. (2002) Learning from demonstration: The role of visual search from video and point-light displays. *Journal of Sports Sciences*, 20, 253–269.

Houlton, C. (2002) Qualitative sports using quantitative assessments: diving, a case study. UWIC, Cardiff: Unpublished undergraduate dissertation. B.Sc. Coaching Science.

Howells, G. (1993) Patterns of play in elite women's hockey. Unpublished undergraduate dissertation. B.A. S.H.M.S. Cardiff: UWIC.

Hubball, J. (1999) *Notational analysis of elite level female 800 m runners*. UWIC, Cardiff: Unpublished undergraduate disserttion. B.Sc. Coaching Science.

Hubbard, M. and Alaways, L.W. (1989) Rapid and accurate estimation of release conditions in the javelin throw. *Journal of Biomechanics*, 22, 583–595.

Hughes, C. (1973) *Football Tactics and Teamwork*. Wakefield: E.P. Publishing Co. Ltd.

Hughes, C. (1987) *The Football Association Coaching Book of Soccer Tactics and Skills*. London: Queen Anne Press.

Hughes, C. (1996) *Soccer Skills: Tactics and Teamwork*. London: Diamond Books.

Hughes, M. (1985) A comparison of the patterns of play of squash. In I.D. Brown, R. Goldsmith, K. Coombes and M.A. Sinclair (eds), *International Ergonomics '85* (pp. 139–141) London: Taylor & Francis.

Hughes, M. (1986) A review of patterns of play in squash. In *Sports Science* (edited by J. Watkins, T. Reilly and L. Burwitz), pp. 363–368. London: E & FN Spon.

Hughes, M. (1988) Computerised notation analysis in field games. *Ergonomics, 31*, 1585–1592.

Hughes, M. (1993) Notational analysis of football. In *Science and Football II* (edited by T. Reilly, J. Clarys and A. Stibbe), pp. 151–159. London: E & FN Spon,

Hughes, M.D. (1995a) Using notational analysis to greate a more exciting scoring system for squash. in: G. Atkinson and T. Reilly (eds) *Sport, Leisure and Ergonomics*, London: E & FN Spon., 243–247.

Hughes, M. (1995b) Computerised notation of racket sports. In T. Reilly, M. Hughes and A. Lees (eds), *Science and Racket Sports*. E & FN Spon: London, pp. 249–256.

Hughes, M.D. (ed.) (1997) *Notational Analysis of Sport – I & II*, Cardiff: UWIC.

Hughes, M. (1997) Computerised notation systems in sport. In M. Hughes (ed.) *Notational Analysis of Sport – I & II*, Cardiff: UWIC, pp. 27–43.

Hughes, M. (1998) The application of notational analysis to racket sports. In *Science and Racket Sports II* (edited by A. Lees, l. Maynard, M. Hughes and T. Reilly), pp. 211–220. London: E & FN Spon.

Hughes, M.D. (ed.) (2000a) *Notational Analysis of Sport – III*, Cardiff: UWIC.

Hughes, M. (2000b) Do perturbations exist in soccer? In M. Hughes (ed.) *Notational Analysis of Sport – III*, Cardiff: UWIC, pp. 16–24.

Hughes, M. (2001a) Perturbations and critical incidents in soccer. In M. Hughes and F. Tavares (eds) *Notational Analysis of Sport IV*, Porto: Faculty of Sports Sciences and Education, University of Porto, Portugal, pp. 23–33.

Hughes, M. (2001b) From analysis to coaching – the need for objective feedback. UKSI Website: *www.uksi.com*, November.

Hughes, M. (2002) Analysing patterns of play in soccer and other team sports. UKSI Website: *www.uksi.com*, January.

Hughes, M. (2002) How to develop a notation system. UKSI Website: *www.uksi.com*, September.

Hughes, M. (2002) Using analysis to examine rule changes and game structures in individual racket sports. UKSI Website: *www.uksi.com*, July.

Hughes, M. and Bartlett, R. (2002) Editorial – Special edition on performance analysis. *Journal of Sports Sciences*, 20, 735–737.

Hughes, M. and Bartlett, R. (2002) The use of performance indicators in performance analysis. *Journal of Sports Sciences*, 20, 739–754.

Hughes, M. and Bell, K. (2001) Performance profiling in cricket. In M. Hughes and F. Tavares (eds) *Notational Analysis of Sport IV*, Porto: Faculty of Sports Sciences and Education, University of Porto, Portugal, pp. 176–183.

Hughes, M. and Billingham, N. (1986) Computerised Analysis of Patterns of Play in Field Hockey. *National Conference of Psychology*. Patiala, India.

Hughes, M. and Blunt, R. (2001) Work-rate of rugby union referees. In M. Hughes and F. Tavares (eds) *Notational Analysis of Sport IV*, Porto: Faculty of Sports Sciences and Education, University of Porto, Portugal. pp. 184–190.

Hughes, M. and Charlish, P. (1988) The development and validation of a computerised notation system for American football. *Journal of Sports Sciences*, 6, 253–254.

Hughes, M. and Clarke, A. (1994) Computerised notational analysis of the effects of the law changes upon patterns of play of international teams in rugby union. *Journal of Sports Science*, **12**, 2, 181.

Hughes, M. and Clarke, S. (1995) Surface effect on patterns of play of elite tennis players. In *Science and Racket Sports* (edited by T. Reilly, M. Hughes and A. Lees), pp. 272–278, London: E & FN Spon.

Hughes, M. and Crowley, A. (2001) Success in sports acrobatics as a function of complexity of skills and time. *Journal of Human Movement Studies*, 40, 161–170.

Hughes, M. and Cunliffe, S. (1986) Notational Analysis of Field Hockey. *Proceedings of the BASS Conference*, September, Birmingham University.

Hughes, M. and Feery, M. (1986) Notational Analysis of Basketball. *Proceedings of BASS Conference*, September, Birmingham University.

Hughes, M. and Franks, I.M. (1991) A time-motion analysis of squash players using a mixed-image video tracking system. *Ergonomics*, **37**, 23–29.

Hughes, M. and Franks, I.M. (1997) *Notational Analysis of Sport*. London: E & FN Spon.

Hughes, M.D. and Franks, I.M. (2001) *pass.com*. Cardiff: UWIC.

Hughes, M. and Franks, I.M. (2002) Analysis of passing sequences, shots and goals in soccer. *Journal of Sports Science*. (Submitted, June).

Hughes, M. and Hill, J. (1996) An analysis of referees in the men's Rugby Union World Cup, 1991. In M.D. Hughes (ed.) *Notational Analysis of Sport – I & II*, Cardiff: UWIC, pp. 161–167.

Hughes, M. and Knight, P. (1995) Playing patterns of elite squash players, using English and point-per-rally scoring. In T. Reilly, M. Hughes and A. Lees (eds), *Science and Racket Sports*. E & FN Spon: London, pp. 257–259.

Hughes, M. and Lillywhite, G. (2000) A comparison of forward performance profiles in the 1991 and 1995 rugby union World Cups. In M. Hughes (ed.) *Notational Analysis of Sport – III*, Cardiff: UWIC, pp. 207–219.

Hughes, M. and McGarry, T. (1989) Computerised notational analysis of squash. In M. Hughes (ed.) *Science in Squash*. Liverpool Polytechnic.

Hughes, M. and Moore, P. (1998) Movement Analysis of Elite Level Male Serve and Volley Tennis Players. In A. Lees, I. Maynard, M. Hughes and T. Reilly (eds) *Science and Racket Sports II*. London: E & FN Spon, pp. 254–259.

Hughes, M. and Murray, S. (2002) Performance profiling in squash and other individual sports. UKSI Website: *www.uksi.com*, March.

Hughes, M. and Nicholson, A. (1986) Analysis of tactics in inland dinghy racing. *Proceedings of the BASS Conference*, September, Birmingham University.

Hughes, M. and Robertson, C. (1998) Using computerised notational analyisis to create a template for elite squash and its subsequent use in designing hand notation systems for player development. In A. Lees, I. Maynard, M. Hughes and T. Reilly (eds), *Science and Racket Sports II*. E & FN Spon: London, pp. 227–234.

Hughes, M. and Robertson, C. (1998) Using computerised notational analyisis to create a template for elite squash and its subsequent use in designing hand notation systems for player development. In A. Lees, I. Maynard, M. Hughes and T. Reilly (eds), *Science and Racket Sports II*. E & FN Spon: London, pp. 227–234.

Hughes, M. and Sykes, I. (1994) Computerised notational analysis of the effects of the law changes in soccer upon patterns of play. *Journal of Sport Sciences*, 12, 1, 180.

Hughes, M. and Tavares, F. (eds) (2001) *Notational Analysis of Sport – IV*, Porto: Faculty of Sports Sciences and Education.

Hughes, M. and Taylor, M. (1998) A comparison of patterns of play between the top under 18 junior tennis players in Britain and the rest of the world. In *Science and Racket Sports II* (edited by A. Lees, I. Maynard, M. Hughes and T. Reilly), pp. 260–264. London: E & FN Spon.

Hughes, M. and Webber, G. (2001) Case study of the performance of an elite squash coach. In (eds M. Hughes and I.M. Franks) *pass.com*, Cardiff: CPA, UWIC, pp. 153–174.

Hughes, M. and Wells, J. (2002) Analysis of penalties taken in shoot-outs. *eIJPAS International Journal of Performance Analysis Sport (Electronic)*, 2, 55–72.

Hughes, M.D. and White, P. (1997) An analysis of forward play in the men's Rugby Union World Cup, 1991. In M.D. Hughes (ed.) *Notational Analysis of Sport – I & II*, Cardiff: UWIC, pp. 183–192.

Hughes, M. and Williams, D. (1988) The development and application of a computerised Rugby Union notation system. *Journal of Sports Sciences*, 6, 254–255.

Hughes, M. and Williams, J. (2002) Using analysis to examine rule changes and game structures in team sports. UKSI Website: *www.uksi.com*, May.

Hughes, M., Adair, S. and Beeston, D. (2000) Midfield and defensive performance profiles in the 1994 World Cup for soccer. In M. Hughes (ed.) *Notational Analysis of Sport – III*, Cardiff: UWIC, pp. 129–141.

Hughes, M., Cooper, S.-M. and Nevill, A. (2002) Analysis procedures for non-parametric data from performance analysis. *eIJPAS*, 2, 6–20.

Hughes, M., Dawkins, N. and David, R. (2000) Perturbation effect in soccer. *Notational Analysis of Sport III*, Cardiff: CPA, UWIC, pp. 1–14.

Hughes, M., Dawkins, N. and Langridge, C. (2000) Perturbations not leading to shots in soccer. In M. Hughes (ed.) *Notational Analysis of Sport III*, Cardiff: CPA, UWIC, pp. 108–116.

Hughes, M., Evans, S. and Wells, J. (2001) Establishing normative profiles in performance analysis. *Electronic International Journal of Performance Analysis of Sport*, 1, 4–27.

Hughes, M., Franks, L.M. and Nagelkerke, P. (1989) A video system for the quantitative motion analysis of athletes in competitive sport. *J. Human Movement Studies*, 17, 212–227.

Hughes, M., Kitchen, S. and Horobin, A. (1997) An analysis of women's international rugby union. In M. Hughes (ed.) *Notational Analysis of Sport – I & II*, Cardiff: UWIC, pp. 125–134.

Hughes, M., Robertson, K. and Nicholson, A. (1988) An Analysis of 1984 World Cup of Association Football. In *Science and Football* (edited by T. Reilly, A. Lees, K. Davids and W. Murphy), pp. 363–367. London: E & FN Spon.

Hughes, M., Wells, J. and Matthews, C. (2000) Performance profiles at recreational, county and elite levels of women's squash. *Journal of Human Movement Studies*, **39**, 85–104.

Hughes, M., Cooper, S.-M., Nevill, A. and Brown, S. (2003) An example of reliability testing and establishing performance profiles for non-parametric data from perform-ance analysis. *International Journal of Computers and Sports Sciences*, *1*, (In press).

Hughes, M., Dawkins, N., David, R. and Mills, J. (1997) The perturbation effect and goal opportunities in soccer. *Journal of Sports Sciences*, **16**, 20.

Hughes, M., Dawkins, N., David, R. and Mills, J. (1998) The perturbation effect and goal opportunities in soccer. *Journal of Sports Sciences*, *16*, 20.

Hughes, M., Ponting, R., Murray, S. and James, N. (2002) Some example of computerised systems for feedback in performance analysis. UKSI Website: *www.uksi.com*, October.

Hunter, P. and O'Donoghue, P. (2002) A Match Analysis of the 1999 Rugby Union World Cup. In (eds M. Hughes and I.M. Franks) *pass.com*, Cardiff: CPA, UWIC, pp. 85–90.

Hunter, P. and O'Donoghue, P. (2002) A match analysis of the 1999 Rugby Union World Cup. In (eds M. Hughes and I.M. Franks) *pass.com*, Cardiff: CPA, UWIC, pp. 85–93.

Hutchinson, A. (1970) *Labanotation – The System of Analysing and Recording Movement.* London: Oxford University Press.

Ichiguchi, M. (1981) Analysis of techniques in World amateur wrestling games Greco-Roman in 1979. *Bulletin*, School of Physical Education, Tokai University, 11, 53–58.

Ichiguchi, M., Kasai, S., Nishiyama, T., Takenouchi, T., Mitsukuri, T. and Saito, M. (1978) A basic study on recordimg method and information analysis of wrestling games. *Bulletin*, School of Physical Education, Tokai University, 8, 31–43.

Ichiguchi, M., Ogawa, K. and Iwagaki, S. (1978) Analysis of techniques in Wrestling games. *Bulletin*, School of Physical Education, Tokai University, 8, 45–56.

Ichiguchi, M., Ogawa, K. and Iwagaki, S. (1979) Analysis of techniques in Wrestling games. *Bulletin*, School of Physical Education, Tokai University, 9, 93–107.

Imwold, C.H. and Hoffman, S.J. (1983) Visual recognition of a gymnastic skill by experi-enced and inexperienced instructors. *Research Quarterly for Exercise and Sport*, 54, 149–155.

Jackson, N. and Hughes, M. (2001) Patterns of play of successful and unsuccessful teams in elite women's rugby union. In (eds M. Hughes and I.M. Franks) *pass.com*, Cardiff: CPA, UWIC, pp. 111–119.

Janeira, M. (1988) Perfil Antropométrico dos basquetebolistas dos 13–15 anos e sua relação com os níveis de eficácia do jogo. Dissertação Apresentada às Provas de Aptidão Pedagógica e Capacidade Científica. Faculdade de Ciências do Desporto e de Educação Física – Universidade do Porto.

Janeira, M. (1994) 'Funcionalidade e estrutura de Exigências em Basquetebol. Um estudo univariado e multivariado em atletas séniores de alto nível'. Dissertação Apresentada às Provas de Doutoramento. Faculdade de Ciências do Desporto e de Educação Física Universidade do Porto.

Janeira, M. and Maia, J. (1991) 'Análise factorial à estutura do corpo e ao padrão de distribuição do tecido adiposo sub-cutâneo em basquetebolistas de elite. In Jorge Bento e António Marques (eds), *As Ciências do Desporto e a Prática Desportiva*. Vol II, pp. 123–30. FCDEF-UP

Japheth, A. and Hughes, M. (2001) The playing patterns of France and their opponents in the World Cup for association football, 1998, and the Championships, 2000. In (eds M. Hughes and I.M. Franks) *pass.com*, Cardiff: CPA, UWIC, pp. 277–285.

Jinshan, X., Xiaoke, C., Yamanaka, K. and Matsumoto, M. (1993) Analysis of the goals in the 14th World Cup. In (eds T. Reilly, J. Clarys and A. Stibbe), *Science and Football II*. London: E & FN Spon, pp. 203–205.

Johansson, G. (1975) Visual motion perception. *Scientific American*, **232**, 76–89.

Johnson, R.B. (1987) *A reliability test of the computerised coaching analysis system*. Unpublished master's thesis, University of British Columbia, BC, Canada.

Johnson, R.B. and Franks, I.M. (1991) 'Measuring the reliability of a computer-aided systematic observation instrument.' *Canadian Journal of Sports Sciences*, 16, 45–57.

Kasai, J. and Mori, T. (1998) A qualitative 3D analysis of forehand strokes in table tennis. In *Science and Racket Sports II* (edited by A. Lees, I. Maynard, M.D. Hughes and T. Reilly), pp. 201–205. London: E & FN Spon.

Katz, L., Liebermann, D.G. and Morey Sorrentino, R. (2001) A preliminary analysis of coaches' attitudes to the use of technology and science in sport. In (eds M. Hughes and I.M. Franks) *pass.com*, Cardiff: CPA, UWIC, pp. 77–81.

Kazdin, A.E. (1978) Methodological and interpretive problems of single-case experimental designs. *Journal of Consulting and Clinical Psychology*, 46(4), 629–642.

Kearney, J.T. (1996) Training the Olympic Athlete. *Scientific American*, **June**, 52–63.

Kelly, A. and Hubbard, M. (2000) Design and construction of a bobsled driver training simulator. *Sports Engineering*, 3, 13–24.

Kenyon, G.S. and Schutz, R.W. (1970) Patterns of involvement in sport: A stochastic view. In G.S. Kenyon (ed.), *Contemporary Psychology of Sport*, Chicago, Athletic Institue.

Kernodle, M.W., Johnson, R. and Arnold, D.R. (2001) Verbal instruction for correcting errors versus such instructions plus videotape replay on learning the overhand throw. *Perceptual Motor Skills*, 92, 1039–1051.

Knapp, B.J. (1963) *Skill in Sport – The Attainment of Proficiency*. London, Routledge & Kegan Paul Ltd.

Knudsen, D.V. and Morrison, C.S. (1997) *Qualitative Analysis of Human Movement*. Champaign, IL: Human Kinetics.

Krebs, H.I., Hogan, N., Aisen, M.L., Volpe, B.T. (1998) Robot-Aided Neuro-Rehabilitation. *IEEE Transactions in Rehabilitation Engineering*, 6, 75–87.

Kreighbaum, E. and Barthels, K.M. (1990) *Biomechanics: A Qualitative Approach for Studying Human Movement*. New York: MacMillan.

Kugler, P.N., Kelso, J.A.S. and Turvey, M.T. (1980) On the concept of coordinative structures as dissipative structures: 1. Theoretical lines of convergence. In G.E. Stelmach and J. Requin (eds), *Tutorials in motor behavior* (pp. 3–47). Amsterdam, Elsevier.

Laban, R. (1975) *Laban's Principles of Dance and Music Notation*. London: McDonald & Evans Ltd.

Lacy, A.C. and Darst, P.W. (1985) Systematic observation of behaviours of winning high school head football coaches. *Journal of Teaching in Physical Education*, 4(4), 256–270.

Ladany, S.P. and Machol, R.E. (eds) (1977) *Optimal Strategies in Sports*. Amsterdam. North Holland.

Lai, Q. and Shea, C.H. (1998) Generalized motor program (GMP) learning: Effects of reduced frequency of knowledge of results and practice variability. *Journal of Motor Behavior*, 30, 51–59.

Land, M.F. and McLeod, P. (2000) From eye movements to actions: how batsmen hit the ball. *Neuroscience*, 3, 1340–1345.

Lapham, A.C. and Bartlett, R.M. (1995) The use of artificial intelligence in the analysis of sports performance: A review of applications in human gait analysis and future directions for sports biomechanics. *Journal of Sports Sciences*, 13, 229–237.

Larder, P. (1988) *Rugby League Coaching Manual*. London: Kingswood Press.

Larsen, O., Zoglowek, H. and Rafoss, K. (2000) An analysis of team performance for the Norwegian women soccer team in the Olympics in Atlanta 1996. In (ed. M. Hughes) *Notational Analysis of Sport III*. Cardiff: CPA, UWIC, pp. ?????.

Lee, T.D., Swinnen, S.P. and Verschueren, S. (1995) Relative phase alterations during bimanual skill acquisition. *Journal of Motor Behavior*, 27, 263–274.

Lee, T.D. and Carnahan, H. (1990) Bandwidth knowledge of results and motor learning. *The Quarterly Journal of Experimental Psychology*, 42, 777–789.

Lee, T.D., Swinnen, S.P. and Serrien, D.J. (1994) Cognitive effort and motor learning. *Quest*, 46, 328–344.

Lees, A. (2002) Technique analysis in sports: A critical review. *Journal of Sports Sciences*, 20, 813–828.

Lees, A. and Nolan, L. (1998) The biomechanics of soccer: A review. *Journal of Sports Sciences*, 16, 211–234.

Lees, A., Maynard, I.W., Hughes, M.D. and Reilly, T. (1998) *Science and Racket Sports II*. London: E & FN Spon.

Leippe, M., Wells, G. and Ostrom, T. (1978) Crime seriousness as a determinant of accuracy in eyewitness identification. *Journal of Applied Psychology*, 63, 345–351.

Lewis, M. and Hughes, M.D. (1988) Attacking play in the 1986 World Cup of Association Football. *Journal of Sports Sciences*, 6, 169.

Liao, C. and Masters, R.S.W. (2001) Analogy learning: A means to implicit motor learning. *Journal of Sports Sciences*, 19, 307–319.

Liddle, S.D. and O'Donoghue, P.G. (1998), 'Notational Analysis of Rallies in European Circuit Badminton', In *Science and Racket Sports II* (Editors Lees, A., Maynard, I., Hughes, M. and Reilly, T.), E & FN Spon.

Liddle, S.D., Murphy, M.H. and Bleakley, E.W. (1996) A comparison of the demands of singles and doubles badminton among elite male players: a heart rate and time/motion analysis, *Journal of Human Movement Studies*, 29(4), 159–176.

Liebermann, D.G. (1997) Temporal structure as a primitive of movement for skill acquisition. In *Proceedings of the World Conference of Sport Psychology* (edited by M. Bar-Eli and R. Lidor), Wingate Institute, Israel, pp. 496–499.

Liebermann, D.G., Maitland, M.E. and Katz, L. (2002) Lower-limb extension power: how well does it predict short distance speed skating performance? *Isokinetics and Exercise Science*, 10, 87–95.

Liebermann, D.G., Raz, T. and Dickinson, J. (1988) On intentional and incidental learning and estimation of temporal and spatial information. *Journal of Human Movement Studies*, 15, 191–204.

Liebermann, D.G., McClements, J., Katz, L., Franks, I.M. and Hughes, M. (2002) Advances in the application of information technology to sport performance. *Journal of Sports Sciences*, 20, 755–769.

Locke, L.F. (1984) Research on teaching teachers: Where are we now? *Journal of Teaching in Physical Education*, Monograph #2, Summer.

Luhtanen, P.H. (1993) A statistical evaluation of offensive actions in soccer at World Cup level in Italy 1990. In (eds T. Reilly, J. Clarys and A. Stibbe), *Science and Football II*. London: E & FN Spon, pp. 215–220.

Luhtanen, P.H., Korhonen, V. and Ilkka, A. (1997) A new notational analysis system with special reference to the comparison of Brazil and its opponents in the World Cup 1994. In (eds T. Reilly, J. Bangsbo and M. Hughes), *Science and Football III*. London: E & FN Spon, pp. 229–232.

Luhtanen, P., Belinskij, A., Häyrinen, M. and Vänttinen, T. (2002) A computer aided team analysis of the euro 2000 in soccer. *EIJPAS*, *1*, 74–83.

Luke, M. (1989) Research on class management and organization: Review with implications for current practice. *Quest*, *41*, 55–67.

Lynch, G., Wells, J. and Hughes, M. (2001) Performance profiles of elite under 17 and under 19 female juniors. In (eds M. Hughes and I.M. Franks) *pass.com*, Cardiff: CPA, UWIC, pp. 195–202.

Lyons, K. (1988) *Using Video in Sport*. Huddersfield: Springfield Books.

Lyons, K. (1992) 'The Use of Notational Analysis in Sport'. *In Touch*, Autumn.

Lyons, K. (1996) Lloyd Messersmith. In M. Hughes (ed.) *Notational Analysis of Sport – I & II*, Cardiff: UWIC, pp. 49–59.

Lyons, K. and Hughes, M.D. (1996) The science of chaos. *New Scientist*, July.

Maclean, D. (1992) Analysis of the physical demands of international rugby union. *Journal of Sports Sciences*, 10(3), 285–296.

Magill, R.A. (1989) *Motor learning: Concepts and applications*. Wm. C. Brown Publishers, Iowa.

Magill, R.A. (2001) *Motor learning: Concepts and applications* (Sixth International Edition). Singapore: McGraw-Hill International Editions.

Magill, R.A. and Schoenfelder-Zohdi (1996) A visual model and knowledge of performance as sources of information for learning a rhythmic gymnastics skill. *International Journal of Sport Psychology*, *24*, 358–369.

Magill, R.A. and Wood, C.A. (1986) Knowledge of results precision as a learning variable in motor skill acquisition. *Research Quarterly for Exercise and Sport*, *57*, 170–173.

Maia, J. (1993) Abordagem Antropométrica da Selecção em Desporto – Estudo multivariado de indicadores bio-sociais de selecção em andebolistas dos dois sexos, dos 13 aos 16 anos de idade. Dissertação Apresentada às Provas de Doutoramento. Faculdade de Ciências do Desporto e de Educação Física – Universidade do Porto.

Maia, J. (1989) 'Estudo Cinantropométrico do Andebolista Sénior da 1ª Divisão Nacional'. Dissertação apresentada às provas de Aptidão Pedagógica e Capacidade Ciêntífica. Faculdade de Ciências do Desporto e de Educação Física – Universidade do Porto.

Malpass, R. and Devine, P. (1981) Guided memory in eyewitness identification. *Journal of Applied Psychology*, *66*, 343–350.

Mancini, V.H., Wuest, D.A. and van der Mars, H. (1985) Use of instruction and supervision in systematic observation in undergraduate professional preparation. *Journal of Teaching in Physical Education*, *5*, 22–33.

Marascuilo, L.A. and Busk, P.L. (1987) Loglinear models: A way to study main effects and interactions for multidimensional contingency tables with categorical data. *Journal of Counseling Psychology*, *34*, 443–455.

Markland, R. and Martinek, T.J. (1988) Descriptive analysis of augmented feedback given to high school varsity female volleyball players. *Journal of Teaching in Physical Education*, *7*, 289–301.

Marques, F. (1990) A definição de critérios de eficácia em Desportos Colectivos. Dissertação Apresentada às Provas de Aptidão Pedagógica e Capacidade Científica. Faculdade de Motricidade Humana – Universidade Técnica de Lisboa.

Marshall, K. and Hughes, M. (2002) Changes in elite women's rugby union from 1994 and 2000. In (eds M. Hughes and I.M. Franks) *pass.com*, Cardiff: CPA, UWIC, pp. 119–127.

Marshall, R.N. and Elliott, B.C. (2000) Long axis rotation: The missing link in proximal-to-distal sequencing. *Journal of Sports Sciences*, *18*, 247–254.

Martens, R., Burwitz, L. and Zuckerman, J. (1976) Modeling effects on motor performance. *Research Quarterly*, 47, 277–291.

Martin, M., Thomas, C. and Williams, J. (2002) Mapping the world game of rugby
union. In (eds M. Hughes and I.M. Franks) *pass.com*, Cardiff: CPA, UWIC, pp.
94–102.

Masters, R.S.W. (1992) Knowledge, knerves and know-how: The role of explicit versus
implicit knowledge in the breakdown of a complex motor skill under pressure. *British
Journal of Psychology*, 83, 343–358.

Masters, R.S.W. (2000) Theoretical aspects of implicit learning in sport. *International
Journal of Sport Psychology*, 31, 530–541.

Masters, R.S.W. and Maxwell, J.P. (2003, in press) Implicit Motor Learning, Reinvestment and Movement Disruption: What You Don't Know Won't Hurt You? In A.M.
Williams, N.J. Hodges and M.A. Scott (eds), *Skill Acquisition in Sport: Research, Theory
and Practice*. London, UK: Routledge.

Mawer, M. (1990) It's not what you do- it's the way that you do it! Teaching skills in
physical education. *British Journal of Physical Education*, Summer, 307–312.

Maxwell, J.P., Masters, R.S.W., Kerr, E. and Weedon, E. (2001) The implicit benefit of
learning without errors. *Quarterly Journal of Experimental Psychology*, 54A, 1049–1068.

Mayhew, S.R. and Wenger, H.A. (1985) Time-motion analysis of professional soccer.
Journal of Human Movement Studies, 11, 49–52.

McClements, J.D., Sanderson, L.K. and Gander, B.E. (1996) Using immediate kinetic
and kinematic feedback measured by the Saskatchewan Sprint Start System to improve sprinting performance. *New Studies in Athletics*, 11, 137–139.

McCorry, M., Saunders, E.D., O'Donoghue, P.G. and Murphy, M.H. (1996) A Match
Analysis of the Knockout Stages of the 1995 Rugby Union World Cup. World Congress of Notational analysis of Sport III, Antalya, Turkey.

McCullagh, P. (1987) Model similarity effects on motor performance. *Journal of Sports
Psychology*, 9, 249–260.

McCullagh, P. and Weiss, M.R. (2001) Modeling: Considerations for motor skill performance and psychological responses. In R.N. Singer, H.A. Hausenblas and C.M. Janelle
(eds), *Handbook of Sport Psychology: Second edition* (pp. 205–238) Wiley Publishers.

McDonald, M. (1984) Avoiding the pitfalls of player selection. *Coaching Science Update*,
41–45.

McGarry, T. and Franks, I.M. (1994) A stochastic approach to predicting competition
squash match-play. *Journal of Sports Sciences*, 12, 573–584.

McGarry, T. and Franks, I.M. (1995) Modeling competitive squash performance from
quantitative analysis. *Human Performance*, 8, 113–129.

McGarry, T. and Franks, I.M. (1996a) Analysing championship squash match play: In
search of a system description. In S. Haake (ed.) *The Engineering of Sport*. Rotterdam:
Balkema, pp. 263–269.

McGarry, T. and Franks, I.M. (1996b) In search of invariance in championship squash.
In M.D. Hughes (ed.) *Notational Analysis of Sport – I & II*, Cardiff: UWIC, pp. 281–
288.

McGarry, T. and Franks, I.M. (1996c) Development, application and limitation of a
stochastic Markov model in explaining championship squash performance. *Research
Quarterly for Exercise and Sport*, 67, 406–415.

McGarry, T. and Franks, I.M. (1996d) In search of invariant athletic behaviour in
competitive sport systems: An example from championship squash match-play. *Journal
of Sports Sciences*, 14, 445–456.

McGarry, T., Khan, M.A. and Franks, I.M. (1999) On the presence and absence of behavioural traits in sport: An example from championship squash match-play. *Journal of Sports Sciences*, 17, 297–311.

McGarry, T., Anderson, D.I., Wallace, S.A., Hughes, M.D. and Franks, I.M. (2002) Sport Competition as a dynamical self-organizing system, *Journal of Sports Sciences*, 20, 771–781.

McKenna, M.J., Patrick, J.D., Sandstrom, E.R. and Chennells, M.H.D. (1988) Computer-video analysis of activity patterns in Australian rules football. In T. Reilly, A. Lees, K. Davids and W. Murphy (eds), *Science and Football*. London: E & F Spon.

McKenzie, T.L. (1981) Modification, transfer, and maintenance of the verbal behavior of an experienced physical education teacher: A single-subject analysis. *Journal of Teaching in Physical Education*, Introductory Issue, 48–56.

McKenzie, T.L. and Carlson, B.R. (1984) Computer technology for exercise and sport pedagogy: recording, storing and analyzing interval data. *Journal of Teaching in Physical Education*, 3, 17–27.

McKenzie, T.L., Clark, E.K. and McKenzie, R. (1984) Instructional strategies: Influence on teacher and student behaviour. *Journal of Teaching in Physical Education*, Winter, 20–28.

McNamara, M. (1989) *Match Analysis of Womens Hockey*, Cardiff Institute of Higher Education. Unpublished undergraduate dissertation.

Medley, D. (1979) The effectiveness of teachers. In P. Peterson and H. Walberg (eds), *Research on Teaching: Concepts, Findings and Implications*. Berkeley, CA: McCutchan.

Meltzoff, A.N. and Moore, M.K. (1977) Imitation of facial and manual gestures by human neonates. *Science*, 198, 74–78.

Mendes, L. and Janeira, M. (2001) Basketball performance – multivariate study in Portuguese professional male basketball teams. In Hughes, M.D. and Tavares, F. (eds) (2001) *Notational Analysis of Sport – IV*, Cardiff: UWIC, pp. 103–111.

Merians, A.S., Jack, D., Boian, R., Tremaine, M., Burdea, C., Adamovich, S., Reece, M. and Poizner, H. (2002) Virtual reality-augmented rehabilitation for patients following stroke. *Phys Ther.*, 82, 898–915.

Messersmith, L.L. and Bucher, C.C. (1939) The Distance Traversed by Big Ten Basketball Players. *Research Quarterly.* 10(1) 61–62.

Messersmith, L.L. and Corey, S.M. (1931) Distance Traversed by a Basketball Player. *Research Quarterly.* 2(2) 57–60.

Messersmith, L.L., Laurence, J. and Randels, K. (1940) A Study of Distances Traversed by College Men and Women in Playing the Game of Basketball. *Research quarterly.* 11(3) 30–31.

Metzler, M. (1979) The measurement of academic learning time in physical education. Unpublished doctoral dissertation, The Ohio State University, Columbus.

Metzler, M. (1981) A multi-observational system for supervising student teachers in physical education. *The Physical Educator*, 3, 152–159.

Metzler, M.W. (1984) ALT-PE micro computer data collection system/version 1.0 [Computer program]. Blacksburg, VA: Metzsoft.

Metzler, M. (1989) A review of research on time in sport pedagogy. *Journal of Teaching in Physical Education*, 8, 87–103.

Michaels, C.F. and Carello, C. (1981) *Direct Perception*. Englewood Cliffs, NJ: Prentice-Hall.

Mikes, J. (1987) A Computer Breakdown of %-age Basketball. *Scholastic Coach.* 57(4) 52–55.

Miller, A.W. (1992) Systematic observation behavior similarities of various youth sport soccer coaches. *The Physical Educator, 49,* 136–143.

Miller, B. and Edwards, S. (1983) *Assessing motor performance in hockey: a field based approach.* Paper presented at British Society of Sports Psychology Conference, Birmingham, February.

Miller, B.P. and Winter, E. (1984) Specifity and netball performance. *Report for the All England Netball Association,* June.

Miller, G.N. (1988) *Observational accuracy in sport.* Unpublished masters' thesis, University of British Columbia, BC, Canada.

Miller, S.A. and Bartlett, R.M. (1993) The effects of increased shooting distance in the basketball jump shot. *Journal of Sports Sciences,* **11,** 285–293.

Miller, S.A. and Bartlett, R.M. (1996) The relationship between basketball shooting kinematics, distance and playing position. *Journal of Sports Sciences,* **14,** 245–253.

More, K. (1994) *Analysis and modification of verbal coaching behaviour: the utility of a data driven intervention strategy.* Unpublished Masters' dissertation, University of British Columbia, BC, Canada.

More, K.G. and Franks, I.M. (1996) 'Analysis and modification of verbal coaching behaviour: The usefulness of a data driven intervention strategy'. *Journal of Sports Sciences, 14,* 523–543.

More, K.G., Franks, I.M., McGarry, T. and Partridge, D. (1992) Analysis of coaching behaviors: The effectiveness of using a computer-aided system. Paper presented to the Canadian Society for Psychomotor Learning and Sport Psychology, Saskatoon, Saskatchewan.

More K.G., McGarry, T., Partridge, D. and Franks, I.M. (1996) 'A computer-assisted analysis of verbal coaching behavior in soccer'. *Journal of Sport Behavior, 19,* 319–337.

Morris, P. and Bell, H. (1985) An analysis of Individual Performance in Hockey. *Carnegie Research Papers,* 1(7), 18–22.

Morris, S.J. and Paradiso, J.A. (2002) Shoe-integrated sensor system for wireless gait analysis and real-time feedback. In *Proceedings of Second Joint EMBS/BMES Conference,* Houston, Tx, Oct. 23–26 2002, pp. 2468–2469.

Mosteller, F. (1979) A resistant analysis of 1971 and 1972 professional football. In J.H.Goldstein (ed.) *Sports, Games and Play.* New Jersey: Lawrence Erlbaum Associates, pp. 371–401.

Murray, S. and Hughes, M. (2001) Tactical performance profiling in elite level senior squash. In (eds M. Hughes and I.M. Franks) *pass.com,* Cardiff: CPA, UWIC, pp. 185–194.

Murray, S., Maylor, D. and Hughes, M. (1998) The effect of computerised analysis as feedback on performance of elite squash players. In A. Lees, I. Maynard, M. Hughes and T. Reilly (eds) *Science and Racket Sports II.* London: E & FN Spon, pp. 235–240.

Mustain, W.C. (1990) Are you the best teacher you can be? *Journal of Physical Education, Recreation and Dance,* February, 69–73.

Nawrat, C. and Hutchings, S. (1996) *The Sunday Times Illustrated History of Football.* London: Hamlyn.

Neisser, U. (1982) *Memory Observed.* San Francisco: W.H Freeman and Co.

Nevill, A.M., Atkinson, G., Hughes, M.D. and Cooper, S.-M. (2002) Statistical methods for analysing sport performance and notational analysis data. *Journal of Sports Sciences,* **20,** 829–844.

Newell, K.M. (1981) Motor skill acquisition. *Annual Review of Psychology, 42,* 213–237.

Newell, K.M. (1991) Motor skill acquisition. *Annual Review of Psychology, 42,* 213–237.

Newell, K.M. and Corcos, D.M. (1993) *Issues in Variability and Motor Control.* Champaign, IL: Human Kinetics.

Newell, K.M., Carlton, M.J. and Antoniou, A. (1990) The interaction of criterion and feedback information in learning a drawing task. *Journal of Motor Behavior*, 22, 8–20.

Newell, K.M., Morris, L.R. and Scully, D.M. (1985) Augmented information and the acquisition of skill in physical activity. In R.J. Terjung (ed), Exercise and sport science reviews, 13, 235–261.

Newtson, D. (1976) The process of behaviour observation. *Journal of Human Movement Studies*, 2, 114–122.

Ocansey, R. (1988) An effective supervision guide for supervisors: A systematic approach to organizing data generated during monitoring sessions in student teaching. *The Physical Educator*, 45(1), 24–29.

O'Donoghue, P. (2001) Notational analysis of rallies in European club championship badminton. In M. Hughes and F. Tavares (eds) *Notational Analysis of Sport IV*, Porto: Faculty of Sports Sciences and Education, University of Porto, Portugal. pp. 225–228.

O'Donoghue, P. and Ingram, W. (2001) Notational analysis of the cause of elite tennis players approaching the net in men's and ladies' singles at grand slam tournaments. In M. Hughes and F. Tavares (eds) *Notational Analysis of Sport IV*, Porto, Portugal, pp. 248–256.

O'Donoghue, P. and Liddle, D. (1998) A notational analysis of time factors of elite men's and ladies' singles tennis on clay and grass surfaces. In *Science and Racket Sports II* (edited by A. Lees, I.W. Maynard, M.D. Hughes and T. Reilly), pp. 241–246, London: E & FN Spon.

O'Donoghue, P. and Parker, D. (2002) Time-motion analysis of FA Premier League soccer competition. In (eds M. Hughes and I.M. Franks) *pass.com*, Cardiff: CPA, UWIC, pp. 258–261.

O'Donoghue, P.G. (2001) The CAPTAIN System. In M. Hughes and F. Tavares (eds) *Notational Analysis of Sport IV*, Porto, Portugal, pp. 239–249.

O'Donoghue, P.G. (2001) Time-Motion Analysis of Work-Rate in Elite Soccer. In M. Hughes and F. Tavares (eds) *Notational Analysis of Sport IV*, Porto, Portugal, pp. 71–79.

O'Hare, M. (1995) In a League of Their Own. *New Scientist*, 30 September 1995, Number 1997, 30–35.

Ohashi, J., Togari, H., Isokawa, M. and Suzuki, S. (1988) Measuring movement speeds and distances covered during soccer matchplay. In T. Reilly, A. Lees, K. Davids and W. Murphy (eds), *Science and Football*. London: E & F Spon.

Oliveria, J. (1997) Playing Two on Two. A Descriptive Study in Young Basketball Players Aged 13–14. *Notational analysis of sport I & II* (1997), UWIC Cardiff, pp. 221–225.

Olsen, E. and Larsen, O. (1997) Use of match analysis by coaches. In *Science and Football III* (edited by T. Reilly, Bangsbo, J. and Hughes, M.D.), pp. 209–220. London: E & FN Spon.

O'Shea, R. (1992) *An analysis of the tries scored in the 1991 Rugby World Cup.* Cardiff Institute of Higher Education. Unpublished undergraduate dissertation.

O'Sullivan, M.M. (1984) The effects of inservice education on the teaching effectiveness of experienced physical educators. *Dissertation Abstracts International*, 44, 1724–A.

Otago, L. (1983) A game analysis of the activity patterns of netball players. *Sports Coach*, 7, No. 1, 24–28.

Paese, P.C. (1984) Student teacher supervision: Where we are and where we should be. *The Physical Educator*, 41, 90–94.

Palmer, C., Hughes, M. and Borrie, A. (1994) Centre pass patterns of play of successful and non-successful international netball teams. *Journal of Sports Sciences*, 12, 2, 181.

Paradiso, J., Hsiao, K. and Hu, E. (1999a) Interactive Music for Instrumented Dancing Shoes. In *Proc. of the 1999 International Computer Music Conference*, pp. 453–456.

Paradiso, J., Hu, E. and Hsiao, K.Y. (1999b) The CyberShoe: wireless multisensor interface for a dancer's feet. In *Proc. of the International Dance and Technology 99* (IDAT99), Tempe, AZ, Feb 26–26, 1999.

Parker, A. and Hughes, M. (2002) Notational analysis of male and female performance in the 100 m. In (eds M. Hughes and I.M. Franks) *pass.com*, Cardiff: CPA, UWIC, pp. 365–373.

Parsons, A., Mullen, R. and Hughes, M. (2002) Performance profiles of male rugby union players. In (eds M. Hughes and I.M. Franks) *pass.com*, Cardiff: CPA, UWIC, pp. 129–137.

Partridge, D. and Franks, I.M. (1989) A detailed analysis of crossing opportunities from the 1986 World Cup. (Part I) *Soccer Journal*. May–June, pp. 47–50.

Partridge, D. and Franks, I.M. (1989) A detailed analysis of crossing opportunities from the 1986 World Cup. (Part II) *Soccer Journal*. June–July, pp. 45–48.

Partridge, D. and Franks, I.M. (1990) A comparative analysis of technical performance: USA and West Germany in the 1990 World Cup Finals. *Soccer Journal*, Nov–Dec, 57–62.

Partridge, D. and Franks, I.M. (1993) Computer-aided analysis of sport performance: An example from soccer. *The Physical Educator*, 50, 208–215.

Partridge, D. and Franks, I.M. (1996) Analyzing and modifying coaching behaviours by means of computer aided observation. *The Physical Educator*, 53, 8–23.

Patrick, J.D. and Mackenna, M.J. (1988) CABER – a computer system for football analysis. In T. Reilly, A. Lees, K. Davids and W. Murphy (eds), *Science and Football*. London: E & F Spon.

Pearce, M. and Hughes, M. (2001) Substitutions in Euro 2000. In (eds M. Hughes and I.M. Franks) *pass.com*, Cardiff: CPA, UWIC, pp. 303–317.

Pelcher, T. (1981) Computer analysis of champion athletic performance. *Research Quarterly*. 45, 391–397.

Penner, D. (1985) Computer volleyball stats. *Volleyball Technical Journal*, VIII, 116–127.

Pereira, A., Wells, J. and Hughes, M. (2001) Notational analysis of elite women's movement patterns in squash. In (eds M. Hughes and I.M. Franks) *pass.com*, Cardiff: CPA, UWIC, pp. 223–238.

Perl, J. (2002a) Game analysis and control by means of continuously learning networks. *International Journal of Performance Analysis in Sport*, 2, 21–35.

Perl, J. (2002b) Adaptation, antagonism and system dynamics. In G. Ghent, D. Kluka and D. Jones (eds). *Perspectives. The multidisciplinary series of physical education and sport science*, 4, pp. 105–125. Oxford: Meyer & Meyer Sport.

Pettit, A. and Hughes, M.D. (2001) Crossing and shooting patterns in the 1986 and 1998 World Cups for soccer. In *Pass.com* (edited by M. Hughes and I.M. Franks), pp. 267–276, Cardiff: CPA, UWIC.

Phillips, D.A. and Carlisle, C. (1983) A comparison of physical education teachers categorized as most and least effective. *Journal of Teaching in Physical Education*, 2(3), 55–67.

Pinto, D. (1995) 'Indicadores de *Performance* em Basquetebol – estudo descritivo e preditivo em cadetes masculinos'. Dissertação apresentada às provas de Mestrado em Ciências do Desporto, na área de especialização de Desporto de Crianças e Jovens. – FCDEF-UP.

Pollard, R., Reep, C. and Hartley, S. (1988) The quantitative comparison of playing styles in soccer. In T. Reilly, A. Lees, K. Davids and W. Murphy (eds), *Science and Football*. London: E & F Spon.

Potter, G. (1996a) Hand notation of the 1'994 World Cup. In M. Hughes (ed.) *Notational Analysis of Sport – I & II*, Cardiff: UWIC, pp. 113–122.

Potter, G. (1996b) A case study of England's performance in the Five Nations' championship over a 3 year period (1992–1994). In M. Hughes (ed.) *Notational Analysis of Sport – I & II*, Cardiff: UWIC, pp. 193–202.

Potter, G. and Carter, A. (1995) Performance at the 1995 Rugby World Cup. In Tau, C. (ed.) *Rugby World Cup 1995*, International Rugby Football Board: Bristol.

Potter, G. and Carter, A. (2001a) From whistle to whistle: A comprehensive breakdown of the total game contents. In M.D. Hughes (ed.) *Notational Analysis of Sport – III*, Cardiff: UWIC, pp. 209–215.

Potter, G. and Carter, A. (2001b) The four year cycle: A comparison of the 1991 and the 1995 rugby world cup finals. In M.D. Hughes (ed.) *Notational Analysis of Sport – III*, Cardiff: UWIC, pp. 216–219.

Potter, G. and Hughes, M. (2001), Modelling in competitive sports. In M. Hughes and F. Tavares (eds) *Notational Analysis of Sport IV*. Cardiff: U.W.I.C., pp. 67–83.

Potter, M. (1985) *Notation of Schoolgirl Netball*. Bedford College of Higher Education. Unpublished undergraduate dissertation.

Poulton, E.C. (1957) On prediction in skilled movements. *Psychological Bulletin*, 54, 467–478.

Pritchard, S., Hughes, M. and Evans, S. (2001) Rule changes in elite badminton. In (eds M. Hughes and I.M. Franks) *pass.com*, Cardiff: CPA, UWIC, pp. 213–225.

Purdy, J.G. (1974) Computer analysis of champion athletic performance. *Research Quarterly*, 45, 391–397.

Purdy, J.G. (1977) Computers and sports: From football play analysis to the Olympic games. In S.P. Ladany and R.E. Machol (eds) *Optimal Strategies in Sports*. Amsterdam, North Holland: pp. 196–205.

Putnam, C.A. (1993) Sequential motions of body segments in striking and throwing skills – descriptions and explanations. *Journal of Biomechanics*, **26**, 125–135.

Ramsden, P. (1993) 'Learning to Teach in Higher Education.' London: Routledge.

Read, B. and Edwards, P. (1992) *Teaching Children To Play Games*. Leeds: White Line Publishing.

Rebelo, A.N. and Soares, J.M.C. (1996) A comparative study of time-motion analysis during the two halves of a soccer game. In M. Hughes (ed.) *Notational Analysis of Sport – I & II*, Cardiff: UWIC, pp. 69–72.

Rebelo, A.N. and Soares, J.M.C. (1996) Endurance capacity of soccer players during pre-season and during playing season. In M. Hughes (ed.) *Notational Analysis of Sport – I & II*, Cardiff: UWIC, pp. 73–78.

Reep, C. and Benjamin, B. (1968) Skill and chance in association football. *Journal of the Royal Statistical Society*, Series A, **131**, 581–585.

Reep, C., Pollard, R. and Benjamin, B. (1971) Skill and chance in ball games. *Journal of the Royal Statistical Society*, **134**, 623–629.

Reilly, T. (ed.) (1997) *Science and Soccer*. London: E & FN Spon.

Reilly, T. (ed.) (2003) *Science and Soccer II*. London: E & FN Spon.

Reilly, T. and Thomas, V. (1976) A motion analysis of work-rate in different positional roles in professional football match-play. *Journal of Human Movement Studies*, 2, 87–97.

Reilly, T., Bangsbo, J. and Hughes, M. (eds) (1997) *Science and Football III*. London: E & F Spon.

Reilly, T., Clarys, J. and Stibbe, A. (eds) (1993) *Science and Football II*. London: E & FN Spon.

Reilly, T., Hughes, M. and Lees, A. (eds) (1995) *Science and Racket Sports*. London: E & FN Spon.

Reilly, T., Lees, A., Davids, K. and Murphy, W. (eds) (1988) *Science and Football*. London: E & FN Spon.

Richers, T.A. (1995) Time-motion analysis of the energy systems in elite and competitive singles tennis. *Journal of Human Movement Studies*, 28, 73–86.

Rico, J. and Bangsbo, J. (1996) Coding system to evaluate actions with the ball during a soccer match. In M. Hughes (ed.) *Notational Analysis of Sport – I & II*, Cardiff: UWIC, pp. 95–90.

Riera, J. (1986) *Análisis cinemático de los desplazamientos en la competition de baloncesto*. In Rev. Investigatión y Documentatión sobre Ciencias de la E.F. y Deporte 3, 18–25.

Rink, J. (1993) *Teaching Physical Education forLlearning*. St. Louis: Mosby.

Rizzolatti, G., Fogassi, L. and Gallese, V. (2001) Neurophysiological mechanisms underlying the understanding and imitation of action. *Nature Reviews – Neuroscience*, 2, 661–670.

Rosenthal, R. (1963) On the social psychology of the psychological experiment: The experimenter's hypothesis as unintended determinant of experimental results. *The American Scientist*, 51, 268–283.

Ross, D., Bird, A.M., Doody, S.G. and Zoeller, M. (1985) Effects of modeling and videotape feedback with knowledge results on motor performance. *Human Movement Science*, 4, 149–157.

Rothstein, A.L. and Arnold, R.K. (1976) Bridging the gap: application of research on videotape feedback and bowling. *Motor Skills: Theory Into Practice*, 1, 35–62.

Rothwell, J. (1994) *Control of Human Voluntary Movement*. Cambridge: Chapman & Hall Publishers.

Rushall, B.S. (1977) Two observation schedules for sporting and physical education environments. *Canadian Journal of Applied Sport Science*, 2, 15–21.

Russell, D. (1986) *A study of passing movements in relation to strikes at goal in Association Football*. Bedford College of Higher Education. Unpublished undergraduate dissertation.

Sailes, G. (1989) A comparison of three methods of target orientated hitting on baseline ground stroke accuracy in tennis. *Journal of Applied Research in Coaching and Athletics*, 4, 25–34.

Salmoni, A., Schmidt, R.A. and Walter, C.B. (1984) Knowledge of results and motor learning: A review and critical reappraisal. *Psychological Bulletin*, 95, 355–386.

Sanderson, D. J. and Cavanagh, P.R. (1990) Use of augmented feedback for the modification of pedaling mechanics of cyclists. *Canadian Journal of Sports Sciences*, 77, 245–251.

Sanderson, F.H. (1983) A notation system for analysing squash. *Physical Education Review*, 6, 19–23.

Sanderson, F.H. and Way, K.I.M. (1979) The development of objective methods of game analysis in squash rackets. *British Journal of Sports Medicine*, 11(4), 188.

Sanderson, L.K., McClements, J.D. and Gander, B.E. (1991) Development of apparatus to provide immediate accurate feedback to sprinters in normal training environment. *New Studies in Athletics*, 6, 33–41.

Schaal, S. (1998) Learning from Demonstration. *Technical Report*, Georgia Inst. of Technology, *www.cc.gatech.edu/fac/Stephan.Schaal*.

Schaal, S. (1999) Is imitation learning the route to humanoid robots? *Trends in Cognitive Sciences*, **3**, 233–239.

Schmidt, R.A. (1988) *Motor Control and Learning: A Behavioural Emphasis*. Champaign, IL: Human Kinetics Publishers.

Schmidt, R.A. and Lee, T. (1999) *Motor Control and Learning*. Champaign, IL: Human Kinetics.

Schmidt, R.A., Lange, C. and Young, D.E. (1990) Optimizing summary knowledge of results for skill learning. *Human Movement Science*, **9**, 325–348.

Schmidt, R.C., Carello, C. and Turvey, M.T. (1990) Phase transitions and critical fluctuations in the visual coordination of rhythmic movements between people. *Journal of Experimental Psychology: Human Performance and Perception*, **16**, 227–247.

Schmidt, R.C., O'Brien, B. and Sysko, R. (1999) Self-organization of between-person cooperative trials and possible applications to sport. *International Journal of Sport Psychology*, **30**, 558–579.

Schmidt-Nielsen, K. (1984) *Scaling, Why is Animal Size so Important?* Cambridge: CUP.

Schutz, R.W. (1970a) Stochastic processess: Their nature and use in the study of sport and physical activity. *The Research Quarterly*, **41**, 205–212.

Schutz, R.W. (1980) Sport and mathematics: A definition and delineation. *Research Quarterly for Exercise and Sport*, **51**, 37–49.

Schutz, R.W. and Gessaroli, M.E. (1987) The analysis of repeated measure designs involving multiple dependent variables. *Research Quarterly for Exercise and Sport*, **58**, 132–149.

Schutz, R.W. and Kinnsey, W.J. (1977) Comparison of North American and international Squash scoring systems-A computer simulation. *Research Quarterly for Exercise and Sport*, **48**, 248–251.

Scully, D. (1988) Visual perception of human movement: The use of demonstrations in teaching motor skills. *British Journal of Physical Education*, Research supplement No. 4.

Scully, D.M. and Newell, K.M. (1985) Observational learning and the acquisition of motor skills: Toward a visual perception perspective. *Journal of Human Movement Studies*, **11**, 169–186.

Segrave, J.O. and Ciancio, C.A. (1990) An observational study of a successful Pop Warner football coach. *Journal of Teaching in Physical Education*, **9**, 294–306.

Shannon, C.E. and Weaver, W. (1949) *The Mathematical Theory of Communication*. Chicago, IL: University of Illinois Press.

Sharp, R. (1986) Presentation: Notation Workshop in the Commonwealth Games Conference on Sport Science. Glasgow.

Shea, C.H. and Wulf, G. (1999) Enhancing motor learning through external-focus instructions and feedback. *Human Movement Science*, **18**, 553–571.

Shephard, R.J. (1999) Biology and medicine of soccer: An update. *Journal of Sports Sciences*, **17**, 757–786.

Sherwood, D.E. (1988) Effect of bandwidth knowledge of results on movement consistency. *Perceptual and Motor Skills*, **66**, 535–542.

Sherwood, D.E. and Rios, V. (2001) Divided attention in bimanual aiming movements: Effects on movement accuracy. *Research Quarterly for Exercise and Sport*, **72**, 210–218.

Siedentop, D. (1984) The modification of teacher behavior. In M.P. Pieron and G. Graham (eds), *Sport Pedagogy*, Champaign, IL: Human Kinetics, pp. 3–19.

Siedentop, D. (1991) *Developing teaching skills in physical education* (3rd ed.) Mountain View, CA: Mayfield.

Sinclair, G.D. (1989) Feedback analysis profile. In P.W. Darst, D.B. Zakrajsek, V.H. Mancini (eds), *Analyzing PhysicalEeducation and Sport Instruction*, Champaign, IL: Human Kinetics, pp. 361–368.

Skrinar, G.S. and Hoffman, S.J. (1979) Effect of outcome on analytic ability of golf teachers. *Perceptual and Motor Skills*, **48**, 703–708.

Smith, P. (1992) *Computerised analysis of water-polo*. Unpublished Dissertation, B.Sc. Sports Science, Liverpool John Moores University.

Smith, R.M. and Loschner, C. (2002) Biomechanics feedback for rowing. *Journal of Sports Sciences*, **20**, 783–791.

Smith, R.E., Smoll, F.L. and Hunt, E. (1977) A system for the behavioral assessment of athletic coaches. *Research Quarterly*, **48**, 401–407.

Smith, R.M., Galloway, M., Patton, R. and Spinks, W. (1994) Analyzing on-water rowing performance. *Sports Coach*, **17**, 37–40.

Soar, R.S. and Soar, R.M. (1979) Emotional climate and management. In P.L. Peterson and H.J. Walberg (eds) Research on Teaching: Concepts, findings and implications. Berkeley, CA: McCutchan.

Spinks, W., Reilly, T. and Murphy, A. (2002), *Science and Football IV*. London: E & FN Spon.

Stanhope, J. and Hughes, M. (1996) An analysis of scoring in the 1991 Rugby Union World Cup for men. In M. Hughes (ed.) *Notational Analysis of Sport – I & II*, Cardiff: UWIC, pp. 167–176.

Steele, J.R. and Chad, K.E. (1991) Relationship between movemnet patterns performed in match play and in training by skilled netball players. *Journal of Human Movement Studies*, **20**, 249–278.

Steele, J.R. and Chad, K.E. (1992) An Analysis of movement patterns of netball players during match play: implications for designing training programmes. *Sports Coach*, **15**, 21–28.

Stockill, N.P. (1994) A three-dimensional cinematographic analysis of cricket fast bowling: A study of junior and senior fast bowling techniques. Unpublished Master's thesis, the Manchester Metropolitan University.

Stretch, R.A., Bartlett, R.M. and Davids, K. (2000) A review of batting in men's cricket. *Journal of Sports Sciences*, **18**, 931–949.

Stretch, R.A., Buys, F., Du Toit, D.E. and Viljoen, G. (1998) Kinematics and kinetics of the drive off the front foot in cricket batting. *Journal of Sports Sciences*, **16**, 711–720.

Suinn, R.M. (1980) *Psychology in sport – methods and applications*. Burgess, USA.

Swinnen, S.P. (1996) Information feedback for motor skill learning: A review. In H.N. Zelaznik (ed.), *Advances in motor learning and control* (pp. 37–66). Champaign, IL: Human Kinetics.

Swinnen, S., Schmidt, R.A., Nicholson, D.E. and Shapiro, D.C. (1990) Information feedback for skill acquisition: Instantaneous knowledge of results degrades learning. *Journal of Experimental Psychology: Learning, Memory, and Cognition*, **16**, 706–716.

Swinnen, S.P., Lee, T.D., Verschueren, S., Serrien, D.J. and Bogaerds, H. (1997) Interlimb coordination: Learning and transfer under different feedback conditions. *Human Movement Science*, **16**, 749–785.

Swinnen, S.P., Verschueren, S.M.P., Bogaerts, H., Dounskaia, N., Lee, T.D., Stelmach, G.E. and Serrien, D.J. (1998) Age-related deficits in motor learning and differences in feedback processing during the production of a bimanual coordination pattern. *Cognitive Neuropsychology*, **15**, 439–466.

Swinnen, S.P., Walter, C.B., Lee, T.D. and Serrien, D.J. (1993) Acquiring bimanual skills: Contrasting forms of information feedback for interlimb decoupling. *Journal of Experimental Psychology: Learning, Memory and Cognition*, **19**, 1328–1344.

Tang, H.P., Abe, K., Katoh, K. and Ae, M. (1995) Three-dimensional cinematographical analysis of the badminton forearm smash: Movements of the forearm and hand. In *Science and Racket Sports* (edited by T. Reilly, M.D. Hughes and A. Lees), pp. 113–118. London: E & FN Spon.

Taylor, M. and Hughes, M. (1998) Analysis of elite under-19 tennis players. In *Science and Racket Sports II* (edited by A. Lees, I. Maynard, M.D. Hughes and T. Reilly), pp. 211–220. London: E & FN Spon.

Taylor, S. and Hughes, M.D. (1988) Computerised notational analysis: a voice interactive system. *Journal of Sports Sciences*. **6**, 255.

Templin, D.P. and Vernacchia, R.A. (1995) The Effect of Highlight Music Videotapes Upon the Game Performance of Intercollegiate Basketball Players. *The Sport Psychologist*, **9**, 41–50.

Tharp, R.G. and Gallimore, R. (1976) What a coach can teach a teacher. *Psychology Today*, **25**, 75–78.

Thomas, C., Williams, J. and Martin, M. (2001) Mapping the world game of rugby union. In (eds M. Hughes and I.M. Franks) *pass.com*. Cardiff: CPA, UWIC, pp. 91–110.

Thornton, S. (1971) *A Movement Perspective of Rudolph Laban*. London: McDonald & Evans.

Tina, P.M. (2001) Performance indicators of basketball – a study of their impact for winnings. In Hughes, M.D. and Tavares, F. (eds) (2001) *Notational Analysis of Sport – IV*, Cardiff: UWIC, pp. 123–126.

Tiryaki, G., Cicek, S., Erdogan, A.T., Kalay, F., Atalay, A.T. and Tuncel, F. (1997) The analysis of the offensive patterns of the Switzerland soccer team in the World Cup, 1994. In M. Hughes (ed.) *Notational Analysis of Sport – I & II*, Cardiff: UWIC, pp. 91–98.

Todorov, E., Shadmehr, R. and Bizzi, E. (1997) Augmented feedback presented in a virtual environment accelerates learning of a difficult motor task. *Journal of Motor Behavior*, **29**, 147–158.

Treadwell, P.J. (1988) Computer aided match analysis of selected ball-games (soccer and rugby union) In T. Reilly, A. Lees, K. Davids and W. Murphy (eds), *Science and Football*. London: E & F Spon.

Treadwell, P.J. (1992) The predictive potential of match analysis systems for rugby union football. In T. Reilly (ed.), *Science and Football II*. London: E & F Spon.

Treadwell, P.J. (1996) Building knowledge in sports science: the potential of sports notation. In M. Hughes (ed.) *Notational Analysis of Sport – I & II*, Cardiff: UWIC, pp. 43–48.

Underwood, G. and Macheath, J. (1977) Video analysis in Tennis Coaching. *British Journal of Physical Education*, **8**, 136–138.

Van der Mars, H. (1989) Observer Reliability: Issues and Procedures. In P.W. Darst *et al.* (eds) *Analyzing Physical Education and Sport Instruction*. Champaign, Ill.: Human Kinetics.

Van Hal, L. (1999) in *http:www.ndirect.co.uk/~Dav Reece/vball/news-let*

van Rossum, J.H.A. (1997) Motor development and practice: The variability of practice hypothesis in perspective. Amsterdam: Free University Press.

Vander Linden, D.W., Cauraugh, J.H. and Greene, T.A. (1993) The effect of frequency of kinetic feedback on learning an isometric force production task in non-disabled subjects. *Physical Therapy*, **73**, 79–87.

Vereijken, B. (1991) *The dynamics of skill acquisition*. Meppel: Krips Repro.

Vickers, J.N. (1996) Visual control when aiming at a far target. *Journal of Experimental Psychology: Human Perception and Performance*, 2, 342–354.

Vickers, J.N. and Adolphe, R.M. (1997) Gaze behaviour during a ball tracking and aiming skill. *International Journal of Sports Vision*, 4, 18–27.

Vincent, W. (1999) *Statistics in Kinesiology*, Champaign, Ill.: Human Kinetics.

Vogt, S. (1996) The concept of event generation in movement imitation – neural and behavioral aspects. *Corpus, Psyche et Societas*, 3, 119–132.

Waddell, D.B. and Gowitzke, B.A. (1977) An analysis of overhead badminton power strokes using high speed bi-plane photography. Communication to the International Coaching Conference, Malmö, Sweden, 3–7 May.

Wade, A. (1967) *The F.A. Guide to Training and Coaching*. London: Heineman.

Wells, G.L. and Leippe, M. (1981) How do triers of fact infer the accuracy of eyewitness identifications? Using memory for peripheral detail can be misleading. *Journal of Applied Psychology*, 66, 682–687.

Wells, G.L. and Loftus, E.F. (1984) *Eyewitness testimony: Psychological perspectives*. London: Cambridge University Press.

Wells, J. and Hughes, M. (2001) Movement analysis of elite women squash players. In (eds M. Hughes and I.M. Franks) *pass.com*, Cardiff: CPA, UWIC, pp. 175–184.

Werner, P. and Rink, R. (1989) Case studies of teacher effectiveness in second grade physical education. *Journal of Teaching in Physical Education*, 8, 280–297.

Whaley, G.M. (1980) The effect of daily monitoring and feedback to teachers and students on academic learning time-physical education. *Dissertation Abstracts International*, 41, 1477–A.

Wilson, A.M. and Watson, J.C. (2003) A catapult action for rapid limb protraction. *Nature*, 421, 35–36.

Wilson, G. (1987) A Case for Hockey Statistics. *Hockey Field*, 74, 161–163.

Wilson, G. (1987) A Case for Hockey Statistics: As seen through the eyes of a computer. *Hockey Field*, 74, 191–194.

Wilson, K. and Barnes, C.A. (1998) Reliability and validity of a computer based notational analysis system for competitive table tennis. In A. Lees, I. Maynard, M. Hughes and T. Reilly (eds) *Science and Racket Sports*. London: E & FN Spon, pp. 265–268.

Winkler, W. (1988) Match analysis and improvement of performance in soccer with the aid of computer controlled dual video systems (CCDVS). In *Science and Football* (eds T. Reilly, A. Lees, K. Davids and W. Murphy). London: E & FN Spon.

Winkler, W. (1992) Computer-controlled assessment- and video-technology for the diagnosis of a player's performance in soccer training. In T. Reilly (ed.), *Science and Football II*. London: E & F Spon.

Winkler, W. (1996) Computer/video analysis in German soccer. In *Notational Analysis of Sport – I & II* (edited by M. Hughes), pp. 19–31.Cardiff: UWIC.

Winstein, C.J. and Schmidt, R.A. (1989) Sensorimotor feedback. In *Human Skills* (edited by D.H. Holding), pp. 17–47. New York: Wiley.

Winstein, C.J. and Schmidt, R.A. (1990) Reduced frequency of knowledge of results enhances motor skill learning. *Journal of Experimental Psychology: Learning, Memory and Cognition*, 16, 677–691.

Winstein, C.J. and Schmidt, R.A. (1990) Reduced frequency of knowledge of results enhances motor skill learning. *Journal of Experimental Psychology: Learning, Memory, and Cognition*, 16, 677–691.

Winterbottom, W. (1959) *Soccer Coaching*. Kingswood: The Naldrett Press.

Winters, J.M. and Woo, S.L-Y. (1990) *Multiple Muscle Systems: Biomechanics and Movement Organization*, N.Y.: Springer-Verlag.

Withers R.T., Maricic, Z., Wasilewski, S. and Kelly, L. (1982) Match analyses of Australian professional soccer players. *Journal of Human Movement Studies*, 8, 158–176.

Wollstein, J. and Neal, R. (1993) Video analysis of squash swings: part one racket preparation variables. *Sports Coach*, 16(3), 26–33.

Wolpert, D.M., Ghahramani, Z. and Jordan, M.I. (1995) Are arm trajectories planned in kinematic or dynamic coordinates? An adaptation study. *Exp. Brain Res.*, 103, 460–470.

Wulf, G. and Weigelt, C. (1997) Instructions about physical principles in learning a complex motor skill: To tell or not to tell. *Research Quarterly for Exercise and Sport*, 68, 362–367.

Wulf, G. and Prinz, W. (2001) Directing attention to movement effects enhances learning: A review. *Psychonomic Bulletin & Review*, 8, 648–660.

Wulf, G. and Schmidt, R.A. (1996) Average KR degrades parameter learning. Journal of Motor Behavior, 28, 371–381.

Wulf, G. and Shea, C.H. (2003, in press) Understanding the role of augmented feedback: The good, the bad, and the ugly. In A.M. Williams, N.J. Hodges and M.A. Scott (eds), *Skill acquisition in sport: Research, theory and practice*. London, UK: Routledge.

Wulf, G., Lee, T.D. and Schmidt, R.A. (1994) Reducing knowledge of results about relative versus absolute timing: Differential effects on learning. Journal of Motor Behavior, 26, 362–369.

Wulf, G., Shea, C.H. and Matschiner, S. (1998) Frequent feedback enhances complex motor skill learning. *Journal of Motor Behavior*, 30, 180–192.

Wulf, G., McConnel, N., Gärtner, M. and Schwarz, A. (2002) Feedback and attentional focus: Enhancing the learning of sport skills through external-focus feedback. *Journal of Motor Behavior*, 34, 171–182.

Yamanaka, K., Hughes, M. and Lott, M. (1993) An analysis of playing patterns in the 1990 World Cup for association football. In T. Reilly (ed.), *Science and Football II*. London: E & F Spon, pp. 206–214.

Yeadon, M.R. and Challis, J.H. (1992) *Future Directions for Performance Related Research in Sports Biomechanics*. London: the Sports Council.

Young, D.E. and Schmidt, R.A. (1992) Augmented feedback for enhanced skill acquisition. In G.E. Stelmach and J. Requim (eds) *Tutorials in Motor Behaviour II*. North Holland: Amsterdam, pp. 677–694.

Zaal, F.T.J.M. and Michaels, C.F. (1999) Catching and judging fly balls in CAVETM. In *Studies in Perception and Action V* (edited by M.A. Grealy and J.A. Thompson), pp. 148–152. Manwah, NJ: Lawrence Erlbaum.

Index

actions 110
allometric scaling 171
American football 61, 115, 117, 285
analysis 3, 129, 132, 189–203; game
    strucures 172–87; system 111
Anova 72, 190, 202, 203
Ariel 42, 49
Armstrong & Hoffman 1979 13
association football 277, 279, 282, 285–6,
    288, 295–6, 301
Attentional focus 34
attitudes, of coaches 57
Augmented information 17, 39, 293
Australian Rules Football 291
Automated systems 43, 46

Badminton 74–5, 98, 293, 295, 300
Bandura 277
Bangsbo 67
Bartlett 4, 42, 166–9, 182, 186
basketball 124, 151
Benesh 275
biomechanical indicators 166, 175, 177,
    182, 185, 187
Bland and Altman 4, 190–200
boxing 146
Bruno 147–51

CABER system (computer analysis) 294–5
Carroll 27, 276–7
Carroll and Bandura 27, 276–7
Carter 73, 74, 181, 277
Centre for Performance Analysis
    (Cardiff) 60
Centre for Sport Analysis (Vancouver) 103
chance 228, 233
Choreology 275
Clifford and Hollin (1980) 13–14
Coach Analysis Instrument (CAI) 250
coach effectiveness 6, 243–4, 246
coaching 12

coaching process 6, 11–13, 81, 107;
    effective verbal strategies 251; feedback
    1, 17, 265–6, 269, 271, 276–301;
    intervention 281, 292; recall 8, 14–15,
    26, 28, 29, 33, 39, 241, 247; systematic
    observation 243–92; verbal strategies
    251
computer controlled video 280
computerised notation 80–103
computerised systems 10, 74, 80, 85, 104,
    107, 265, 286
computerised-video feedback 104
Computerised Coaching Analysis System
    (CCAS) 280, 287
concept keyboard 83, 90–1, 99, 103, 72
Cooper xv, 189, 285–6, 292
cricket 128
cricket notation system 128
Croucher 96, 278

dance notation 169
data: analysis 9, 122–8, 141–65, 189–204,
    256–72; collection systems 118, 126;
    presentation 128, 141–65, 195,
    264–70; summary 113, 119, 126, 134
develop a notation system 3, 118, 183
digitisation board 247
digitisation pad 85, 97, 102, 103, 272
Downey 62, 278
Dufour 85, 278
DyCoN 241
dynamic conditions 50
Dynamical Systems vii, 227, 236–7
Dynamically Controlled Network 238

eIJPAS 60
evaluation of performance 109, 253
Evans 5, 74, 205–23
examples of notation systems 3, 141–65
extrinsic feedback 9
eye movement technology 56–7

eyewitness 8, 13–14
eyewitness testimony 13

feedback 8–15, 17–39, 40–58, 134–8, 166–8, 244–56, 258–71; augmented 2, 17, 19–25, 39, 293; temporal 51–5
field hockey 71, 96, 108
fitness training 51, 169
flowchart 6, 110, 112, 166, 172–87
force sensors 55
Franks and Goodman (1986a and b) 10
Franks and Miller (1986) 8, 14
Franks and Nagelkerke (1988) 11, 102, 104, 134, 280
Franks, Elliot and Johnson (1985) 8
Franks, Goodman and Paterson (1986) 10
Franks, Johnson and Sinclair (1988) 11
Franks, Wilson and Goodman (1987) 10
Frequency Distributions 65, 90, 104, 134
Frequency tables 118, 120, 121

game structures 70, 172, 187, 284, 285
General or Summary Data 134
General steps in analysis 132
Goodman 10, 97, 102, 108, 109, 113, 115
graphical user interface 91, 103
Grehaigne 85, 86

Hand notation 3, 10, 60–2, 66–9, 71–4, 78–80, 118, 127, 139, 151, 221, 245, 265, 285, 295
hierarchical structure 108, 109
historical perspective 3, 60
Hodges 8, 17–40
Hong 92, 93
Hughes & Charlish (1988) 10
Hughes & Cunliffe (1986) 10
Hughes & Franks (1989) 10

implicit learning 37
Imwold & Hoffman (1983) 13
individual sports 141–51
International Journal of Performance Analysis of Sport (see eIJPAS) 60
inter-operator 191, 196–200, 202–3, 210, 217
intra-operator 98, 197–9, 201, 209, 217
intrinsic feedback 9
Introduction 1
Invasion Games 178

javelin 27, 44, 167, 171

Katz 57
Kelso 237, 279, 281, 287
kinematic model 53

kinematic parameters 43
knowledge of performance (KP) 9, 17, 20
knowledge of results (KR) 1, 9, 17, 19
Kohonen Feature Map 238, 239
Kruskal-Wallis 197, 202–3

Laban 287, 299
Laser technology 50
Lees 62, 168, 170, 181, 185, 187
Leippe, Wells and Ostrom (1978) 14
Liebermann 40, 51–4, 167
limit of error 210, 214
Lissajous figures 31–2
Luhtanen 86, 87
Lyons 61, 72

McDonald (1984) 14, 290
McGarry 4, 10, 12, 17, 90, 93, 95, 96, 228–43
Magill 22–4
Magill & Wood 19
Malpass and Devine (1981) 14
Markov 8, 21, 95, 237–43
Martina Navratilova 143, 145
match classification indicators 175
match indicators 4, 166, 169, 180, 185
Measuring Coaching Effectiveness 243–56
Messersmith 61
Messersmith and Bucher 61
Miller 8
model 92, 94, 107, 113, 172, 228–43; sport performance 106, 288, 292, 294; sports contests, see above
modification of behaviour 248, 251, 256
Moore 41, 62
More 7, 12, 15, 28, 244–57
motor control 40, 170, 187, 293, 297
movement analysis 62, 69, 73, 74, 78, 94
Murray 92, 191–4, 264–70

Nagelkerke 11, 90, 102, 104, 134, 189, 248
Neisser (1982) 8
net and wall games 4, 166, 172–4
netball 70, 95, 160–5
Neural Networks 227, 238, 240–2
Nevill 4, 42, 61, 171, 173, 189–203
Newell (1981) 9
Newtson (1976) 15
Nicola J. Hodges, see Hodges
non-dimensional ratios 170, 187
normative profiles 187, 205, 222, 285
notation: computerised notation systems 80–103, 207–8, 265; hand notation 9, 59–80, 260; systems 2, 3, 4, 59–106, 107–17, 118–40, 141–65, 207–8, 260, 265

O'Donoghue 94, 95, 99, 101, 206
Observation systems 245, 271
Olsen 67, 172, 181 526
operational definitions 67, 128, 213
optimization 278
outcomes 107–10, 125–8

Partridge 10, 68, 83, 85–7, 134, 136, 181, 257, 259, 261
penalties (soccer) 68–70
percentage difference 79, 193, 197, 199, 210, 215–17, 220
percentage difference calculations 193, 210
performance 61–102, 166–86, 205–23, 245–52, 258–72
performance indicators 4, 166–7, 169–70, 172, 177–9, 174, 181–4, 186–8, 180, 269–70, 284, 299
Performance Profiling 5, 7, 94, 209, 263, 284, 292; tactical 263, 292
performance template 212
Perl 5, 228–43
Pettit and Hughes 67, 180–1, 263
Potter 73, 74, 206
Power Pad 90, 97, 103
Presentation 132–4, 141–65, 207–22, 265–9
purposes of notation 81

QWERTY keyboard 89, 97, 99, 103, 265

racket sports 59, 62, 92, 112, 169, 176–8, 189
Read and Edwards 172, 173
Reep 65, 66, 182, 206, 229
Reep and Benjamin 65, 66, 181, 206, 227–8
Reilly 10, 59, 67, 69, 82, 84, 92, 139, 174, 177, 189, 237, 261, 321, 342
Reilly and Thomas 10, 69–70, 82, 127, 139
reliability 4, 5, 7, 66, 73, 97, 98, 99, 128, 129, 167, 170, 189–203, 205–7, 259
review of the literature 2, 38, 59–106
Ross, Bird, Doody and Zoeller (1985) 296
Rothstein and Arnold (1976) 9, 39
Rugby Union 72–3, 99–101, 139, 180–1, 196, 198, 206, 221, 271, 276–7, 284–6, 289–90, 298–9

Sanderson 10, 55, 63–5, 88, 91, 112, 113, 128, 138, 176–8
Sanderson and Way 10, 63–4, 88, 104, 112–13, 128, 138–9
scatter diagrams 118, 119, 121
Schmidt 2, 8, 20–6, 52, 184, 239, 244
Schutz 287, 297

sequential logic 109
sequential systems 118
Sequentially Dependent Data 138
Siedentop 243–5, 250, 253, 256
Skrinar & Hoffman (1979) 13
Smith, Smoll and Hunt (1978) 298
soccer 64–70, 81, 136, 139, 154–60, 179–83, 238, 258–64
squash 44, 60, 63–4, 88–94, 102, 112–13, 127, 135–6, 139, 173, 175, 191–4, 205, 207–10, 215–17, 228, 229–30, 237–40, 264–9
Statistical processes and reliability vii, 201
Steffi Graf 143
stochastic 5, 91, 98, 228, 229, 232–236, 238, 240, 242
striking and fielding games 4, 166, 172, 183–5
summary data 132, 134, 190, 204, 208, 266
Swinnen 20–6, 29
system design 209, 257, 265
systematic observation 243–6, 248, 250, 271, 277–8, 287, 289, 292

tactical: indicators 166–87; performance profiling 263–8
Tavares 60, 77, 84
Taylor & Hughes (1987) 10, 103, 169, 174
teaching effectiveness 243
team 3, 113, 151–66
team analysis 114, 289
technical indicators 4, 166–87
tele-remote training 49–50
tennis 20, 35, 37, 52–3, 56, 62, 91, 94–5, 111, 117, 127, 141–5, 169, 171–2, 175, 177, 178, 182, 206, 252
temporal feedback 51–3
Tiryaki 85, 87
Tyson 147–50

verbal coaching strategies 251
video 2, 9, 40–58, 201, 244–6
video feedback 9–10, 18, 26, 34, 41–2, 85
virtual reality 26, 46–9
voice entry of data 103
volleyball 35, 36, 56, 97–8, 178, 224–5, 254

water polo 109, 113, 122
Wells 5, 14, 15, 68–70, 90, 205–23, 263
Wells and Leippe (1981) 14
Wells and Loftus (1984) 13
Winkler 85, 169, 300

Yamanaka 85, 287, 301